PENGUIN AFRICAN LIBRARY
Edited by Ronald Segal

South Africa:
An Historical Introduction

Freda Troup was born and received her early
education in South Africa, where she has travelled
fairly extensively. She has contributed articles to a
number of South African magazines such as
Africa South, *Fighting Talk*, and *Forum*, and has
also written a book entitled *In Face of Fear:
Michael Scott's Challenge to South Africa*.

D0958584

FREDA TROUP

South Africa
An Historical Introduction

Penguin Books

Penguin Books Ltd, Harmondsworth,
Middlesex, England
Penguin Books Australia Ltd, Ringwood,
Victoria, Australia
Penguin Books Canada Ltd,
41 Steelcase Road West, Markham, Ontario, Canada
Penguin Books (N.Z.) Ltd,
182–190 Wairau Road, Auckland 10, New Zealand

First published by Eyre Methuen 1972
Published with revisions in Penguin Books 1975
Copyright © Freda Troup, 1972, 1975

Made and printed in Great Britain by
Cox & Wyman Ltd,
London, Reading and Fakenham
Set in Monotype Plantin

Contents

Contents

List of Illustrations

PLATES

DRAWINGS

List of Illustrations

CARTOONS

MAPS (*drawn by William Bromage*)

> *Note:* The maps reflect the geographical references throughout the text as a guide to the reader and are not necessarily limited to any particular period.

FAMILY TREES

Preface

Issues so current as those of attitudes to racial conflicts in southern Africa must be of obsessive interest to South Africans. As one, of British origin, I have sought an understanding in our country's history; and this book is a creaming off of some of the work on that history that is accumulating in great and valuable profusion. Being the product of my White South African birth and conditioning I cannot put my Black countryman's point of view on our history, and his own stating of it, in the main, is still to come: I can only proffer my own up-dated White version. There lies the success of White South African policies: that we have a variety of versions.

In what follows answers may, I think, emerge to such urgently topical questions as: Why ban the Springboks? Why boycott fruit from the RSA? Why not act against Russia, India – any other country we don't approve of? One factor which I have recognized with unexpected and shocking clarity is the extent of the responsibility that rests on British Governments and people. It was only when British forces took a part that many of the African peoples, so desperately defending their independence, were defeated; without British aid the Trekkers might well have lost out. When Britain had the power to check and control discrimination she did not. Much current legislation, if not introduced, at least has precedents set by British administrations. The South African Native Affairs Commission set up by Milner before Union, most of its members impeccably British, many of them noted for their sympathies with the 'Native people', laid clear guide-lines which, in the event, were to govern the policies of successive administrations on franchise, land and labour – on segregation, apartheid, in short – from that day to this. Then, in the Act of Union, Britain finally relinquished responsibility for Africans. English-speaking South Africans have generally supported discriminatory legislation whether under Botha, Smuts, Hertzog, Malan, Strydom, Verwoerd or Vorster. The British of Natal háve been as crudely racial towards the African and Indian communities as the most domineering of Boer settlers. United Kingdom companies are making huge profits, British people drawing huge dividends, from South Africa only because the workers whose labour provides the profits are remorselessly underpaid, and because the whole machinery of government prevents any betterment, whether by acquiring improved skills and productivity or by conventional industrial action such as is available to workers in Britain – and in South Africa if they are White.

The tragedy and shame of it is that for so long there was such a fiercely glowing faith in British rule and British justice. People after people, when they realized they could not keep their independence, chose to ask Britain above all nations for protection. 'The Great Queen' and 'the British flag' were trusted symbols; the hopeful (and disappointed) deputations of chiefs to Westminster and the petitions directed with patient persistence to HMG were expressions of faith. When Dr Abdurahman, Coloured leader in the Cape, saw the threat implicit in the reconciliation of Boer and Britain after the war, he declared, 'Did not our gracious king promise protection to the Natives ? Is not the British flag synonymous with justice and freedom ?' Years later, when what had been salvaged from that reconciliation was about to be torn away, Professor D. D. Jabavu, member of a distinguished African family, made a last appeal: the franchise, he proclaimed despairingly, was 'a treasured gift of justice from Queen Victoria'. These were not words spoken in irony.

ACKNOWLEDGEMENTS

I wish to acknowledge gratefully the long-suffering advice and support of many friends. In particular, I would express my thanks to Dr Shula Marks for her cool, hard look at my manuscript and invaluable guidance. The shortcomings are entirely mine.

Notes on Names and Spelling

NOTE ON NAMES

A glossary of some terms with a confusingly idiosyncratic usage in South Africa may be helpful to the reader:

South African applies only to White nationals who are also referred to as

Europeans, whether born in South Africa, Europe or elsewhere, and is further divided into:

English-speaking, including South African and foreign born, and

Afrikaans-speaking, generally South African born of Dutch descent.

Afrikaans is the main official language of South Africa, Dutch in origin with French, Malay and English influence.

Afrikaners (once Afrikander, but this now only refers to a breed of cattle) are South Africans of basically Dutch origin.

Boers, meaning farmers, was extended from the time of the Great Trek to include, loosely, all Afrikaners or, more precisely, Republican Afrikaners. Since Union it has passed out of English use.

Africans in international usage applies to one indigenous section of the population (more explicitly, South African Africans) and it is preferred by them to

Bantu, which is a linguist term referring to a group of languages and was loosely applied to the people speaking them. It was adopted officially as scientifically and objectively more in keeping with apartheid than

Native, the term previously in official use and still current among English-speaking Whites. Although on the face of it strictly correct, the term acquired a very illogical usage, referring only to Africans (even those not born in South Africa and leading to terminological curiosities such as 'foreign natives') and *never* to the White South African born. The word acquired a derogatory connotation and consequently Africans object strongly to its use.

Kafir (Kaffir, Caffre) is Arabic for 'unbeliever' and was adopted by White settlers on the Eastern Frontier for those tribes they were in early contact with, particularly the Xhosa. From there it spread with the Trekkers all over South Africa and was applied with increasingly contemptuous undertones to all Africans, to whom its use is abhorrent.

Khoikhoi, their own name for themselves, is preferred to *Hottentot*, more usually used by Whites and which has become abusive. They were the first people the Dutch settlers came in contact with.

San is the Khoikhoi name for the *Bushman* and now generally preferred for reasons as above.

Cape Coloured are the people of mixed racial origin, predominantly indigenous Khoikhoi and Malay slaves with varying admixtures of African and White. The Cape Coloured are considered a group on their own and are now found living all over South Africa. They are sometimes disparagingly called *Hotnots*.

Indians are the descendants of the indentured labourers and, though mostly South African born of several generations, they are only reluctantly accepted as a part of the South African population and are sometimes slightingly called *Coolies*.

Asiatics, the South African version of the international *Asians*, refers generally to all people from the East, though the Japanese, with whom South Africa has profitable trade relations, are granted an 'honorary White' status.

Tribe is used loosely to denote traditional social groupings with a common history or a common allegiance to a chief.

Non-Europeans, and later *Non-whites*, have been customary terms used to include Africans, Coloureds and Indians, in fact, all who are not white, in matters relating to all those groups.

However, with the recent increasing identity of interests among these population groups in South Africa the preferred term is

Blacks in referring collectively to Africans, Asians and Coloureds (and seems no less precise than the application of White to all from Sicily to Scandinavia).

Race in the South African sense refers generally to skin colour differences, black, brown, coloured or white; but sometimes it is also used to distinguish between Afrikaans-speaking and English-speaking Whites.

Reserves, in South African usage, refer to tracts of land demarcated for occupation exclusively by Africans. They are frequently either naturally very barren or have become so through generations of gross overcrowding, over-stocking and primitive land usage. These tribal areas, in present government thinking, are to form the 'Bantu homelands' where 'separate development' will take place. There is a distinct 'through the looking-glass' atmosphere created by current terminology when contrasted with reality; further examples include the titles of Acts: 'The Abolition of Passes' . . . 'Extension of University Education' . . . 'Promotion of Bantu Self-government'.

NOTE ON SPELLING

The spelling of African names is complex and confusing because the various African languages have been reduced to writing generally by missionaries of various denominations and nationalities, working with different peoples. English, French and Germans would render the same name from, say Tswana or Xhosa speakers, phonetically into almost unrecognizably dissimilar forms: Chaka, Tshaka and Shaka; Moselikatze, Msiligazi, Mzilikazi; Sekukuni, Secocoeni, Sekhuknune. Chief Lutuli expressed his own preference for the omission of an 'h' in his name. There is now an attempt to standardize spelling.

Population figures (June 1974)

Africans	17,712,000
Asians	709,000
Coloureds	2,306,000
Whites	4,160,000
Total	24,887,000

Department of Statistics (quoted *Cape Times*, 18 September 1974)

Abbreviations

AAC	All Africa Convention
AME	American Methodist Episcopal Church
AMWU	African Mine Workers' Union
ANC	African National Congress
APO	African People's Organization
BAD	Bantu Administration and Development Department
BOSS	Bureau for State Security
BPC	Black People's Convention
BSA	British South Africa Company
CNE	Christian National Education
COD	Congress of Democrats
CP	Communist Party
DRC	Dutch Reformed Church
FAK	Federasie van Afrikaanse Kultur Verenigings
HNP	Herenigde Nasionale Party
ICJ	International Court of Justice
ICU	Industrial and Commercial Workers' Union
ISL	International Socialist League
LMS	London Missionary Society
NAD	Native Affairs Department
NP	Nationalist Party
NRC	Native Representative Council
NUSAS	National Union of South African Students
OAU	Organization of African Unity
OB	Ossewabrandwag
PAC	Pan African Congress
PDL	Poverty Datum Line
RDB	Reddingsdaadbond
SABRA	South African Bureau of Race Affairs
SAIC	South African Indian Congress
SAP	South African Party
SASO	South African Students Organization
SWAPO	South West Africa People's Organization
TUC	Trades Union Congress
UDF	Union Defence Force
UN	United Nations
UNO	United Nations Organization
UP	United Party
WNLA	Witwatersrand Native Labour Association

Map I. Southern Africa showing present-day political boundaries

1 The Country (before 1652)

I. THE LAND

Africa has always fired the imagination of men in Europe. Herodotus, five hundred years before Christ, told with some scepticism of Phoenician voyages of discovery. The Latin Pliny, in the first years of our era, said there was always something new out of Africa, and Sir Thomas Browne, fifteen hundred years later, declared that all Africa and her prodigies were within us. Shakespeare sang of Africa and golden joys. Dickens's philanthropic Mrs Jellyby, inattentive to her household, was looking far away into Africa, while Browning contemplated the rising of Jupiter, silent over Africa. Embers of the obsession glow recurrently in the literature. Down the centuries men sought adventures and riches. Myth mingled extravagantly with fact and somewhere in Africa was sited Ophir, the biblical source of fine gold, King Solomon's mines.

Africa has proved to be a land of tremendous promise and challenge, far beyond men's dreams. Africa is the second largest continent after Asia and one-fifth of the land surface of the globe. Africa contains great forests of valuable hardwoods and of rubber, cork and palms. Its vast savannahs and grasslands pasture huge herds of wild and domestic animals. Its seas and lakes are rich in fish. Its varied climates allow the abundant production of most agricultural crops: cocoa, coffee, banana, ground-nuts, cotton, tobacco, sugar; maize, millet, wheat and barley; all tropical and temperate fruits; the citrus, vines and olives of the winter rainfall lands; dates of the desert oases.

In Africa's ancient rock structures are found almost all of commercially desired minerals: most of the world's diamonds, more than half the world's gold, and copper, iron, chrome, zinc, aluminium, uranium and many others, rare and essential to modern industry.

Africa is amply supplied with potential power: oil in the north, coal in the south and almost everywhere hydro-electric possibilities totalling perhaps 40 per cent of the world potential. Its surface and underground water, if wisely used and conserved, would irrigate many thousands of acres to augment an erratic rainfall. Its 330 m. people, though densely crowded in some small areas, in general are sparsely spread. With good management Africa could be largely self-supporting and could contribute notably to the food supplies of the world.

Yet despite the prodigal natural endowment of Africa, its populations are among the poorest in the world; in 1959 for instance some $8\frac{1}{2}$ per cent of the world's people had only a 4 per cent share of the world trade. The average income per head of the population of Ghana, then the second richest country after South Africa, was about £54 and in many countries it was £15–£20. The cause of this inequity lies basically in the interaction of geography and history.

Africa, 11,000,000 square miles in area and 5,000 miles from northern shore to southernmost point, straddles the equator and extends as far into the southern hemisphere as it does into the northern, but with very different human consequences in opposite latitudes. The continent consists of a high plateau of ancient rocks, surrounded by a lower broken coastal belt. The interior plateau rises from about 1,000 feet in the north and west to 3,000 feet, and in places much more, in the east and south. The plateau is edged by an escarpment which drops to the surrounding coastal areas and is particularly high and steep along its south-eastern edge, forming the high Drakensberg range. The high eastern part of the plateau is broken and confused by the bifurcating Great Rift Valley of East Africa which runs for 4,000 miles into Asia Minor and contains most of the East African lakes, the Red Sea and the River Jordan. The Rift Valley is edged by volcanoes and contains some of the most fertile soil in all Africa.

Some half-dozen very large rivers (besides innumerable small ones) – the Nile in the north, the Niger, the Congo and Orange in the west, the Zambezi and the Limpopo in the east – make their long ways across the highlands and cascade down the scarp in series of waterfalls and rapids. The north-western edge of the plateau is bounded by the folds of the Atlas Mountains, structurally part of the great folded mountain ranges of Europe and Asia. On the south the parallel ranges of the Cape cross the coastal belt from west to east.

The large extent of Africa north and south of the equator gives a wide range of climatic conditions and variety of vegetation. The equatorial rain forest, which includes the Congo Valley, merges into temperate woodland and savannah to north and south. These in turn change into bushveld and wide grassland and then into the sand and rock expanses of the Sahara in the north and the desert and semi-desert of the Namib, the Kalahari, Namaqualand and the Karroo in the south. Beyond these to the north and south are the winter rainfall areas of the Mediterranean littoral and the Cape Peninsula.

A huge arc of high savannah and grassland swings through East Africa round the basin of the Congo into South Africa, the high temperatures normal to such latitudes being very much modified by the altitude.

Configuration and climate together explain why Europe should have remained for so long ignorant of conditions in Africa and why Africa persisted in European minds as the dark continent. The desert was always discouraging, though never entirely a barrier to man's movement, and its occupation for long centuries by Muslims made it a sufficient barricade on the north against outsiders. Even when navigation was sufficiently advanced to allow voyagers down the west coast of Africa, they went no further inland than the low-lying malarial plains. The 19,000 miles of stretched and unindented coastline (less than that of Europe, only one-third of Africa's size) offered few harbours. Ships could not penetrate much beyond the mouths of rivers, great and wide though some of these were, because of the sandbanks that obstructed them or of the rapids by which they made their unruly descent from the hidden interior. Inside Africa itself, on the other hand, there was much movement of the inhabitants, often along the river valleys, and the eastern grasslands from Egypt and Ethiopia south were to prove a highway of migration and of

3

fundamental importance to the settlement and historical development of southern Africa.

South Africa, the broad peninsular end of the continent, is at
present the most highly developed and richest country in Africa.
It lies almost entirely outside the tropics, the plateau of the
interior being between 4,000 feet and 6,000 feet above sea level.
The landscape is mainly of undulating stretches of grassland or
bush broken by frequent characteristic *kopjes* or hills. The plateau
is rimmed on the east by the great north–south escarpment of the
Drakensberg which drops to the coastal plain, between 50 miles
and 250 miles wide, of Natal and the Eastern Cape and culminates
in the mountains of Lesotho, in places over 10,000 feet high.
South-westwards the fall from interior to coast is no longer a
well-defined scarp. The edge crumples into a series of parallel
east–west folded ranges, traversed by swift, narrow, deeply cut
and densely wooded rivers which offer no easy ways for human
transit, though movement and settlement in the lowlands between
the ranges and along the coast is easy.

Most of the interior drains westwards into the Orange River.
This flows wide, shallow, sluggish, except in the fast upper reaches
in Lesotho, through country so dry that for long stretches of its
course in winter the river breaks up into a chain of pools and
waterholes; it descends through a deep gorge over falls from the
plateau to the coast. It is useless for navigation but offers no great
impediment to movement and is important as a source of water-
power in its upper reaches and of irrigation in the arid country
through which it mostly flows. In contrast, the streams of the east
and south are short, deep and rapid and drain into the Indian
Ocean.

The rainfall in South Africa comes mainly in the summer, from
December to March. Brought on the eastern trade winds, it is
heavy on the east coast, on the Drakensberg and on the southern
ranges, and lessens inland and in the lee of the mountains, so that
the country becomes increasingly dry towards the west. In
consequence, the east and south coasts and slopes are thickly
wooded, particularly in the valleys where liane-tangled forests
often enclose splashing waterfalls and scampering monkeys.
Away from the streams the trees frequently have been felled

and the countryside is densely populated and heavily grazed.

West of the Drakensberg scarp the vegetation thins to the thorn-bush of the low-veld where there is little surface water but the land is verdant after summer rain and gradually dries to drought yellows and ashy grey. In warmer, wetter parts towards the Limpopo and Rhodesia the bush becomes a more luxuriant parkland of mopani and umbrella-thorn trees; in drier parts fleshy candelabra Euphorbia are as grotesque as the boulder-piled hills among which they stand. Westwards the bush gradually disappears, giving way to the undulating grass ocean of the high veld – a dazzling green after rain and shimmering gold for most of the year, covering much of the Transvaal and Orange Free State provinces. The land has been recklessly used and erosion has made harsh inroads. Now, in a thriftier generation, afforestation, contour cultivation and a scattering of small, glittering dams testify that man can intelligently exercise his first birthday gift of dominion over his environment.

Still further west, as the country becomes progressively drier, the grasslands pass into the arid Kalahari where thornscrub survives and any precipitation brings a quick and brilliant flowering that soon withers, and to the Namib desert of Namibia, South West Africa. The extreme western Cape Province juts into the belt of westerly winds, winter rainfall and mediterranean vegetation and agricultural economy as apparent in many orchards and wide vineyards. The maquis-type bush of the Cape hinterland desiccates to the north into the Kalahari semi-desert; and northeastwards the Karroo country, which lies enfolded in the ranges of the south, is covered with the unpromising low scrubby karroo-bush, succulent and highly nutritious for sheep. This is a land of great horizons, flat-topped distant blue hills, sunsets of unparalleled magnificence and magically evocative solitude. Farmsteads lie far out of sight one from another, tree-shaded, beside a spring or a wind-pump to lift water to fill a dam and irrigate a few acres. It is a country whose austerity, as likely as not, repels the passing stranger but commands the passionate devotion of those whose roots are there.

The altitude of much of the interior plateau tempers the climate of its sub-tropic latitude. The summer's heats are reduced by cooling evening storms, the winters are sunny, crisp and sharp at night and the country is particularly attractive to men of northern Europe.

This is a land that before and long after the coming of men carried an abundant wild life: large and small antelope, giraffe, buffalo, zebra, elephant, rhinoceros, baboons; the carnivores that prey on them, lion, leopard, jackal, hyena; and birds in splendid variety. But most have vanished before the predatory guns of men, to be now preserved in national parks.

Man has also played havoc with the vegetation. Primitive shifting cultivation was extravagant with land but there was plenty of it; hoeing was superficial and the earth was given time to recover. But the march of civilization changed this by pinning men to their plots and providing relentless cultivation techniques. Trees did not grow again where once they had been; plough replaced hoe; grazing was restricted and devastating; natural vegetation thinned and lost its moisture-retention powers. Desiccation and soil-erosion became regional disasters to which governments and people have only lately awakened.

The ancient rocks of Africa, richer in the minerals upon which modern life is based than any comparable area of the earth, tend, in many parts, to break down into a soil poor in nutritional content when the natural balance is disturbed.

The bush, the grasslands and the rivers of Africa harbour a variety of diseases, the incidence of which modern science is reducing. Many, however, continue to flourish in rural, backward and poverty-stricken areas where ignorance and lack of hygiene still prevail. Malaria, sleeping-sickness, hookworm, bilharzia and dysentery are all scourges that go back far in the life of the peoples and, along with the consequences of poor feeding, for centuries have had an immeasurably debilitating effect on their victims – often almost entire populations – causing the sapping lethargy and the low output which has for so long been regarded by Whites as a hallmark of the African.

The physical facts of Africa's situation, the interaction of topography, climate, vegetation and disease, have been of profound importance in the distribution of people and in their fates.

2. FIRST MEN AND MIGRATIONS

Scientists in many spheres – palaeontology, geology, zoology, biology, anthropology, archaeology, linguistics and pre-history – are patiently cooperating on a huge assignment. Each brings his newly-found, jagged, highly coloured, unrelated bits of know-ledge to fit into the communal jig-saw puzzle that will one day tell us our origins. Already a great deal is seen with reasonable certainty and much more, though subject to expert disagreement and continual revision, is confidently guessed at. As the picture becomes more coherent it develops a particular relevance to Africa and makes nonsense of many current theories and beliefs about race and race purity.

Among the more exciting of recent discoveries are the fossils found in East and South Africa which suggest, unexpectedly but convincingly, that it was there that man evolved. The great plains with fluctuating climate and changing vegetation may, over geological aeons, have provided the challenging natural conditions that induced a section of herbivorous primates to leave the Eden of sheltering forests and embark on a roaming, hunting life of hardship.

The fossil remains of a primate who lived perhaps 25,000,000 or 30,000,000 years ago near Lake Victoria have been found and named Proconsul. He seems to have been 'unspecialized', physically uncommitted to any one particular mode of life, equipped to live either in the trees or on the ground: that is, more adaptable to environmental vagaries than the run of animal life. He may well have been the common ancestor of both ape and man. His descendants, in order to survive the rigours of 12,000,000 years of drought, accommodated themselves, some to living as vegetarians in the forests; others, such as carnivores, hunted in groups and learned to walk upright with hands freed to acquire skills. Eventually this led to the use and the making of weapons and tools and so, 'with his seeing eye, understanding ear and skilful hands' to the shaping of his own destiny.

In the next 20,000,000 or so years the African uplands were probably inhabited by many different groups of primates, evolving, differentiating, struggling to survive; some were

7

defeated; others adapted successfully to changing conditions.

Fossils of *Australopithecus* – Man-Ape of the South – have been found in great numbers in South and East Africa, some branches vegetarian, some also carnivorous. Though their brains were smaller than has been generally accepted for man, the flesh-eaters of perhaps 750,000 to 2,500,000 years ago, at most 4′ 6″ tall, apparently walked upright, could run and could throw. They lived in small groups round shallow lakes in semi-arid grasslands. They were scavengers; but they also formed hunting bands. Possibly earlier forms armed themselves with thighbones of their antelope victims and selected and used pebble tools, while later-developing but co-existing types – *homo erectus* and *homo habilis* – the upright and the dextrous men of South and East Africa respectively – were shaping bone and pebble tools, giving a fresh context to Benjamin Franklin's two hundred-year-old criterion: 'Man is a tool-making animal'. At any rate, the great quantities of early stone tools found over South and East Africa – far more than anywhere else – taken with other evidence, makes it seem very likely that pre-sapient man, 'the self-conscious animal', was being shaped. In the dawn mists of history and over an inconceivably long time, multiplying groups of emergent men struggled with nature, practised and extended their skills and, as they became more confidently and securely established in their world, they wandered over Africa, overflowed into Europe and Asia and ebbed back. They defeated, outlived or assimilated the various less adaptable cousins they met, to produce in due time the different races that were to people the earth. Under constant challenge they used their brain and by use developed it: a brain at length capable of a Hamlet, a Dachau, the book of Genesis or the atom bomb. Along the line too, they found the knowledge of good and evil, which must be reinterpreted in each generation and by each individual.

The evidence becomes more abundant. By perhaps 50,000 BC a number of 'pre-sapient' types of men (Neanderthal man in North Africa, Rhodesian Man in southern Africa and Kanjera, a more sapient-type man in East Africa, among them) were established all over Africa. They had probably by now discovered the use of fire and had invented a great variety of specialist tools

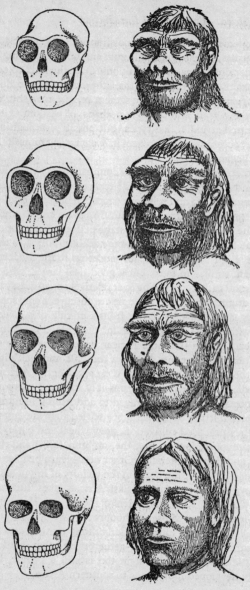

Eight line drawings (four skulls and four faces) to illustrate the four phases of human cranial and facial evolution. From top to bottom: australopithecine, pithecanthropine, neanderthaline and sapient.

and implements – grubbing tools, spearheads, chisels, knives, bone needles, thread, vegetable gum and fibre – enabling them to live under diverse natural conditions. Over the next 20,000 years some strains better adjusted than the rest began to dominate: *homo sapiens*, not so much the sapient or wise man, but the man with the big brain and capable, perhaps, of wisdom. The others disappeared as individual types, but possibly through assimilation they accentuated differences in *homo sapiens* himself. Modern 'races' began to emerge.

By 10,000 BC *homo sapiens* was dominant everywhere in Africa, living in larger groups than his predecessors, with rudimentary social organization and religious concepts, burying his dead with a care that would enable remote future ages to know something of him. The predominant type to establish itself over most of Africa from the Sahara, through Ethiopia and East Africa to the Cape, was the 'Big Bushman' probably ancestral to the modern San or Bushman, similar in looks but a good deal larger, who lived as hunters and gatherers ranging over relatively open grassy lands.

The origins of the Negro people are obscure. Some speculation has suggested that they derive from a mixing of a *homo sapiens* group with another vanished strain; their blood grouping shows a connection with the same African ancestral stock as the San. They inhabited territory between the Nile and the Niger from where they spread over most of West and Central Africa, people of woodlands and rivers who possibly in a wet climatic phase after 5000 BC became encouraged to add fishing to hunting and so were enabled to lead lives more settled than the nomad San. Later they practised cultivation, grew wheat and barley in more temperate zones, domesticated the sorghum, millet and rice of the tropics and they proliferated. Other non-Negro peoples possibly developed further to the north in the vicinity of Egypt and groups may have settled around the East African lakes. Further to the south were the Khoikhoi, Men of Men, the Hottentot, who looked like the San, whose neighbours they were, except that they were taller, and they spoke a different tongue; they also followed the roaming life of the hunter-gatherers and they herded sheep and cattle as well. Their origin too is still a puzzle, but they possibly developed indigenous to southern Africa.

Homo sapiens may have evolved in Africa and from there spread out over the world and back again. But it was in the great fertile river valleys of Asia Minor that he first discovered the techniques of animal breeding and plant cultivation which enabled him to abandon his wandering life. He settled down, began to live in large groups, to accumulate material possessions and wealth, to trade, to discover how to use metal and to evolve complex social organizations – in short, began to become civilized. From Asia Minor the new skills and practices filtered out in all directions along migrants' paths and trade routes, and penetrated up the Nile and across the desert far into Africa.

Egypt became great when her people fused their African tradition with farming techniques learned around 6000 BC–5000 BC from Asia Minor. This fusion made the growth of a large settled population possible in the fertile Lower Nile Valley and a complex political organization was required to administer the growing numbers and wealth. At last Bronze-Age Egypt was destroyed by drought and invading Assyrian cohorts. Byron's 'the sheen of their spears . . . like stars on the sea', had been the first glint of sunlight on wrought iron, the new metal with which *homo sapiens* would revolutionize his life on earth. The civilization of Egypt, however, was preserved for a thousand years by the Kushites of the Sudan. They had learned from the Assyrians the potent secret of iron and in Meroë (near modern Khartoum) iron ore and fuel for smelting it were abundant. From there knowledge of iron-working was diffused by trade, migration and conquest far and wide in Africa.

Cultivation of wheat and barley spreading out from the Nile valley and the later domestication, further south, of tropical grains, sorghums, millets and dry rice, permitted a slow build-up of population among the Negroes of the Sudan and Central and West Africa. One theory is that the growing use of iron, giving improved tools, weapons and boats and more efficient hunting, fishing and transport, enabled groups of perhaps only several hundred in all, when pressure was heavy, to break through the barriers of Nile swamp and equatorial forest and move rapidly south of the equator to the Katanga area. There they found lightly wooded, well-watered country similar to their distant homeland where life could follow the traditional pattern and the ample endowment of gold, copper and iron made for increasing technical efficiency and wealth. From this centre they could spread afield, even towards the coast, and when at the beginning of our era the Indonesian colonists of Madagascar introduced valuable East Indian food crops – yam, banana and coconut – to the African mainland they were ready to adopt them. This greatly improved food supply enabled their numbers to multiply further and accelerated their long dispersal. Groups of energetic, resourceful Iron-Age farmers, their original Negro characteristics becoming variously modified by those of the peoples they came in

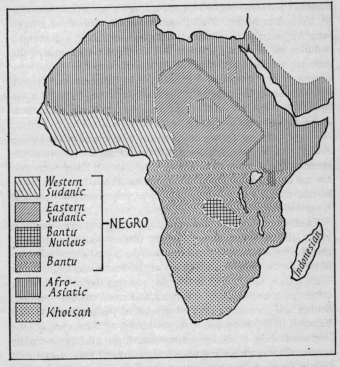

Map II Distribution of Peoples according to Language Groups

contact with – such as the earlier indigenous peoples of the interior and the oriental colonists of the east coast – continued their movement to north and to south until they became the predominant inhabitants of Africa south of the equator. That, at any rate, is the chain of events suggested on complex linguistic evidence and supported by archaeology and early historical documents. This new, late-coming entity in Africa's population spoke a derivative of their original western Sudanic tongue, which splintered into a large group of allied languages now classified as Bantu (this being their own word for 'the people'). Bantu was the name given by Whites also to the people who spoke those languages.

Arab traders were active along the east coast of Africa during the first millennium AD. They valued more highly even than the fine gold found in those parts the iron produced by the Africans of the interior. They took it to India to be forged into steel and from there to Damascus, where it was tempered and made into swords and chainmail which could eventually arm the Saracens against the crusaders of western Europe. By Islamic times kingdoms of marked sophistication by contemporary European and Eastern standards existed in Africa, and those of the east and centre have a relevance to the past of southern Africa.

The sites of ancient mineral workings – copper, gold and iron – are widely spread over modern Zambia, Rhodesia and the northern part of South Africa. Amongst them, mysterious and splendid, stand ruins of stone – fortresses, temples, palaces. The most renowned of these are the Zimbabwe ruins of Rhodesia, a few hundred miles north of the Limpopo River. White men from the south came on these ruins in the nineteenth century and were baffled; they believed them to have been built by a vanished people from the East, or even by Phoenicians, so improbable did it seem that the African people living primitive lives around them could ever have been craftsmen skilled enough to build so grandly.

But Great Zimbabwe is an indigenous African achievement, founded and inhabited for over a thousand years by Bantu-speaking Iron-Age people. The early Karanga-speaking inhabitants may have come into Rhodesia about AD 850 from the Congo, settling among indigenous San and earlier Iron-Age people whom they employed as herders and smiths. Further immigration of Bantu Mbira from Lake Tanganyika brought advanced techniques and ideas and an elaborate society developed. They improved the earlier rough stone buildings, a skill stimulated no doubt by the abundantly available material in the rock-strewn countryside. They erected impressive and elaborate stone temples to serve complex religious systems based on beliefs in a supreme deity and on cults of spirit worship in which kings as well as priests or mediums had important functions. From the mid-fifteenth century onward there was great building, mining and commercial activity and rising prosperity. With the increase in their numbers they spread and dominated ever wider areas between the Zambezi and the Limpopo. The central chieftainship imposed authority over surrounding areas until the loose Karanga confederacy of many subject states was created. After a successful campaign in 1450, the ruler (and his successors) became known as Monomotapa (*Mwene Mutapa*), a corruption of an equivocal praise-name meaning 'master pillager'. He moved the head-quarters of his dominions from Zimbabwe to a more central site on the Zambezi. A ruling and exclusive clan of the Karanga, possibly with priestly functions, was probably the Rozwi. They had built up great power and close trading relations with the Arabs of the coast. Towards the end of the fifteenth century a Rozwi chief broke away from the Monomotapa and established the rival Changamire dynasty in the south and based on Zimbabwe, while the Monomotapa retained a shrinking ascendancy in the north-east.

Arabs pursuing their centuries' old trade, exchanging cloth, beads, porcelain and eastern luxuries for Monomotapa's gold, iron, ivory and silver, brought to the coast accounts of the great state he kept and of riches untold which suggested to Europe that there was the land of Ophir and which lured the Portuguese to inland conquests. Portuguese inroads and the rivalry of the Changamire (whose domains the Portuguese never controlled though they traded with them) upset the political stability of the area. The Monomotapa declined in power after a defeat in about 1700 and became a puppet of the Portuguese. The Rozwi kingdom retained its independence until, towards the middle of the nineteenth century, it was defeated by invasions of fierce

Nguni people from the south. The invaders destroyed the old civilization so completely that Whites, crossing the Limpopo less than a hundred years later, could only speculate wildly on the origin of the bush-submerged ruins. Legends of Ophir and King Solomon's mines revived and a company was formed to 'explore' over forty-three ruins, offering blankets in exchange for the betrayal of the tribal heritage. No one knows what they came on or looted and melted down, for no golden treasure has been found in later archaeological investigations of Zimbabwe.

The picture of that civilization, however, was filled in when a burial trove of fine golden objects was found in 1932 in an unplundered hilltop fortress at Mapungubwe, south of the Limpopo in the Northern Transvaal. This seems to have been the home of a people broadly contemporary with those of Zimbabwe and whose way of life was similar. This community reached its heyday in the fourteenth or fifteenth century and established a rich and varied culture there. The area seems also to have been an important religious and commercial centre until it too was destroyed by the northward sweep of Ndebele warriors (a branch of the Nguni), early in the nineteenth century.

While notable empires were building up at focal points the slow, desultory, southerly drift of groups of Bantu-speaking iron-working people continued for most of two thousand years. They drove their herds, stopped seasonally to sow and harvest, and settled at last where they found space and a location to suit them. In their wanderings they met with, mixed with, settled among, influenced and were influenced by earlier inhabitants – earlier-coming Bantu peoples, perhaps, or the indigenous San or Khoi-khoi. According to circumstances and contacts their physical, cultural and linguistic characteristics became varied.

People familiar with the working and use of iron were probably settled in the Transvaal by the last half of the first millennium. Their physical type is unknown. They may have been Khoisan who learned the techniques from further north, but more likely small groups of Bantu-speaking immigrants settled among the local populations introducing them to the art of metal working and to cultivation and stock rearing. By the eleventh century Iron-Age communities were widely established in the Northern

South Africa: An Historical Introduction

and Central Transvaal: in the Zoutpansberg, Witwatersrand and Rustenberg areas and in Swaziland.

The Bantu-speaking people of South Africa today fall into two main language groups, the Sotho-Tswana and the Nguni, with differences of culture within their broad similarities. They probably acquired their modern tribal structure after centuries of movement, adaptation, assimilation and regrouping. They may stem from two different peoples in the north: the Nguni, who set greater store by their cattle, from a mixing of East African cattle people with cultivators of the southern savannah; and the Sotho, for whom cattle are important but less ritually significant, from more agriculturally orientated societies of Central Africa. Or they may have come of the same early Iron-Age people of the Transvaal and developed differently, influenced by different groups of the indigenous population.

The ancestors of the Sotho may have been the earliest Iron-Age inhabitants in South Africa or they may have crossed the upper Limpopo, avoiding the tsetse-fly areas, between the eleventh and twelfth centuries, assimilating with earlier Iron-Age people. They have probably occupied their present areas, Botswana (Tswana), Lesotho and the Free State (Southern Sotho) and the Northern and Eastern Transvaal, since before 1600. The Venda and Lemba peoples of Northern and Eastern Transvaal speak languages related to Sotho and to Karanga and are thought to have moved into South Africa perhaps in the fifteenth or sixteenth centuries. The Venda may be an offshoot of the Rozwi, while the Lemba, skilled metal workers and potters, are markedly non-Negro in appearance and may be descendants of people once trading intensively with the east coast.

The Nguni group includes the Swazi, Zulu, Pondo, Thembu and Xhosa peoples, living mostly east of the Drakensberg, through Natal to the eastern Cape Province, and the Ndebele of the Transvaal. They have no tribal memories of a distant homeland; their early connections north of the Limpopo have not been traced, perhaps because they were a mainly nomad cattle people leaving not much mark of their passing, but they have apparently been living in their present area for many centuries. The southern Nguni are known to have been settled on the Natal coast by the

16

end of the sixteenth century. By tradition they lived in the Drakensberg foothills on the upper reaches of the Umzimvubu for many generations before that.

So by the middle of the seventeenth century when the Dutch were making their first settlement in the extreme south-west the Bantu-speaking people, contrary to popular belief, had been living in the northern, central and eastern parts for as much as several hundred years.

The Bantu Africans vary widely in appearance. From the basic Negro stock they inherit the dark skin, long oval-shaped head and broad prominent face. While some individuals and tribes look almost pure Negro, others have the light yellow colour or high cheekbones of San or Khoikhoi ancestors. Others again, especially among the eastern tribes with the bearing and features of Mediterranean sculpture, show evident reminders of the passage and sojourn of adventurers from Arabia and south-east Asia. Yet others reveal later fugitives of many races from the Cape and Whites, shipwrecked along the southern coasts, among their forbears.

The culture and complex social organization – broadly similar among all, though with variation in details from people to people – were distinctive and often very different from those of Europe. The differences have given rise to fundamental misunderstanding and conflict. Many elements of the old tribal way of life endure today but they are frequently much modified and often stultified and emasculated by the impact of the West.

In the days of their old independence Bantu-speaking Africans were pastoral and agricultural people living, in normal circumstances, in settled communities, bound by birth or allegiance to a hereditary chief in an elaborate social and political organization. The family was the basic unit and consisted of a man and his wife or wives, their children and various dependants. Plural marriages were common, as they are in many rural non-mechanical societies, where the day-to-day maintenance of the family unit requires many hands. Among the Nguni the families lived in scattered homesteads which consisted of a group of huts, usually ranged in an arc, with that of the head of the family in the centre, those of the wives and other members of the household on either side, all surrounding the *kraal* or cattle enclosure. The Sotho often lived in very large villages surrounded by gardens and cattle posts. At the very centre of life were the cattle. They represented the status and wealth of the head of the family and had both ritual and economic significance. Though milk was used, the cattle were seldom slaughtered except for social or ritual feasting. Marriages were legalized by the transfer of a certain number of cattle from groom to bride's father, and these *lobola* cattle were often provided collectively by the tribe for a chief's main marriage which would secure the succession. These cattle established the husband's title to the children of the marriage and guaranteed its stability. They had frequently to be restored if the bride's conduct was unsatisfactory or forfeit if the husband's fell short of accepted standards. The growth of the practice of exchanging cattle associated with polygyny in a patrilineal society may in part explain the periodic rapid increase in population and rise to power and wealth of certain chiefly families at the expense of their poorer neighbours, perhaps when groups of cattle people settled among hunters or cultivators.

Age was respected and the elders were the repository of the traditions and accumulated wisdom of the people. Children were loved and indulged in infancy, disciplined in adolescence and prepared for adult responsibilities in the harsh testing of circumcision or initiation schools.

All land was vested in the chief and administered by him on behalf of the tribe. He parcelled out areas for habitation and cultivation to the headmen who made allotments to each family; pasturage was in common. The wives of the household each had their own plots and granaries and to them traditionally fell the tasks of agriculture while the men hunted, looked after the cattle, or went to war. Possession of land was retained until it fell into disuse when it reverted to tribal ownership. The chief had no rights to alienate tribal land; he could only grant usufruct. Europeans had no comprehension of this basic fact any more than the African had of the European's claim to individual ownership, and much disastrous misunderstanding and embitterment resulted.

The chief governed his tribe and administered law, usually with the advice of his counsellors, elders or headmen, and with the consent of the people. There would be much open discussion of matters affecting the community before decisions were taken, and justice was administered in open tribal gatherings. A chief's status and the size of his tribe depended on the people's approval and acceptance, and the followers of an unpopular chief defected and melted away to his rivals. Military tyrants such as the Zulu Shaka, who, at the time of European penetration, was wreaking havoc in the east, were far from typical. As provision was made for the hiving off of the discontented so there were also formulae for the acceptance of aliens either by absorption or in some form of vassalage.

Most Bantu peoples had some conception of a supreme being who controlled the natural order, which helped to make them receptive to Muslim and Christian teachings. But their religious beliefs and practices centred largely on the worship and propitiation, sometimes through powerful mediums, of the ancestors whose spirits, for better or worse, hung about the home, and whose goodwill had to be kept. This fostered a great sense of the unity of the family, past and present. Two sorts of magic were recognized: there were witches with supernatural powers to harm others, who when identified, were exterminated; and there were medicine-men (and women) and diviners whose gifts were beneficent, whose skill was often considerable and whose office was frequently hereditary.

Generally in mountain fastnesses or on the inhospitable desert edges, but also sometimes in closer and amicable association with their more powerful neighbours, lived small and scattered groups of San, dwarfed and direct descendants of the proud first men who once roamed the African homelands almost unchallenged, but were now ousted from all but those parts where life was most difficult. The San are small in stature – few are taller than five feet – yellow in colour with triangular faces, bright eyes and tightly curled peppercorn hair; the men have protuberant stomachs, the women immensely fat buttocks, which perhaps, like the camel's hump, is a storage device for lean seasons. These distinctive physical characteristics of the San served to emphasize their strangeness to European eyes. They wandered in loose clans of 300 at most, forming hunting bands under a chief, with rights (well recognized by other San tribes and by their Khoikhoi neighbours) over a particular territory: to the water-holes within it and to the game drinking at the water. Long conditioning to subsistence living enabled them still to follow man's primeval mode of life. They hunted game and their enemies with poisoned arrows. They kept no domestic animals other than dogs; they did not cultivate; they caught reptiles and insects and they gathered edible roots and leaves and berries. When food was plentiful they gorged and when it was scarce they stoically starved. They forever wandered gathering and hunting. They had no settled home but lived in the flimsiest of reed shelters or in caves. They wore animal skins, fur inside in the winter time, and ornaments of leather or ostrich shell. Family ties were weak; children had to fend for themselves early; the old and sick were perforce abandoned when they could no longer keep up the nomad pace.

The San's four unrelated languages had small vocabularies, full of strange clicks. They were a cheerful people and loved to dance on both social and ritual occasions; they were born story-tellers and actors, brilliant mimics; above all they and their ancestors painted and carved, leaving for us to find in the caves where they sheltered the lively, vivid rock engravings and paintings that are among the art wonders of the world.

The San, the little hunters, wrote Dorothea Bleek, had never been known to attack stronger races save in defence of their country, but for this had been fighting a losing battle for thousands of years: against men who herded animals and, in search of pasture, invaded their hunting grounds; against men who planted grain and took over the water places; against men armed with iron spears and guns and whom they held off with their long knowledge of the African wild and their deadly poisoned arrows until they were forced to retreat before superior numbers. But Africa was vast and there had always been deserts and mountains where the cattle and grain men could not exist, but where the San could continue to hunt rock rabbits, lizards and locusts and so survive. Even today some still live like this in the Kalahari desert and the dry lands of South West Africa. Some of them, too, came to terms with their neighbours, attached themselves in a dependent status to the more successful Khoikhoi and Bantu (and, much later, to the Whites) as hunters, trackers and herdsmen in return for some economic security.

The origins of the Khoikhoi are unknown. Tribal tradition holds that, displaced by others, they drove their herds south-westwards, their faces always to the setting sun. Like the San, however, they are probably descended from sections of the basic indigenous late Stone-Age population of South Africa, who came under the influence of early Iron-Age farmers and metalworkers and adopted a pastoral way of life. They closely resembled the San in appearance except that they were a good deal taller. They were more elaborately organized in small clans loosely knit into hordes of between a few hundred and a couple of thousand individuals. They spoke many different dialects of a click language. There was often rivalry between the chiefs and struggles between clans for pasturage. Each clan had its own recognized territory and strangers were expected to get permission to hunt or pasture their animals upon it. As well as being hunters, the Khoikhoi were skilful pastoralists, driving their large herds of fat-tailed sheep and long-horned cattle to and fro in search of water and grass. They were good craftsmen too, making mats, pots, baskets and ornaments of shell, ivory and grass. Some seem to have acquired a knowledge of iron-working, but mostly they preferred to barter their spear and arrow heads from others rather than smelt themselves. They wore clothing of skins and greased their bodies with animal fat which gave them a smell often repellent to Europeans. Their main foods were milk, wild vegetables and game. They slaughtered their cattle only for feasts, but some would train them as pack or riding animals. Their camps were more permanent than those of the San, their huts elaborately made and portable in contrast to the rough disposable shelters of the San. Their social organization was complex, with features resembling that of the San and unlike the Bantu-speakers. They recognized a supreme being, but they did not practice ancestor worship and the chiefs had no priestly function. Though the San were traditionally hunters and the Khoikhoi largely herders, there are no hard and fast distinctions; hunters were known who spoke Khoikhoi dialects, herders who resembled San.

Along the common boundaries in the south-east San, Khoikhoi

and later-coming Nguni people established an equilibrium. At times they were in conflict, but in the main they adjusted to each other and the age-old blending process slowly continued. There was some inter-marriage and some tribes of mixed origin developed.

3. EARLY TRAVELLERS

From the time when man first produced food or artefacts surplus to his own needs and discovered that these could be bartered for other men's products, he has found routes to follow in pursuit of commerce. The Nile penetrated deep into the interior of the African continent and carried traffic up and down from time immemorial. Well-worn routes west and south across the Sahara were followed by convoys of camels and chariots, finding harbour and refreshment at the scattered oases. For thousands of years men launched out on the seas, hugging the coasts in cockle-shells, drifting on the currents and learning to sail with the prevailing winds.

From about 2000 BC, the Egyptians conquered, traded with, settled amongst and married into the peoples of distant regions to west and south. From these remote areas knowledge and goods and individuals filtered back along the trade routes, bringing new influences to bear on Egypt. Egyptian fleets, too, made their way out of the Red Sea and reached along the eastern coast of the continent, at least as far as the 'Cape of Spices' or the 'Horn of the South', Cape Guardafui in Somaliland. In a great series of temple reliefs near Luxor, the ships of Queen Hatshepsut are shown being loaded for a return voyage 3,000 years ago with

marvels of the land of Punt (Ethiopia): all goodly fragrant woods of God's land, heaps of myrrh-resin, with fresh myrrh trees, with ebony and pure ivory, with green gold of Emu, with cinnamon wood ... incenses ... eye-cosmetics, with apes, monkeys, dogs and skins of the Southern panther, with natives and their children.[1]

Even then, in the first light of history, there was traffic in slaves and gold, merchandise that was to be woven into the fabric of African history.

About 600 BC Pharaoh Necho of Egypt sent a Phoenician fleet to sail through the Red Sea and south, and return through the

1. Basil Davidson, *Old Africa Rediscovered*, p. 47.

Pillars of Hercules, the Straits of Gibraltar. Herodotus, writing some 150 years later, relates:

> On each occasion when autumn time came round, they put to shore, sowed grain in the soil of whatever part of Libya (Africa) they had reached on their voyage, and waited until reaping time. They then harvested the corn and sailed on. When two years had passed in this fashion, they doubled the Pillars of Hercules in the third year and came to Egypt. They made a statement, which other men may believe, of course, but not I, that in sailing round Libya they had the sun on their right hand.[2]

Since most authorities are even more sceptical about this voyage than Herodotus, we do not know whether or not the Phoenicians were the first people to circumnavigate Africa.

Less spectacularly but more surely, Hanno, the Carthaginian, eighty years after Necho's expedition, sailed in the opposite direction into the Atlantic to found Punic settlements along the west coast of Africa as far as Sierra Leone. These Phoenicians, jealous of their commercial connections, destroyed their records and did all they could to block the profitable way to rivals; and later the links with the Mediterranean weakened and the colonies disappeared.

Greek pilots, about 500 BC, first made the voyage from Europe through the Red Sea to India. On their earlier journeys clinging to the coasts, the Greeks gradually learned to use the monsoon winds which blow regularly in certain months, north-east or south-west, and will carry ships in either direction according to the season. When Carthage was at last destroyed and Rome became supreme, trading ships of Rome and Alexandria also made the passage to India. Soon there were regular sailings along the east coast of Africa, reaching perhaps as far as Dar-es-Salaam by the first century AD, and a fairly detailed knowledge of the coast had been gathered.

Once beyond the Red Sea, the ships of Europe were on the trading thoroughfare of the world. From the time of the Queen of Sheba, 1000 BC, the states on the south coast of Arabia had grown wealthy, trading with Africa across and beyond the Red Sea which for centuries they dominated. Later merchant princes from southern Arabia, who traced their descent from Sheba, journeying

2. *Cambridge History of the British Empire*, Vol. VIII, p. 56.

in search of commerce rather than loot or conquest, established trading stations along the East African coast. There they were to learn the local language, probably an early Bantu form, marry the local women and create the Swahili culture, a synthesis of African and non-African. In time, famous cities of wealth and luxury grew up along the coast. By the first century AD there were regular sailings, a busy coming and going along the monsoon routes between India, Arabia and the east coast of Africa.

Europe, however, with the collapse of the Roman Empire and the sweeping conquests of northern barbarians, had become concentrated on internal struggles and readjustments. By the fourth century the Indians, Arabs and Abyssinians had closed the Red Sea to Roman navigators. Europe's ships disappeared from the eastern seaways and all memory of what lay south of the Sahara faded into mists of legend, myth and dark ignorance for over a thousand years.

With the coming of Islam in the seventh century the Indian Ocean became even more an Indo-Arabian closed sea and, for about 900 years, inaccessible to western Europe. Muslims founded the towns of Brava and Mogodixo, on the Somali coast, and drove their Arab predecessors and half-Arab descendants to become the middle men in the trade with the interior which began to flourish. By the end of the first millennium the site of Sofala, near Beira, was reached and a settlement made when gold was found to be available.

In his book, *Meadows of Gold*, El Mas'udi of Baghdad tells of the Arabs and Persians in the tenth century passing along the monsoon trade routes from Madagascar and East Africa to Malabar and Ceylon, and of the sectional squabbling of the Arab settlers. He describes the native inhabitants of the coast, the Zanj – the Blacks, making no distinction between those of Khoisan, Bantu or other origin. He gives a picture of a vigorous, energetic people living inland from Sofala, agriculturalists and cattle-owners, skilled workers in gold and iron, who hunted elephants for ivory and traded gold, ivory, iron, panther-skins and tortoise-shell with the Arabs of the coast.

Not only were Arabs and Persians active in the commerce of the coast. From India, Indonesia and China ships constantly made the perilous voyage. The Indonesians colonized Madagascar and possibly sites on the African mainland early in the Christian era. Between the twelfth and fifteenth centuries huge Chinese fleets were crossing the Indian Ocean. Travellers' accounts that have survived, exotic food plants that took root and excavated fragments of the porcelain, beads, glass and coins left by Oriental seamen in exchange for the luxury products of Africa, all tell the same story.

Of all this long traffic between the civilizations of the East and Middle East with African kingdoms whose power and wealth derived from knowledge and skill in the working of metal, little was known in Europe, enclosed first in its own Dark Ages and then cut off by the crescent of Islam.

4. CHRISTIANITY AND COMMERCE

When a population becomes too great for its homeland to contain it, due perhaps to an adverse change in climate or an advance in successful adaptation to environment, movements of people in search of new homes and living-space will generally follow. Sometimes these movements are gradual, long sustained and apparent only after time has passed; others are more an inevitable bursting of bounds with consequences that can be cataclysmic. The migrants progressively displace their neighbours and fall on settled, and often more civilized but less virile, peoples, setting up waves of disturbances that die out only far from the centre. The continual flux which formed the tribes of Africa naturally also influenced events elsewhere. The Roman Empire, which had for so long kept in imperial fashion the peace of the Western world, shattered under assaults of barbarians pressing down from the north and left a fragmented Europe slowly to mould national identities in the shade of the Dark Ages.

Similar population pressures in Asia coincided with the emergence of Mohammed, the prophet, in 622 and projected the Arabs into a world role. A vigorous proselytizing Muslim flood swept into the vacuum left by Rome: from Asia Minor west into Egypt; along the Mediterranean coast and into Spain and Portugal; across the Sahara into the open uplands south of the desert; and southward into the East African coastlands. Islam was carried also to the East, into northern India and Malaysia and almost encircled the Indian Ocean. The Muslims established societies of high culture and brilliant artistic and intellectual achievement.

Throughout the twelfth century expeditionary forces comprising the flower of Christendom went in vain against them. Behind the crusades, like later wars, was a mixture of motives, the commercial imperative underlying the strident religious call to arms. Byzantium, weakened by centuries of Christian dissension, fell to the Saracens in 1453. The westward and northward flow of Arab and Turk was not checked until 1565 by the Knights of St John behind their bastions in Malta and over a hundred years later at the gates of Vienna. But in the far west the force of Muslim advance spent itself in the thirteenth century against a renascent Christendom in Spain and Portugal.

After the Middle Ages, western Europe began to awaken in the first light of a new learning. Scientific and technical advance was stimulated by the intellectual challenge of the Muslim world: Arab science and mathematics and forgotten classical knowledge were brought to cross-fertilize medieval scholarship. Men of the West, with broadening horizons, began to shake off the blinkers of orthodoxy and to take up again where the ancients had left off. Military successes against the infidel made them bold to discover and conquer new worlds. Barred by Muslim hegemony from the old trade routes to east and south of the Mediterranean, new adventurers at last made the passage round southern Africa sought by Hanno nearly 2,000 years earlier. Ships of the West burst suddenly into the long-closed Indo-Arabian commercial precinct of the Indian Ocean, taking Islam in the rear. History was given a fresh and fateful direction.

Portugal, a narrow territory on the western seaboard of the Iberian peninsula, moved into the lead of European progress. For three centuries, with Spain, she fought the Muslim enemy, welded herself into a nation in the process and emerged in the fifteenth century with the Moors finally defeated and driven out. A relatively poor and hilly country with a long Atlantic coast-line and cut off landwards to the north and west by Spain, Portugal developed her fisheries and sea-going trade and organized her navy, using all that in the intimate contact of centuries of domina-

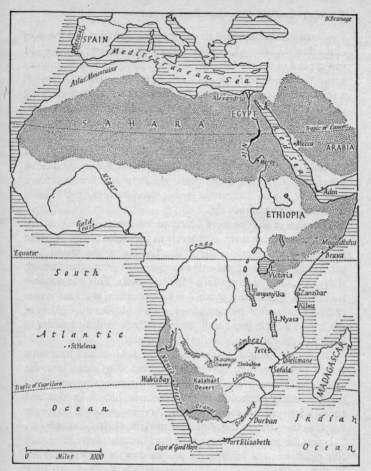

Map III Africa and the Mediterranean

tion and struggle she had learnt of Arab geography, navigation and mathematics.

In this environment a young prince grew up. Born in 1415, half-Portuguese, half-Anglo-French, grandson of John of Gaunt, he was to go down in history as Henry the Navigator. He was intelligent, curious, inquiring; religious and acquisitive, rich and a visionary; fascinated by astronomy, mathematics and the tales of mariners. Later to be called 'a Renaissance Cecil Rhodes', he was typical of his time in the dawning spirit of scientific inquiry in the West and the turning of its fruits to profit. He built himself an observatory on a rocky promontory and spent his days studying charts, talking to seafarers, cartographers and instrument-makers, and reading reports by Marco Polo and the Arab writers of the day, of the trade of the Indian Ocean, of the cities and riches of the East. Convinced by all his researches that Africa could be circumnavigated, he sent out his fleets. The captains sailed along the unknown West African coast, either to perish or to return with information that would enable their successors to press a little further on each voyage.

The men of Europe were falling under the spell of commerce which was to drive them excessively in succeeding ages. Western Europe's long severance from the Eastern world meant that products of the East could only be acquired at great price through the middle-man of the eastern Mediterranean. This was not only for the trade in luxury goods – silks, porcelain, precious stones and perfumes – but for necessities in a world where the spices of the Indies were in great and commercially rewarding demand to keep food palatable through the long winters.

Of course, the gold of Guinea glittered. Gold had long been traded from the West African coast, carried by Arab caravans across the Sahara to Morocco and the Mediterranean coasts. Gold was becoming important in the economic life of Europe and necessary to pay for goods from the Arabs who would no longer barter as the Africans did. And here too Islam held the monopoly.

It was the gold trade that began the Portuguese rise to wealth. But profit was not initially the sole motive for the expeditions. Elation at the military defeat of Islam was accompanied by a missionary zeal to convert the Muslim and indeed all heathen peoples. In addition there was Prester John, the legendary Christian monarch with a realm and great wealth somewhere in the African interior – perhaps a confusion of the old Christian kingdom of Ethiopia with that of the gold-producing Monomotapa – and for a time one of the purposes of African exploration was to find him and enlist his support against the infidel. The missionary incentive was given added zest when the Popes, Nicholas V and Calixtus III, granted remission of sins to all who took part and gave to the Portuguese sole rights of seizing the people of Africa with a view to converting them to Christianity.

The Portuguese Government rewarded Henry the Navigator with a monopoly of the African trade and 5 per cent of the profits and within the next few years 1,000 slaves were taken into Portugal. By the time Henry died in 1460, the Gold and Slave Coasts had been reached and the shores from Cape Bojador to Sierra Leone explored and mapped.

Little is known of this early exploration. The Portuguese, like the trading Carthaginians before them, may have deliberately destroyed records and followed a policy of secrecy to conceal the source of the new wealth from competitors. It was a monopoly worth preserving. In 1469, for instance, a Fernao Gomes was leased the trade of the Guinea coast for five years provided he explored 100 leagues of unknown coastline each year. This he did and imported a thousand slaves annually into Portugal.

Under successive rulers the Portuguese pushed on with the exploration of Africa. The lure of trading profits soon eclipsed proselytizing enthusiasm. One emissary travelling eastwards overland reached the spice marts of Malabar, in India, and, returning with Arab traders to Abyssinia, sent back messages that Africa could be rounded: the captains were to ask for Sofala and the Island of the Moon and there they would find pilots for Malabar.

In 1487 Bartholomew Dias set out with two caravels and a store-ship, under orders to sail on and not stop to trade along the coast. He took with him West Africans captured on an earlier expedition and samples of silver and gold and spices. On 8 December, four months after leaving Lisbon and sailing close to the coast he reached Walvis Bay. A storm then drove him far out to sea and when it was spent he sailed east without reaching land. He therefore turned north and arrived at Mossel Bay, which he called the bay of Cowherds. These ashy-yellow brown people, Khoikhoi, whose language his captive West African Negroes did not know, drove their herds away in terror and pelted the Portuguese with stones as they landed. Dias retaliated and killed one with a bolt from a cross-bow.

The trend of the coastline was eastwards and Dias followed it to the mouth of either the Kowie or the Great Fish River. Here, as the voyage had been hard and the men were restive, they turned back. On the return voyage, in May 1488, they discovered the Cape, but it remains uncertain whether Dias called it Cabo Tormentoso, the Stormy Cape, or the Cape of Good Hope. They reached Lisbon in December 1488, after a voyage of sixteen months and seventeen days, having proved the Cape could be rounded and India accessible.

The next expedition was planned with great care by King Manoel, the Fortunate. He chose as leader Vasco da Gama, an able soldier and experienced administrator, supplied him with credentials as Ambassador to the ruler of Calicut and instructions to establish friendly relations and make a commercial treaty. Da Gama was equipped with two of the best pilots of the day, who had made the voyage with Dias, three ships, a store-ship, 170 men and the latest maps, charts and astronomical instruments. Instead of hugging the coast as had been customary, da Gama, relying on charts and instruments and on the knowledge of winds and currents gained by Dias and his pilots, made out across the ocean. Less than four months later, on 5 November 1497, he made landfall at St Helena Bay, just north of the Cape. There the seafarers met Khoikhoi who again were hostile when the men landed to draw water. The expedition sailed on, past Dias's furthest point, touched a new coast on Christmas Day and called it Natal. Pressing on, da Gama put in at the mouth of a small stream which he named Copper River. Here he found the local people black and very different from the Khoikhoi further south and so friendly that he called their country the Land of the Good Folk. This was probably a little west of Capa das Correntes and in the neighbourhood of Delagoa Bay. (Between 1552 and 1593, a century after da Gama, survivors of successive shipwrecks reported meetings with, apparently, Nguni people settled in Pondoland near the present Port St Johns and Umtata.) From them the Portuguese learned of the great Black kingdom of Monomotapa, further to the north and inland.

At Kelimane the expedition, the first Europeans to arrive by sea and from the south, was received with astonishment, and with courtesy until the Arab traders realized that here were formidable commercial rivals.

Da Gama completed the voyage to India on the monsoon. On the way back to Portugal (with a cargo of spices which paid the cost of his voyage sixty times over) he made an alliance with the Sultan of Malindi who was at odds with the rulers of Kilwa and Sofala. Back on the coast again in 1502, he compelled the Sultan of Kilwa to accept Portuguese suzerainty and to pay tribute.

For the next three-quarters of the sixteenth century the Portuguese scoured the eastern and western coasts of Africa for valuable trade and were ruthless in pursuit of their objective. Zanzibar and Brava were subdued. De Almeida was appointed Viceroy of India in 1505 and one of his tasks was to secure the east coast trade, building fortresses as had been done on the west coast. He defeated the navy of the Sultan of Egypt and put Portugal in command of the eastern seas for a hundred years. He destroyed Mombasa and conquered Kilwa and Sofala. Mozambique became the seat of government and settlements were made at Sena and Tete at the head of navigation of the Zambezi. From here missionaries were sent to the Karanga and strenuous efforts were made to capture their gold trade. The Portuguese gained control of much of the wealth of the Sofala hinterland. The three-year captaincies of Sofala have been calculated to have been worth, on modern standards, £300,000, and this was only a cut: the total profits must have been enormous. But the Arabs still managed to keep some of the trade and much of their smuggling eluded the Portuguese.

The first missionary was murdered in 1561 by the Karanga who were incensed by religious attacks on their traditional practices and whose hostility was encouraged by jealous Arab traders. Eight years later, when unrest in the interior interrupted the flow of gold, the Portuguese ruler, Sebastian, remembering earlier papal obligations laid on his people to spread Christianity, decided on an expedition of retribution. To be sure of proper sanction for his action, he called a conference of lawyers and theologians, the *Mesa da Consciencia*, to pronounce in January 1569 on the international morality of the project. The King of Portugal, they found, might justly make war on the Monomotapa:

the missionary, Father Silveira, and other Portuguese had been murdered; Monomotapa had robbed them and had sheltered the Moors (Arabs), the enemies of the Christian faith and the instigators of these crimes. Besides these motives there must be

in the King who represents a public person obliged to defend his state and subjects from all injuries, an upright intention of spreading the Gospel in those parts. This conversion and salvation of souls must be the principal end in view ... and not the increase of empire, or the personal glory and profit of the prince, or other private interests.[3]

This opinion provided a formula to define and rationalize colonial policy for 400 years and set a precedent for 'the just war' of later days.

The Monomotapa, however, discreetly accepted the Portuguese terms. He agreed to expel the Muslims, to allow the Gospel to be preached and to hand over the ownership of some of the mines. But the Portuguese found the gold costly to extract and the natives, afraid that the land as well as the gold would be taken, would not reveal the whereabouts of many of the ceded mines. The Portuguese also suffered a series of defeats at the end of the seventeenth century at the hands of the Rozwi Changamire.

Away on the west coast, too, the Portuguese made their conquests. They subdued Angola, sought rumoured silver supplies, found heathen souls for conversion and salvation and heathen bodies for slavery. But the southern coasts of Africa, between Angola and Mozambique, offered little to attract them, and with treacherous currents and battering storms were best avoided.

The turn of the fifteenth century had been busy and successful beyond dreams for the explorers from Europe. Within five years of Bartholomew Dias rounding the Cape of Good Hope, Christopher Columbus had discovered the West Indies: and in 1497 Cabot sailed to Canada and da Gama found the Cape route to India. In 1500 Portugal annexed the vast new country of Brazil. It is one of the unhappy juxtapositions of history that the empty spaces of the West should have fallen to the Europeans in their mood of acquisitive, arrogant expansionism, at the same moment as comparatively populous Africa. By mid-century sugar cultiva-

3. *Cambridge History of the British Empire*, Vol. VIII, p. 97.

tion was under way in Brazil and in desperate need of labour. The Portuguese had conducted a lucrative trade in slaves from their first contacts with the African coasts, but now they were dealing in a commodity which, for making men rich, would far eclipse gold and silver and spices for the next quarter of a millennium.

Slavery had always existed in Africa. Strong tribes held weak tribes in subjection; migrant invaders conquered sedentary and often more civilized people, marrying their women and enslaving their craftsmen; rich men kept poor men, sometimes their poor relations, as servants. The Arabs had a long experience of draining men off from Africa into servitude, but it was a system of domestic slavery and the numbers involved relatively small. The Europeans, however, with their guns, their more efficient organization, their lust for gain and the insatiable demand for labour of the new plantation colonies of Portugal, and later of those of Britain, Holland and France, gave the trade a dimension that changed the face of Africa.

The full number of people taken from Africa to be sold into slavery can never be known with accuracy, but there are figures which indicate the appalling scale of the traffic. In 1444 the first consignment of slaves was taken from Senegal to Lisbon. Between 1486 and 1641, rather over 150 years, 1,389,000 slaves were taken from Angola, i.e. 9,000 a year. In the sixteen years between 1575 and 1591, 2,000 a year went from Angola alone to Brazil. Between 1580 and 1680, Brazil absorbed 1,000,000 slaves from Angola and Mozambique, that is 10,000 a year for 100 years. Between 1783 and 1793 the slave traders of Liverpool made 900 voyages, carrying 300,000 slaves worth £15m., giving a net return of £12m. or £1m. a year.[4]

'If there were no buyers there would be no sellers' is one writer's view. 'The European traders taught the African to sell other Africans as they had taught them to sell gold-dust and ivory . . . for third rate articles'[5] – and for cheap brandy and costly (as they would prove in the end) guns.

Africa and the shores of the Indian Ocean were never the Paradise Gardens. Men struggled and fought, seeking both social

4. Davidson, op. cit., p. 120.
5. James Pope-Hennessy, *Sins of the Fathers*.

good and personal gain: there were the rich and the poor, the powerful and the enslaved. But on the whole life in these parts before the coming of the Whites, was ordered. The trading vessels of India, Persia and Arabia followed the age-old routes in search of commerce and not of conquest. They brought their goods of cotton and silken cloth, porcelain, beads, perfumes and spices to Africa and in exchange took away gold, ivory, iron, slaves, monkeys and leopard skins. The Arabs formed their colonies; they settled; they mixed with the local population and gave their own colouring to the existing culture of the coast. Warfare in Africa and India in those days, it has been shown, was often – not always – subject to conventions designed to give victory with a minimum of casualties, 'ritualized combat' Dr Desmond Morris calls it. A way of retreat for the vanquished was left open, for without hope men gain a desperate valour and sell their lives dearly.

Europe changed all that. Its men, made arrogant by their new conquests of nature, greedy for maximum gain, armed with gunpowder broke into this world. They looted and sacked and relentlessly killed those who did not submit. They used cruelty and torture in a deliberate policy of terrorization. White intrusion and the massive development of the slave trade coincided with a time of movement and migration among the peoples of Africa, and chaos reigned. The old conditions were forgotten and Africa was known only as savage, dark and perverse, locked in brutish misery.

In the middle of the sixteenth century Portugal became subject to Spain. The African east coast was neglected: the colonists became undisciplined and corrupt, the settlements decayed and were sacked by Bantu invasions. Arab revival further reduced their power and Portuguese interest centred increasingly on Brazil, with Angola as a dependent source of labour. On the east coast they retained their colony of Mozambique.[6] Other sea-faring nations in western Europe, too, were beginning to overtake the Portuguese lead and to challenge her supremacy in the Atlantic and Indian Oceans.

6. Paradoxically, Portugal and Spain, the first European colonial powers in Africa, were the last to retain their old-style colonies.

2 The Company (1652–1795)

I. DUTCH EAST INDIA COMPANY AND WHITE SETTLEMENT

As Portugal came under Spanish domination in the latter part of the sixteenth century, the Dutch provinces of the north were banding together under the leadership of William of Orange in the struggle to free themselves from Spain's stranglehold. Lisbon had succeeded Venice as the great European centre of East–West trade and Philip II of Spain, hoping to subdue the rebellious Protestant Netherlands, closed the port of Lisbon to their traders. Undaunted, the Dutch set off themselves for the East and soon challenged the declining Portuguese influence in the Indian Ocean.

The Netherlands – the Lowlands – was a low-lying, fertile country, criss-crossed by the channels of the Rhine delta, with an immensely long indented coast line in relation to its size. By the turn of the sixteenth century, the Dutch were an industrious and prosperous people. They were able farmers and capable fishermen and seafarers. Situated on the then trading cross-roads of Europe, they possessed a strong commercial bent and high educational standards – Flemish and Jewish financiers, refugees from persecution in Catholic Spain, made Amsterdam the banking centre of the West. Powerful commercial companies grew up, and as the Dutch provinces united politically so the rival companies abandoned their competition and amalgamated to form the Dutch East India Company, which received its Charter from the government in 1602.

The government of the United Provinces held a large share in the Company and many of the leaders of the legislature were directors. It leased to the Company a monopoly of trade and took a cut of the profits. Only Dutchmen were permitted to hold shares, but small investors were encouraged so as to spread interest as widely as possible and to involve a large section of the people in the Company's commercial fortunes. The direction of policy lay with the governing Council of Seventeen, selected by the States-General from lists submitted by the Estates of the Provinces and subject to review by a Vigilance Committee of eight directors at The Hague.

The Company acquired wide interests all round the Indian Ocean and as far east as Japan. Its headquarters were established in Batavia and within its dominions it behaved much as a sovereign state. It sent out expeditions of exploration, acquired colonies and fought wars in defence of its monopolistic commercial empire. The Far Eastern colonies were rapaciously exploited; the Company would limit production or even destroy crops in order to maintain price levels. It paid very high dividends, the average in the first half of the seventeenth century being as much as 25 per cent. Officials of the Company who were woefully poorly paid not unnaturally made the most of their many opportunities to advance their personal fortunes; corruption permeated its structure and contributed eventually to its collapse.

The Dutch East India Company's motives were strictly and relentlessly commercial; its purpose was to acquire valuable trade and to establish a monopoly in its spheres from which all competitors should be excluded. The Dutch were not crusaders as the early Portuguese ostensibly were. Their mercantile fortunes were not carried forward on any wave of evangelizing fervour and their old quarrel with Catholicism made their relations with the Muslim world far smoother than those of the Portuguese had ever been. They were attracted to Africa by the gold of Sofala and Mozambique, but their main interest centred on the crops of the tropics, particularly the spice trade of the East, and on the lucrative traffic in slaves.

Dutch ships, sailing more boldly than the Portuguese on the prevailing winds, found the Cape a convenient point on voyages both ways. More and more frequently during the early seventeenth century they tended to call there for water and fresh meat obtained by barter from the Khoikhoi, who by this time were becoming used to trading with passing ships. Above all they wanted the green wild sorrell to remedy scurvy, the dreaded scourge which decimated crews on those long voyages without fresh food. So habitual became their movements that an elementary postal system was established on the coast and letters were left under inscribed 'post-office' stones (now collected in South African museums) for the crews of following vessels in either direction to pick up and deliver.

In 1647 the *Haarlem* was wrecked in Table Bay. The valuable cargo was salvaged and the crew left to guard it until another ship was sent to pick them up. Like Necho's Phoenicians 2,000 years earlier, they grew the food crops they needed and found conditions favourable. They got on well with the local Khoikhoi, unlike their Portuguese predecessors. Two crew members, Janssen and Proot, produced South Africa's first blue book, on the suitability of the Cape for a refreshment station. They reported to the directors that vegetables and fruit could be abundantly produced, the sick recovered quickly in the clement climate, the natives were friendly if well treated and the cattle were cheap. They suggested that the profits from possible seal and whale fishing could be made to pay the cost of a settlement, and they emphasized the strategic importance of the position for the defence of the Company's trade routes.

The directors considered this enthusiastic report and decided to establish the much-needed half-way house at the Cape.

Some five years after the wreck of the *Haarlem* and 154 years after Vasco da Gama's voyage, Jan van Riebeeck, a tough, much-travelled and very able ship's surgeon, set sail from Holland with three small ships, the *Goede Hoep*, the *Dromedaris* and the *Reiger*, to found at the Cape 'a depot of provisions', to enable the ships of the Company 'to refresh themselves with vegetables, meat, water and other necessities, by which means the sick on board may be restored to health'.[1]

Arriving in Table Bay on 6 April 1652, van Riebeeck began to carry out the Company's instructions. He was to set up a fort to be called Good Hope, lay out a garden and establish friendly relations with the natives. On them he must depend initially for

1. *Cambridge History of the British Empire*, Vol. VIII, p. 114.

his meat supplies. Cattle and sheep would be bartered – probably
for such articles as copper wire and beads, the accepted currency
then in trading with indigenous people.

Even before his expedition landed, van Riebeeck published his
first Ordinance – and the first law to be proclaimed in South
Africa, presciently enough concerned with race relations. It
forbade provocation or ill-treatment of the natives on any pretext.
All offenders, 'whether they be in the right or in the wrong',
would receive fifty lashes in the presence of the natives to prove
the friendly intentions of the authorities. This concern was more
to ensure the supply of cattle for the Company than from any
great tenderness towards the Khoikhoi whom van Riebeeck
himself described as 'a faithless rabble' and 'dull, stupid, lazy and
stinking'.[2]

Van Riebeeck had only ninety men, soldiers and sailors, to do
all the work and provide the defence of the station. They were, he
complained, 'as raw as the whole world has ever seen', and he had
to be his 'own engineer, delver, gardener, farmer, carpenter,
mason, etc'.[3] The men, under harsh discipline, for their part
loathed their conscript servitude, reckoned they got no more pay
whether they worked hard or loafed and they deserted – to
passing ships or to tribes of the interior – at every opportunity.

The new settlement made small progress in its first years. It
failed to fill adequately the revictualling function expected of it
and was proving a too costly experiment to the Company. It was
soon apparent that the area of occupation was too restricted and
the labour force of service men insufficient, as well as inefficient,
for profitable farming. The soil and the climate near the shore
were found unsuitable for agriculture and the lands were subjected to raids by Khoikhoi.

Van Riebeeck almost from the beginning had pressed for the
project to be run on a different basis, suggesting in turn imported
Chinese, free settlers and slaves. It became increasingly obvious
to him that only free and independent farmers, whose livelihood
and future depended on their own efforts, could be successful.
They would not have to be paid as the soldiers were, and the

2. E. A. Walker, *A History of Southern Africa* (1959), p. 33.
3. *Cambridge History of the British Empire*, Vol. VIII, p. 115.

garrison could be reduced and freed for its proper function. He also urged the importation of slave labour which would cost less than European unskilled workers.

The Company, however, was firmly opposed to the establishment of a settler colony, for they had found in the East that such people were intent on furthering their own interests, tended to trade to their own advantage and, if in any number, threatened serious economic competition to itself: in fact, they possessed those very qualities likely to make the settlement less of a liability. But van Riebeeck pressed his views at every opportunity and at last the directors capitulated. In 1657 nine Free Burghers were settled on Khoikhoi lands in the Liesbeeck valley, in the same year as the first dozen slaves were brought in from the east. Each was given a farm of 13 *morgen*[4] (28 acres) free of land tax for twelve years. In return they had to undertake to remain on their land for twenty years; to take turns in cooperating with the garrison in defence; to pay one-tenth of their cattle in return for pasturage; to sell their cattle only to the Company; to pay the Khoikhoi no more for cattle than the Company paid and to have no other dealings with them; to grow no tobacco, the importation of which was a Company right; to sell no vegetables surplus to their own or the Company's needs to ships until these had been in port for three days.

The settlers at first had found three clans of Khoikhoi of under 1,000 men, and all in the environs of the Cape, but they soon came in contact with other tribes further inland. Van Riebeeck fought a constant and losing battle trying to keep his men apart from the clans in order to prevent barter and endless friction between the two groups. Private trade with the Khoikhoi for such alluring and profitable commodities as ivory, rhinoceros horns, ostrich eggs, turtles, was forbidden because it distracted settlers from the main purpose of providing for the Company's wants. Private cattle barter was forbidden to ensure that prices to the Company did not rise and in an effort to discourage all contact with the tribes. Tobacco planting was forbidden, ostensibly because the Khoikhoi raided the plantations and this led to reprisals and trouble, but also because it was a valuable Company

4. 1 *morgen* = $2\frac{1}{9}$ acres.

monopoly and not to be trespassed upon. In an attempt to
enforce separation, to keep the colonists in and the Khoikhoi out,
the settlement's 6,000 acres, which was intended to be the full
extent of the Colony, was enclosed by a hedge of bitter almonds
from the Salt River mouth to the mountains behind Wynberg
(some of it still stands today, a reminder of the country's first
failure in apartheid).

Van Riebeeck would, but for the Company's specific instructions otherwise, have favoured the simple solution to his difficulty
of seizing the Khoikhoi cattle and shipping the Khoikhoi to the
Indies as slaves. As it was he had to learn to live with his problem
and a great part of South African history consists of his efforts
and those of his successors to do that.

There was more than one contemporary view of the Khoikhoi.
John Maxwell, an early English traveller, found that 'their
Native inclination to idleness and a careless life will scarce admit
of either Force or Rewards for reclaiming them from that innate
Lethargick humour'.[5] On the other hand, Janssen and Proot, who
had lived among them after the shipwreck of the *Haarlem*, wrote
in their report to the Company in 1648, before ever it had been
decided to make a settlement in the Cape:

> Others will say that the natives are brutal and cannibals, from
> whom no good can be expected ... This is a vulgar error ... We are
> convinced that the peasants [of Holland] ... were their cattle shot
> down or taken away, without payment, would not be a hair better than
> these natives, if they were not obliged to respect the law ... The kill-
> ings of our people is undoubtedly caused out of revenge by the natives
> when their cattle is seized ... The uncivil and ungrateful conduct of
> our people is therefore the cause ...[6]

This relates, of course, to people making calls at the Cape for
supplies before the Company took over but it suggests tensions in
relations from the beginning.

The independent burghers very soon became resentful of the
Company's restrictions and in 1658 drew up a memorial of their
grievances, described by the authorities as a document 'full of

5. E. A. Walker, op. cit., p. 36.
6. K. L. Roskam, *Apartheid and Discrimination*, p. 17.

sedition and rebellion'.[7] In particular, they refused to work the land until grain prices were fixed, 'since we will not be slaves of the Company . . . If we are to remain on our land we will not be forced by anybody, no matter whom, in our farm work.'[8] They gained their point on the grain price but other restrictions persisted. The Company jealously defended its economic prerogatives and the colonists, upon whom they bore heavily, complained, but eventually settled down with the Company in an uneasy truce, which gave way from time to time to open hostility.

When van Riebeeck, ten years later, left the Cape on transfer further east, the little village of De Kaap was well established, guarded by a fort, surrounded by gardens and farms and including the seeds of all the human problems which grew rank in the years to come. The Colony on one reckoning contained about 130 free citizens or burghers and their hired servants and at least twenty-three slaves, many of them Muslims, either political prisoners or criminals sent from the Company's eastern possessions. It contained also detribalized Khoikhoi who were filtering in as servants, and half-castes, for three-quarters of the slave children were half-breed: the creation of the Cape Coloured people had begun.

Most of the freemen were unmarried; European women were scarce in the Colony and the orphans van Riebeeck had asked for from Holland, 'lusty farm wenches', had been reluctant to face the voyage and hardships of the Colony even to acquire a husband. Van Riebeeck had therefore recommended mixed marriages in conformity with the practice in the Company's possessions further east. Jan van Wouter is recorded as having married Catherine, the freed daughter of a slave, Antonie of Bengal. One of the early Dutch Reformed Church missionaries, the Rev J. H. Schmelen, married a 'pious Hottentot woman'.[9] Best known is the marriage of the famous hunter, van Meerhof, to Eva, the Christian Khoikhoi. Eva is reputed to have 'gone to the bad' after her husband's death, but one of her children married a European in Mauritius.

7. *Cambridge History of the British Empire*, Vol. VIII, p. 122.
8. ibid., p. 121.
9. W. P. Carstens, *Africa South: III*, No. 2, p. 50.

The administrative machinery of the Colony in its early days was comparatively simple. Headed by a Commander (the post being later raised to a governorship), a Council of Policy and, later, a Council of Justice was formed of Company officials appointed by the Governor in consultation with the Council of India. As they became necessary, a High Court, a Matrimonial Court and an Orphans' Chamber were established upon which in due course the Free Burghers were given a small representation. A Fiscal, responsible directly to the Seventeen, was appointed to control the finances of the Colony, to check corruption and private trade, to regulate the administration of justice and act as public prosecutor. Much later, when the new settlement of Stellenbosch was founded, the post of Landdrost, also answerable to the Company, was created. His function was that of Rural Magistrate; he was Chairman of the Court of Heemraden to which four colonists were appointed, and which was responsible for local administration and justice.

There was continual friction between the Company and the colonists. The latter, discontented with the low price fixed for wheat under the Company monopoly, turned more and more from unrewarding agriculture to cattle-rearing which yielded big profits. Despite the tyrannical control of the Company, there was constant trading across the border with the Khoikhoi and smuggling to the ships in harbour.

The ships of France and other trading nations were following the Cape route to the East in growing numbers and the Company began to take steps to counter any possible foreign threat to the station by increasing its population and so building up both defensive and economic strength. A new and vigorous governor was appointed.

In 1679, Simon van der Stel, himself of mixed race, son of a governor of Mauritius and Monica, his Indian wife, arrived at the Cape. He was a man of immense energy, an ardent Dutch patriot, born in the East, brought up in the Company's administration and imbued with all its ways.

Van der Stel began his task with great reforming zeal. He found that the colonists, despite the Company's attempts to corral them, were spreading further and further outside the settlement's confines in search of pastures and of new holdings for their sons. He extended the settled area and founded the new village of Stellenbosch, thirty miles from Cape Town, beyond the sand flats and in the fertile valley of the Eerste River. He introduced modern agricultural methods and under his leadership the Colony at last began to produce a sufficiency of wheat which before long turned into a surplus. He produced good wine and tried to persuade the colonists to improve the quality of their product. He saw the urgent need for afforestation, insisted on replacement of felled trees and planted the oaks which survive today to give areas of the Cape their air of settled security. The conservative farmers opposed many of his reforms and refused to augment their fat-tailed flocks with the woolled sheep which were to profit later generations.

The population gradually swelled as Company servants took their discharge. Settlers from Europe entered only slowly because the selective immigration policy demanded men of good conduct and sound Protestantism, subjects of the Dutch Republic or of German princes not engaged in sea trade.

An infusion of new blood came, however, from elsewhere. French Huguenot refugees, in flight from the persecution of

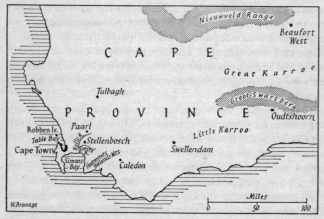

Map IV Cape Colony – Western Province

Louis XIV after the revocation of the Edict of Nantes in 1685, were pouring into Holland. Those who wished it and would take the oath of allegiance were given a free passage as settlers to the Cape. They received advances for equipment to be repaid when it was possible to do so. They had to undertake to remain in the Cape for at least five years, and were to be treated as if they were freeborn Dutchmen. Not more than two hundred of these people arrived between 1688 and 1700, one-sixth of the total Free Burgher population of the Cape, but they were to have a social and economic importance for the future of the Colony far beyond their number. They were of a better social class for the most part than the Dutch and German settlers, 'industrious people, satisfied with little', skilled vine and olive cultivators or artisans, mostly young and married with no other fatherland to which they could turn. The 200 Huguenots were, to their chagrin, initially scattered among 600 Dutch and Germans in the new settlements of Drakenstein and Franschhoek. It was not the Company's intention to nurture a cluster of French subversives, particularly at a time when France was building up international power and relations with the Dutch were bad, so all protests at the dispersal were ignored. Children were educated bilingually until they had a mastery of Dutch and a French-speaking sick-comforter was appointed for the sake of the elderly; but the far-sighted policy was to let the French language die out as soon as possible so that it could not become a disruptive nationalistic focus, and to speed the fusion of diverse elements. This was entirely successful. The only individual French characteristics that survive are in the physical features of many of the Afrikaner people and the spelling of many surnames.

The process of welding several nationalities into one people was hastened by common grievances. During its first fifty years the Colony had suffered from persistent under-production. The soil was poor, the rainfall erratic, and the colonists lacked the skilled workers and advanced techniques of Europe. They struggled on, confined in area and chronically short of labour, for small rewards against the Company's monopolistic stranglehold. They were poor, many of them in debt and some on charity. The Colony could not produce enough to satisfy the Company's demands, to supply the ships or to pay its own way. Production costs were high and quality low. There was no great staple such as sugar or timber on which the prosperity of colonies in the New World was built. Wool, olives, silk, coffee, sugar, tobacco, all were at one time or another tried and so far had failed. In addition, venality remained endemic amongst the underpaid officials throughout the Company's empire; the few attempts to stamp it out were unavailing, for it permeated to those in high office. All who could were busy feathering their nests and the more powerful their position the more successfully were they able to do so.

The Cape was no exception and with the coming of the van der Stels, the father and the son, who succeeded him in 1699, both Batavian born and brought up in the Company's tradition, there was plenty of opportunity for the ill-disposed to make allegations of graft.

The unhappy governors, exploited like the rest, were the channel through which the Company's regulations, restrictions, edicts, and complainings were transmitted. They were blamed by their superiors and often very sharply rebuked for expenses incurred and the failures of the settlers to come up to expectations, while they were also the focus of all the settlers' resentment of the irritations and cheeseparing policies of the absent Company. Both van der Stels, and other senior officials, acquired wide acres, great vineyards and huge herds, much of it granted officially by visiting commissioners, though contrary to Company's rules. The splendid estates of Groot Constantia and Vergelegen, with their lovely homesteads and every manifestation of the ample gracious living available in a slave society, were the creations of Simon and Willem Adriaan van der Stel. But they were intelligent, industrious and enterprising men. The younger had for ten years before his appointment to the Cape held high office in Amsterdam. In addition to being a fine horticulturist like his father, he well appreciated the possibilities of stock-farming and reserved an area large enough to provide eighteen cattle-posts to pasture his herds out beyond the Hottentots' Hollands when granting grazing licences on the frontiers to farmers. His wheat production was one-third of the whole. He eventually owned one-third of all the vine stocks in the Colony. The chief gardener of the Company and fifty or sixty of its servants and one hundred of its slaves, it was alleged, cultivated his estates and his building materials came from the Company's stores. The van der Stels together with a few leading officials owned one-third of the Colony's 12,000 morgen of farm land, equivalent to the holdings of two hundred burghers. Willem Adriaan van der Stel then was accused of cornering the market in wine and corn, and, by changing the terms of the valuable meat concession, he made an implacable enemy of the previous holder and this at a time when the burghers were suffering a new and severe set-back of over-production and inadequate markets for their produce.

Resentment seethed among the farmers who, in 1706, empowered one of themselves, Adam Tas, secretly to compile a memorial of their complaints against the governor to be sent direct to the Seventeen in Holland. Van der Stel got wind of the discontent and sent soldiers by night to raid Tas's house where they seized a draft of the memorial and other documents. The leaders were arrested. Five of them were sent to stand trial in the Netherlands. Every sort of intimidation – solitary confinement, threats of torture and banishment – was used to induce the others to retract. Van der Stel vigorously defended himself on every count but the case never came to court in Amsterdam and the allegations long persisted. The country districts were in a state of rebellion and the Seventeen were thoroughly alarmed. They ordered the discharge of all prisoners and the dismissal of the governor and certain other officials. Company servants were again forbidden to own land or to trade, while individual settlers were not to be allowed to acquire too much land or become rich and powerful. It was decided for the time being not to send out more settlers to swell the ranks of future malcontents.

Their opposition to this 'unsupportable yoke' drew the farmers of different national origins together as nothing else could have done. Half the signatories of the memorial were French and it was noted almost as symbolic that of nine banished colonists, three were Dutch, three French and three South African born; and, of the three who died during the trouble, one was of each group. Van der Stel acknowledged that this was a revolt not of townsmen but of farmers and blamed *de boeren*, tacitly recognizing the fore-runners of the sturdy, independent, self-willed people that were to form the core of the modern *Boere Nasie*.

The Company's troubles persisted. It could not assume, in the turbulent state of Europe, that the Cape could be relied on to defend itself. Nor could the various commissioners sent on inspection devise a way of making the Colony economically self-supporting. The prayer of one of them, van Rheede, for 'something rich to be discovered or something profitable to be contrived'[10] would be answered only some two hundred years later with the discovery of diamonds and then of gold.

It was not only that the settled farmers were showing an independence and ability to resist official tyranny. The authorities were acquiring other problems. The abundant big game of the hinterland was an irresistible lure to the men of the frontier. Permits granted for hippo hunting not only allowed them to pursue an occupation more attractive than tilling infertile fields, but gave cover for secret trading with the Khoikhoi. Early in the Colony's history addiction to the hunter's life developed among the frontiersmen who lived, as their descendants were to continue to do until the present day, gun in hand and they were excellent shots. The severest legislation could not stop them and contemporaries complained that game within ten or twelve days' journey from the Cape was in danger of extermination.

At the same time increasing population and increasing herds and exhaustion of the pastures drove even the settled farmers to look for new grazing grounds. To obtain enough grass they rented land on the frontier where they would go with their cattle, camping in their wagons or building rude huts. The older landed farmers would remain in their homesteads, sending their sons to the cattle-posts and a younger generation grew up roving and independent, eventually to acquire land for themselves beyond the parents' horizons.

Any understanding of the Afrikaner character and of the influences and impulses which enabled this remarkable people to withstand first the hostility of the people around them and then, much later, the hostility of a great part of the world, must be looked for in their past. The basic factor in the evolution of the

10. *Cambridge History of the British Empire*, Vol. VIII, p. 132.

Afrikaner Volk was their deep rooting in seventeenth-century Calvinism. The original settlers emigrated from a Netherlands which had been nourished on this stern doctrine for a hundred years.

Calvin, born in 1509, a Frenchman, lived most of his life in Switzerland. He was a man of a highly austere intellect, a reformer who sought to purify the individual and to permeate every department of life with religion. On to the Stoic pursuit of virtue for its own sake he grafted St Augustine's doctrine of predestination which held that God had fore-ordained certain of mankind, the Elect, to eternal life and others to damnation. He taught his followers that they were a chosen people with a great destiny in the providential scheme. In attempting to restore the religious life of early Christians, he introduced considerable lay participation in Church government; he also followed early Christian practice in barring the unworthy from the sacraments. This required an inquisition which worked through a mixed council of clergy and laity; it had great powers to penalize private lives and beliefs and caused much cruelty and suffering. Adultery, blasphemy and heresy were all punishable by death and Calvin himself acquiesced in the burning at the stake of his Unitarian friend Servitus for heresy. Sped by the vernacular Bibles turned out on the recently invented printing press and the growing number of people able to read, this teaching spread from Calvin's Geneva through northern Europe, where reformers such as Erasmus and Luther had paved the way, and took an especially firm hold in the Netherlands. There it became a unifying force in the Dutch struggle for freedom from the autocratic domination of Spain that stood for the hated authority of Rome and its contemporary malpractices.

It was this rigid doctrine of Calvin that the industrious, independent Hollander settlers took with their Bibles to the Cape. Mostly simple folk – farmers, artisans, fishermen – they had little education or culture. Educational facilities were slow to develop in the Cape, and as *trekboers*, or graziers, wandering farmers (and later Voortrekkers) dispersed, they left religious organization behind and became self-reliant in spiritual as well as all other resources. *Die Boer met sy Bybel en sy roer*, with his Bible and his gun, was a true image of the generations spreading out over the land. Through all vicissitudes the trekboer clung to a basic literacy, instilled by a parent or itinerant schoolmaster – enough to read the Bible which was a necessary qualification for church membership. Each child's day began and closed with a large household gathering – parents, uncles, aunts, cousins, Khoikhoi and African servants, visitors, hangers-on – to hear father or grandfather read a portion of Scripture, render an extempore prayer and together sing a hymn or psalm. His earliest understanding was of those nomad Jews brought, with servants, flocks and all their possessions, safely out of Egypt; who wandered in the wilderness, beset by heathen enemies, seeking their promised land. How could his own people – divinely chosen as Calvin taught they were – not be providentially guided, protected, granted vast acres, great herds, many sons and, at last, victory over the heathen? Like the Jews they stood against barbarian hordes on the one hand and on the other, first the monopolistic Company and then the British who, like the Roman conqueror, pursued them with an alien law and culture. They developed qualities of amazing endurance and self-respect which hardened into obstinacy, resistance to new ideas, mistrust of foreigners and contempt for inferiors. Without any formal education, faculties of intellect and imagination remained mostly latent.

Lichtenstein, who travelled in the Cape at the beginning of the nineteenth century, described the trekboers' 'joyless existence' (and, except for the stimulus of constant skirmishing, the Voortrekkers' was to be little different). 'In an almost unconscious inactivity of mind,' he wrote, 'without action, without useful effect upon a wider circle of mankind, beyond the little circle which his own family formed around him, the South African colonist of these parts spends his solitary days and by his mode of life is made such as we see him.'[11]

As the more ranging pioneers, the trekboers, moved further from the amenities of civilization, so they learned to do without them. Crops were grown only for their own use; sale of grain to the Company declined; they came to depend increasingly on cattle destined for the Cape market; they would live on venison

11. C. W. de Kiewiet, *A History of South Africa,* p. 18.

and milk and honey, hunting or trading with the Khoikhoi to supplement their wants. A proclamation as early as 1692, attempting once again to curb those who lived by cattle-rearing and barter, condemned them for following a 'lazy, sluggardly life, to the detriment of the common weal'.[12] But it was in vain. Generations of hardy, self-reliant nomads developed, regarding the possession of plenty of land as a natural right of all free men, restlessly moving with their herds, continually at war with wild beasts and hostile tribes and later resenting all administrative authority as an interference with their personal liberty. In a prophetic moment, Simon van der Stel warned his successor, his son: 'the whole of Africa would not be sufficient to accommodate and satisfy them'.[13]

2. SERVANTS AND SLAVES

From the first moment of settlement the colonists had been in bartering, bickering contact with the indigenous people of the south. It was, after all, their recognition of the Khoikhoi as substantial cattle-breeders that made the settlement, in large part, attractive to the Dutch. The administration might, for economic and political reasons, try to enforce segregation of White from Non-white but the whole White migration, once begun, would follow its inexorable course. From the beginning settlement was an exercise in race relations.

The Europeans soon came up against the San who lived in the more inhospitable and inaccessible areas into which they had been pressed by the southward and eastward expansion of other better equipped and more numerous peoples. Because their ways of life and requirements were different, the hunting San and the herding Khoikhoi had established an uneasy sort of equilibrium with each other and with their environment, based on recognition and acceptance of each other's living space – the areas where each had rights to hunt or to pasture their beasts. With Khoikhoi (and with Bantu-speaking) peoples individual San not infrequently formed a relationship, hunting and herding in return for a security they

12. *Cambridge History of the British Empire*, Vol. VIII, p. 136.
13. ibid., p. 135.

could not otherwise achieve. This balance was to be destroyed by the new insatiable interloper. The San generally welcomed the passing hunter who acted with civility, but they resented and resisted the intrusion of strangers on the hunting-grounds and water-holes which traditionally they regarded as their own. Between the White settlers and the Stone-Age San there ensued a collision of customs and outlooks so far apart that no point of understanding was to be found. The Whites drove their herds into wide and, apparently, almost unoccupied lands to graze and water at pools where only wild beasts drank. The San saw these strangers settling themselves, without a by-your-leave, permanently on their hunting-grounds, devouring their pastures, occupying their water-holes, shooting off their game – and they retaliated. To them the White man's munching herds were so much lazy game; they hunted them and attacked the owners. The Whites, unaware of their trespass, regarded the San as untamable wild men. An implacable hostility developed. The shadowy desperate San with their hunting skills and deadly arrows were a dangerous foe.

In fighting the San the commando system, which was to play so important a part later against Black adversaries and, still later, against British troops, was evolved by the settlers. From the earliest days it was accepted that burghers banded into mounted posses should take their share with the garrison of the defence of the community. Out on the frontier and far from officially provided protection, men knew that they must take care of themselves. Punitive expeditions were organized by the Boers, generally with Khoikhoi support, to deal with the San. A register was kept of all White men of sixteen years of age and over, who served under officers of their own choice, each man providing his own mount and rations, Khoikhoi often accompanying them as servants and guides. All were unpaid. Once the government had sanctioned any expedition and provided ammunition for it from the Company's stores, they were independent. The system was simple and cheap, and in fighting against the San the leaders of the commandos acquired the training, techniques and veldcraft which served them in later wars against stronger adversaries. These expeditions continued throughout the eighteenth century and until 1827. Generally, they decimated the San clans they rode against or seized the people, including the children, to 'apprentice' them as servants, for the Colony's hunger for labour was always unappeased and the San were extremely reluctant unless forced to work for the Whites. In the 1770s, when the White movement to the north-east was barred by desperate San resistance, a massive drive was made against them. Contemporary reports give an idea of the scale of some of these actions. In 1774 a commando of 250 armed and mounted White men killed 500 San and captured 239. One commando leader admitted that in six years his commando had killed or captured 3,200 San; another had been in actions which annihilated 2,700. San were regarded as outlaws. Towards the end of the century, in a government attempt to prevent their total extermination, a reward was offered of £3 per head for San of any age and either sex captured alive and handed over to the authorities to be imprisoned for life on Robben Island.

The San were soon to play no further direct part in the history of South Africa. Some of their blood contributes to the genetic cocktail in the veins of the Cape Coloured people. They survive in very small numbers, perhaps 50,000 in all, in the Kalahari desert and in South West Africa where they are, like the game, officially protected, visited from time to time and written up by anthropologists, and occasionally a small group of them has been exhibited at some international fair. Those who remain hold for us an unquenchable fascination, for in them we see as far back as we ever can into our own past.

The Khoikhoi were the first people with whom the European settlers had come in contact. They were then spread round the South African coast in the better watered areas from the Swakop River in the west to the Keiskama in the south-east. In addition to caring for their great herds, some of the clans were active as middlemen between other Khoikhoi and the Bantu-speaking peoples beyond, exchanging metal and beads from the far interior and from European ships for cattle and dagga (a variety of hashish, marijuana, 'pot', much prized then as now), a commerce that was extended to include the White newcomers, with their strident demands for cattle. They soon understood the distinctions between early Company rule within its fixed boundary and the Free Burghers' steady encroachment. Seeing the Europeans ploughing up their old pastures and building houses, they naturally asked, 'Where were they then to live ?'[14] Because the cattle trade was vital to the Whites and the Company had forbidden all punitive action against Khoikhoi malefactors, they dared take what reprisal they could by skilfully stealing tobacco plants and raiding cattle-posts. Unlike the Company's servants, the settlers would not submit to this. Taking the law into their own hands, for instance, they seized the chief of a band suspected of cattle stealing and 'hanged him by the neck from a beam' until he confessed where the stolen cattle were.[15] The Khoikhoi were also accused of the murder of a herdsman and of harbouring runaway slaves and before the South African settlement was ten years old it emerged successful from its first colonial war over the dispossession of the Khoikhoi of their grazing grounds in the Liesbeeck valley.

The Khoikhoi sued for peace, and tried to regain rights to their pastures, 'standing upon it that we (the Dutch) had gradually been taking more and more of their land, which had been theirs since the beginning of time . . . Asking also, whether, if they came to Holland, they would be permitted to do the like.'

The Commander argued that if their lands were restored there would not be enough grazing for both nations. The Khoikhoi replied 'Have we then no cause to prevent you from getting more cattle ? The more you have the more lands you occupy. And to say the land is not big enough for both, who should give way, the rightful owner or the foreign invader ?'[16] Van Riebeeck made it clear 'that they had now lost the land in war and therefore could only expect to be henceforth deprived of it . . . The country had thus fallen to our lot, being justly won in defensive warfare and . . . it was our intention to retain it.'[17]

Twelve years later, in another attempt to end the constant friction by putting a legal gloss on an existing situation, the

14. *Cambridge History of the British Empire*, Vol. VIII, p. 123.
15. ibid., p. 123.
16. *ibid* p. 124.
17. Roskam, op. cit., p. 16.

Company agreed to buy from the clans all the land north and east from Saldanha Bay to the Hottentots' Hollands for goods to the value of £1,600. Of this sum only £9 12s. 9d. was ever paid. The final war, again over land rights, with Chief Gonnema followed from 1673–7.

The effect of their encounter with White civilization was disastrous for the Khoikhoi. Some wary clans trekked away to the interior. Others remained on the frontiers, trafficking with the Whites while more and more of their numbers became detribalized and absorbed into the Colony. As they recklessly traded away their cattle their poverty increased. They were very susceptible to White men's diseases. A fever epidemic in 1687 hit them hard and the smallpox outbreak of 1713 carried them off in hundreds. Inside the Colony they were protected by by-laws; some became Christians; the children to begin with went to school with White and slave children. But these cheerful improvident African nomads, stripped of their grazing lands, their herds, their free life and social cohesion, were eventually absorbed into the lives of the settlers; they became herdsmen and labourers, domestic servants, wagon drivers, draftsman, interpreters – with other clans and then with Bantu – for trekboers and missionaries; they became good shots and excellent horsemen; they turned hunters and trackers for their masters, soldiers for the government; they sold firewood; they begged tobacco or illicit liquor, became vagabonds, lived by their wits. They were to form the basis of the labour force of the Cape. The clans vanished and, enslaved by the invaders, the Khoikhoi ceased as a unit to have significance in the racial groupings of South Africa. They live strongly on, however, in the Cape Coloured people, derived from the fusion of all that had made the Khoikhoi in the distant past with Malay and African slaves and with their White masters: the latest creation in the genesis that is Africa.

The conditions which made slave labour seem necessary in other colonies did not exist in the Cape. The climate was suitable for White workers and there was then no plantation development of the tropical crops, such as sugar or tea, which demand a large supply of labour. But the Colony lay between the two great slave-trading coasts on east and west and the traditions of the

Company and of its servants, grown up in the East Indies, was attuned to the labour of slaves. The Company's inflexible control of prices and the relatively high wages required by White labourers who were scarce, reduced the profits of the settlers and inevitably stimulated the cry for slaves.

The first slave on record, Abraham of Batavia, was in the Colony the year after van Riebeeck landed. Twelve slaves are recorded in 1657, from Madagascar and Java. The next year 174 Angolans were taken off a captured Portuguese ship and later in the year another 228 arrived. From then on, slavery was to be the practice of the Cape until the Emancipation in 1834, the best part of 200 years. An opportunity of reversing its direction was lost in 1717, when the Company considered an overhaul of its policy. Dominique de Chavonnes, brother to the governor, argued that the Colony could support 150 White artisans. Their work would be more efficient and would therefore prove cheaper than slave labour. The greater White population would allow a reduction of the garrison, would create a larger internal market, would necessitate the break-up of the farms into small units and would 'breed habits of industry' in the Whites. He was completely out-voted at the time, partly on the grounds that further immigration would only add to the poverty then prevalent in the Cape; but his far-seeing judgement was to be vindicated by many experts in a day when correction of the trend was a far more basic and controversial operation. The slave section of the community, for all its position of bondage, was to have a quite fundamental influence on the course of events in South Africa: in the physical contribution to the racial amalgam, in the modifying of language and customs and in the moulding of race attitudes that would underlie and distort all future social, economic and political affairs. As time went by their economic role as the labouring class was gradually taken over by Khoikhoi and increasing numbers of Coloureds.

All slaves were imported by the Company, which kept those it needed, hired out some of the remainder and sold others at £6 per head, payable in wheat. For the most part Angolans were not favoured. They frequently escaped into the interior to be harboured by the Khoikhoi or Nguni and, with a sufficient knowledge of conditions in the country, often made their getaway. The colonists relied more on East Africans and Madagascans and on Malays from the Dutch East Indies. Some of the latter were criminals, many more were political prisoners and one, Sheikh Joseph who came in 1682, had been the leader of a revolt against Dutch rule in the Indies. He was revered in his day and his tomb near False Bay is still a place of Muslim pilgrimage. Generally speaking the Malays, who were frequently highly skilled, were the artisans of the Colony, those of mixed breed (often Khoikhoi with an infusion of White) were the domestic servants, living closest to their masters, while it was the lot of the black Africans to toil in the lands through the heat of the day.

It is said that slaves in South Africa were not treated with undue cruelty – not as compared with conditions in the American plantations, nor in an age generally indifferent to the concept of human dignity and particularly conscious of the sanctity of property – be it potatoes or chickens in a field, landed acres or human souls – and capable of barbaric retribution for infringements of the codes. Slaves were, of course, valuable at the Cape and difficult to replace. The labour of those who were skilled was often hired out, and many were heavily mortgaged by their masters. Then, as in later days, servitors who were industrious, respectful and docile were highly prized and well cared for. But they must not get ideas above their station. The law of the day was harsh on all transgressors and particularly so on servants and slaves. Whipping, chains, branding and loss of ears were punishments for quite minor offences, while murderers and rapists were broken at the wheel or hanged. The High Court condoned torture if necessary. Not until 1799 were breaking at the wheel and slow strangulation abolished. On the other hand owners were allowed to administer only 'ordinary' beatings; floggings had to obtain official permission. Burghers could be punished for the illtreatment of slaves and slaves who, with good cause, took their masters to court were sold by public auction to protect them from reprisals.

In the early days the distinction in the Colony, as in the Indies, was not between White and Black, but between Pagan and Christian and no Christian could be held in slavery. White men walked publicly in the streets with slave women. The sick-comforter, lay precursor of the predikant, taught the slaves the Dutch language and Christian precepts and great efforts were made to convert. In 1677 it was decreed that all slave children under the age of twelve should go to school, which they did alongside Whites and Khoikhoi, but the next year a separate school was set up for these children with a Non-white master. No half-breed child could be kept in servitude and most of the slave children of the Colony were of mixed blood. Manumissions were frequent. Skilled slaves could hire out their services in their free time and earn money to buy their freedom. The population of freedmen and half-castes grew rapidly and the situation was reflected in the legislation that ensued.

From 1685 new restrictions were imposed. The right of the baptized to emancipation was changed to a favour, the Cape Town Church Council concurring. Heathen freedmen who were regarded as being idle were re-enslaved. Only Dutch-speaking half-castes could claim emancipation as of right, at twenty-five years of age for men and twenty-one for women. 'Foreign' slaves qualified after thirty years' service and 'native' slaves after the age of forty on payment of £8 6s. 8d., though they were not to be freed unless their owners guaranteed that they would not be a charge on the public funds for a period of ten years. In this year, too, marriage between White and Black (but not half-caste) was forbidden.

There was from time to time unrest among the slaves and an occasional revolt. One of these, as late as 1808, was planned by two Irishmen and two slaves. The Whites backed out and the others led a band of 326 rebellious slaves in a forlorn attack on Cape Town with its garrison of 5,000 soldiers. Five leaders were hanged and the bodies exposed as a warning to others; fifty rebels were flogged or sentenced to life imprisonment in chains, and the rest, after being made to watch the executions, were sent back to their masters.

For the most part, throughout the eighteenth century and until emancipation, legislation relating to slaves veered according to the direction of the breeze of change both at home and abroad. In the middle of the century laws became more onerous. It was decreed that every slave, even if unarmed, who raised a hand against his master be put to death. All slaves travelling between rural and urban areas must carry 'passes' from their masters. When Company rule at the Cape came to an end in 1795 there were more slaves than Whites and they formed the mass of the Colony's labour force. During the first British occupation, however, slaves were only landed by permit and the succeeding Batavian Republic, intending to begin a gradual abolition, followed the practice. After the abolition of the slave trade in 1807, slaves could no longer be sold or replaced so that their value increased and their conditions improved, their new state emphasizing the rigours of their old. Good treatment was ordered and judges exercised supervision; conversion was encouraged; provision was made for the education of the children; property rights for slaves were recognized; evidence of baptized slaves was given equal weight with that of 'Christian people'; punishment was to be mild and 'domestic', limited to twenty-five lashes only, once only a day; hours of field-workers were restricted to twelve in summer and ten in winter; married slaves and their children were not to be separated. The 1820 settlers from Britain were not allowed to own slaves at all. A register and a Guardian of Slaves were provided by the Nineteenth Ordinance of 1826 and strongly resisted by the masters. The White population of the Cape began to outnumber the slaves.

The slaves, as they were freed, drifted in to reinforce that new substratum already beginning to form which was the Cape Coloured people. The evolution of a new people is a creative marvel, but in South Africa it is a phenomenon we have been able to witness as a living historical process to which our fathers, grandfathers, great-grandfathers have made their contribution.

The Cape Coloureds are derived from a basic mixture of Khoikhoi, San and Malay slave, with a strong infusion of the blood of the black African and of the White master. Though, after the very early days of settlement, it became unlawful for Whites to marry with pure breed Blacks, marriage between Whites and half-castes was permitted for 300 years and associations outside marriage have never ceased. The old Dutch farmers lived in patriarchal fashion and many exercised patriarchal rights in biblical style, though in South Africa the dominant race self-consciously kept itself an exclusive aristocracy. The Cape Coloureds are extremely varied in physical type, individuals displaying every mixture of feature of the progenitors as well as appearing pure African, Khoikhoi, Malay, or – and this has special significance – European. Many have been light-skinned enough to 'pass' into the privileged White community, tactfully ignored by their darker brothers and sisters. In this way, despite spasmodic attempts in earlier days and intensive efforts more recently to prevent it, dark blood flows liberally in White men's veins. It has been estimated that anything up to one-third of the White South African population, including some of the oldest and most prominent families, has submerged Coloured blood. Every now and then there is a scandal and embarrassment when chance genes produce a dark 'throw-back' in a White family to be explained away or sent abroad.

The Cape Coloureds, numbering now nearly 2,000,000, for all their humble position are the truest South Africans, wholly evolved in the Cape. Their status over the generations has changed from slavery to serfdom. Underpaid, under-nourished, under-educated, and above all under-esteemed, with limited opportunities and few prospects, they have acquired the reputation in the more northerly parts of South Africa of being lazy, drunken, thieving and unreliable. But the Whites of the Cape regard them with more affectionate if exasperated tolerance, as well they might, since for generations Coloureds have been their childhood playmates and their companions and mentors in the outdoor life. Many a White South African child has been enveloped in comfort and affection in the warm and often ample bosom of a Coloured or African nannie. The mother tongue of the Coloureds is Afrikaans, for many generations a 'kitchen' language, evolved from Dutch by master and slave and with Malay and African language contributions to its vocabulary. Their religion is Dutch Reformed. Much of traditional Cape cooking is oriental in character. They have greatly influenced each other, these half-brothers, and they are caught indissolubly in equivocal love–hate bonds.

Generations of dependence on slave and serf labour had

profound consequences for South Africans. From the very beginning, free colonist and bond worker existed side by side and the servile class, whatever its race composition, was never White. Van Imhoff, the Governor-General of the Dutch East Indies, visiting the Cape in 1743, after nearly 100 years of slavery, noted that, 'having imported slaves every common or ordinary European becomes a gentleman and prefers to be served rather than to serve', many considering it 'a shame to work with their own hands'.[18] Not that they were lazy, as their passion for hunting and their achievements on the Great Trek bear out. But land was cheap and labour was cheap, and needs and ambitions were limited. A privileged landed class grew up dependent upon a disproportionately large number of servants and slaves whose labour was inefficiently used, whose standard of living remained low and opportunities restricted. This contributed nothing to reducing the prevailing poverty of the Colony by providing a larger market or higher production. With slaves doing the skilled work there was no place for the emigrant artisan class which contributed so much to the development of other colonies, nor was there opportunity in the skilled trades for younger sons of Whites, who, as they came of age, sought not work but land. This increased the restless tendency to movement into the interior. In the Cape the result was economic stagnation. The White young, sons and daughters of Hollanders and Huguenots, the most industrious and independent of peoples, were reared in these conditions; inevitably and from very early days they grew up with an implanted contempt for the labouring classes here identified with the Blacks, who were held in an effacing bondage which tended to eliminate individual worth. Physical labour was 'Kafirs' work' and the Black men who did it were fit only for that. These attitudes entered the national soul and were eventually to spread from slave lands to infect a great portion of the White world.

3. EXPANSION AND CONFRONTATION

The problem of the eighteenth century was radically different from that of the settlement's first fifty years. The population

18. Walker, op. cit., p. 85.

increased, the Colony expanded, labour was more available and agricultural methods had improved. Consistent under-production now gave way to periods of over-production alternating with seasons of drought, crop failure and disease until, in the latter part of the century, rare periods of almost riotous prosperity were erratically sandwiched between devastating slumps.

The wine and the wheat of the Cape were of poor quality which neither Europe nor the Company's eastern dependencies wanted, even if transport costs had not priced them out of the market. In any case ships for Europe from the East were generally already fully laden and unable to take on further cargoes at the Cape and the Company was indifferent to the colonists' needs. There was too small an internal market to absorb agricultural produce. Constant balance of payment problems drained currency off all the time to pay for excess of imports over poor and unreliable exports. In the circumstances the Colony could build up capital only slowly, while the Company, already past its heyday, did little to foster development or even to improve internal transport and communications; on the contrary, in protecting its monopoly it resisted innovation, put brakes on trade and prevented the creation of any significant industry. The commercial and administrative systems of the Cape were now obsolete as well as corrupt, the administration top-heavy with officials versed in all the malpractices of the Dutch East India Company. The Company's power lay in the hands of the 'Patricians', a small number of wealthy families in the far-away Netherlands and their great political influence prevented the States-General from instituting a projected inquiry into the affairs of the Company. Dividends were very large, 25 per cent in the early half of the century and 12 per cent in the later part, but the Company all the while was piling up a huge debt.

In the second part of the century the European powers were engaged in almost endless conflict. In the course of the Seven Years War, Britain backed Prussia against a Catholic combination of Austria, Russia, Spain and France, took on and defeated France in the overseas territories, and emerged in 1763 from the Treaty of Paris with great possessions. Wolfe's triumph on the Heights of Abraham secured Canada; Senegal and the French slave trade passed to Britain; and Clive found a rich empire in India. A decade later Britain was engaged in putting down a revolt in the American colonies – an internal and domestic affair, so it seemed, until the colonists made it international by calling in allies and forcing Britain to fight the Spanish, French and Dutch on distant fronts. The colonies won their independence and Britain lost much of her earlier gains in the West.

But ill though the winds in the north were and whatever the tribulations of Europe, the Cape (then, as did South Africa in later, greater wars beyond her borders) prospered on the whole from these clashes. European conflict and, in particular, Anglo-French economic rivalry in India brought their fleets, based on St Helena and Mauritius respectively, from time to time into Cape waters and with them further brief periods of unwonted prosperity. Wheat export and wine production increased. Official permission was still required to trade with foreigners and not unnaturally these rare opportunities were exploited to the full; the Cape earned a discouraging reputation for excessive prices and official corruption and inefficiency. Much of the trade was clandestine and smuggling was common. Towards the middle of the eighteenth century a long depression was relieved by the visits of a succession of English fleets on the way to India. Then a slump set in again, producing financial chaos and many bankruptcies. By 1770 things were as bad as they had ever been.

Discontents, bred in times of economic distress, had lain dormant during the good years. Now they stirred again under the authoritarian rule of the governors and were aggravated by the excessive use of powers of deportation. Radical ideas were in the air and drifted into the Cape from the ferment of pre-revolution France and the jubilant new American nation. The colonists, in any case, already had considerable experience of local self-government: their representatives sat with the *landdrost* on the court of *heemraden*; the colonists of the interior were virtually independent in defence matters; their church organization was democratic. The powers of the central government, on which they had only consultative status weighed more heavily on the people of the west than on the easterners of the frontier who, in effect, were beyond its control.

A burgher group in Cape Town formed the Cape Patriot movement in 1779 to press for reforms and, by-passing the local autocrats, they went straight to the powers in Amsterdam. They exposed the corruptness of local officials and complained of the arbitrary imposition of fines. They complained of the confused state of the law based, as it was, on innumerable *placaaten*, proclamations, and asked, as had French and American revolutionaries, for it to be codified. They demanded further and more efficient representation on the Council of Policy and the High Court, the right of appeal to Amsterdam instead of to Batavia because of distance and delays, and the ending of powers of banishment without trial. Other requirements were more parochial, mainly economic and entirely limited to the settlers' narrow interests and foreshadowing political demands of much later days. These included demands for more churches in the hinterland; liberty to flog slaves without reference to the fiscal; the use only of Whites to arrest burghers; free-trade with the Indies and slaving rights in Madagascar; an end to the keeping of shops by freed Chinese or Javanese prisoners who allegedly received goods stolen by slaves; and restrictions on the rights of foreigners in the Cape. Some small gains were then achieved: the right to six seats on the High Court, some voice in the care of roads, taxation and fixing of prices, and some not very substantial trade concessions. (But within a few years of the collapse of the Company most of their aims would be realized.)

Two years later a large French fleet sailed in to hold the Cape from the English and a French regiment was stationed at Cape Town. Then began an era of unprecedented and inflated prosperity. Wealth was amassed in Cape Town and its environs, augmented by the new issues of paper money, and the standard of living soared. It was fortunately in an age of cultivated taste. There was a building boom in Cape Town and the new rich on the crest of that wave built themselves many of the white-gabled, stately homesteads shadowed by ancient oaks, surrounded by orchards and vineyards which give the Cape valleys their serene charm today. But Britain regained her naval supremacy in the East and the French left the Cape.

The authorities in the Netherlands were preoccupied with

more urgent concerns than the problems and complaints of the distant colonists. The days of the Company were numbered. It was deeply in debt and up against resolute British and French commercial competition in the East. A commission was sent to organize an economy drive at the Cape, to produce a higher revenue and reduce expenditure. The result was increased taxation – taxes on slaves and wine, new customs duties, wagon duties, auction fees, port fees – and large scale retrenchment. The people were urged to less ostentatious living and greater personal economies. All to no avail. The Company was £10m. in debt, and in 1794 it declared bankruptcy, plunging the Cape into a state of economic collapse. Building stopped, slaves were sold or discharged, debts piled up, property was valueless. In 1792 only 25 per cent of rents due on loan farms were collected. A great many of the people of Cape Town were ruined.

Against a background of economic confusion and depression the Colony inexorably extended. Over-production had become chronic and it was impossible in normal times for the small local market to absorb the whole. Men now naturally turned more and more from the agricultural farmers' round of heavy toil for small return to the untrammelled life of the cattle rancher. Trade with the Khoikhoi though forbidden was irresistible and men traded. Under screen of hunting expeditions they had long been pushing far into the interior to conduct their traffic. At first it was the Colony's settled freehold farmers who ran their herds on the distant cattle-posts. Their overseers or their sons went in charge of the grazing to live for months at a stretch in wild and lonely places. In time sons and grandsons knew only this free life; facing the dangers of wild animals and hostile clans, they became increasingly resourceful, headstrong and defiant, excellent shots and a law unto themselves. Gradually cattle production in the Colony increased, the colonists with herds prospered and meat supplies became less dependent on the vagaries of the Khoikhoi trade but more demanding of land and labour.

After the first decade of the eighteenth century the granting of grazing licences had changed into the granting of loan farms on the frontier. The grazing licence became a 'recognition' fee or rent acknowledging the Company's ownership, though occupation was generally in perpetuity and even those in arrear were seldom evicted. Although they had initially been an adjunct to a freehold farm in the Colony, more and more loan farms were acquired by men who had no other property, sons of the colonists and others eased out of the populous settled areas of the Western Cape. What has been called the first Great Trek had begun.

The farmer who claimed a new farm would measure off his hide or allotment by walking his horse from his chosen centre for half an hour in each compass point direction, and this in effect would amount to about 6,000 acres. It was said he felt crowded if he could see the smoke from a neighbour's chimney. He would build himself a small house of sun-dried bricks and thatch, stabling for his horses and kraals for the herds, all near the essential spring or *fontein*. He could sell his leasehold rights at the value of the development, the *opstal*, homestead or visible proof of occupation, but he could not sub-divide. In a country where land was still plentiful and cheap, while labour and capital were scarce, each man came to look on the possession of one or more of these farms of 6,000 acres as his birthright. The system led to a rapid, leap-frogging dispersion of the trekboers and the striding advance of the Colony's frontiers. Settlement moved out towards the mountains; northwards in the direction of the Namaqualand droughtlands and, even more persistently, eastwards along the valleys folded in the ranges of the Cape towards the heavy rainfall areas of the east. In its first 150 years the Colony spread its frontiers 500 miles from the west coast to the Great Fish River and 300 miles north from Cape Town. Calvinia was settled in 1735; by 1771 Somerset East was reached and the settler van was penetrating beyond Algoa Bay. There was ample game for the shooting, articles like ivory and skins for trade, and the climate was temperate and equable. The trekboers pushed forward, the Company followed behind, its laws unenforceable, and never quite catching up.

By the turn of the century the White population, more than half of it now of German origin, was distributed surprisingly equally between four administrative districts: 6,261 in the Cape Town district; 7,256 in the fertile Stellenbosch area; and the new *drostdies* (magistracies) of Swellendam and Graaff-Reinet held

3,967 and 4,262 White people respectively in their jurisdiction. Living inextricably in the most intimate relationship of master and servant among these 22,000 Whites were over 25,000 slaves, mostly in the old Cape Town and Stellenbosch areas, Graaff-Reinet having less than 1,000 slaves. There were about 15,000 Khoikhoi, of whom 14,000 were in the new eastern districts, many as servants and labourers and others existing as they could in the settled areas. In addition there was an unknown number of San and Khoikhoi living freely and traditionally in the remoter parts of the Colony. Already the ratio of White to Non-white was 1:2, a ratio destined in the next 150 years and despite all the efforts of optimistic legislators, to double.

In their outward movement the Boers pressed hard on the San, who gave way before them, fighting until they were in the end virtually eliminated. But the trekkers generally flowed over and around the Khoikhoi's lands, netting numbers of them in the settled areas. Along with the amenities of civilization the trekkers had for the most part left slaves behind them and many more of the detribalized, landless, impoverished Khoikhoi became the White man's servants. The trekboers found them excellent herds-men and trackers, skilled in finding water and in defending the herds against wild animals and valuable allies in hunting down the unforgiving, marauding San.

In 1702 a party of about ninety Whites and Khoikhoi servants from Stellenbosch on a trading expedition had met and, in the first Boer–Bantu clash, brushed with a party of Xhosa tribesmen near the banks of the Fish River, 500 miles away. It was one of the momentous confrontations of history. But it was not until the middle of the eighteenth century that White trekboers, pushing eastwards, encountered substantial numbers of Xhosa tribesmen making their slow way west along the coastlands.

The Xhosa people were organized under a number of chiefs of varying strength and consequence, the senior of whom exercised some ceremonial domination but, unlike some of the great kingdoms of the Bantu-speaking people to the north, among the Xhosa and their Nguni neighbours no political overlordship was recognized. Groups were frequently embroiled over issues of land or cattle or authority and sections would splinter off, forming new

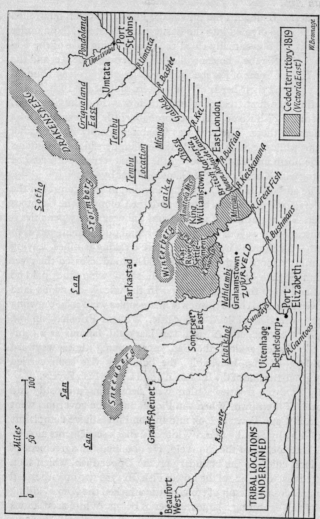

Map V Cape Colony – Eastern Province

W.Bromage

Ceded territory 1819
(Victoria East)

TRIBAL LOCATIONS
UNDERLINED

Miles
0 50 100

DRAKENSBERG

Sotho

San

San

San

San

Stormberg

Sneeuberg

Winterberg

Gaika

Tembu Location

Tembu

Griqualand East

Mfengu

Xhosa

Galeka

Pondoland

Port St Johns

R.Umzivubu

R.Umtata

Umtata

R.Bashee

R.Kei

East London

R.Buffalo

R.Keiskamma

R.Great Fish

R.Bushmans

Mfengu

Umtata Mss.

King Williamstown

British Kaffraria

Queenstown

Kat River Settlement

Fort Beaufort

Tarkastad

Somerset East

Khoikhoi

Ndhlambi

Grahamstown

ZUURVELD

R.Sundays

R.Gamtoos

Uitenhage

Bethelsdorp

Port Elizabeth

Graaff-Reinet

R.Groote

Beaufort West

chiefdoms. In about 1740 the sons of Phalo, the chief, quarrelled and the tribe divided into the Eastern and Western Xhosa under Gcaleka, who eventually ruled the people living east of the Kei River, and Rarabe who controlled those between the Kei and the Fish Rivers. Some of Rarabe's followers later hived off and hunted and pastured their herds on the western side of the Fish. But at the time the first trekboers made their way into the Suurveld, west of the Fish River, there was probably little permanent Xhosa settlement there. The area was inhabited mainly by Khoikhoi groups while the San still lived in some numbers in the mountains to the north and east. However, the Xhosa were reported to be mixing with Khoikhoi on the Gamtoos River by 1772.

The authorities in 1770, still attempting to keep control of the settlers, fixed the eastern boundary of the Colony on the Gamtoos River. But regardless of the law and the very heavy penalties – confiscation of wagons and goods, corporal punishment and even death – for flouting it, more and more trekking families, leaving the most remote of the loan farms far behind, crossed the river and made their homes in the wide grasslands where they paid no rent and were their own masters. In the uneasy no-man's-land between the two rivers the newly met peoples were soon brawling over possession of land and cattle. William Prinsloo, an old elephant hunter, and Adriaan van Jaarsveld, famous as a commando leader against the San, were among those wayward frontline settlers. Inevitably, the boundary was soon carried forward to the line of the Bushman's and Upper Fish Rivers.

By 1778 the frontier settlers were demanding a drostdy and church of their own. When van Plettenburg, the governor, went up from Cape Town to look into this and investigate complaints of raiding by San, he found White and Black settlements already well interlocked in the Suurveld. He obtained the agreement of the local chiefs to the boundary on the Upper Fish, which soon shifted east to the line of the Lower Fish. In 1780 two unauthorized commandos in pursuit of stolen cattle attacked the Xhosa, killing many and capturing a large number of beasts. White accusations of cattle thefts and Xhosa complaints of White misbehaviour abounded. Finally, in 1781, van Jaarsveld formed a commando and by a deceit routed the tribesmen, driving them back over the

XHOSA CHIEFS
Phalo (Palo)
(d. *circa* 1775)

Gcaleka←··········(quarrelled···········→Rarabe
(East of the Kei)   *c.* 1740   (West of Kei to Fish)
                                              d. *c.* 1781

Khawuta   Mlawu   Ndlambe
                                              (Regent for Gaika
                                              d. 1828)

Hintsa   Ngqika (Gaika)
(ruling before 1809   (d. 1829)
d. 1835)

Sarili   Sandile   Maqoma   Tyhali
(d. 1893)   (d. 1878) (d. 1873)

Sigcawu
(d. 1902)

Upper Fish River and capturing over 5,000 head of cattle which the victorious commando members shared. This was the first of a long series of nine Wars of Dispossession, the 'Kafir', Xhosa or Frontier Wars, to be fought between advancing White settlers and the tribesmen, mostly the Xhosa, in defence of their land.

Much of the trouble that was to smoulder and flare on the Eastern Frontier for the next thirty years was due partly to the influence of a few more than usually intractable frontiersmen who lived where and as they wished, ignoring both the demands of authority and the rights of members of other races, and stirring up trouble where it suited them. The newly created landdrost of Graaff-Reinet was instructed to keep peace with the tribes, check Kafir robberies, recall the burghers to the colonial side of the Fish River and put an end to their journeys in Kafirland. But there was no police force to support these decrees. Eastward penetration by farmers and traders went on and Xhosa were now working in increasing numbers on White farms far to the west, even near Swellendam. Rarabe died about 1785, leaving his son Ndlambe as regent for his infant grandson, (Ngqika) Gaika. Not all the Rarabe tribesmen recognized Ndlambe's authority and in increasing numbers the disaffected crossed over the Fish River. A commando drove them back, but the district authorities were under standing orders to avoid conflict and the commando was disbanded.

Honoratus Maynier, secretary and later landdrost at Graaff-Reinet, was sent in 1789 to investigate the explosive situation developing on the border. He was a man who hated cruelty and injustice, very much a product of the liberal climate of the outer world of his time. But many of the autocrats of the frontier mistrusted him and resented his authority. In time his humanity caused him to be branded as a follower of Rousseau and a protagonist of his 'noble savage' ideas. In fact Maynier did his best with the means at his disposal and within the limitations of his day. He blamed San raids very largely for the prevalent unrest and sent the commandos against them. Though £3 per head was paid for live captives, 600 of them were killed.

With the tribesmen, however, Maynier, very conscious of the dangers and suffering that would ensue from provoking a snow-balling of hostilities, strove to keep the peace. He had no illusions about their marauding activities, but he was also very well aware of the faults of the colonists. He was able to make peace with the Xhosa, allowing them to remain on the frontier 'without prejudice to the ownership of Europeans'. He tried to establish the rule of law and to prevent gross injustices between the Boers and their Khoikhoi servants and in their dealings with the Xhosa. But with no police force to control either White or Black, he had to rely on the erratic support of the quarrelsome and insubordinate commandos which, in order to limit their excesses, he reduced to the minimum size required for the purposes in hand. His efforts were often frustrated by the actions of undisciplined individualists among the settlers.

The administration, long stages behind these pioneers, doggedly followed its policy of separation which continued to prove singularly ineffective. The trekkers were pursued and bombarded with proclamations fixing boundaries already out of date. In 1793, an official placaat recapitulated all those since 1677 when hunting parties were active and which had banned, for instance, barter and trading across the frontier or the paying of Khoikhoi in sheep or giving them money lest they pay cash for their tobacco instead of trading cattle for it. In 1739, after a settler revolt against the administration's support of the Namaqua in a dispute with Whites and Kkoikhoi, all intercourse with natives of all tribes and nations had been forbidden. Now again in 1793 all cattle barter and intercourse with the tribes was banned; all Whites were forbidden to go beyond the Baviaan's River or the Tarka district (eastern tributaries of the Upper Fish); prohibited were the sale of fire-arms to Africans and the ill-treatment of Khoikhoi who were not to be separated from their families; and all offenders were to be arrested and reported to the fiscal. On the other hand, any natives found with arms were to be dealt with as vagabonds. It was quite useless. No laws could promote segregation against the economic logic of the situation. Even 'segregation by force of arms', as Professor S. F. N. Gie has put it, did not work, not then nor in much later years when the police went armed. But for the moment there was an official separation on the Eastern Frontier which was no separation.

The drought of 1793 sent some thirty Boer families trekking across the Fish River in search of pasture. The Xhosa were short of grain and those in the Suurveld had also lost their cattle in the drought. The Whites accused them of stealing cattle, 'eating up' pastures, killing off the game and enticing away their servants. The Xhosa complained of White misbehaviour and accused many of the frontier despots of brutal assaults, robbery, murder and of taking their women as concubines. In addition there were complaints about the Boers' treatment of their servants – both Khoikhoi and the Xhosa going into service who were assaulted, half-starved, their wages, cattle or children often withheld if they wished to end their service.

Soon fighting began.[19] The colonists from the beginning had used Khoikhoi servants as allies against less tractable Khoikhoi and against the San. Now they began to play off the tribes against each other. A privately raised burgher commando, with Ndlam-

19. Second Xhosa War 1793.

be's help, seized Xhosa cattle. Some of the Boers and Ndlambe's force then pulled out. The Xhosa retaliated, putting the commando to flight and overrunning the farms between the Zwartkops and the Fish Rivers, killing farmers and servants and driving off cattle across the Fish. The chief promised to respect the border but refused to surrender the booty. Maynier himself joined a punitive commando raiding as far as the Buffalo. But the results were indecisive and he concluded another peace similar to the earlier one and based on the *status quo*. This 'benevolence' enraged the farmers who also knew that in Cape Town they were held largely responsible for the border troubles. After fruitlessly petitioning the administration they revolted against Company restrictions and control. Resentful over the unresolved frontier situation and the 'perverse' and dangerous native policy of Maynier they drove him out, refused to pay rents and taxes and declared they would follow their stolen cattle into Kafirland. Under van Jaarsveld's leadership in 1795 they set up the Republic of Graaff-Reinet, the first in a long succession of breakaway republics. The people of Swellendam followed suit.

In that same week a fleet of British warships sailed into Simon's Bay.

As a result of the wars of the European powers over the last 100 years the balance of power had changed. First the American Revolution and then the French Revolution near the end of the century had largely grown out of the new ideas taking shape about the nature of men and their relationship to each other and to the world they lived in; and they, in turn, contributed to the further development and spread of those ideas and the making of that world. By then, too, the other more stealthy and even more far-reaching *bouleversement*, the Industrial Revolution, was well advanced along its course, making more insistent than before the competition for raw materials, markets, outlets and opportunities for growing populations.

Britain and France had emerged as the great mercantile rivals, pushing the Dutch off the sea-routes and competing for the bankrupt East India Company's overseas trade and possessions. In 1793 French Republican forces overran Belgium and threatened British trade with Europe. Soon, in alliance with Holland

and Spain, Britain was at war with France. The Netherlands was split into two political factions: the exiled Prince of Orange led the conservative group, while the Patriots, then in power as the Batavian Republic, supported revolutionary France. Britain feared the French would succeed to the Dutch control of the Cape, creating a military and commercial menace to her new Empire in India and to her flourishing trade with the East and with the rapidly developing territories in the Americas.

A large British force compelled the Dutch Governor of the Cape to capitulate in April 1795. Southernmost Africa was now to be stripped of its role of secluded kitchen garden to a commercial company and thrust more and more into the flux of world affairs, from then always to be influenced by and to exert influence upon events in an international context.

3 The Colony (1795–1884)

The series of British governors who took control of the new and complex possession were mostly capable and conscientious, but their administration could not be fully effective; Britain had undertaken to return this Colony to the Dutch at the end of the war and the home government regarded the Cape as a fortress defending external interests and not as a colony to be developed. From the beginning, too, they suffered the shortage of funds that, together with indecision as to the Colony's function, was to bedevil its progress.

The first governor, General Craig, vigorous, honest and humane, saw the main need was for firm rule. His administration was conservative and his sway just, strongly paternal and far from popular. Earl Macartney, who followed on in 1797, was one of the most experienced of British administrators with a high reputation for efficiency and integrity. He began by sweeping away the worst abuses of Company rule. Fixed salaries for officials replaced the old system of fees and perquisites. An end was made of monopolies and of restrictions on the sale of goods to ships and on internal and coastal trade. Trade with British possessions was stimulated. Private enterprise was encouraged and small industries began to take shape – a little milling, some forestry, some whaling. But agriculture remained the economic basis of the country. Here there was the perennial story of glut and depression. 1795 had produced bumper crops and a large and ill-advised export, for a series of poor years followed in which grain had to be imported. Nevertheless revenue rose and, freed from the old Company restrictions, the economic life of the Colony began gradually to flow into the stream of world trade that passed its shores. Cape society welcomed the new age and the legal, economic and administrative reforms that it brought. Life in the capital began to set in a traditional colonial mould, with the opulence, the gay round and social functions inevitable with a regiment quartered in the locality.

But the new regime inherited all the old border problems: the stubborn independence of the burghers, the pressure of the Africans and the unrest among Khoikhoi and slaves.

The districts of Cape Town, Stellenbosch and Swellendam soon took the oath of allegiance. The new frontier republic of Graaff-Reinet delayed, and its leaders held out for a year. Craig promised an amnesty but refused to recognize their elected heemraden and, to the request of the farmers that they be allowed into Kafirland to search for stolen cattle or to occupy vacant lands beyond the Fish River as far as the Koonap 'or, if it could be, unto the Kat', he gave a stern rebuke.

With what face can you ask me to allow you to occupy lands which belong to other people? What right can I have to give you the property of others, and what blessing or protection could I expect from God were I to cause or even to encourage such a gross and glaring act of injustice ?[1]

The tribes' claim to the land they then inhabited was recognized early on, but the problem for the British authorities, as for their predecessors, remained of how to stabilize the frontier. Whatever treaties were made with the chiefs, whatever penalties were threatened for the farmers, nothing could alter the ways of the borders where White and Black were now mixed in an explosive ferment. The administration, though far from revolutionary, was not uninfluenced by the egalitarian and humanitarian concepts which were transforming ideas about the relations between men, and those were disturbing innovations in the confined isolation of the Cape. The immediate need for firm and stable government required in the official view that all – Khoikhoi, slaves, unruly Blacks and stiffnecked Whites – must be brought under the rule of law. While acknowledging that there should be 'an exact subordination' among slaves, the British authorities proposed to

1. *Cambridge History of the British Empire*, Vol. VIII, p. 177.

the Cape Court of Justice a relaxation of the customary punishments. The Court replied (much as had the West Indian slave-owners) that the mere deprivation of life was not a sufficient deterrent 'unless accompanied by such cruel circumstances as greatly aggravate their bodily sufferings',[2] and that any mitigation would make the colonists fear for their own safety; but rewards might safely be offered to slaves for good work performed. Craig reported this to London and his successor, Macartney, was instructed to put a stop to practices such as torture of slaves and Khoikhoi on suspicion in criminal proceedings and breaking at the wheel.

The general position of the Khoikhoi was worsening. Full-blood Khoikhoi were theoretically free men, but within the Colony they were almost entirely landless and only two Kaptijns still held land for their clans. Many were underpaid or unpaid labourers on White farms, miserably poor and at constant odds with their employers. Children of slave-Khoikhoi unions were 'provided for' under the apprenticeship system, becoming virtually serfs of the owners of the slaves. Khoikhoi and Basters were expected to take part in the country's defence and Basters not employed by colonists had to enrol and pay taxes exactly as had the burghers. (The Basters were groups, generally Afrikaans-speaking, originating in the late eighteenth century from unions of trekkers and Khoikhoi women along the remote Orange River borders.) Tribes that retained their organization – Korana, Grigriqua, Namaqua – were leaving the Colony and moving into the dry north and west to settle in the Orange River Valley, the Kalahari or South West Africa. Bands of Khoikhoi, half-breeds, escaped slaves, White deserters and outlaws roamed the wild Orange River area. A northern frontier had never been defined and the Company had left it to the burgher commandos to punish raids by San who lived in some numbers in the mountains of north and north-east, provided each 'straf commando' was reported after it had taken place. Some San worked as cattle-herders and servants, but mostly they were shot or driven away.

On the eastern borders skirmishing never ceased. Only when it became particularly intensive and prolonged and government

2. *Cambridge History of the British Empire*, Vol. viii, p. 177.

forces were called in to reinforce the commandos were hostilities raised to the status of war. The Xhosa were living beside the Bushman's River well into the Suurveld and raiding across the Gamtoos, while burghers had crossed the Fish and settled on the banks of the Koonap. Macartney, who tried to impose more stable conditions, offered to remit rent to those who returned to their farms in the Colony, but the well-watered lands under the Winterberg were too great a magnet for the Whites, while Rarabe's people were afraid to go from the Suurveld back over the Fish into the domain of Ngqika with whom they were in feud.

Trouble began again in 1799 when van Jaarsveld, the commando leader, was arrested on a charge of forgery. Coenraad Buis, another of the colourful frontier characters, led a revolt of a section of the Graaff-Reinet burghers, rescued van Jaarsveld, demanded his discharge, liberty to graze their cattle at night beyond the Fish River and permission to go over the border to claim runaway servants. General Vandeleur defeated the rebellious group, captured van Jaarsveld and sent him with his son and nineteen others to Cape Town to stand trial for treason.

Then, returning south to Algoa Bay, he was attacked[3] by Xhosa tribesmen who were pillaging up and down the country, driving out the farmers and terrorizing the Graaff-Reinet area; they may have feared that he meant to drive them out of the Colony or they may have been encouraged by the rebellious Whites to make trouble. They were joined by large numbers of resentful Khoikhoi servants, often armed with guns and mounted, who had seized the opportunity of the confusion to decamp. The alliance, long-feared by Maynier, between the hard-pressed Xhosa and the Khoikhoi, who were able marksmen and familiar with Boer fighting methods, was formidable for the Whites. The colonists, however, gave little support to the troops; they were short of ammunition, thoroughly demoralized, quarrelling among themselves and generally unable to submit to any authority, administration or commando leader.

General Dundas, the acting-governor, came to the rescue but, under instructions to keep the peace, he pursued the well-worn paths of conciliation. Well might he say, 'There must be justice

3. Third Xhosa War, 1799–1803.

for all or there will be trouble'.[4] The British Government, deep in the French war, had not troops nor money for the pacification of the frontier in addition to maintaining the fortress at Cape Town. He sent Maynier back once more to Graaff-Reinet as Resident Commissioner to try to establish better relations between the races. Maynier managed to persuade a majority of fugitive Whites to reoccupy their farms, but he was less successful in getting them to cooperate in an orderly self-defence. He tried to enforce the laws prohibiting intercourse with the Xhosa, while agreeing that they should remain 'peacefully' in the Suurveld. He allowed only the minimum effective commando forces into Xhosa territory in pursuit of stolen cattle, but his efforts to make friends with Ngqika were frustrated by the activities of the more undisciplined of the Boers living in Kafirland.

In his attempt to bring the war to an end Maynier not only ordered strong measures against Khoikhoi vagrants and the Xhosa; he tried also to get them back into employment on the farms and to make their working conditions more tolerable. He required the registration of service contracts (the beginning of a long chain of masters' and servants' legislation), and enforced a compliance with terms of agreement and the payment of wages, low though these were; and amongst other contentious concessions he allowed servants and slaves to worship in White churches on Sunday afternoon. Not only was the deplorable treatment of servants by Whites a potent source of Khoikhoi discontent, but landlessness was another major factor in their debasement, utter poverty and consequent maraudings. In 1801 a temporary location or reserve on the Zwartkops River was set aside for those not in service and several hundreds settled there with the Reverend Johannes van der Kemp of the London Missionary Society. But raiding the Whites persisted. There was another burgher insurrection and the collapse of what measure of security had been achieved. Maynier was recalled (later to be cleared of all the wild charges his enemies had laid against him). Other commando attacks on the armed bands were unsuccessful and the Whites again fled in panic, their farms abandoned. Instructions issued to commandos illustrate the abuses in warfare at the time:

4. E. A. Walker, *A History of Southern Africa*, p. 132.

enemy huts were not to be fired nor corpses mutilated lest there should be reprisals; women and children were not to be harmed, but returned safely to their homes as White women had lately been by the Xhosa.

In the meantime away in Cape Town, Prinsloo and the van Jaarsvelds had been condemned to death, but Dundas, still conciliatory and risking a London reprimand, wisely reprieved them.

Distant events again took control of the fortunes of the Colony. Britain and France made peace and in terms of the Treaty of Amiens the Cape was restored to France's allies, the Dutch Batavian Republic, in February 1803.

The Batavian Republic, sprung from the French Revolution, was infused with advanced political ideas. Its brief regime in the Cape introduced a gust of liberal administration and reform and a more constructive colonial policy in sharp contrast to the previous British preoccupation with the military aspects. Jacob de Mist, a member of the Batavian Council for Asiatic Possessions and a distinguished lawyer, was sent as Commissioner-General to examine relations between the Cape and the Netherlands and with him went Lt-Gen Jan Willem Janssens as governor. A strong and uncorrupt administration was established with a Council of four salaried officials and a secretary to assist the governor. The High Court was converted into a body of seven professional lawyers, independent of the executive, with a qualified attorney-general replacing the fiscal as public prosecutor. The protection of the law was extended equally to all religious communities. The Cape Dutch Reformed Church was somewhat liberalized by the arrival of theologians from the Netherlands. Plans were made to improve the standard of education. But the religious burghers were outraged by the introduction of civil marriages, performed by landdrosts and heemraden, though this was a considerable convenience in a land of great distances and isolation; and they were scandalized by the transfer of schools from church to government control, for education to a basic literacy was necessary for church membership and so was looked on as a part of religion. Changes of this sort were seen as an assault by French revolutionary liberalism on Boer Calvinism.

De Mist tried to make agricultural practice more scientific, to improve the quality of the sheep and wine for export and lay the foundations of wool production. To offset the lack of money and shortage of skilled labour which held up development, more cash was put into circulation by an increased note issue. He and Janssens both believed it to be a disastrous mistake to try to build a progressive economy on a structure of slave labour and that it was not too late to substitute White immigrants, but the colonists would not hear of this.

Both officials visited the eastern region in search of a solution to its defiant problems. Van Jaarsveld had died in prison but his companions had been released and Graaff-Reinet was well disposed to the administration. Janssens found roving Khoikhoi bands were anxious to settle on land of their own. He allotted more Reserves to them and moved van der Kemp's mission to Bethelsdorp near the future Port Elizabeth, as Dundas had originally intended. He further improved their working conditions and again ruled that Khoikhoi were to enter service only on definite contract terms recorded by competent officials. Two farmers were banished from the frontier for harsh treatment of their labourers. From then on the Khoikhoi of the Colony increasingly entered service. As they were assimilated more and more into the burghers' institutions they became more than ever allies of the Whites, for indeed they had little choice.

The frontier Xhosa proved more intractable. Ngqika again acknowledged the boundary of the Fish River, but as the western tribes refused after protracted negotiations to move from the Suurveld there was little Janssens could do but reiterate the old bans on intercourse. To strengthen the central administration and make its writ run on the borders, de Mist created two new districts with drostdies at Uitenhage in the south and at Tulbagh in the north-west. He regularized the form of local government that had already been developed and established the office of *veld-kornet*, an appointment made on the landdrost's recommendation, with military and civil duties in the wards – each a six-hour ride in diameter – into which each district was divided. The form of local government that emerged was to be the model for the Voortrekker Republics of a later day. But while they demanded more protection of the central authorities, the burghers at the same time resented measures of this kind as an interference with their independence. In any case de Mist admitted that the reforms he wished to introduce were far ahead of public opinion. Events in Europe were impinging once again and, short of forces and money, there was little more the enlightened Batavians could do.

Britain now was fighting for survival as a maritime and imperial power as Napoleon rose to pre-eminence, all but uniting Europe under French hegemony, forging a mighty empire, shutting Britain out from the commerce of Europe and threatening her eastern trade. When Napoleon's plans for the invasion of Britain foundered his energies turned eastwards. Holland was his ally and it remained vital to Britain that the Cape should not fall to the French. In January 1806, an overpowering British force reoccupied the Cape. The occupation was ratified nine years later at the Congress of Vienna in a peace settlement which cost Britain £6m. in payments to various powers in compensation or as contributions to fortifications. Against this sum, in order to soothe British public opinion, was offset the advantageous acquisition of the Cape Colony, and this gave rise to the widely accepted fiction that Britain had bought the Colony.

The first thirty years of this fresh occupation were to bring the Cape indisputably under British rule and integrate it into the imperial system of which it would remain a part for the next 155 years. The main elements of population, the *personae* for the multi-act drama that would be played out over those years, were now assembled in its boundaries.

More efficient administration gave rise to an improving economy in the Western Cape, increasing commercial contacts abroad and a more cosmopolitan outlook among the urban inhabitants. But the inevitable extension of the rule of law to the frontiers of the permanent colony which was now replacing the temporary fortress of a few years earlier and to its Black inhabitants was resisted by the men of the borders. Whether welcome or not, British rule irreversibly introduced the secluded tip of southern Africa to the economic and political realities of the day and opened it wide to changing ideas.

But if French ambitions were to be eventually defeated there was for the present no room for liberal experiment in the government of this outpost. The terms of the capitulation, however, guaranteed to the people their existing laws, privileges and forms of worship under a conservative British rule, likely to be more acceptable to them than the advanced reforms of Batavia. The governor, as representative of the Sovereign, ruled autocratically, subject only to the Secretary of State for the Colonies, months distant by sea in England. Legislative and executive authority rested in him, with control over the appointment, promotion and pay of all officials. Salaries for the top jobs were high and the administration costly for so poor a community.

But the first years of the occupation, when garrisons were stationed on the peninsula and fleets had to be provisioned, were again years of agricultural prosperity. Only after the end of the wars, when troops and navies withdrew, would the Cape fall back into the old economic slump. Now civic amenities were extended, internal and external mail service provided, roads and bridges improved, street lighting and piped water introduced into Cape Town, a library and a museum established and hospital services brought up to date. Educational standards remained very low until Lord Charles Somerset, governor from 1814 to 1826, recruited schoolmasters and ministers from Calvinist Scotland who laid the foundations of what was to become a highly developed educational system. His attempts, however, to impose English as the official language, especially in the schools and courts, on a population of 43,000 Dutch and 8,000 English aroused a strong and enduring hostility.

The removal of trade restrictions stimulated the economy; the cattle in the Colony increased rapidly and the wine industry began to prosper. The abolition of the trade in slaves increased their value and owners' profits from their hire. Finance reforms brought order to the chaotic international currencies and paper money in circulation; the introduction of British currency in 1825, taking the Cape into the imperial monetary system, caused immediate individual hardship and consequent unpopularity, but gave eventual benefit.

The Earl of Caledon, the first civil governor after the second occupation, as aware as de Mist of the need to make government effective throughout the Colony, made important legal innovations. Though the High Court had reverted to its non-professional standing as before Batavian rule, Roman-Dutch law remained the basic law of the Colony, and its court procedures were observed in general until the radical reforms of 1827. But the High Court was now to sit according to English practice with open doors, which was some compensation to British merchants who resented being subjected to Roman-Dutch law. Two judges of the High Court were to go on circuit to the drostdies to hear civil and criminal cases and to draw up a report on conditions in each district, while the landdrosts were to make annual visits of inquiry to each veld-kornet's ward to hear the complaints of farmers and Khoikhoi. The anarchic frontier was thus brought under some judicial surveillance by the central government.

To protect the Khoikhoi and increase the labour supply, an attempt to reconcile irreconcilables, Caledon promulgated the Hottentot Code of 1809, in effect the first pass laws. The Code abolished what remained of their tribal system by bringing the Khoikhoi under colonial law, and strengthened in their favour the laws relating to work contracts, giving them rights of appeal to the heemraden. But any advantages were made null by insistence that they should find 'a fixed place of abode', which could only increase the dependence on White farmers (who were protected from 'wanton or malignant' accusations), while their right to land was withheld, and a certificate or 'pass' from the landdrost was necessary before they could cross district boundaries. Infringement brought them under the vagrancy laws. Every White could demand the pass of any Black and no pass could be issued before a labour agreement had been made. The landdrosts administering the laws were generally farmers themselves and inclined to treat Khoikhoi as vagrants in order to force them into service or to refuse them passes.

Cradock followed this up, theoretically to protect Coloured children. In 1812 he ruled that all Khoikhoi children who had been maintained to the age of eight by their parents' masters were to be 'apprenticed' to those masters for a further ten years. In this way whole families could be indentured for long periods while successive children grew up. Somerset was to extend this by authorizing the landdrosts to apprentice orphans. The net result was to reduce the Khoikhoi population to the status of serfs at the disposal of local officials. Though technically under the law, if they tried to invoke it against employers they were kept in jail until the case came up. The heemraden tended to sympathize with the accused masters and punishment was heavy if accusations failed to be proven. The choice before the Khoikhoi was to trek over the frontiers, to take work on the farms or to go to the missions.

Caledon's extension to the frontier, in 1811, of the annual circuit was to have long-resounding consequences. The circuit of 1813, to become well known as the Black Circuit, was charged with investigating serious allegations by missionaries and officials of ill-treatment of Khoikhoi by the masters. Van der Kemp, one of the main accusers, had died the year before and his colleague James Read had to carry the burden of the accusations. Read was an honest and sincere man, dedicated to his work, but his education was limited and he was considered over-enthusiastic and easily misled. Possibly many fewer cases would actually have been brought to court if he had had more experience of the legal processes, of the difficulties of proving charges often some years old, of the confused evidence likely to be given by illiterate people in an unfamiliar milieu, and of the difficulty of finding witnesses among those likely to remain at the mercy of their masters and the local officials. In any event, only eight of the sixty-two Europeans charged of crimes of violence against their servants were convicted; others were found guilty of withholding wages, cattle or children; and one death sentence was passed but later commuted. This provided proof enough of abuses, and of the people's need, to justify the inquiry. But it was also sufficient to enrage the White population. Nearly a hundred of the most respected families in the frontier were implicated and numbers were involved and inconvenienced by charges laid by slaves and Khoikhoi, encouraged (that is what specially rankled) by Christian missionaries. It became an event of tremendous significance to be built in to the *volk* mystique so potent in a later day. In addition, the cases received great publicity in England and helped form a picture then building up of burgher brutality which the frontier farmer much resented.

Nevertheless, the circuits continued to attempt to establish law in the outlying regions and to bring the insubordinate burghers under its sway. When Frederick Cornelius Bezuidenhout, charged with cruelty to a Khoikhoi servant, had ignored two previous summonses, twelve men of the Hottentot Corps under White officers were sent to arrest him. Bezuidenhout resisted and was killed. His brother, Johannes, and his friends swore at his funeral to avenge him by driving the British and their Khoikhoi employees out of the border and to establish a republic. They failed to get help, not only from the burghers but also from Ngqika, the Xhosa chief whose support they twice sought, offering him the Suurveld in exchange for his help and for the land on the Kat River which they coveted. In 1815 sixty of the insurgents were surrounded at Slachter's Nek by a combined force of burghers and soldiers. Johannes Bezuidenhout fought it out. Forty-seven rebels were tried by a specially appointed Commission. Six were condemned to death and thirty to banishment. Many of the sentences, delivered by the Dutch judges administering the harsh Roman-Dutch law, were mitigated by the British Government, but five of the death sentences were allowed to stand as a warning against armed rebellion. The mass of the local population supported the law in this issue and the Xhosa refused to be involved against the British; apart from the attention drawn by the grisly bungling of the execution, the event was not regarded as important by contemporaries. But twenty years later the victims became martyrs in the hagiology of the Voortrekkers.

Friction between the peoples on the frontier remained constant as ever. The Khoikhoi were now detribalized, landless, rootless and at odds with their masters. The Xhosa, hard-pressed for land, quarrelled among themselves with a turmoil of warring tribes behind them and their way forward blocked by Whites. They established themselves where they could and augmented their herds as they might – mostly by plundering the Whites, who took their cattle back again – with interest if they could. The Boers were at loggerheads with both Khoikhoi and Xhosa and baffled by an authority which, so it seemed to them, inadequately protected them, but deprived them of their old power to protect themselves and preached unnatural doctrines of natural rights. More loan farms were being abandoned. Cradock, Caledon's successor, determined to clear the Suurveld of the 20,000 followers of Ndlambe, who had fled there from Ngqika, and the Gunukwebe (half-Xhosa, half-Khoikhoi people allied to the Rarabe) already settled there, who now claimed the territory between the Fish and Sundays Rivers by right of conquest. Only when he sent up a large force of British troops to stiffen the burghers were they finally driven over the Fish.[5] He built a series of forts between Cradock and Grahamstown and offered farms on favourable terms in an attempt to increase White settlement on the frontier. But neither forts nor denser settlement put a stop to the two-way border raids and cattle lifting.

It had become practice in White–Black hostilities for each to find allies in other groups; Whites hunted San with Khoikhoi trackers; Griqua and Xhosa enlisted White outlaws and deserters in their cause; Khoikhoi regiments were formed for the defence of the Colony. Now the authorities began to take sides in inter-tribal rivalries, arm factions against one another, make treaties with chiefs, exact from them concessions, make them presents and eventually were to subsidize them so that they became vassals and at last civil servants, a pattern that was followed until the tribes were conquered.

About this time a prophet, Makanda, appeared among the Xhosa, perhaps the first Black South African nationalist to stand out with clarity. He established a hybrid religion of his own in reaction to Christianity. His pantheon of gods commanded that the Whites be driven into the sea:

> To chase the White men from the earth,
> And drive them to the sea.
> The sea that cast them up at first,
> For Ama Xhosa's curse and bane,
> Howls for the progeny she nursed
> To swallow them again[6]

as his advancing army sang. In an attempt to unite the western

5. Fourth Xhosa War, 1811–12.
6. Edward Roux, *Time Longer than Rope* (2nd edn.), p. 13.

Xhosa, he joined Ndlambe against the weaker and unpopular Ngqika who, routed at the Battle of Amalinde in 1818, called on the governor for help. Government forces, in this the Fifth Xhosa War, crossed the Fish and, joined by some of Ngqika's men, drove Ndlambe and Makanda into the forests and drove off some 23,000 cattle to be shared by the colonists and Ngqika. Ngqika was again defeated by Makanda and Ndlambe who, 'following the tracks of their cattle' (in the old punitive tradition), went over the Fish and carried the war into the Colony, 10,000 of them recklessly investing Grahamstown in 1819. They were forced right back over the Fish and as far as the Kei. Many were killed, their homes fired and all their cattle captured by the Whites. Ndlambe went into hiding. The government forced on other chiefs acknowledgement of Ngqika as Paramount Chief and in an oral treaty with him all the country between the Fish and the Keiskamma was pronounced Neutral Territory (its name and status soon to be unilaterally changed to the Ceded Territory).

Makanda gave himself up. 'People say that I have occasioned this war. Let me see whether delivering myself up to the conquerors will restore peace to my country.'[7] A group of his councillors vainly offered themselves in exchange. He was one of the early political opponents of South African governments to be sentenced to life imprisonment on Robben Island. On Christmas Day, not long after, he organized a mass escape. The boat overturned and the men swam for the shore, encouraged by the great voice of Makanda who clung to a rock until he was swept off and drowned. But the Xhosa refused to accept the fact of his death and he remained a legend.

Thomas Pringle, the 1820 Settler, later recorded this contemporary Xhosa account of events of the Eastern Frontier and their view of relations between themselves and Boer and British during the forty-odd years – from their first drifting across the Fish River at the end of the 1770s to settle in any number on the colonial side until their reckless attack on Grahamstown – of struggle for possession of the Suurveld:

Speaking with dignity and with great feeling, the black man said:

7. Edward Roux, *Time Longer than Rope* (2nd edn), p. 14.

'The war, British chiefs, is an unjust one. You are striving to extirpate a people whom you forced to take up arms. When our fathers and the fathers of the Boers first settled in the Suurveld they dwelt together in peace. Their flocks grazed on the same hills: their herdsmen smoked together out of the same pipes; they were brothers . . . until the herds of the Xhosa increased so as to make the hearts of the Boers sore. What those covetous men could not get from our fathers for old buttons, they took by force. Our fathers were *men*; they loved their cattle; their wives and children lived upon milk; they fought for their property. They began to hate the colonists who coveted their all, and aimed at their destruction.

Now, their kraals and our fathers' kraals were separate. The Boers made commandos on our fathers. Our fathers drove them out of the Suurveld; and we dwelt there because we had conquered it. There we were circumcised; there we married wives; and there our children were born. The white men hated us, but could not drive us away. When there was war we plundered you. When there was peace some of our bad people stole; but our chiefs forbade it. Your treacherous friend, Gaika, always had peace with you; yet when his people stole, he shared in the plunder. Have your patrols ever found cattle taken in time of peace, runaway slaves or deserters, in the kraals of our chiefs? Have they ever gone into Gaika's country without finding such cattle, such slaves, such deserters in Gaika's kraals? But he was your friend; and you wished to possess the Suurveld. You came at last like locusts.[8] We stood; we could do no more. You said, 'Go over the Fish River . . . that is all we want'. We yielded and came here.

We lived in peace. Some of our bad people stole, perhaps; but the nation was quiet . . . the chiefs were quiet. Gaika stole . . . his chiefs stole . . .his people stole . . . You sent him copper; you sent him beads; you sent him horses, on which he rode to steal more. To us you sent only commandos.

We quarrelled with Gaika about grass . . . no business of yours. You sent a commando, you took our last cow . . . you left only a few calves, which died for want, along with our children. You gave half of what you took to Gaika; half you kept yourselves. Without milk . . . our corn destroyed . . . we saw that we must ourselves perish. We plundered and we fought for our lives. We found you weak; we destroyed your soldiers. We saw that we were strong; we attacked your headquarters, Grahamstown . . . and if we had succeeded, our right was good, for you began the war. We failed . . . and you are here.

8. The attack in 1818.

We wish for peace; we wish to rest in our huts; we wish to get milk for our children; our wives wish to till the land. But your troops cover the plains, and swarm in the thickets, where they cannot distinguish the man from the woman and shoot all.

You want us to submit to Gaika. That man's face is fair to you but his heart is false. Leave him to himself. Make peace with us. Let him fight for himself . . . and *we* shall not call on you for help. Set Makana at liberty; and Islambi, Bushani, Kongo and the rest will come to make peace with you at any time we fix. But if you will still make war, you may indeed kill the last man of us . . . but Gaika shall not rule over the followers of those who think him a woman.'⁹

In a further attempt to secure the Suurveld border about 5,000 British, the 1820 Settlers, were brought from post-war industrial Britain, where unemployment was high, and settled in the loop of the Fish River, on farms of 100 acres quit-rent. There was soon discontent. Their farms were ludicrously uneconomic beside the vast 4,000 acres owned by the Boers and they were forbidden slave labour. Blight, drought, flood and Xhosa depredations made it a hard struggle for even the few professional farmers among them, and before three years were out two-thirds of the original number had drifted to the towns. There was no further effort to get British immigrants, the majority of whom went to Canada and Australia. The 1820 Settlement was to have important results all the same. Those who remained on the land increased their holdings and, turning largely to woolled sheep in which the Dutch had shown no interest, laid the foundations of a great wool industry. Others, mainly artisans, earned good wages in the towns. Others became traders, turning Grahamstown and the newly founded Port Elizabeth into prosperous commercial centres and taking trade goods on wagons to the farms and far into Kafirland. Because English was then the official language of government they retained their cohesion and identity and were not as a national group submerged like the earlier Huguenots and the Germans had been. These settlers were too few in number to reshape some 150 years of Dutch rule and influence, but, better educated and more sophisticated than the old frontier population and maintaining their European links, they set a stamp of British

9. ibid., p. 14.

customs and institutions on the development of the country, in the establishing of schools and libraries, for example, and on the course of South African architecture, literature and science. The cleavage had begun between rural Dutch and urban English which was later to have great political significance.

Besides this the 1820 Settlers had come from a Britain in which a spirit of liberty was abroad, echoing the American Declaration of Rights and reacting against the authoritarianism of Napoleon, and in which administrative reform was freely discussed. Some of this leaven they brought to the political life of the Colony, while their friends and their influence in the United Kingdom compelled a greater attention there to Cape affairs. The Settlers themselves soon absorbed the prevailing attitudes to the Black people and their liberal agitation did not, except with rare individuals, include benefits for African or Coloured. When the Settlers in the Eastern Province attempted to ventilate their grievances, Somerset, who was autocratic and very unpopular, forbade meetings and clamped down on all freedom of speech. Indignation swelled and a memorial of complaints was sent to the British Government, contributing to its decision to send out a commission of inquiry and to the introduction of some political, economic and constitutional reforms.

2. EMANCIPATION, MISSIONARIES AND TURMOIL

Racial problems and conflicts had become no longer a marginal but a paramount preoccupation in South Africa, even before the beginning of the nineteenth century, and have to be seen in the context of what was taking place elsewhere in Africa and in the contemporary world.

Before the end of the seventeenth century, while the slave trade was still quite small, English clergy and English Quakers had been protesting at its horrors. In America, the Quakers of Pennsylvania abolished slave-owning among themselves. Within a hundred years of the first stirrings, an English court in 1772 found the 'domestic institution' of slavery illegal in England and set free 14,000 Negroes living with their masters there. By 1781, the Anti-Slavery Committee had been formed with the support of

Bishop William Wilberforce, the friend of Pitt. In 1807, the year after Britain returned to the Cape, the United States Congress and the British Parliament, as almost the last act of the Ministry of All the Talents, abolished the slave trade. The penalties for infringement of the law were first a fine, then transportation and finally hanging, which at last killed the traffic. In their anti-slavery campaign the task of the philanthropists, as they were known, was certainly made easier because at this time the sheer profit in slaves was stifling other forms of commerce in Africa and new enterprises could not be started until trading in slaves was ended. In addition the efficacy of slavery was being questioned and the massive demand for the importation of new slaves into the West Indian plantations had begun to flag. Strong public pressure in Britain resulted in the introduction in 1833 of a Whig Ministry Bill for the Emancipation of Slaves. By the end of 1834, 800,000 slaves throughout the British Empire were to be freed and £20m. was set aside to be paid to owners in compensation.

The moral and religious forces which gave the anti-slavery movement its drive and its appeal were a result of a conjunction of circumstances in the 'age of enlightenment'. The ideas and ideals of the political revolutions fermented speculation on the nature of man and stimulated the growth of liberalism. A new middle class of wealthy and influential traders and manufacturers grew out of the Industrial Revolution: men untrammelled by the shibboleths of the aristocracy, men whose business interests gave them a knowledge of conditions in the colonies, who had connections among settlers, missionaries and others working in distant fields, men from whose ranks many of the new breed of philanthropists derived. The Methodists preaching the doctrine of divine grace, the Evangelicals asserting the value of the individual human soul, were rooted in this same stratum. A belief in the equality of all men in the sight of God and increasing knowledge of 'lesser breeds without the law' gave an impetus to missionary activity and to religion an influence it had not had since the Portuguese set out to discover new lands and to save souls.

As slaves had become rarer and more costly in the Cape, employers looked increasingly to the previously despised Khoikhoi to fill their labour requirements. Soon the concern over the conditions of slavery was extended to the state of the Khoikhoi. This concern was increased by the reports received from missionaries; the influence exerted on the British Government was reflected back to mould events and passions in the Colony and start an interaction between external and internal pressures that has not yet ceased.

The first mission to the Khoikhoi between 1737 and 1744 had been fifty years in advance of its time. George Schmidt, an unordained Moravian, tried to establish a station at Baviaan's Kloof, beyond the Hottentots' Holland hills. He made little headway with the Khoikhoi and roused the animosity of farmers and officials and the jealousy of the Dutch Reformed Church, then at odds with the Moravians in Cape Town. Effective missionary endeavour had only begun at the Cape with Dr Johannes van der Kemp, the Hollander friend of de Mist, a medical man turned parson and member of the newly formed London Missionary Society (LMS), non-denominational in form but with steady Congregationalist support and wide middle-class connections in Britain.

Dundas, during the first occupation, had recognized that one root of the Khoikhoi trouble was lack of land, and, attempting to remove this element from the causes of upheavals in the east, had enabled Dr van der Kemp to establish the first missionary institution on the frontier. This policy had been pursued by de Mist and stepped up by the authorities after the second British occupation. Van der Kemp, who founded the famous Institution for Hottentots at Bethelsdorp, near Port Elizabeth in 1803, was a remarkable man with a gift of being able totally to identify himself with the people among whom he worked: he dressed and lived as the Khoikhoi, ate their food and married 'a woman of Madagascar extraction', the daughter of a slave woman, an example which was followed by his colleague, James Read, who married a recently baptized Khoikhoi girl. His influence among the Khoikhoi was great and for long after his death they regarded all missionaries as 'Jankanna's children'. But the way of life, marriages and activities of van der Kemp and Read did nothing to commend missionaries to the settler population. They soon resented the institutions. Though these did not provide for more than a third of the total Khoikhoi population, it was believed that they drew off potential labour, harboured squatters, encouraged habits of idleness and casual labour in those who preferred to work for themselves rather than at low pay for Whites. It was now that the rather special settler connotations of 'vagrant' and 'idleness' crystallized to linger persistently. Nor did the support van der Kemp and Read gave to the complaints of Khoikhoi servants against the injustices they suffered sweeten relations and the missionaries' part in the events of the Black Circuit was yet another very black mark in the mounting tally. By 1816 there were some twenty L M S missionaries at work on the frontiers and many other sects were becoming active; missionaries were beginning to settle also among the Xhosa; Khoikhoi and Xhosa grievances were increasingly ventilated.

On the distant northern boundaries remnants of Khoikhoi tribes who had left the Colony and outlaws and fugitives were uniting or fighting, creating areas of lawless confusion along the Orange River and at the beginning of what came to be known as the 'Missionary Road', skirting Botswana, to Central Africa. Missionaries persuaded many of these factions to settle under the more able and amenable leaders, whose names have found a place in local history, among them Cornelius and Adam Kok and Andries Waterboer. They formed the little Griqua republics on the northern banks of the Orange River – Griqualand, Campbell and Philippolis – with their own codes, courts and coinages and each with a missionary as adviser and diplomat. The authorities, and particularly Somerset, disliked these activities of the missionaries, some of whom, like the Boers and from not dissimilar causes, had indeed become very independent. Nor could their safety be guaranteed outside the frontiers, so restrictions were placed on their movements. The L M S, worried by reports of conditions in these outposts, sent out John Philip in 1819 as superintendent of all their stations in South Africa, an appointment with consequences which echoed down the years.

John Philip was born in Scotland in 1775, son of an independent hand-weaver of some education and wide reading. He was a weaver himself but, unable to stomach the customary child labour, he set up on his own and became prosperous. Caught up in the religious revival, he trained for the Congregational Church, was a minister for fifteen years in Aberdeen and acquired two honorary degrees in theology from American universities. He had matured in the years of the Industrial Revolution and associated with growing working-class populations struggling for rights and demanding a living wage. He must have been acquainted with the anti-slavery movement of the 'Clapham sect' to which such distinguished and resourceful political campaigners as Wilberforce, Macaulay and Buxton belonged, and which became the model for the hundreds of voluntary movements which were to flourish in Britain. These reformers made a powerful pressure group and they developed methods of parliamentary lobbying, press publicity, open-air meetings, and briefing of Members of Parliament, as techniques for their 'agitation'. The movement was catholic in its membership, passionate evangelical Christians working with Rationalists and atheists and any who subscribed to the same aims. This experience Philip brought with him in 1819 to the Cape where he was to dominate politics for the next thirty years, to be hated by contemporary White South Africans as a meddlesome parson, a radical and negrophile and to become for later generations a symbol of all these things and the arch-enemy of the Afrikaner people.

He was, in fact, conservative in his political views, an advocate of middle-class respectability, anxious where possible to co-operate with authority and slow to take action until convinced of its absolute necessity; then he would speak his mind and was quick to take up cudgels. He was intolerant of opposition and his attitude to the Blacks was often paternal and despotic. He felt much sympathy with the frontier Whites in the depredations they suffered at the hands of the Blacks. In many of his views he followed van der Kemp, and he was energetic, had the right contacts abroad for getting a hearing, and the times were favourable. He made long and frequent journeys among the scattered mission stations and corresponded copiously with other missionaries and with other denominations. Few people in any sphere had acquired so wide an experience of South African conditions or an equal grasp of the contemporary situation, though he may have had an exaggerated belief in the extent of his actual influence on

British policy. Sometimes he was misled, hasty in judgement or too optimistic, but his overall assessment of relations between the races was marvellously prophetic in his day and valid still in ours. In him the Afrikaners saw concentrated all that threatened the destruction of their attitude to life. He set a standard for those later involved in the field of race relations to measure themselves against. Among the missionaries, then and for long after, were almost the only people who worked with and spoke up for the African. Authoritarian and paternalistic though many of them were, they built some frail bridges of understanding, trust and respect which somehow survived great stresses until in later days, as with the Clapham sect, secular groups were to join in the task and in large degree take it over.

Through his friendship with the acting-governor, Sir Rufane Donkin, Philip soon got the ban lifted on missionaries going beyond the frontier. Within two years of his arrival, he was sending to his friends in the United Kingdom carefully gathered information on the disabilities of the Khoikhoi which persuaded the Clapham sect and the interdenominational missionary conference at Exeter Hall that the causes of Khoikhoi and slaves were one and the same. He concluded that it was the law itself, even more than the application of it, that was at fault and that inequality was built in to the legal system. He began to collect evidence of irregularities on the part of the public and the officials.

Philip formed a high opinion of the capabilities of both Khoikhoi and African and believed that, given equal opportunity, they were the equal of Europeans; but he also believed that until they were sufficiently advanced in Western civilization they should be separated from Whites and protected from White rapacity. British opinion was much influenced by his *Researches in South Africa*, published in 1828; but the inaccuracies it contained, though these were generally of detail and did not affect the perceptiveness of his general argument, were taken hold of by the farmers of the frontier, adding fuel to their flaming anger.

Philip's demands for the Coloured people were straightforward enough. He demanded the abolition of vagrancy and pass laws which put the Khoikhoi at the mercy of White officials. He asked for them, he said, 'nothing but the power of bringing their labour to a fair market'. This, the then Secretary of State commented, 'includes everything else'. He demanded that they should have opportunity for education from the missionaries and land from the government, without which they would not have the economic basis necessary to improve themselves. 'The Abettors of the present system seem never to have contemplated the aborigines of the Colony as consumers',[10] a factor only recently grasped by industrial and commercial tycoons and still obscure to the politicians and public at large. Finally and primarily, it was his creed that all free persons of colour should have equality in law with Whites, for without this there could be no hope of civilization or advancement.

Philip had some powerful and militant allies in the Colony, among them the British Thomas Pringle and John Fairbairn and colonial-born Andries Stockenström. Thomas Pringle, an 1820 Settler, poet and journalist (later to become secretary of the Anti-Slavery Society), Fairbairn, one of the recently enlisted Scottish teachers and Abraham Faure, a Dutch Reformed Church minister, made the first attempt to establish a free press in the Cape. In 1824 they obtained licences and launched a bi-lingual magazine and a newspaper, the *South African Commercial Advertiser*, which were printed by George Greig on a mission press borrowed from Dr Philip. Almost immediately they fell foul of the governor by refusing to submit to censorship in reporting libel actions involving himself. He shut both papers down and a long and, for future South Africa, a classic struggle for press freedom started. Somerset made a personal vendetta out of it and closed Pringle and Fairbairn's Academy, 'that seminary of sedition', where he alleged they taught 'the most disgusting principles of republicanism'.[11] Not until 1828, after a long fierce fight, was a free press ensured by an ordinance based on English law.

Meanwhile, the rising unpopularity of Somerset's autocratic methods led to some curb on him. An Advisory Council was established in 1825, composed of six officers appointed by the Secretary of State (to which two colonists were added in 1827).

10. Walker, op. cit., p. 169.
11. ibid., p. 160.

They might debate only topics the governor laid before them and he was able to overrule them, but he had to justify to the Secretary of State any decision he took against the Council's advice.

The liberalizing trend, reflecting movements of opinion abroad, was to touch, often only lightly, most aspects of South African life. The Charter of Justice of 1827 recast the judicial system. An independent Supreme Court was set up consisting of the Chief Justice and three assistant judges, all professional lawyers, with a nine-member jury in criminal cases. There was right of appeal to the Supreme Court and to the Privy Council in London. English court procedure and criminal law were introduced, mitigating the harshness of Roman-Dutch law. A professional attorney-general was substituted for the fiscal. A magistrate and civil commissioners replaced the courts of the landdrost and heemraden; but they were poorly paid and not of sufficient standing to control the frontier, nor were they representative of the burghers in times of grievance. Demands for public representation were refused on grounds that the population was too widely scattered, that there were too few experienced individuals to participate and that the colonists' representatives would be obstructive in matters of Black welfare. 'The British Government recognized that slaves without freedom, Hottentots without rights and a Kafir frontier without peace were issues which had precedence over representative assemblies.'[12]

The Fiftieth Ordinance was promulgated in 1828 on the eve of the attainment of Emancipation. The legislation was based on a memorandum drawn up by Andries Stockenström, now the Afrikaner landdrost of Graaff-Reinet. All former restrictive laws including the pass laws were rescinded. All free persons of colour were given the right (but not necessarily the means) to own land. The Khoikhoi from now on were at liberty to withhold their labour and choose their master and were no longer subject 'to any compulsory service to which other of His Majesty's subjects are not liable, nor to any hindrance, molestation ... or punishment of any kind whatsoever under the pretence that such person has been guilty of vagrancy or any other offence unless after trial in

12. C. W. de Kiewiet, *A History of South Africa*, p. 35.

due course of law'.[13] Apprenticeship without parental consent was forbidden and Khoikhoi servants could keep their children with them without contracting them into service. At the insistence of Philip, who knew his South Africans, the legislation was entrenched: no alteration could be made without the consent of the King-in-Council. His wisdom became all too soon evident, when within six years a new draft vagrancy law, passed in the Cape by a narrow majority, was disallowed in Britain. But Philip was still not satisfied; on principle he opposed legislation for one class or section of the population.

The emancipation of the Coloureds, soon to be followed by that of the slaves, gave rise to great uneasiness and discontent among the White population, particularly in the frontier areas where the dread of Khoikhoi equality with Whites was reinforced in troubled times by real physical dangers. Soon, however, those most disaffected were to trek away out of the Colony, taking with them their grievances, and the situation was accepted for the time being by those who remained. Little more would be heard of the Khoikhoi problem until it became the Cape Coloured problem of a century later. But Philip's far-seeing comment at the time of emancipation was: 'If the Abolitionists fail to follow up the advantages lately gained . . . those that come after us will have to fight all our battles over again . . . and destroy a species of colonial bondage which will arise out of the ashes of the monster which has now been destroyed.'[14]

Having won some redress for those within the Colony, Philip turned his attention to relations with the Xhosa on the frontier where by 1834 a calamitous situation was developing. Refugees from upheavals in Natal and north of the Drakensberg were adding to the overcrowding and unrest and there was continual acrimonious passage of White and Black regardless of bureaucratic barriers until war[15] broke out once more. Maqoma, regent for Ngqika's son Sandile and one of the ablest and most far-sighted of chiefs, had been driven out of his lands on the Kat River and Khoikhoi settled there. He came back into the Colony with 12,000

13. *Cambridge History of the British Empire*, Vol. VIII, p. 290.
14. W. M. Macmillan, *Africa Emergent*, p. 16.
15. Sixth Xhosa War, 1834–5.

men and ravaged the country as far as Algoa Bay and Somerset
East. He was not turned back until Sir Harry Smith rushed up
with a British contingent to still the panic of the colonists and
drive Maqoma back beyond the Kei into Gcaleka territory, where
Hintsa now ruled. Hintsa, suspected of complicity, was made to
pay a large fine in cattle, and then or 'while escaping' was killed
by a White; his son, Sarili (Kreli), was installed as a successor.
Maqoma was imprisoned on Robben Island. D'Urban created
Queen Adelaide Province between the Keiskamma and the Kei
(only to abandon it a year later); the inhabitants were disarmed
and given reserves.

The Mfengu (beggars), or Fingo as the Europeans knew them,
were an amalgam of fugitives from the north-east who found food
and shelter as servants among the Xhosa and Thembu. They had
lost their old tribal cohesion and, beginning to resent their
subordinate status as herders of Xhosa cattle, took readily to
Western missionaries and their teachings (though not necessarily
to conversion), partly perhaps as an expression of social revolt.
The war gave them the opportunity, supported by their missionaries, to ask for British protection. Seventeen thousand of them
were settled, as were Khoikhoi, on lands in the Ceded Territory
confiscated from the Xhosa, many of whose cattle, entrusted to
their care, they had taken: so this measure, leaving Mfengu and
Xhosa neighbours, contributed nothing to frontier peace. But
under British protection and with missionaries, schools and
training colleges, the Mfengu were to advance in westernization
and to produce many outstanding African intellectuals of a later
day. Apart from Khoikhoi and Mfengu reserves, the Ceded
Territory was given out in farms to Whites.

Philip's view was not, as so often it has been represented, that
the 'innocent Kafir' was the victim of the cruel colonists, but that
the policy of military reprisals by White on Black was ineffective
for the protection of both. He had urged that the government
should take full civil responsibility for both colonist and African,
and guarantee security and civil rights to all. In demanding that
the African should be protected from encroachment and dispossession by the White, he advocated (while it might still have
been possible) the geographic separation of Black and White. At

the time of the war, convinced that the rule of law could be entrenched only by adequate magistrates and police and never by commandos, he made it clear that he had no objection to the advance of the frontier, 'provided that the natives have their land secured to them', for except as British subjects 'they cannot otherwise be saved from annihilation'.[16]

The missionaries, early in the field and in a time of uncertainty and disruption for the tribes, acquired great influence, became largely identified with the tribes they settled with and were often strongly partisan in inter-tribal disputes. Sometimes, too, they could involve the tribes in the imported rivalries of the various White missionary societies, inflaming dissensions at times when unity would have better served the people in the face of White advance. But they also gave devoted service. Their motives were on the whole good, their dedication and sacrifice heroic, their understanding and methods often lamentable. Without anthropological grounding or natural sensitivity, many were narrowly dogmatic in a narrow and dogmatic age, and unwittingly destructive of good and stabilizing elements of African life. Their denominational rivalry confused the people. Many of them came to accept the current White colour attitudes and in so doing dissipated much of the trust hard-won by their predecessors. At best, through the education and medical services they gave, they opened windows to let a light of rational thought into dark corners and struggled to alleviate suffering and disease. They reduced the many languages to writing. They translated the Bible into the various tongues and added to the African's great oral tradition literacy and a literature. They recorded tribal memories to boost racial self-esteem and, through schooling, gave to many the key to the full treasure house of human wisdom and the ground base for advanced intellectual achievement. Though dishearteningly few converts may have been made, the missions continued to circulate the most subversive of tracts, the vernacular Bible, and to give currency to English, the *lingua franca* of revolution. In church and school those able sang rousing hymns, learnt about Jesus, Shaka, Moshweshwe and Karl Marx, read newspapers, wrote newspapers, demanded higher education,

16. *Cambridge History of the British Empire*, Vol. VIII, p. 312.

demanded greater equity. The new literacy, though, meant mostly that a good many people acquired a harmless accomplishment which made them more useful to their White employers. A grounding was given in crafts and in agriculture into which, contrary to tradition, men were now brought. Produce or labour had to be sold to obtain the growing necessities, such as clothing, fuel and light, new foods, cash, which changing times created. So increasingly the people were trading with, borrowing from and working for Whites. The missionary and the trader were the African's first sponsors into Western life: the farmer and policeman followed hard on.

Later, Christianity and its missionary advocates became widely and often deservedly discredited among Blacks as an arm of colonial exploitation and White discrimination. At the same time the reputation Philip and others acquired and the passionate hostility they engendered among Whites tended to inhibit some who might have followed along his path. But the spirit was to survive with constant infusions from abroad and, more rarely, from South Africa. The brave work of individuals was always recognized and the occasional turbulent priest or political prelate taking a stand on principle, speaking out against injustice, was to acquire a widespread respect inside and outside Africa. Churchmen over the years kept directed on the Africans the world's fitful concern and, by leading them on to the not always comfortable or welcoming fringes of international Christendom, were to bring them and their problems finally into the heart of the United Nations a century and a half after van der Kemp began his labours.

The slow amelioration during the 1820s in the condition of the slaves, on paper at any rate, as a prelude to emancipation caused much general concern among owners and the legal ironing out of the distinction between master and servant added to the hostility felt towards the missionaries who, with their connections with overseas philanthropists, were held largely responsible. When emancipation at last came in 1834 the owners of the 40,000 slaves in the Cape, instead of the £2¾m. of compensation expected, received only £1½m. and that payable partly in government stock and in London where most of the owners had no connections.

Townsmen could make their claims through the banks but countrymen had to rely on brokers, generally at heavy discount, and many whose slaves were their security faced foreclosure of mortgages. The colonists largely disregarded the long warning of emancipation and the ample opportunity given to prepare for it. Nor did they take account of the fact that all slaves were obliged to remain apprenticed to their former masters for a further four years, while many continued in their employment long after that at wages very little more than the cost of their keep had been. A huge and ineradicable resentment, quite out of proportion to the actual cash losses, understandably festered to inflame other grievances of the colonists. Ten years later £6,000 remained still unclaimed.

In 1832 a British Whig government had granted the Colony a measure of White self-government, with an executive council composed of governor and twenty-four officials; and a legislative council of governor, four officials and from five to seven nominated colonists, with power to initiate laws, to consent to new laws and taxes, and allowing free debate. The governor retained his control of nominations, his casting vote and a veto. But by 1836, with the refractory issue of emancipation disposed of, it was possible to allow the beginnings of representative local government with the election of Boards by urban householders. The municipal boards were subject to no legal colour bar in theory and set a precedent for later Cape legislation. But in practice the householder qualification ensured White domination of councils.

During the decade in which these events were occupying men's minds in the extreme south, it happened that not only the tremendous missionary impulse of the nineteenth century, but also the time of great White expansion both coincided with a period of unusual turmoil among the Bantu-speaking people northwards and eastwards in southern and central Africa. Into this the Whites were moving, knowing and understanding nothing of what was going on, although these events were even then making their impact distantly on the frontiers of the Colony.

Among the numerous Nguni tribes which had for some centuries been settled in the warm, well-watered, fertile area of northern Natal, the Mthethwa occupied the coastal area south of the Umfolosi River. Towards the end of the eighteenth century Dingiswayo, a man of unusual organizing ability, succeeded to the chieftainship. He was particularly successful in reshaping the structure of tribal military power. The traditional local circumcision schools were replaced by the conscription of all the young men into central age-group regiments, their loyalty directed exclusively to the chief and their home ties loosened. This large body of well-organized and disciplined full-time warriors gave Dingiswayo a marked advantage over his neighbours whom, either by force of arms or peaceably, he united into a considerable confederacy with himself as paramount over the area between the Umfolozi River and the Tugela. By conscripting the young men of the vassal states he added to the strength of a loyal army and consolidated his rule.

What external forces gave impetus to the period of nation-building initiated by Dingiswayo and made possible his achievement are not yet clear. There could very likely have been a build-up of population, cattle and soil exhaustion, again associated (as when the Bantu peoples began their wide dispersion centuries before) with the introduction of a new and improved food crop – in this case maize, a high-yielding and pest-resistant grain – from the Portuguese at Delagoa Bay around the end of the seventeenth century. The arrival of White settlers in the south and, later, the west may have blocked the traditional splintering movement and made some sort of social reorganization imperative. It may be, too, that Dingiswayo and his successors fought their campaigns in order to control the Nguni trade in cattle, ivory (a royal monopoly), gold and tin, with the Portuguese at Delagoa Bay, and that this gave them the wealth and prestige wherewith to command the loyalty of viceroys and councillors and to consolidate the kingdom. There is also speculation that Dingiswayo in his youth may somewhere have associated with Whites, perhaps on a trading trip to Delagoa Bay, where he learned something of European military methods. But whatever the sources and causes, he applied his ideas with notable success.

The wife and young son, Shaka, of the ruler of the chiefdom of the Zulu, a small western satellite, had taken refuge with the Mthethwa. Shaka, illegitimate, rejected by his father, ridiculed and humiliated by his companions, enlisted in Dingiswayo's army and found scope for his great military gifts. Joining in a plot to murder his brother and with Dingiswayo's help, he succeeded to the Zulu chieftainship in 1818. He seems to have had an original mind and military flair exceeding that of his patron whose military system he adopted with added refinements, so concentrating great power in his own hands. He formed a standing army of men who lived permanently in special barrack villages and were expected to remain celibate until allowed to marry when over the age of forty, and whose regional loyalties became attenuated by

ZULU ROYAL HOUSE

MTHETHWA

Jobe
|
Dingiswayo
(Protector of
Shaka)

Senzangakhona
(d. 1816)

Shaka   Dingane   Mpande
(d. 1828)   (d. 1840)   (d. 1872)
|
Cetshwayo
(d. 1884)
|
Dinuzulu
(d. 1913)
|
Nkayishana (Solomon)
(d. 1933)
|
Cyprian Bhekuzulu

time. They were rigorously trained and disciplined and fought with high morale and dedicated valour. Shaka devised his famous crescent battle formation – a central regiment, flanked by two 'horns' which would encircle the enemy, with reserves in the rear. He stripped off his soldiers' sandals, leaving them barefoot for speed and mobility. After the death of Dingiswayo, Shaka absorbed the Mthethwa confederacy, greatly extended his domains and within ten years of his accession ruled over the whole of Natal north of the Tugela and west to the Buffalo, with an army of perhaps some 40,000 men. He eliminated most possible rivals, often, unlike Dingiswayo and traditional practice, killing women and children when expedient. The old tribal units remained under closely supervised hereditary or nominee headmen. The unity of the kingdom was ensured by Shaka's control of the army. Captured cattle were loaned out (as was often done) to the regiments, who could use the milk, but the beasts remained the chief's and he was immensely rich. He maintained his position in large part by terror; executions and massacres – in displeasure or for pleasure – were common enough events. He became a cruel, sadistic and widely feared tyrant. By 1824 most of central Natal was devastated and made a desolate no-man's-land between him and the colonists whose guns were beginning to alarm him. He remained, however, on friendly terms with the handful of White adventurers who traded under his protection from their base at Port Natal (Durban), though he failed in an attempt to make contact with the British Government.

Fugitives streamed before Shaka's victorious armies. Some, the Mfengu among them, fled south to the White frontiers. Others grouped as far from his range as they could under new chiefs, many of whom had fought with or against him and had adopted or adapted his methods. Some of these carried reverberations of Shaka's conquests far and wide in southern Africa, as they sought to create for themselves tolerable living conditions again.

The events known as the *difaqane* (forced migration) or *mfecane* (the crushing) were set in motion. Sobhuza, a northern neighbour of Shaka, retired to the mountainous country north of the Pongola where refugees strengthened his Dhlamini people, already a synthesis of Nguni and Sotho; here he formed a Zulu-type army and laid the foundation of the Swazi kingdom. Other leaders with small bands of perhaps a hundred men moved further afield, gathering more followers as they went, living by mauling the populations through whom they passed, seizing crops and cattle and leaving trails of desolation, until they found a place to settle. Shoshangane went north, laying waste Portuguese settlements on the way to found the Gaza kingdom between Delagoa Bay and the lower Zambezi, where his people lived until, being refused British protection, they were destroyed by the Portuguese in 1895. Zwangendaba went through the Lebombo foothills and into Rhodesia, devastating the old Rozwi kingdom and destroying Zimbabwe in 1830 and killing the Mambo, the ruler. He moved north again in 1835 to establish at length the Ngoni kingdom on the western side of Lake Malawi and extending northwards to Lake Tanganyika, some 2,000 miles from the people's place of origin. There they survived conflicts with German and British colonists.

Other leaders, Mpangazita and Matiwane, crossed the Drakensberg into the south-eastern high veld carrying the turmoil to the Southern Sotho. Here in 1822 they fell on the Tlokwa under MaNthatisi (Mantatis), an able woman who acted as regent for her son, Sekonyela, and whose amazonian exploits were to become legendary. For the next few years the hordes of these three were at each other's throats and ravaging the area along the Orange and the Caledon: settlements were abandoned, cattle destroyed, fields lay uncultivated, areas were littered with human bones, even cannibals abounded among the starving. In 1825 Mpangazita was killed in battle with Matiwane and his followers dispersed. Matiwane, after further fighting, went back across the Berg to harry the people of Southern Natal and the Cape frontier until a colonial force defeated him in 1828, and his people swelled the ranks of the Mfengu. MaNthatisi and Sekonyela, impoverished by the long wars, settled in a defensive position near the north-west borders of Lesotho and began to build up into a new chiefdom.

The utter collapse of the old order among the Southern Sotho gave a man of humble birth but unusual political acumen his chance. Moshweshwe, born in about 1786, became embroiled in the troubles. With his followers eventually he retreated to Thaba Bosiu, an easily defended hilltop in the Lesotho heights and from there, after he had defeated Matiwane, his reputation spread widely. Sotho and Nguni survivors flocked to put themselves under his protection. From there, with judicious military activity and diplomatic and conciliatory policies, he built up population strength, prestige and cattle wealth, until by the early 1830s his people were renowned as BaSotho, *the* Sotho. Learning from

Griqua adversaries, he bartered from them guns and horses in the management of which his people became adept. Hearing of missionaries, he sent to 'buy' one and soon men of the Paris Evangelical Mission, allied to the L M S, attached themselves, and churches and schools were built. The missionaries became his advisers and diplomats, and all who met him were deeply impressed by his intelligence and sensitivity. Sekonyela, his poor neighbour, soon resented his presence and success and other survivors of the mfecane began to ally themselves with the one or the other, boding trouble for the future.

North of the Vaal about four Sotho hordes of peoples who had been displaced, in their turn attacked the Tswana peoples. One group was routed by armed and mounted Griqua; another, the Kololo, fought its way north-west to the Zambezi where Livingstone eventually met them.

The most formidable leader in the Transvaal was Mzilikazi, one of Shaka's subordinates who defied him in 1822 and fled with 200 or 300 men to settle in the Eastern Transvaal high veld where he rapidly increased his following. In 1825, in a period of drought and harassed by Shaka, he moved near to the site of Pretoria and here he extended his suzerainty from beyond the Limpopo south to the Caledon River and west to Tswana territory. He, too, amalgamated Nguni and Sotho refugees and, with a Zulu-type army of up to 5,000 warriors, his Ndebele kingdom of 30,000 square miles became the dominant power in the high veld. But he was still too close for comfort to the Zulu and was also subject to Griqua attack, so in 1836 he settled still further west at Mosega near Zeerust until the approaching Voortrekkers added to his enemies and he led his people over the Limpopo. There he was to found the Ndebele (Matabele) kingdom among the Shona of Rhodesia, descendants of the Karanga confederacy, destroying the remnants of the Rozwi empire. Though Mzilikazi was despotic in his methods, like others caught up in the mfecane his main search was for security; he seems to have been considered gentle, intelligent, brave and a born leader, and anxious to be on good terms with the Europeans, who remarked favourably on the standard of law and order he maintained.

From the kaleidoscopic convulsions of these twenty turbulent years of revolution fresh groupings and patterns began to take shape. The influence of this renaissance spread wide over southern and central Africa and large new kingdoms, often composed of a variety of peoples, emerged – some of them to consolidate and withstand the greater social and economic disturbances that still lay ahead, as Whites with horses and wagons, guns and gin, invaded the lands they lived in.

3. GREAT TREK AND GREAT CONQUESTS

The Great Trek of 1836, which was to become so central an event in South African affairs as almost to institute a new calendar, was no isolated sudden exodus. The whole life of the Colony had been an inexorable flowing, first east and then north. The Great Trek was a conscious, reasoned acceleration of the old unordered drift for a sufficient period to have a character and be enclosed in dates, the motives for it well known and recorded. The immediate causes were many and often interrelated. First of all there was overcrowding, difficult to understand in so vast a country unless one recalls the size of the individual farms. A new generation grew up to whom the Colony could give no more 6,000 acre farms at rentals of fifty shillings, the Boer's birthright. Land shortage for the eastern farmers had been aggravated by the arrival of the 1820 Settlers in the Suurveld, a run of drought years, the new system of land tenure and the rising costs of land which had hitherto been free, apart from the negligible recognition fee. Eastward expansion was blocked by the hostility of the tribes. The government had vacillated; Queen Adelaide Land, between the Keiskamma and the Kei, was first annexed to give hope of new farms, then abandoned and returned to the Xhosa. To the north, however, over the Orange River and in the Free State area, frontier farmers in the habit, legal or no, of seasonal trekking and later specific expeditions of investigation, the *commissie trekke*, all reported limitless stretches of unoccupied grazing land. It must have happened without any other cause as part of the inevitable process. Piet Retief, the great leader, is said to have told the Zulu chief Dingane (so soon to be his executioner), that the Colony was too small and the Boers were becoming landless.

But besides the antique impulse of the land-hungry, the frontier people were disillusioned with a government in which they had no part and whose suppression of their language and enforcement of English in the schools and courts embittered them, and which was unable to provide them with the security demanded on the frontier and yet was unwilling to give them a free hand to protect themselves by the tried old commando methods. They resented the extension of the central administration, more or less efficiently, to the districts; they chafed at its limitations on their free-ranging across the boundaries, on their punitive expeditions after stolen cattle, on their trade and labour relations with the Xhosa, and, particularly, on their absolute control over their domestic Coloured employees. The existence of missionary institutions constantly reminded them of the creaming off of potential Khoikhoi labour and the supposed harbouring of ne'er-do-wells. Indeed they were experiencing a substantial labour shortage stemming from the emancipation of Khoikhoi and slaves. Some also suffered severe financial losses, although most of the Voortrekkers from the eastern districts possessed few slaves; but all were enraged and humiliated by the liberalization of the Hottentot laws: the abolition of vagrancy, the requirements of written contracts, limitations on punishments and the new rights of Non-whites to take Whites to court. They were bitter about the criticism abroad of their race policies, for which they blamed the accounts of 'missionaries and other prejudiced people'. They deplored the new laws which destroyed correct relationships, which gave Coloureds an 'ungodly equality'[17] with Christians, Black with White, servant with master, and aggravated the White man's sense of danger. By the time the Trek took place the whole economic and social structure of the Cape was based on colour discrimination and the conviction that as a race (as a White race) they could not have survived – and could not survive – without it. Attempts by British administration, missionaries, and liberal politicians to modify the structure were seen as a planned destruction of a people.

So they trekked. Piet Uys, who led one of the trekking parties, said: 'We have been deprived of all our domestic authority over

17. Walker, op. cit., p. 200.

the apprenticed coloureds in our homes and in our farms, and this has made these coloureds so insolent that we are no longer secure in our property and even our lives.' Anna Steenkamp, kinswoman of Piet Retief, another leader, complained not only of the 'unending plundering and stocktheft of the kaffers and their proud and defiant attitude', but also of 'the scandalous and unjust procedures in regard to the freeing of our slaves', and especially of 'their being placed on an equality with Christians, contrary to the laws of God and the natural differences of race and religion, so that it was intolerable for any decent Christian to bow under such a burden; wherefore we rather moved away in order to preserve the purity of our doctrines'.[18]

Piet Retief himself, in the Manifesto he published before his party left, complained of the losses caused by emancipation and by constant Kafir raids and thefts and declared:

We are resolved, wherever we go, that we will uphold the just principles of liberty; but whilst we will take care that no one shall be in a state of slavery, it is our determination to maintain such regulations as may suppress crime and preserve proper relations between master and servant ... We quit this Colony under the full assurance that the English Government ... will allow us to govern ourselves without its interference.[19]

'They fancy,' wrote an observer, 'they are under a divine impulse', a truth that has remained valid; and with equal perceptiveness he added, 'The women seem more bent on it than the men'.[20]

The Voortrekker parties were extremely small by comparison with the westward migrations in the United States. Nonetheless, one-sixth of its White population left the Colony. Between 1836 and 1846, perhaps some 14,000 people trekked, 2,000 of them in September 1837 – 'the flower of the frontiersmen',[21] D'Urban, the governor called them. They pulled up their roots which, for many with trekking already in the blood, were not very deep. A few abandoned their farms but most sold out well, and the

18. Gustav Preller, *Voortrekkermense II*, p. 30.
19. E. A. Walker, *The Great Trek*, p. 105.
20. E. A. Walker, *A History of Southern Africa*, p. 200.
21. ibid., p. 195.

proverbial exchange of a farm acquired free for (in those times) a
scarce wagon and span was considered not a bad bargain. But
their capital was mainly mobile : their families and basic furniture,
a few chairs, perhaps, some carpets and the old kists in the
wagons, Khoikhoi and African servants accompanying them and
driving the cattle, the goats and the sheep.

An idea of the substance of some is found in the records. 113
people from Tarka took with them £60,000 worth of stock; and
twenty-nine small parties or families owned between them 6,156
cattle and 96,000 sheep. Equally, their losses were heavy. One
group of twenty-seven families lost to the Ndebele 96 horses,
4,671 cattle and 50,795 sheep. Their wants were simple. For many
frontier families bread was no longer a staple diet. Game was
plentiful for the shooting. They had milk and meat. Ammunition
which they had been accumulating for some time, was adequate
if not squandered. Their movement was unimaginably slow.
They might average five miles a day, the pace of their grazing
sheep and goats, but the creaking wagons could not go much
faster. Now and then at mountain passes or rivers difficult to ford
the wagons were man-handled over in sections with all their
contents and rebuilt on the other side. At good water and grazing
they might remain for weeks, resting themselves and the animals.

They set out in small, generally neighbourhood, groups of
twenty or thirty families to join beyond the frontiers into larger
companies under a chosen leader, usually a well-known figure in
the Colony. The parties went from the eastern districts almost due
north, crossing the middle Orange and Caledon Rivers, skirting
the rich grain uplands of Lesotho to the east where Chief Moshweshwe was welding assorted refugee groups into a people, to
converge on Thaba Nchu, headquarters of Moroka, Chief of the
Rolong and friendly to the Whites. West of the route, along the
Orange River, there lay the fertile territories of the Griqua under
Adam Kok and Waterboer, and beyond them the desert. Ahead
stretched the great grass plains of the High Veld, extending from
the Orange River to the Vaal and from the Vaal River to the
Zoutpansberg range edging the Limpopo valley. Into this area,
recently devastated by the mfecane and an apparently vacant
waste of ruined buildings and whitening bones, survivors of its

old population were beginning to return from exile or hiding to reoccupy their old lands or to settle in more defensible positions; many of them were to find that the emigrant Whites had forestalled them. This area into which the Voortrekkers were pressing was encircled by other populous regions: the Ndebele and behind them on the western and north-western desert fringes the Tswana (Bechuana) people; to the north the Pedi, the Venda and others; eastwards the emerging Swazi kingdom, the Tsonga of the lowlands and the Zulu regiments, still powerful under Dingane, who had assassinated and succeeded to his brother Shaka in 1828; and south-east the Southern Sotho (Basuto), the Pondo and others on the colonial frontier.

For the next seventy years South Africa presents a picture of fluid boundaries, vacillating allegiances and responsibilities, kaleidoscopic flux of populations and shifting race relations – Afrikaner–British, Afrikaner–African, British–African and Africans all vieing with one another.

The Voortrekkers were primarily seeking land on the expansive scale to which they had grown accustomed. They were also moving away from the Colony and its detested laws and in so doing they cut themselves increasingly off from the economic and material trends of the Colony and the industrial and intellectual climate of the day. They took, Professor de Kiewiet has said, deep into the nineteenth century 'the non-literary, non-industrial habits of the eighteenth century'.[22]

Despite the frequent quarrelling and disagreement of Boer leaders, despite the irresolute, stop-go colonial policy of British Governments, great land tracts were constantly annexed to the Whites until by the turn of the century southern Africa, from the Atlantic to the Indian Ocean, from the Cape coast to the Zambezi, was under White occupation and suzerainty. Within two years the Voortrekkers had flowed round the main concentrations of Africans in face of the fiercest opposition. In fourteen years they had settled in most of the best parts. Their persistent ubiquity was to make South Africa ultimately Boer in character and race segregation impossible, and was greatly to complicate White–Black relations. They took with them the old problem of the

22. de Kiewiet, op. cit., p. 56.

eastern frontier and the dichotomy of solution, dependent on who was in power and what the prevalent influences were in distant London. There, for the most part, humanitarian and philanthropic forces had played themselves out and Britain was hard put to maintain her expanding colonial responsibilities in Canada, Australia and New Zealand – colonies with more promise of ultimate prosperity and independence of the British exchequer than South Africa with its contentious nomads.

The Great Trek went in four main streams. The first to leave, in September 1835, was Louis Trigardt, who had been settled on the banks of the Kei, far outside the Colony, and was suspected of illegal activity with the tribes. He and Jan van Rensburg, who joined him, led their groups over the Orange River and gradually made their way through the Orange Free State and up to the Zoutpansberg Mountains where they parted. Van Rensburg's group pushed on north and, weakened by malaria and sleeping sickness, were wiped out by hostile tribes (perhaps Tsonga or Pedi) in the lower Limpopo valley. Trigardt's party, decimated by fever, turned south-east and struggled on to Delagoa Bay, from where the survivors reached Port Natal by sea in 1839.

In February 1836, Hendrick Potgieter took a party from Tarka across the Orange, to be joined by a group from Colesburg (in which was the ten-year-old Paul Kruger). He then set off from their base camp (on land bought from a chief in the northern Orange Free State for twenty-nine head of cattle), to find Louis Trigardt. Meanwhile Mzilikazi, still at Mosega and already sorely harassed by both Zulu and Griqua bands, was much disturbed by reports of the influx of Voortrekkers. He had generally been well disposed to passing White strangers, but numbers of Whites with families and stock, unannounced and apparently taking possession of large tracts of land, was another matter. He sent out patrols, one of which destroyed a group of Potgieter's people, possibly mistaking them for Griqua. On Potgieter's return another force attacked his laager at Vegkop and drove off all his oxen. In this open or lightly wooded terrain the Whites had considerable advantages in fighting the African. Their horses gave them mobility; their guns in the hands of mounted men out-ranged the assegai and stabbing spear, deadly though these often were when used at close quarters by disciplined and desperate tribesmen. Though often it was the train of wagons and households and the implicit announcement of occupation, settlement and dispossession that provoked attack, the impediments with which the trekkers travelled were turned to account too. They developed their laager system of defence: when danger threatened a party of trekkers, the wagons were ranged and bound in a compact circle enclosing households and if possible animals. From the confines of this mobile fort men as desperate as their attackers defended their beleaguered families, women and older children loading the guns and often firing them too. Not only were tactics evolved in this relentless warfare, but an attitude of mind was cast – a tendency when opposition was expected to draw together in a mental laager – which was to live on long after it had become an anachronism.

After the serious loss of his draught animals and strengthened by a new party from the Cape led by Piet Uys, Potgieter retaliated and attacked the Ndebele centre at Mosega, killing 400 people and capturing 7,000 cattle. Ten months later he attacked and defeated Mzilikazi's main force, after which Mzilikazi and his followers retreated over the Limpopo to settle in the old kingdom of Monomotapa already shattered by the passage of Zwangendaba. Here they seemed well out of range of White and Black enemies for a little while. The Voortrekkers, and particularly Potgieter's people, thereafter laid claim by right of conquest to a great part of the High Veld which they regarded as having been Mzilikazi's domain.

Potgieter was now joined by a new party from Graaff-Reinet led by Gerrit Maritz, a man of some education and legal experience, but ambitious and wilful. Together at Thaba Nchu they set up their first primitive republic. The people – *Het Volk* – elected Maritz landdrost and, later, President of the Volksraad.

Piet Retief of the Winterberg (and author of the Manifesto) with 400 followers swelled the number now scattered along the Vet River. The ablest of the Voortrekker leaders, Retief was elected Commandant-General and Governor of the new republic. The Articles of Winburg were drawn up to regulate the religious and community life of the people. Retief formulated his native policy which forbade the shedding of innocent blood and the taking of San children as apprentices without their parents' permission. He made oral treaties with neighbouring chiefs, which probably included permission for Whites to occupy land, probably in return for some recompense.

When other parties from Uitenhage and Beaufort West came up the strength of the fledgling republic was between 4,000 and 5,000 fighting men. But neither Potgieter nor Uys had been given any official position under the new constitution and soon jealousies and quarrelling divided the leaders, all with different aims in view, and Potgieter set up another centre at Potchefstroom, across the Vaal.

A large number of emigrants moved east towards the Drakensberg. Retief with a small party went ahead down into Natal, where he found the Voortrekkers would be welcomed by the British and Coloured ivory hunters and traders who had been based on Port Natal (later Durban) since 1824. He then turned north into Zululand to treat with Dingane. Dingane seemed prepared to grant him land, possibly the whole of Natal, if he would recapture for him cattle stolen by Sekonyela. Retief by a trick took not only Sekonyela's cattle, but his guns and horses as well. He found his followers and Maritz's, who were under instructions to await his return on the High Veld, already impatiently streaming down the valleys and fanning over the lush promised land of Natal.

Dingane had tried to maintain generally friendly relations with the Whites, mainly traders and missionaries, in the area. From them he sought to acquire guns and horses, for, like Mzilikazi, he was becoming filled with anxiety by these new White interlopers whose hunger for land and cattle and whose guns and military success were alarming. He knew of the White advances on the Eastern Frontier, had heard of their routing of Mzilikazi and tricking of Sekonyela. He was informed that in numbers they were now occupying territory before ever it had been granted, and he was confused by rival claims to land coming from local Whites.

Retief, although warned of danger, rode with a party of about seventy White companions and thirty Coloured servants back to Dingane, handed over the cattle but held on to Sekonyela's guns and horses in the face of Dingane's demands. Dingane made the

115

grant of Port Natal and all the land between the Tugela and the Umzimvubu Rivers. Then, in a desperate bid to preserve land and independence, he seized his chance to massacre the whole group of guests still within his kraal, seizing their arms and mounts. His *impi*, regiments, then fell on Voortrekker encampments scattered over the land and before reinforcements from the High Veld could arrive, some 350 of the 3,500 Natalians were killed and the British swept out of Port Natal.

Retribution was appalling. On the 16 December 1837, from their laager on the banks of what thereafter was named the Blood River, a commando of 500 Voortrekkers under Andries Pretorius, a later-comer from the Colony and an experienced leader, slaughtered 3,000 Zulu at a cost of three white men wounded. Before the battle the devout Voortrekkers took a vow if given victory to hold an annual service of thanksgiving. Dingaan's Day (more appropriately renamed the Day of the Covenant) became charged with vibrant religious and national emotions, with strong racial overtones.

Shortly after this victory a White mounted detachment broke out of a Zulu ambush, killing a thousand Zulu fighting men with the loss of five Voortrekkers. To restore his men's morale, Dingane made an attack on the Swazi. This was unsuccessful and his half-brother Mpande, with a following of 17,000 defected to the Voortrekkers. Together they inflicted yet another defeat on Dingane who fled to Swaziland, to be in his turn murdered there. The Voortrekkers drove off 36,000 cattle and a thousand Zulu children as apprentices. Mpande became King of the Zulu, but temporarily vassal to the Boers.

By 1840 Pretorius had founded the Voortrekker republic of Natalia with its capital at Pietermaritzburg and a volksraad acting as legislature, executive and court of appeal and empowered to appoint commandant, landdrost and heemraden. The High Veld republics of Winburg and Potchefstroom joined with Natalia in loose federation, all similar in structure and almost innocent of central control, and gained briefly their long-desired outlet to the sea. But the republics were now running very short of funds and could employ few officials and no police. Division and factiousness persisted, with quarrels about such matters as land and apprentice allocations. Citizenship of Natalia was reserved to those of European descent, born at the Cape and Dutch-speaking. Other Whites were accepted on conditions, including a certificate of good conduct. Non-whites had no rights in settled parts except as servants.

Within the republic of Natalia at this time were about 6,000 Whites and 20,000 Africans whose numbers were rapidly increasing, despite stringent attempts to control the influx – mostly persons displaced by the bitter ravages of war and now returning to their homes. Headmen were under pain of death to report newcomers, who were forbidden to build a hut on or near a White man's farm. The Zulu within the borders were evenly shared out as labourers, no more than five native families being supposedly permitted to squat on each White farm, but this was never enforced. Apprentices captured in battle were also shared. Passes had to be carried and service contracts to be entered into within two weeks of leaving the last place of employment. Africans were not allowed to own land, guns or horses. Powers were taken to expel whole clans and a policy of territorial segregation for 'redundant natives' – those not required as labourers on White farms – was adopted. The Fiftieth Ordinance was no more than a memory. In fact, however, there was not the machinery to carry out the regulations or even to keep order.

A commando, in pursuit of cattle stolen possibly by San, but for which the Bhaca on the southern borders of Natal were held responsible, attacked the kraals of Ncaphai, the chief. They killed thirty people, carried off 3,000 cattle and seventeen child-apprentices. Ncaphai's Pondo neighbour and enemy, Chief Faku, felt threatened in turn and appealed to the British Colony for protection against Natalia. The British authorities had been disturbed by the routing of Mzilikazi and shocked by the terrible slaughter of Blood River and the recent 'cattle commando'. They were worried too by the possible scale of the expulsions from Natalia which could greatly exacerbate the continuing racial turbulence there and carry disorder south beyond the Colony's eastern frontier. There was also a growing appreciation of the importance of Port Natal to the defence of the route to India.

Consequently the Boer request for recognition of the independence of the republic of Natalia was refused. After an initial defeat by the republicans, the British reoccupied Port Natal in 1843 and annexed the whole territory. The Natalians were consulted on the form of government to be established, but a colour-bar, further encroachment on native lands and slavery (to which the apprenticeship system approximated) were ruled out. Many Natalians now realized that there would be no independence nor 'proper' race relations and that there was little prospect of security, land and labour in the desired degrees. They began to drift back to the High Veld, some to Potchefstroom, others to Winburg and later to Lydenburg; some formed the little republic of Utrecht on land ceded by Mpande. Within two years the republic of Natalia had withered away.

Sir Peregrine Maitland, the new colonial governor, now administered a much reduced Natal as a district of the Cape. He recognized Faku, the Pondo Chief, as ruler of the territory south of Natal from the Umzimkulu to the Umtata River and between the mountains and the sea. The Tugela and the Buffalo Rivers divided Natal from Zululand to the north and Mpande ceased to be a vassal. The British were now responsible for more than 100,000 Africans in the new district and migrants from Zululand constantly swelled the number. Over half the Black population were squatters on White lands, though many were drafted into reserves demarcated for them. The land shortage was not ameliorated, for the Blacks everywhere were intolerably crowded, while on the alienated lands the speculators had moved in and extensive areas in Natal and on the High Veld were available no more to White or Black.

While the Voortrekkers had been swallowing huge tracts to the north and east of the Colony, trying to establish their republics and warring for land with the tribes, conditions on the Eastern Frontier which they had left behind them were deteriorating. With a change of Colonial Office policy and the growth of the view that annexation was unfair to the Black inhabitants and, even more, was expensive for the Exchequer, Stockenström had been appointed Lieutenant-Governor in 1836 with a brief to 'ensure the maintenance of peace, good order and strict justice on the frontier'.[23] He had abandoned Queen Adelaide Land and made over the Ceded Territory to the chiefs as a loan in perpetuity, acknowledging the 'right to the territory of its then actual possessors'.[24] By treaties with the chiefs between the Keiskamma and the Kei he managed to keep the peace but when he retired his treaty system broke down. Whites were eager as ever for more territory. The murders, inevitable in areas so isolated and inadequately policed, of Khoikhoi herdsmen and, occasionally, of Whites and the constant cattle losses in a country of wild beasts were all indiscriminately blamed on the tribesmen. Changes in treaties enabled colonists to go more freely and further into tribal country in search of lost cattle. New alliances were made with chiefs beyond the Kei: Sarili of the Gcaleka, the senior chief of the Xhosa, and Faku of the Pondo on the western borders of Natal.

The drain-off of the Trek had not abated competition among the Whites for land. As more tribal land was alienated, the more uncontrollable became the pressures in what remained. Beyond the Xhosa the Pondo, and behind the Pondo, Whites from the north-east now as well as the west closed in on the peoples trapped between the Berg and the sea. Tribal leaders sparred and disagreed over policies in their frustration and mistrust of government intentions, and regarded with suspicion the chain of forts erected in the Ceded Territory. Treaties were by all parties more disregarded than honoured. In the confusion there were always Whites fishing to their own advantage, fomenting dissension among the tribes and trading guns and ammunition.

The flash point in 1846, the War of the Axe (1846-7), as so often happens, was a matter remote from the real explosive issues of land. An old Xhosa thief, charged with stealing an axe and on the way to Grahamstown for trial, was forcibly rescued by his kinsmen. When Sandile, Ngqika's successor, refused to return him a disciplinary force was marched into Kafirland against the Ngqika; a long, costly war followed and ended with the pacification of the country to the west of the Kei.

At this point Sir Harry Smith took over as governor, and with

23. *Cambridge History of the British Empire*, Vol. VIII, p. 314.
24. ibid., p. 315.

him came another switch in official policy. Smith was flamboyant, impulsive and impetuously decisive. He had campaigned on the frontier with D'Urban in the mid-1830s, before a period of service in India, and was familiar of old with the country's problems. He was convinced that the only way to establish peace on the troubled borders was to take full responsibility for government. He annexed the old Ceded Territory, between the Fish and Keiskamma Rivers, and made it the new district of Victoria East, where he made a further settlement of Mfengu. Queen Adelaide Province, annexed again and renamed British Kaffraria, was to be administered as a Crown colony, using the chiefs as agents, advised by White magistrates. Most of the lands were reserved for the tribes, but amongst them some White villages and soldier settlements were set up.

It took more than a vigorous policy to reconcile the people to this fresh dispossession. The chiefs had lost much of their authority and discontent was fanned by new interference with old custom, particularly bans on the practice of witch-hunting and on the lobola system, 'the sin of buying wives', the important social function of which the Whites totally failed to understand. A burning drought and a new prophet were adding to the restlessness. The Ngqika, in the north of British Kaffraria, were especially fretful, reacting to trekker pressures further north on the lands of Moshweshwe's Sotho with whom they were in sympathy.

The Eighth Xhosa War, which dragged on between 1850 and 1853, broke out when Smith deposed Sandile, for insubordination. The tribe refused to accept the authority of either European magistrate or African nominee, rebelled when at Christmas 1850 troops went into the reserve to arrest Sandile and for a time had the better of the Whites. The Ngqika were supported by the Thembu and, what greatly disconcerted the authorities, by many of the Kafir police force and some of the Coloured Mounted Rifles. These were reinforced by landless Khoikhoi, usually regarded as allies of the Whites but who were angry and resentful because at the end of the previous war they had not received as generous a share of the spoils as the burghers whom they had supported. Worse, many of the disillusioned burghers refused to come out on commando. Sarili's Gcaleka on the coast beyond the

Kei were thought to be giving assistance to the Ngqika and the Pondo were restive under increasing constriction. Reinforcements at last enabled Smith to subdue the Ngqika who sought refuge in the wooded ravines, while the Pondo, in fortuitous alliance with him, fell on the Gcaleka from behind.

The British Government baulked at the money and men necessary to make Smith's policy of total responsibility effective and replaced him in 1852. His successor, the Hon. George Cathcart, raised a White mounted police force, brought the burghers out again on commando by promising a large share of spoil, shattered the tribes and took 10,000 of Sarili's cattle. Sandile was pardoned and recognized as paramount chief, and the Xhosa were driven over the Kei, their lands in the Amatola mountains and the Kat River area made over to Whites. Only Mfengu and some Thembu now remained in the Colony.

While the Colonial authority was occupied with the turbulence of the Eastern Frontier and in the newly acquired Natal, conditions of total anarchy were developing north of the Cape in the heartland of southern Africa.

During the middle 1840s the great grasslands beyond the Orange River were filled with unstable warring elements. Immediately over the river, in the Griqua republics of Waterboer and Adam Kok, Voortrekkers competed for farms with pre-Trek Boers, farmers who had wandered north in search of grazing rather than driven by political discontents and who still regarded themselves as British subjects and retained connections and loyalties in the Colony. Midway between Orange and Vaal lay the Winburg republic of the Voortrekkers and beyond it, north of the Vaal, Potgieter's republic of Potchefstroom. The two abutted on Pretorius's short-lived Natalia beyond the blue Drakensberg, whose northern folds contained Potgieter's new republic of Ohrigstad, soon to shift to Lydenburg. Scattered bands of San hunters survived in isolated spots. All along the western borders were Tswana tribes still comparatively undisturbed in their unattractive droughtlands. South-east, between Winburg and Natalia, in the almost impregnable mountain core of Lesotho, Moshweshwe was gathering in his Sotho people, with rival chiefs building up their strength around him. Between Winburg and the

Griqua, the Tswana and the Sotho, lay Transorangia, a vast uncontrolled no-man's-land of unruly adventurers and land seekers and a cockpit for all the factious elements.

To the administration in the Cape, Moshweshwe, struggling to stabilize a new community and economy, seemed at this moment to be the main intransigent. He claimed a belt of land running north to the Vaal and a strip of cornland west of the Caledon River where his people lived mixed with rival clans and scattered Boers. In the upper and middle Caledon were the followers of other chiefs antagonistic to Moshweshwe who looked on them as his vassals. Furthermore, the Boers coveted the Caledon cornlands and even aspired to Moshweshwe's mountain pastures, free as they were from horse-sickness.

Sir George Napier, the governor, in 1843 had made treaties with Kok and Moshweshwe, similar to one made by D'Urban with Waterboer nine years earlier, under which, in return for subsidies, both were to keep order in their territories and enforce the Cape Punishment Act of 1836. (This act had been an ineffective attempt to retain authority over the Voortrekkers by making British subjects liable to punishment on their return to the Colony for crimes committed anywhere south of latitude 25°S). The Whites, of course, defied the chiefs' authority and disturbances continued.

Britain hitherto had disclaimed all responsibility for 'emigrant farmers' north of the Orange. Maitland, who had succeeded Napier, attempted even more urgently to end the seething unrest which was seriously disturbing to the farmers in the northern Colony. In 1845 he had introduced an official British presence across the river; he proposed the chiefs divide their domains into an inalienable section under their own rule and an area where the eager Whites could lease quit-rent farms, and he installed a British resident to control the latter.

At this juncture Sir Harry Smith, having established Victoria East and British Kaffraria under the Crown, turned his exuberant attention to the north. He extended the Colony's frontier, hazily defined until now, along the whole length of the Orange River. Then, in 1848, believing many Boers in Transorangia, mostly pre-Trek Boers, would welcome British authority, he proclaimed the Orange River Sovereignty from the Orange to the Vaal. Pretorius fought against this and was defeated in a skirmish at Boomplaats, midway between the Orange River and the Modder.

It is conceivable that if the British had now established a resolute government north as far as the Limpopo the whole country might have been unified and open to the still mildly liberal laws and influences of the Cape and to the trends of the contemporary world. But the British Government, torn between missionary and philanthropist pressures on behalf of the Black peoples and the relentless parsimony of the taxpayers appalled at the huge cost of 'native wars' (and fiercely fending off a proposed rise in income tax from 7d. to 1s.), was resolute only in its economies. Again it retreated and Voortrekker philosophies were able to take hold in the north and eventually seep back to the Cape where fragile Black rights were now about to be constitutionally implanted. For many years past public petitions for representative government had been refused on grounds of constitutional and other difficulties, among them deep cultural differences in the small and scattered White population. When, in 1848, however, the British Government attempted to land a shipload of convict labourers in the Colony, the Dutch and English sections united in a fury of opposition, compelling British capitulation and bringing the two language sections together in common interests. In 1853 the representative Constitution was granted. The colonists pressed for and got low franchise qualifications, occupation of premises worth £25 p.a., or an income of £50 p.a.; the British Government, insisting on a non-racial franchise, opened it to all adult male British subjects: 'All HM subjects without distinction of class or colour, should be united by one bond of loyalty and a common interest.'[25]

The responsibility lay with the British now for preserving the peace with the Sotho chiefs on the borders of the Sovereignty on which its stability, and that of the Cape, depended. The skirmishing continued over the fertile Caledon lands from which Moshweshwe naturally refused to move, despite the official recognition by Major Warden, the incompetent British Resident at Bloemfontein, of the interests of the Whites and the rival chiefs and his

25. Walker, *A History of Southern Africa*, p. 243.

total disregard of the claims of Moshweshwe. Warden attempted with inadequate forces (the commandos gave him no support) to shift the Sotho and was routed by them in 1851 at Viervoet. The Sotho moved into lands they claimed across the Caledon. Warden tried to raise another commando against 'the common enemy of the White man' to 'decide the mastery between the White and Coloured race'.[26]

After Natal had come under British rule in 1845, Potgieter left Potchefstroom and with his followers pushed north-east to found the republic of Ohrigstad on the west slopes of the Drakensberg and beyond the range of the Punishment Act, from where he still hoped to be able to open up a way to the sea. There he was joined by the die-hards of Natal and those of the Trek unremittingly moving from British influence. From there he claimed jurisdiction over the whole Transvaal, but his dictatorial attitude was resented by many, his claim to supremacy challenged and the community split. Once more Potgieter packed his wagons, yoked up his oxen and moved off further into the wilderness of the north. In the Zoutpansberg mountains he founded the dorp of Schoemansdal, to become a centre for the lawless and the tough, those who could hold their own against other inhabitants and who could live on hunting and the trading of ivory beyond the Berg far into the malarial Low Veld. Those who remained behind, defeated by mosquito and tsetse fly, abandoned Ohrigstad in 1850 for the higher, healthier Lydenburg.

The more conciliatory leader, Pretorius, with his Natal experience to guide him, had remained at the head of the community in Potchefstroom and strove to bring the dissident parts of the Transvaal into a unity. The states were weak, divided by rivalry between Potchefstroom and Lydenburg and the jealousies of the leaders, and their populations of 15,000 White people were widely scattered. Authority was divided among three commandant-generals and the only policing was performed by the commandos. The Transvaalers were at odds with the African communities to the west and north and were trying to gain control of the 'Missionary Road' lying between the Voortrekker settled areas and the Tswana tribes and along which the mission-

26. J. S. Galbraith, *The Reluctant Empire*, p. 253.

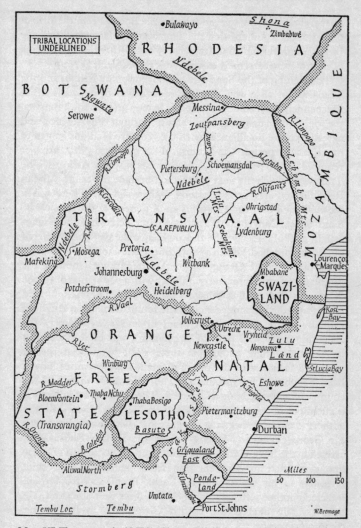

Map VI Transorangia (OFS), Transvaal (SA Republic) and Natal

aries travelled trying to evade the hostile Boers. From the British Government's point of view the Transvaal was far away, its people restless, quarrelsome and implacably anti-British; the problems of control were extremely expensive or insoluble. It gave up.

The signing of the Sand River Convention by Britain and the Transvaal in 1852 was the first recognition to be made of an independent Boer state. By its terms Britain granted the Transvaal the right to manage its own affairs without interference and agreed to make no alliances with the 'coloured nations' north of the Vaal, to permit the Transvaal to purchase what arms it required and to prohibit all trade in arms with the Africans. The Transvaal, which the next year would become the South African Republic, on its part undertook to ban slavery. There was a reconciliation between Pretorius and Potgieter at the time of the Sand River Convention; but soon after achieving their long-sought goal of a recognized independence the two battle-scarred old rivals both died, within a short time of one another.

By this time the Orange River Sovereignty was showing the semblance of an organized community with a population of 10,000 Whites in four or five villages, each with a Dutch Reformed Church predikant and a school. The foundations of an Anglican cathedral were laid in Bloemfontein and a newspaper, the Bloemfontein *Friend* (still in circulation), was established. But land, astonishingly enough in these great wide open spaces, remained far short of the demand for it, large expanses having been bought up by speculators who held more than half the country outside the Non-white areas. The Africans still disputed occupation of what fertile land remained to them and the authorities still sided against Moshweshwe with his weaker rivals. Sir George Cathcart, having settled the Eighth Xhosa War, arrived in the Sovereignty and rounded up a 10,000 head of cattle fine demanded in compensation from the chief. The chief retreated to his stronghold at Thaba Bosiu and from there inflicted another setback upon a British force sent after him. He then astutely offered the British Government a face-saving compromise peace.

Britain, by now again involved in European affairs and war in the Crimea, decided to reduce her South African commitments to the protection of her loyal subjects and the peoples on the Colony's frontier. So, in 1854, Sir George Clerk signed the Bloemfontein Convention granting the Sovereignty independence on similar terms (except the embargo on arms for the Africans) to the Transvaal's. One clause stipulated that no future alliances prejudicial to the Orange Free State would be made by Britain with the Blacks – a proviso which destroyed the treaties with the Griqua. No boundaries were delineated despite Moshweshwe's anxiety and with the removal of British restraints further conflict between the Whites and the Sotho was ensured and would once again have repercussions on the Colony.

The Great Trek had ended, but the Boer dream of total independence from Britain, despite the appearance of things, had still about a hundred years to run, when a new trek would begin into international isolation for ideals similar to those of 1836.

4. BLACK WARS AND PROTECTION

With the signing of the Bloemfontein Convention in 1854 there were five independent Voortrekker republics in South Africa: Zoutpansberg, Lydenburg, the South African Republic (previously Potchefstroom) all sharing a common volksraad, and the Orange Free State and Utrecht. The quarrels, divisions, assertiveness and long inability of the leaders to cooperate reflected the Boer character as it had developed over some 200 years of independence and stubborn individuality. This proliferation of units prevented them from achieving political, defensive or economic effectiveness and gave the Afrikaner a lasting reputation for dissension.

The rivalry between Potchefstroom and Lydenburg and the jealousies of the leaders were aggravated by religious differences. Because the Cape Dutch Reformed Church had from the beginning opposed the Trek and the scattering of Church members that it entailed, no predikants went with the Voortrekkers. They could only get ministers later if they submitted, as Lydenburg was prepared to do, to the authority of the Cape DRC synod. But disputes among the Voortrekkers themselves led to the development within a short time of seven autonomous churches closely similar in doctrine. The *Nederduits Gereformeerde Kerk* (the NGK) was the first Church in South Africa and the largest and most widespread. It eventually consisted of four federated autonomous churches, one in each province, and one in South West Africa. This group is what is generally meant by the Dutch Reformed Church (DRC or NGK). The *Nederduits Hervormde Kerk* was set up in the Transvaal in 1853 to care for those Voortrekkers who, suspicious of the 'liberal influences' for a time active in the Cape NGK, leading to the trial of three theologians for heresy, turned instead direct to Holland for affiliation. This was the official Church of the first Constitution of the Transvaal Republic. The *Gereformeerde Kerk van Suid Afrika,* the 'Dopper Kerk' was established in the Transvaal in 1859, a breakaway from the parent NGK in the Cape, in order to sever the link of Church with State. It was a return to pure Calvinist doctrine, deeply fundamentalist, very puritanical, narrow and rigid in outlook. Its members – one of the staunchest was Paul Kruger – objected to the singing of hymns, as distinct from biblical psalms, at services and abjured many of the ordinary social pleasures. Branches spread to other provinces, but the Church remained small in membership. It was to have, however, disproportionately great importance and permeating influence a hundred years later, for it was to control the University and Theological College of Potchefstroom; many of its members came to hold key positions in education, the ministry and in other spheres.

The Church became more than ever a dominant influence and the centre of the life of the volk, in a way not unlike the central position of the Catholic Church in medieval rural life and its power and prestige depended on the maintenance of pure and exclusive Afrikanerdom. The church spire soared above the dwellings of every sizeable dorp. In the field around the church would gather the covered ox-wagons of the distant farmers who might travel two or three times a year for weeks together to attend the major festivals which were great social as well as religious occasions. The predikant was probably the most educated and cosmopolitan man in the community. He conscientiously went his parish rounds, was informed about all that went on and acquired great influence.

The part of the Church in the life of South Africa cannot be over-stressed. It was to give definition to the character rough-hewn by circumstance, to nurture the self-respect of a dependent, divided, defensive people and guide it into united nationalistic expression. Above all, it provided fundamentalist and scriptural arguments which could later be turned to justify racial discrimination.

Back in the very early days of settlement the NGK had exercised no form of colour bar. Baptized slaves and other Blacks were accepted as church members, the gospel was preached and sacraments administered to White and Black together, though soon it became customary to reserve a part of the seating for Blacks. Initially White and Black girls and boys were taught together, and often continued to be in mission schools until the late nineteenth century, but in 1685 the Company's visiting commissioner, van Rheede, had decreed that a separate school be erected for slave children. By the end of the eighteenth century the 'Non-whites were ministered to as a separate group with a distinctive religious life and needs'.[27] The first meeting of the Presbytery in Cape Town decided that the teaching of the Bible and the spirit of Christianity allowed Coloured converts to take communion along with Christian-born; in some congregations there was no distinction, in others Coloureds came after Whites.

The Synod of 1829 had ruled there should be no colour discrimination at communion; but the need to preach in the vernacular led to separate services being held on the Eastern Frontier. When the DRC Missionary Societies were founded in 1834 to Christianize the Africans (who were coming increasingly into contact with the Whites as the Eastern Frontier advanced) and to group them in parishes, the constitution laid down that members of Native congregations would be admitted to White congregations only where no Black congregations existed. In some remote areas Whites joined Coloured congregations, but before long many of them were demanding separation. In 1855, the Stockenström Church Council refused the request of forty-five White members of the congregation to partake of Holy Communion on a separate Sunday, as this would conflict with the articles of faith

27. DRC *Statements on Race Relations*, No. I (November 1960), pp. 3, 4.

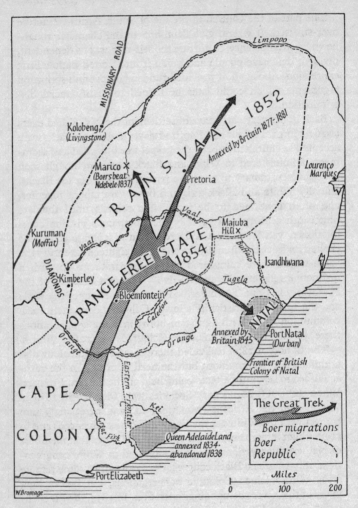

Map VIIa White Migrations

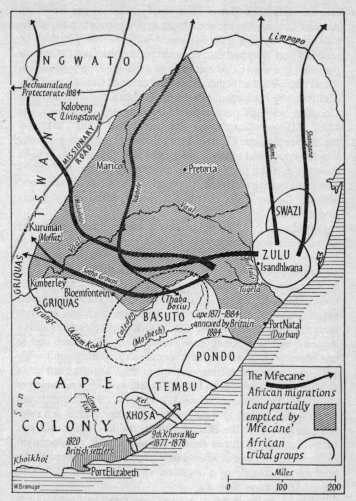

Map VIIb Black Migrations

and the scriptures. But in 1859, on a motion by the Reverend Andrew Murray, Senior, the Albany Synod pronounced it 'desirable and scriptural that our members from the Heathen be received and absorbed into our existing congregations wherever possible; but where this measure, as a result of the weakness of some, impeded the furtherance of the cause of Christ among the Heathen, the congregation from the Heathen . . . shall enjoy its Christian privileges in a separate building or institution'. The DRC Mission Church was not established until 1881 as a separate indigenous Church. From that time missionary activity was to spread, and separate indigenous DR churches were to be founded in many parts of Africa as far away as Malawi (Nyasaland) and northern Nigeria, to proselytize and run hospitals and schools. In the White churches, however, racial exclusiveness intensified.

Outside South Africa the persistent medieval notions that the sons of Ham were cursed by being black and degenerate had been preserved by the need for European imperial societies to justify slavery and plantation economics. Then the philosophers of the Enlightenment, attempting to reconcile the new science and the old theology, debated on whether the races of mankind were individually created or evolved from a common stock and amongst their findings were theories that the dark peoples were either separate and sub-human creations or were degenerate due to environment. The former conclusion was smoothly compatible with current South African versions of the Calvinist doctrine of election and acceptable to the Afrikaner, who in generations of close and conflicting relationships, had even evolved different terms: *mense* (people) for themselves and other Whites and *skepsels* (creatures) for the Blacks. During the late nineteenth and early twentieth centuries much pseudo-scientific corroboration of these theories was produced in Europe and the United States and was to contribute a dogmatic ground-base for racism in South Africa and elsewhere.

In the 1850s South Africa was still a confusion not only of sects and states, but of peoples, policies and aims. In the fluid groupings of the five Voortrekker republics, the more far-sighted leaders campaigned for unity and pursued the lure of an eastward outlet to

the sea, without which there could be no true independence of
Britain. This ambition and the Afrikaners' constantly unsatisfied
appetite for land kept them always in conflict with the African
communities surrounding them. The Cape Colony, Natal and
British Kaffraria were all under British colonial rule. Between
British Kaffraria and Natal, Xhosa, Pondo and Thembu, though
under a fluctuating British influence, still lived on their overcrowded lands and retained their tribal structure, virtually free of
Whites, save missionaries and traders. In the mountainous heart
of the country, the Sotho defended their independence against
all-comers. North of Natal the Zulu had regained a nominal independence and beyond them the Swazi were as yet little affected
by the Whites. From Swaziland, in a great arc through the Zoutpansberg, and west and south were the many tribes recovering
from the storms of the mfecane. On the Orange River the Korana
and Griqua states fast succumbed to White penetration. All were
continually playing off each against the other, White against
White, Black against Black, White against Black, all benefiting as
and where possible from old enmities, old rivalries.

The only stable element in all this was the Cape Colony, but it
was obvious to successive governors that the turmoil and insecurity all around threatened even that, inhibiting real prosperity and
making its defence a constant financial drain on Britain. The
British Government, however, reluctant to meet the expense of
keeping the peace on the immediate colonial borders, boggled, as it
had always done, at the outlay necessary to enforce a *pax Britan-
nica* over the whole seething land, from a large part of which she
had just withdrawn. But against the logic of economics were other
disciplines. There was still, if no longer a liberal conscience, at
least a lingering liberal habit in Britain which fought a more or
less losing battle with political considerations and regard for the
taxpayers and which reacted to suggestions of injustices or ill-
treatment of Africans; and these came in abundantly, if not always
proved to the hilt, from the many missionaries. Then there was a
conviction that British subjects remained British subjects and
under British control however far they wandered, and this had
been accepted by the pre-Trek Boers of the Free State and some of
the less doctrinaire of the Voortrekkers. Above all there was

always the fear that a foreign power might gain a foothold on the east coast, in Natal, and menace the route to India. These divergencies, variously potent, and the different and often conflicting weight they carried with Secretaries of State in London and governors in Cape Town in days when a reply to a letter took at least three months, accounted largely for the vacillations and contradictions in policy during much of the nineteenth century.

The temporary predatory intrusion of the Voortrekkers into Natal had aggravated the general turmoil and the newly acquired British colony presented complex problems. Zulu survivors of the wars were streaming back to their homes there all the time. By 1856 there were about 8,000 Whites – mostly British – and 150,000 Africans.

The shaping of the Native policy of Natal between 1845 and 1875 was largely the work of Theophilus Shepstone who was appointed Diplomatic Agent to the Native Tribes in Natal. He had been brought up among Xhosa on his Wesleyan father's mission station and he was ambitious, strongly paternalistic and convinced of the superiority of the contemporary White way of life. He imported the old separation policy of the Eastern Frontier, setting it into its modern mould. A commission, which included Shepstone and some of the missionaries, established a number of reserves totalling, by the 1860s, 2,250,000 of Natal's 12,500,000 acres, but in addition to the 80,000 Africans initially given homes in these reserves, another 50,000 lived on Crown lands or as squatters on European farms. Shepstone planned to westernize the people by basing industrial and agricultural schools in each reserve and by building a Zulu police force officered by Whites. Apart from the police force his schemes were stillborn for lack of funds. Few magistrates were available, so he evolved a makeshift tribal system and where natural chiefs were lacking himself appointed chiefs to be responsible for law and order under the governor, declared to be the Supreme Chief. In these conditions the Roman-Dutch law of the Whites could not be applied, so he recognized Native law and custom, in so far as these were not repugnant to the dictates of humanity, but left it adaptable to changing conditions. Not until 1878, after he had left the scene, were these codified to be administered as the Natal Code of Native Law by the chiefs assisted by White magistrates, with the right of appeal to the Supreme Chief – the Governor-in-Council. Certain individuals could apply to the governor for exemption from the Code – but not as a right.

When, in 1856, Natal was created a Crown Colony with a legislative council of four official and twelve elected members, the White population was largely British and local government was based on the British system. In theory the franchise, as in the Cape Colony, was colour blind, but the great number of qualifications effectively debarred Africans. A law of 1865 allowed a Natal African to apply for registration if he had been resident in the Colony for twelve years, owned property valued at £50 or paid £10 p.a. in rent, had been exempt from the Natal Code for seven years and could produce a certificate signed by three White electors and endorsed by a magistrate or Justice of the Peace. He was then entitled to petition the Governor-in-Council to grant the privilege of franchise which, after all that, was not infrequently refused. Not more than a dozen or so ever cleared these hurdles to emancipation.

The whole basis of native administration in British Natal thus fundamentally differed from the Cape. Centred on the governor, it was highly paternalistic – even dictatorial; the complex qualifications and frequent opposition of the governor virtually disfranchised the Africans and the use of the Natal Code introduced different laws for Black and White. This system profoundly influenced later legislation and administration, while among the British of Natal, race discrimination soon became as rigid and as harsh as in the Voortrekker republics.

Meanwhile, the other territories were making progress, sometimes painfully slow, towards political equilibrium.

The Orange Free State, after the Bloemfontein Convention, had achieved with its independence a seeming liberty to solve its border problems as best it could. It adopted a constitution, the most liberal and balanced of all the republican constitutions, based in some degree on that of the United States and on the Code Napoleon. The volksraad was elected on a White male suffrage; an elected president with three raad members and two officials formed the executive. The first President, J. P. Hoffman, was chosen because he was on good terms with Moshweshwe, relations with whom were acknowledged to be of central importance to the stability of the new state. But there was little experience of government and, as much British capital had gone with the British administration, financial problems became acute.

Marthinus Pretorius stepped into his father's shoes as the dominant figure in the new South African Republic, but the strife within the Dutch Reformed Church exaggerated political differences and progress was slow. By 1858 a constitution was drafted, the young Paul Kruger being a member of the drafting committee. There was a great deal of conflict and almost war outright before, in 1860, the amended version was accepted by all the Voortrekkers. This, the *Rustenburg Grondwet*, provided for a volksraad of twenty-four elected members and an elected president. The Roman-Dutch Law of the Cape Colony at the time of the British Occupation was accepted as the basis of common law. All offices and membership of the raad were restricted to members of the Dutch Reformed Church. Citizenship was limited to Whites and the Grondwet, true to the principles of the Great Trek, contained the declaration that 'the people desire to permit no equality between coloured people and the white inhabitants either in Church or State'.[28]

Following the Natalia example, the Transvaalers disclaimed authority over border chiefs with whom treaties were made, but in fact they were regarded, as Mpande had been, as vassals. Potgieter had claimed all the lands which Mzilikazi had ruled, and reserves under the command of chiefs or headman were provided for the communities living in the country or returning home to it. But the lands were held only on condition of 'good behaviour' and there was no security of tenure. The Africans were forbidden to own guns, horses or wagons or to make inter-tribal alliances. A labour tax, 'labour at suitable wages when called upon',[29] was imposed, though some favoured chiefs were granted 'burgher rights' to pay taxes in cash and military service. Africans not under any chief had to enter into labour contracts thus coming under pass laws, and no liquor was permitted without the masters' consent.

28. *Cambridge History of the British Empire*, Vol. VIII, p. 389.
29. Walker, *A History of Southern Africa*, p. 277.

By contrast, during this period the Cape Colony, where Sir George Grey became Governor and High Commissioner from 1854 to 1862, made great material progress. The enlarging internal market of the republics buoyed the Cape economy. Wool improved in quality and the export of wool, copper and guano from Namaqualand rose. Internal communications and harbour facilities were extended, the first railway was instituted, the sea-mail to Europe reduced to forty-two days. There were educational advances. The Cape Town public library (to which Grey gave his own valuable collection of books) was built.

Grey was intensely aware that the stability of the Colony hinged on relations between the White states and the still powerful African peoples on their borders and in his view would only be assured by a uniform native policy throughout the whole country. He had little use for the current policy of separation and the consequent incessant conflicts over land. On the Eastern Frontier he tried to open tribal territory to what he believed would be a civilizing influence, by settling Whites among Africans. He encouraged education and the establishment of such institutions as Lovedale where trades and improved agricultural methods were taught. He put the Blacks to work on road building and other public works in the quaint assumption of the time that this would instil an appreciation of the dignity of labour; he believed they would benefit from the example of industrious Whites settled among them. He failed to realize the impossibility of any progress while the disparity in culture, political power, economic opportunity and attitude to landowning existed.

The tribes of the Eastern Frontier, beaten at the end of the war in 1850 but not broken, continued in misery and poverty and hopelessly overcrowded; many people were entirely without lands of their own and dependent on their kinsmen. The disputes were over cattle but the basic contention was about land. The undermining of the authority of the chiefs, the assault on the stabilizing force of custom, the threat to the whole tribal structure during the last fifty years or so and the relentless amputations of land through wars and treaties – all the frustrations of the situation – led to a weirdly tragic act of self-destruction, not uncommon in its nature in Africa but appalling in its consequences.

One morning in March 1856 (according to some of the many versions of the story)[30] a sixteen-year-old Xhosa girl, Nongqause, who lived on the banks of the Kei, went as usual down to a tributary stream to fetch water. There, she reported to her uncle, himself a diviner, she had seen strange people and cattle. He went to investigate and saw a number of Black people (among them his dead brother) who said they were Russians (the Crimean War had just come to a close), the eternal enemies of the White men; they had come from the battlefields beyond the sea where they had been fighting the English with whom they would wage perpetual war and had come to help the Kafirs. They ordered that all cattle were to be killed, all grain destroyed and that no one was to cultivate the land. Then on a certain day great herds of fat cattle would fill the kraals, grainpits would overflow, wagons, clothes, guns and ammunition would be abundant. The skies were to fall, crushing the Whites and all Blacks who had not obeyed. Two suns would appear and come into titanic collision, after which all who wore trousers (this included the once vassal Mfengu, now protégés of the Whites) would be swept away in a whirlwind.[31]

Chief Sarili and Nongqause's uncle believed and, despite bitter disagreement among the people and the desperate efforts of missionaries and other Whites to prevent disaster, they set the example which rapidly spread through the unhappy Xhosa and to many of the Ciskei clans in British Kaffraria. Only the hard-headed Mfengu were not swayed, kept their cattle and bought what others they could.

D-day in August came and went and the people emerged from their wish-fulfilment dream of the millennium into a very harsh reality. It was estimated that at least between 150,000 and 200,000 cattle perished. In the famine that followed perhaps some 20,000 people died of the 100,000 or more between the Fish and the Kei. The tribes were not eradicated; the members left their lands and scattered; many went to inland districts and 30,000 sought work

30. Roux, op. cit., p. 36; *The Oxford History of South Africa*, Vol. I, p. 256; C. Mutwa, *My People*, p. 244–6.

31. Allegations were later made by both Blacks and Whites that the vision was a plot by the other side to provoke war, but these seem to have been groundless.

from farmers in the Colony. When in the following years some filtered home again with their newly earned cattle they found their old lands occupied by European immigrants. They were more cramped than before, the chiefs' authority more eroded. The restless Sarili was banished across the Kei where his land-starved people were penned between the colonial borders and the Pondo. By 1860, 6,000 Whites were settled in British Kaffraria and the land problem of the Africans was more acute than ever. The Xhosa ability to resist White encroachment had been irreparably undermined.

The spotlight now turned to other arenas – the quarrelling and warfare to the north. Marthinus Pretorius was trying to form one single republic, claiming, as the son of his father, to be the rightful head of the Free State. Many Free Staters, chary of the Transvaal extremists, favoured stronger ties with the Colony, while Grey, fearing that a united Afrikaner Republic in the heart of the land would make war on Moshweshwe's Sotho and upset the equilibrium in the Colony, did what he could to circumvent Pretorius. He urged the resumption of British authority over the whole country, possibly in some form of federation of colonies and republics which would prevent the union of the republics and the evils he believed would follow. But the British Government still would not countenance his measures, believing they would mean 'either enormous expense or the independence of South Africa',[32] and independence, it was argued, would lead to the combination of the Whites against the Blacks.

Grey's worries over the independent republics were justified. The Free Staters, bickering with the Sotho over lands on the Caledon River, in 1858 struck at Moshweshwe's stronghold, Thaba Bosiu. Moshweshwe checked them. He was as apprehensive as Grey at the prospect of an Afrikaner union, but he was a subtle and experienced fighter, and had learned to gain what he could by war, and when defeat threatened he switched to skilful diplomacy. He accepted, in the first Treaty of Aliwal North, a compromise boundary by which he gained some territory. He continued to try to improve his position at the expense of the politically divided Boers who were also being harried

32. *Cambridge History of the British Empire*, Vol. III, p. 407.

on the west by the Korana and the western Transvaal tribes.

By 1865 Free Staters and Sotho were again at war; a war in which not only had the Sotho inferior weapons but the Treaty of Bloemfontein was used to ban arms sales to them, though the British well knew that only in the Sand River Convention had such sales been prohibited. The chief petitioned the British Government for annexation as his one hope of keeping the people and their remaining land intact. To gain time, as the commandos were devastating land and homes, Moshweshwe signed the Treaty of Thaba Bosiu and agreed to surrender the conquered territory, though this would deprive his people of much of the economic basis of their subsistence and break the nation. Already thousands of dispossessed refugees, driven by lack of food, were making counter raids and were pouring into the Cape frontier districts. Wodehouse, Grey's successor, foresaw that the destruction of the Sotho kingdom would send hordes of landless starving people roving into the overcrowded areas in and around the Colonies, fomenting turmoil in them.

The harassed Sotho resumed hostilities in 1867. This time after a series of successes the Free State commandos were held only when they laid siege to Thaba Bosiu. Now that White domination looked inevitable, the aged chief settled firmly for British raj rather than Afrikaner boss. Again and again he appealed for the Great Queen's protection; and in a period when British statesmen baulked at the cost and complications of further military investment in southern Africa, his importuning at long last succeeded. In 1868 Wodehouse annexed his territory.

'I have become old . . . I am glad that my people should have been allowed to rest and lie under the huge fold of the flag of England before I am no more.' To the great White Queen Victoria herself he wrote his staggeringly forthright deed of trust: 'My country is your blanket, and my people the lice in it.'[33]

In the second treaty of Aliwal North in 1869, Wodehouse and President J. H. Brand (for the Free State) settled Lesotho's boundaries and future in negotiations which excluded any representative of the people concerned. Moshweshwe lived to see the

33. Margery Perham, *The Times* (London, 5 July 1934).

nation he had so long and laboriously built up preserved[34] though with most of its best lands lopped off. The next year, as South Africa stood unaware on the edge of the new age, he died.

A small girl, playing one day in 1867 on the banks of the Orange River near Hopetown, picked up a pretty stone that was to begin a revolution in the dusty grasslands where until then Whites and Blacks had followed their herds, disputed water and pastures, raided each other's cattle and made war and peace in the time-honoured fashion made familiar to them by their Bible-reading and their predikants and missionaries. Now, men flocked to the area hoping to pick up a fortune. Two years later, in the dry diggings between the Vaal and the Modder rivers where Kimberley stands today, a stone worth £25,000 was found and work began in the mines which were soon to eclipse all other sources of diamonds in the world.

Suddenly, and late, South Africa was pitchforked into the beginnings of her own industrial revolution and the whole historical direction of southern Africa, and for that matter of all Africa south of the Sahara, was deflected. Diggers, prospectors, fortune-hunters and all who followed in their wake – traders, transport-riders, missionaries, gun-runners, canteen-keepers – flooded the area.

The diamond fields were a magnet not only to Whites from all over South Africa and far beyond. The Africans of the south, unsettled by wars, displaced, overcrowded and poor in the lands that remained to them, also flowed in in thousands especially from Lesotho and the restless eastern frontiers. They came primarily to earn money, but also to see the sights, come by a gun (which they acquired in great numbers) and start on the agonizing road which was to take them in some eighty years from the Iron Age into the nuclear era.

The fevered and debilitating streaming of labour from rural to industrial areas had begun in earnest; upon it South Africa's great fortune was to be largely founded and upon it largely was to rest the responsibility for the sapping of White independence and of Black vitality and of much human dignity of both Black and White. The Africans came in poverty and ignorance of White

34. To gain its independence a hundred years later.

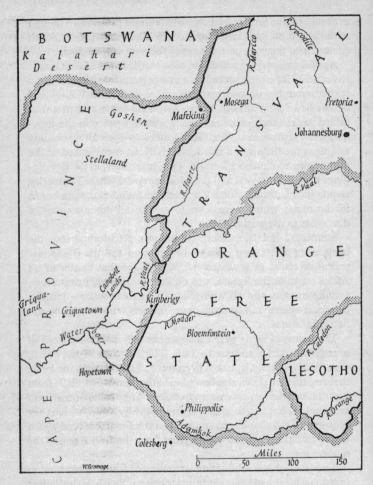

Map VIII The Griqua lands and the Diamond Area

ways, and with lack of technical skills; inevitably they found barriers of colour discrimination, already so depressingly familiar in rural life, raised against them. Double standards were built into urban and industrial spheres with devastating effect. The locations where the Black labourers were forced to crowd, without social or educational amenities and with no hope of betterment, set into the pattern of the future – poverty, starvation, disease, drink, vice and lawlessness.

The worst consequences of this, however, lay far ahead. Kimberley, which began as a turbulent, wild-west free-for-all, was by its very wealth eventually disciplined and reduced to order. By 1871 the Whites alone in the diamond fields numbered more than had taken part in the entire Great Trek. Between 1871 and 1895, some 100,000 Africans with 400,000 dependants found employment in the diggings. In ten years the area produced about £20m. The growth of population, the soaring mining and commercial activity and demand for communications led to a rapid development of railway and harbour facilities and a great rise in the general prosperity of the Cape and the Orange Free State.

The particular shape taken by the economic development of Kimberley (and later the whole development of South Africa) was much influenced by the arrival there in 1872 of a financial genius and political buccaneer.

Cecil John Rhodes, twenty-year-old son of an English country parson and forerunner of the great twentieth-century financial tycoons, was a fortune-hunter of new and remarkable calibre. He had been sent for his health to farm cotton in Natal where he was not particularly successful, and he moved after a year or two to the exciting centre of activity. Within a short time on the diggings he amassed the first £5,000 on which he was to build his great fortune, and in between attending to his interests in Kimberley he pursued his studies at Oxford. Rhodes was a man of astonishing energy, acumen and industry. He sought wealth less for its own sake than for the power it could give. He had a vast vision of imperialism in the years when British imperialism approached its zenith, the daring and ruthless assurance to pursue the vision at whatever cost and the ability to amass the fortune to meet the cost.

For thirty years he was a dominating figure in the economics and politics of southern Africa and gave impetus to movements that are still far from spent.

The nature of the Kimberley diamond deposits was such that there was no place, as there had been on the alluvial deposits, for the individual digger. The elaborate mining necessary demanded complex machinery and capital far beyond his means. The genius of Rhodes contained the imagination and determined ability within the space of ten years to dragoon the other fortune-seeking individualists from many nations into consolidating the seventy-odd companies that had already formed into the single powerful de Beers organization. By the end of the next decade he had acquired the Premier Diamond Mine in the Transvaal and the entire industry was organized with the maximum efficiency and economy; it controlled South Africa's output and the world price of diamonds.

With the discovery there of diamonds, the area around the junction of the Orange and the Vaal suddenly acquired immense importance. This arid region had long been left to the Griqua and to those farmers who had acquired from them land grants and had occupied the water sources. In 1861 Adam Kok had agreed to abandon what land remained to him and to move his people to Nomansland (renamed East Griqualand) south of the Drakensberg between the Colony and Natal. Ownership of the vacated lands in which much of the diamond areas lay was claimed and fiercely disputed by the Orange Free State, the South African Republic and the remaining Griqua chief, Waterboer. A decision became urgent with the flood of diggers and fortune-hunters pouring into the area. The dispute was brought to a head by a clever Coloured lawyer and land-speculator, David Arnot, who saw advantage for himself in British annexation of the territory. The complex case he presented on behalf of the Griqua was accepted in 1871 by the Keate Commission and gave Britain, still half-reluctant to take on more administrative responsibilities, grounds for annexation to protect the rights of Waterboer. This move was not entirely uninfluenced by appreciation of the unwelcome power that possession of the wealth and the growing population of this area would give to the northern republic; and there was the old determination to keep control of the Missionary Road to the African interior.

Against a background of mounting confusion to the north and east, and although the opening of the Suez Canal reduced for the time being its strategic importance, the economic situation of the Cape Colony was steadily improving; the value of the wool export was rising, ostrich farming was becoming profitable in the Eastern Province, and the markets opened by the diamonds of Kimberley and the goldfields of the Eastern Transvaal gave commerce new life.

Throughout the British world the imperial government was strongly encouraging colonial self-reliance in finance and defence and responsibility for adjacent native territories. Its unwillingness in South Africa to be saddled with the administration of the anarchical diamond fields and reluctant to see a Free State–West Griqualand union in economic rivalry with the Cape, turned thoughts once again and urgently to some form of federation for South Africa, perhaps to include the Cape, West Griqualand, the Orange Free State and Lesotho. Responsible government for the Cape was a first step pressed on a reluctant Cape government faced with internal division. The Eastern Province hankered after separation, fearing subjection to the politically dominant West, with a draining of their finances to subsidize western advancement, and convinced that the West lacked understanding of the old ever-present and urgent native problem. However, the Bill for Responsible Government was pushed through the Cape legislature in 1872 with a majority of one by John Molteno who, in a mainly English-speaking Parliament, became the Cape's first Premier, dedicated to the twin causes of Responsibility and elimination of the divisions between East and West. At the same time Eastern anxieties were allayed by provision for equal representation.

The possibility of federation, over which the imperial government in Grey's time had dragged its feet, now became a vital issue, taken up by Lord Carnarvon, the colonial secretary from 1874–8 with an obsessive dedication. His main motive was that of future imperial defence, for he considered the naval base at Simon's Bay to be the most vital British station should the newly opened Suez

Canal ever be blocked, and behind Simon's Bay he wanted a strong united and loyal dominion. Also, though less imperatively, he wished to retain control over White relations with Africans and he may have had vague dreams of a great northward extension of British influence. For once too and briefly, there were no pressing economies to strangle his efforts. The frustrations came from the circumstances within the country, try as he might to turn these to serve his overall purpose. The Cape, destined to be the king-post of the federal edifice, suspected that in a larger connection its own self-government might be compromised and was also very reluct-ant to take over West Griqualand and so fall foul of the Republics. The Keate Award of 1871 had evoked widespread and lasting antagonism in the Republics, exacerbated when a land court, appointed in 1875 to sort out the confusion of land titles, found all the claims made for Waterboer by Arnot were void and much of the evidence on which Keate made his award was unreliable. It was then too late to reverse the decision and £90,000 compensa-tion was paid to the Orange Free State by Britain but this in no way reduced Afrikaner bitterness. Yet, oddly enough, for all the high feeling, no one – not the British, nor the Cape, nor the Or-ange Free State – in fact wanted to take on the burden of admin-istering so chaotic an area as this disputed treasure trove (in which the White diggers had succeeded in getting the issue of licences to mine and deal in diamonds restricted to Whites). Finally, in 1880 the Cape was forced to incorporate the area as a condition under which Molteno was permitted to annex Walvis Bay on the west coast and Tembuland in the east. Meanwhile, the Free State was offended and would not be lured into showing any interest in confederation. The Transvaal too was not to be drawn.

The Sand River recognition of the independence of the South African Republic had by no means produced an ordered society north of the Vaal. The Rustenburg Grondwet had been generally accepted but its writ ran not very far. The Republic was nearly bankrupt and the executive was unable to collect taxes from the anarchic population or to exercise control over the remoter sec-tions. People of all description were flowing into the new-found gold-fields around Lydenburg in the east which brought promise of increased financial stability. President Burgers still dreamed of a rail-link with Delagoa Bay which would give the Transvaal its complete economic independence of Britain and enable it to compete commercially with the Colonies. He tried desperately for foreign assistance and the rising interest of Germany in southern Africa seemed likely to include the Transvaal.

Fresh outbreaks of border disturbances high-lighted, in the British view, the need for a common approach to relations with the Africans. Langalibalele, a semi-independent chief of the Hlubi on the Lesotho borders, was ordered by the Natal authorities to send in his men to register the guns which were being freely acquired on the diamond diggings (an order equivalent to confiscation). The chief temporized, then fled with his following into Lesotho with a large force in pursuit, led by the governor of Natal, Sir Benjamin Pine, and bent on destructive retribution after the loss of three men in a skirmish. They killed Hlubi stragglers, took lands and cattle from a sympathetic but law-abiding neighbouring tribe and sent the men to work on the farms. Langalibalele, betrayed for cattle by a Sotho chief to a Cape force supporting the Natalians, was handed over for trial by Pine himself who, by a special Act of the Cape Parliament, ordered his banishment to Robben Island. Protests to Britain led to the recall of Pine and the transfer to the mainland of the chief. There was widespread official alarm at the possible consequences of other similar revolts. Carnarvon gathered up this evidence of Natal's vulnerability to use in preventing any effort to obstruct his plans. He still hoped to use the Diamond Fields as a bargaining counter to win Free State support.

The Transvaal, constantly skirmishing with African and Griqua around its ill-defined borders, now faced a nearer threat. The Pedi people, whose strength had continued to increase under Chief Sekhukhune by the assimilation of Zulu and Swazi refugees, were accumulating guns from the Diamond Fields and Delagoa Bay. They were spilling out of their well-defended country in the Lulu mountains near the Lydenburg goldfield and raiding Boer cattle. Short of land himself, the chief would not allow gold prospectors any nearer his domain, nor pay certain taxes, nor give up lands claimed by the Republic as part of an 1846 Swazi concession. He repulsed an attack led by Burgers himself without money or sufficient armed men, who then handed over the war to a recruited company of 'filibusters' (Wolseley declared one of the leaders, Abel Erasmus, to be a 'fiend in human form'),[35] who were to pay themselves in looted cattle and land. A war of massacre and unrestrained brutality followed. But Sekhukhune remained undefeated in his mountains.

Further east the able and popular Cetshwayo, who had succeeded his father, Mpande, in 1873, had revived Zulu militancy. Though he was careful to remain in friendly alliance with Shepstone and the Natal Whites, he opposed Transvaal penetration into the Blood River district claimed as ceded by Mpande. To British worry over Sekhukhune's resistance was added the assumption that Cetshwayo too was poised to attack the Zulus' traditional enemies in the Transvaal. The panic cry of the Lydenburg diggers, mostly English, for British protection was exaggerated and even distorted in London (a later petition showed an actual 6,500 against and only 500 for annexation); it reinforced Carnarvon's line of wishful thinking, that the Transvaal was ripe for annexation, that the Free State would then no longer hold out and Confederation would be accomplished.

In January 1877 Shepstone went up to Pretoria with twenty-five mounted police and instructions to investigate conditions and advise. He addressed the volksraad and offered British protection, which Burgers and Kruger rejected. Shepstone then precipitately proclaimed the Transvaal annexed to the British Empire, promising immediate self-government. There was no resistance beyond a formal protest by Burgers who afterwards retired to the Cape, to be succeeded in the leadership by the recently elected Vice-President, Paul Kruger. A scarring resentment remained.

Carnarvon had long been prepared with a draft South Africa Bill for consideration by the various governments. It was not very different from that to be accepted thirty-three years later except that for all Carnarvon's humanitarian posture, the imperial government took even less account of Black interests than the colonials were to do. Sir Bartle Frere was sent out as governor and Carnarvon's unofficial viceroy to push the federal scheme.

35. *Cambridge History of the British Empire*, Vol. VIII, p. 463.

One of Frere's first distractions, however, was on the Eastern Frontier. By 1877 the Xhosa had to some extent recovered from the cattle-killing and once again were finding their confinement intolerable. The Gcaleka crammed on the coast between the Kei and the Umtata were brushing with the Mfengu over the latter's desirable lands. Sarili, remembering his father Hintsa's fate, refused to comply when summoned by the governor. Colonial forces, helped by cattle-eager Mfengu and Thembu, drove the Gcaleka across the Bashee River which bisected their territory. Molteno would have liked to transport them as trouble-makers to St Helena. Frere opposed this as unnecessarily ruthless and a potent source of future discontent. Sarili's army was crushed, the chief deposed and Frere began to disarm the tribe, intending to send White settlers to Gcalekaland. Groups of tribesmen secretly crossed the Kei and infiltrated into the Ngqika location in the north of British Kaffraria to rouse their kith and kin under Sandile to rebellion in which the Thembu joined. The outcome was inevitable. Sandile, though he twice asked for terms, was shot. Sarili fled. The chiefs' long struggle, one of the longest and most determined in Africa, to preserve the independence and cohesion of their people was over. Frere tried to restrain Molteno from breaking up the Gaika location: 'The Gaikas are our fellow subjects not our enemies.'[36] Aware of the ruthless methods of the settlers in conflict with the Blacks, he determined himself to keep control of the costly war which was threatening to spread. He rejected Molteno's demands for control of the colonial volunteers and withdrawal of the imperial troops (what, in fact, the whole self-government policy was to encourage) and exercised his probably constitutional but unprecedented right to dismiss Molteno. The Ngqika location was all the same broken up and sold as farms. Fingoland and Griqualand East were shortly annexed to the Cape and magistrates were introduced throughout the Transkei, the chiefs becoming salaried civil servants, administering the will of the Whites. By 1885, Gcalekaland and Thembuland were annexed to the Cape and British protection was extended over the coasts of Pondoland, where the chief was exacting a toll on passing traffic, and where the Germans too had

36. *Cambridge History of the British Empire*, Vol. VIII, p. 470.

begun to show an interest. The whole of Pondoland was not formally annexed to the Cape until 1894.

Having disposed of the Eastern Frontier problems, Frere turned his attention to Zululand. There Cetshwayo, still embroiled in his boundary disputes, now found the Transvaal a British colony and himself opposing his one-time British allies. He was, so Frere mistakenly understood, the focal point of an extensive Black conspiracy to rise and turn the White men out of South Africa. Frere, believing the disarming of the Zulu and removal of the threat to the White territories would conciliate the Transvaalers and advance the cause of federation, decided on a showdown. Early in 1879 Cetshwayo, while agreeing to surrender lawbreakers and to pay a cattle penalty, ignored an ultimatum which would have resulted in the destruction of the Zulu military machine and his own power, in the break-up of the Zulu nation and, with the acceptance of British Residents, in the loss of all independence. Early in 1879 four British columns under Lt-Gen. Lord Chelmsford entered Zululand. At Isandhlwana they suffered a massacre of 800 Whites and 500 African troops, who fought till their ammunition was done and they had slaughtered 3,000 Zulu warriors. At Rorke's Drift a heroic force of 120 repelled between three and four thousand Zulu, killing 350. Four

Interrogating Cetshwayo's messengers at Dalmain's Farm (Fort Cherry)

months later the reckless young Prince Imperial of France was killed in a skirmish. These battles live as examples of the useless confrontations of African history: numbers and courage against courage and guns. Finally, at Ulundi, the guns won: the Zulu were routed; Cetshwayo was taken and was imprisoned in Cape Town Castle. These events, following on the ecclesiastical storm raised by Bishop Colenso of Natal's doctrinal doubts prompted by his Zulu converts, drew from Disraeli, then the British Prime Minister, the dry comment: 'A very remarkable people, the Zulus: they defeat our Generals; they convert our Bishops; they have settled the fate of a great European dynasty.'[37] And, he might have added, had struck a mortal blow at his own ministry.

The British were still reluctant to take full responsibility. Sir Garnet Wolseley, now in charge, shrewdly divided the Zulu under thirteen petty chiefs, most of them unrelated to the Zulu royal family, with a British Resident, Sir Melmoth Osborn, a man of poor judgement and with restricted authority, to advise. The nominees, selected without regard to existing divisions and relationships, were glad of a chance to extend their own power at the king's expense. Rivalry, injustice and bloodshed soon resulted, but no strong rule could develop to trouble White frontiers. But Wolseley, after making his arrangements for Zululand, had gone on to deal with Sekhukhune, whom the Transvaalers had been unable to subdue. He attacked his stronghold with a large force including African troops and after a tremendous struggle the people were crushed by weight of numbers. The chief was starved out, imprisoned for a time and later murdered by a rival.

With no established authority in Zululand, disorders there turned to anarchy. The British wished no further involvement so Cetshwayo was reinstated in 1883 in a divided and utterly demoralized kingdom and was soon in conflict with one of the sub-chiefs, his cousin Zibhebhu, who had the British Resident's support. Worsted and injured he died the next year. Dinuzulu, his son, succeeded him and with the assistance of Transvaal Boers defeated Zibhebhu and avenged his father. His allies claimed much more land than they had been promised – but with British 'mediation' in discussions at which the Zulu were not

37. *Cambridge History of the British Empire*, Vol. VIII, p. 478.

present, they accepted a large area round Vryheid where three hundred Boers founded the New Republic (among the surveyors of whose boundaries was the young Louis Botha), and relinquished claims down to St Lucia Bay. The situation worsened and the British annexed the rest of Zululand. In 1887 Zibhebhu and his people were allowed to return, displacing many of Dinuzulu's followers and there was trouble again involving government forces against Dinuzulu, who surrendered to the British and, convicted of high treason, was banished to a term on St Helena. The stability as a preliminary to federation that the British hoped for from the subjugation of the Zulu did not materialize. Dinuzulu was to be allowed to return to a fragmented country ten years later, after Natal had incorporated Zululand.

In 1879 the Cape Parliament legislated for the disarmament of Africans within its jurisdiction. The great Queen had passed Moshweshwe's blanket and its uncomfortable inhabitants to the Cape Government in 1871. Now, in view of the disturbed conditions on the White perimeters, Frere demanded the handing in of Sotho guns. To enforce its will the Cape fought the Gun War, or War of Disarmament, unsuccessfully and at a cost of £3m. and threatened to break up some of the territory into farms. In the end the Sotho submitted to arbitration, kept their land intact and retrieved surrendered arms on payment of a licence fee. The Colony was happy to pass the pesky blanket back to Britain. The Sotho gladly agreed to double their tax so as to be free of a Cape government subsidy and any control that might imply. Becoming a Crown Colony in 1844, they retained a tenuous political autonomy, but were increasingly drawn into economic subservience to the White South Africa encircling them.

While the administration was preoccupied with these events and Isandhlwana had advertised the British forces to be far from invincible, the promised self-government for the Transvaal was overlooked. Drought ravaged the impoverished country. Kruger, now the most influential of the Boer leaders, was hostile to Britain; and the speed with which British officials attempted to introduce efficient administration, to collect taxes and restore solvency antagonized the backward, pastoral individualists who still had not moved very far from the Great Trek. Protests against the withholding of self-government and deputations to London having failed, Kruger, Pretorius and General Petrus Joubert set up a temporary republican capital at Heidelberg and declared war on Britain, the Boers' first War of Freedom. Only after spectacular defeats of the British at Bronkhorst Spruit, Majuba and Laing's Nek in the Drakensberg and because neither party wished to become embroiled in costly hostilities, was self-government restored. The terms of the Pretoria Convention of 1881 were modified by the London Convention in 1884, by which Britain retained control of the Transvaal's foreign relations.

The last flickering hope of Confederation, conscientiously tended by Frere after Carnarvon left office, was extinguished. Huge areas of African states were in thrall. Relations between Britain and the Afrikaners, not only in the republics but everywhere in South Africa, could hardly have been worse. In opposing what seemed to them to be British greed, double-dealing and disregard of their cherished traditions, the Afrikaners throughout the country found themselves drawing together in common interest and beginning to discover a nationhood.

4 The Union (1884–1910)

I. GOLD AND A CAPE TO CAIRO VISION

The remarkable development in colonization known vividly and aptly as the scramble for Africa occupied the last third of the nineteenth century. It resulted in the parcelling out of Africa among European powers which, before 1880, had only the sketchiest, if any, footholds scattered the length of the coastline. By 1914 they had carved up amongst themselves almost the entire continent (except for the ancient kingdom of Ethiopia) and acquired some 11,000,000 square miles of colonial territory.

The impetus was given by two countries – Belgium and Germany – which until then had shown no interest in African possessions and seem to have been impelled by motives rather different from those of the old colonizing powers.

Leopold II of the Belgians, grandiose and ambitious, aspired to a personal colonial empire. His attention was focused on the Congo basin by H. M. Stanley, fresh from his explorations there. Leopold intended to build a powerful commercial monopoly. He astutely persuaded the European powers that it was better to have a free trade area under a scientific-commercial African International Association he had founded as cover for his activities, than to let any rival obtain full control. A by-product of his intrigue was the arousing of deep mutual suspicions among the European contenders in Africa, which were stoked by German diplomacy.

Bismarck's interest in Africa seemed to have been initially different from Leopold's. In part he may have wished to deflect French hostility and distract attention from the recently annexed Alsace-Lorraine. But more significant, the political and financial collapse of Turkish and Egyptian régimes, which had been finely balanced under British and French influences, upset the balance of European powers in the Middle East. Britain's overriding concern as always, was the defence of Suez and of imperial and commercial interests in India and the Pacific against possible foreign inroads, particularly by Russia and France. Franco-British co-operation in that region broke down when Britain, in a blundering miscalculation, moved into Egypt to restore order and found herself bogged down in a long crippling occupation. To keep German support against France in Egypt, she was forced to acquiesce in German acquisitions elsewhere. In eighteen months, between 1883 and 1885, Germany had annexed four large areas including South West Africa and parts of East Africa where an agent had rapidly collected treaties, many quite worthless from often bogus chiefs.

The speed of the Belgian and German inroads made it clear that a rapid partitioning of Africa was inevitable. The long-established powers, until now reluctant to become more financially and militarily committed than they could help, were forced to take stock.

There began a reappraisal of the contemporary value of overseas possessions. The swift growing new industrial and capitalist societies were raising barriers of protection; multiplying populations were demanding new sources of raw materials, markets for manufactured goods, areas for capital investment and, in suitable areas, for emigration. The reports of the journeys of Livingstone, Stanley and other explorers aroused interest in the previously unknown African interior. There was a general awakening to the existence of rich mineral troves which the discovery of the diamonds of Kimberley stimulated. A general rise in wealth increased the demand for tropical products – tea, coffee, sugar, rubber. Not only were hardy adventurous individuals spreading far and wide but organized commerce and finance were taking a growing part. Africa seemed to offer almost limitless but, it was becoming obvious, highly competitive opportunities. And where nationals and money were involved the apparatus of government and defence must follow.

At the Berlin Convention at the close of 1884 the great powers recognized Belgium's Congo claims and rapaciously shared out their own spheres of influence. So little of Africa as an entity, so little of its populations was known to the statesmen who carved it up that much of this was done in offices and country houses in Europe, where lines were drawn across maps so inaccurate, so smudged by ignorance, that frontiers could only follow lines of latitude. The people went with the parcels of territory regardless of social affinities, another of the natural resources. The tribes, many of them, put up a powerful resistance when they realized what was happening. Others tried to make their own terms; but they could not win against the moguls of commerce whose day was dawning, any more than earlier generations had succeeded against rancher and prospector. As every land in every sense is a part of the main, so southern Africa could not be uninfluenced by or without influence upon events to the north.

In return for being accommodating over Egypt, Britain gave Germany a relatively free hand in East, in Central, and in South West Africa. South West Africa is a huge semi-arid tract, two-thirds of the size of South Africa, lying between the Orange and the Kunene and Okavango Rivers, the Atlantic Ocean and the Kalahari desert. A hundred years ago pastoral Khoikhoi or Nama tribes occupied the southern part almost to Windhoek, pastoral 'cattle-rich' Herero the centre, and the largely agricultural Ovambo and related communities lived in the northern area. San and Berg Damara clans were scattered in the less desirable areas and, the latter especially, also worked as servants for Nama and Herero. South of Windhoek in the small area of Rehoboth granted them by the Nama, Coloured Basters had lived since, in 1865, they were forced to trek from the lands by the Orange River which they had occupied from the time of their origin at the end of the eighteenth century but to which they could establish no title. Here, in Rehoboth, their haughty independence, like that of their White forbears, made them an acute administrative problem.

South West Africa was explored by Dutch and British from the Cape; LMS missionaries were the first to settle with the tribes and were succeeded by Rhenish parsons in the 1840s. The 1860s was a time of savage Nama–Herero warfare during which the German missionaries and traders appealed for British protection. In 1870 peace was made. Chief Kamaharero, however, had heard the distant rumble of approaching Trekker wagons:

We have no unoccupied land for the admission of any other nation, more especially one who, we have been led to believe, has always looked upon the black tribes with scorn and indignation and who both recognize and practise slavery ... The Boers, like ourselves, have an irrevocable attachment for cattle ... They would require an extensive tract of country.[1]

He signed a deed of cession to Britain which was not taken up. Though Frere urged intervention, all the British Government at that stage was prepared to do was to annex Walvis Bay.

When fighting between the Nama and the Herero began again in 1880, the German Government asked the British for protection for its nationals, but Britain disclaimed responsibility for events outside Walvis Bay. The Germans then founded a trading station at Angra Pequena (Luderitzbucht) and in the next year, 1884, the year of the Berlin Conference, proclaimed a protectorate over 322,000 square miles in South West Africa. Kamaharero signed another deed of cession to Britain which was again rejected. 'The British flag flew here,' he reflected later. 'It waved this way and that; we attached ourselves to it, and we were waved backwards and forwards with it.'[2] He appealed to the Aborigines Protection Society in London, saying that he feared the Germans would destroy his country. This needed no special gift of clairvoyance at that stage of the colonization of Africa.

The Germans paid a great price in money and men to hold a territory that could then absorb only few settlers; but they were hopeful of extending in temperate latitudes. 'For us the Boer States, with the coasts that are their due, signify a great possibility'; and, 'the possession of South Africa offers greater advantage in every respect than the possession of Brazil'; these were thoughts given press currency rather later in Germany. Soon after they were considering their colony's strategic importance 'if war should break out between us and Great Britain'.[3]

Rhodes was thoroughly alarmed by the threat from Germany on the one side and the Transvaal on the other to the road – the old Missionaries' Road to the north – and to the fulfilment of his ranging dreams of expansion. Trekker infiltration enabled him to

1. Ruth First, *South West Africa*, p. 67.
2. ibid., p. 68.
3. Sir Charles Dundas, *South West Africa: The Factual Background*, p. 11.

engineer British acquisition of Bechuanaland in 1885. The southern part, from the Orange to the Molopo River, including most of the two small recently founded Trekker republics of Stellaland and Goshen (parts of which were ceded to the Transvaal) became a Crown Colony until annexed to the Cape in 1895; 'a share of the land was reserved for the Bechuana clans whose rights the expedition had been sent to uphold'.[4] From the Molopo north to 28° S latitude was declared a British Protectorate, the modern Botswana. The Missionaries' Road was kept open and the danger of Germany and the Transvaal joining hands and barring the way from the Cape to Central Africa was for the present removed.

Away to the east, however, the possibility persisted of the Transvaal getting its outlet to the coast and giving an unfriendly power a base. Into Swaziland, the small mountainous kingdom lying between the South African Republic and the Portuguese–Zululand coastland, Boers had for a long time been penetrating by their customary methods of first sending in hunting expeditions, then driving herds to graze over the borders and then, a sure foothold gained, exacting concessions from the local chiefs. For a time the Swazi chiefs had encouraged the Whites as potential allies against the Zulu and from 1875 to 1881 they had virtually controlled Swaziland. The reigning chief, Mbandzeni, rewarded with champagne and other rich presents (and without missionaries or any reliable Whites to advise him), signed a confusion of concessions – even granting away his revenues. The independence of Swaziland had been guaranteed under the London Convention of 1884, but when the now alarmed king asked for British protection it was refused him. In the meantime an agent of Germany had acquired a large concession round St Lucia Bay, the best harbour between Delagoa Bay and Durban, and Britain, invoking an old 1842 treaty with Mpande, occupied the area in 1887, thus further severing the republics from the coast and reducing the possibility of a German base there. Kruger strove to regain a Swaziland overlordship, hoping now for a rail link to Kosi Bay, the only potential harbour that remained.

Protracted negotiations between the Republic and Britain took place between 1891 and 1894 during which Britain offered Kruger

4. *Cambridge History of the British Empire*, Vol. VIII, p. 514.

the administration (but not incorporation) of Swaziland (in spite of the protests of the people) and access to a port at Kosi Bay on condition the Transvaal joined with the Colonies in a Customs Union, permitted the extension of the railways through the republic and renounced activities and expansion in the north and north-west. Finally, in 1895, regardless of official Swazi protests, Kruger was allowed control of the territory, in which by then there were many White settlers, on conditions theoretically safeguarding the interests of the Swazi inhabitants. It was at this time that the German press was threatening intervention and Kruger, at a banquet to celebrate the Kaiser's birthday, announced his intention to regain total independence for the Transvaal with German aid. Britain responded by annexing all south of the Portuguese border between Swaziland and the sea.

Diamonds made capitalists rich and brought pastoralists in thousands into a competitive commercial economy. But on foundations of gold is laid the structure of a great nation of surpassing industrial potential. The discovery, in 1886, of the gold of the Witwatersrand is the central event in the development of South Africa. Rich mineral deposits had been believed to exist in the Transvaal and were sought after for many years. Gold had been worked at the Tati River north-west of the Transvaal for twenty years past and the mines of the Eastern Transvaal had saved that country from bankruptcy in the 1870s and early 1880s. But the gold of the Witwatersrand was something very different from those and from all other deposits anywhere else in the world.

The total area of these gold-bearing deposits is about 170 miles by 100 miles – greater in extent than any other goldfield. The reefs slant deeply below the surface in complex formations. The gold is microscopically fine, uniform in composition and intimately associated with pyrites. The average gold content per ton is lowest of all gold-producing areas. To make this sort of mining pay demands a scientific and technological sophistication that quite rules out the individual methods of the old-style romantic prospector. The enormous deposits of gold and the great difficulties in extraction postulated a long, continuous and even production which was soon to confirm gold rather than silver as an international monetary standard. It was a fortunate conjunction of circumstances that the find came at a time when the necessary heavy machinery, railway development, engineers, scientists, technicians and know-how were readily available. Associated with the goldfields and near by in Natal were abundant supplies of good, cheap coal.

The experience of the diamond fields and the vast capital amassed by the companies there were immediately applied to the development of the Reef. It had taken twenty years to build up the basic financial structure of the diamond industry, but the same magnates accomplished the amalgamation of the gold mines in six years. The companies controlling the mines were organised into groups and the groups united in the Chamber of Mines which looks after the interests common to the industry as a whole: mining regulations, legal, statistical and taxation matters, the health of the employees and above all the recruiting of labour. The formation of the Witwatersrand Native Labour Association (WNLA) and the Native Recruiting Corporation Limited (NRC), to recruit outside and inside South Africa respectively, eliminated competition among the mines for labour and ensured that wages were maintained at a uniform minimum level. Africans, once so hard to induce to work for the Whites, in hundreds of thousands now answered the lyrical call of the NRC, as inscribed above the portals of a Zululand depot: *Abathanda imali, abathanda izinkhomo indhlela elula eya eGoli; nanti iHovisi.* (Lovers of money, lovers of cattle, the road is easy to go to the City of Gold [Johannesburg]; here is the office.)

The economic principle of the desirability of abundant cheap labour, provided exclusively by one section of the people, had developed its local colour in the South African rural feudal system; at Kimberley it was carried into the industrial sphere; on the Witwatersrand it was grafted grotesquely into the heart of a twentieth-century industrial society. Only the existence of this huge cheap labour force made possible the development of the gold mines in the beginning and provided the foundation of individual fortunes and of the phenomenal industrial and commercial prosperity the country was to achieve in the next fifty years. (In 1936, for example the average wage of each of the 47,000 Europeans on the mines was £325 p.a., that of each African labourer £31 p.a.) The Transvaal, which had been almost bankrupt in 1887, had a revenue of £1½m. five years later and by 1896 gold formed 96 per cent of its exports. The dominant position of the Transvaal in the South African economy was assured. But the effect of this hectic urban and competitive cosmopolitan injection into the pastoral patriarchy of the Transvaal is not difficult to imagine. The Boers saw their cherished liberty once more threatened by the British, their religious foundations undermined, Black–White relationships turned over and their young seduced by foreign and unscriptural ideas and ways. They preferred their poverty. Over much of the rest of the country the spectacular development of the Transvaal produced boom conditions. There were steep price rises, keen land speculation, thriving activity in the ports and a great development of the railway system.

Chains of events that had been developing more or less independently in different parts of the country now were becoming tightly tangled, and three outstanding personalities were responsible for designing the pattern.

There was Rhodes. Wealth and financial pre-eminence were for him, deeply involved in gold as well as in diamonds, the means to realize his youthful and audacious ambition of not merely a united southern Africa but of an unbroken area of British imperial domination from the Cape of Good Hope to the Suez Canal. He dreamed of the torch of Western civilization carried into the dark corners of Africa. 'I contend,' he had declared in 1877, 'that we [the British] are the first race in the world and that the more of the world we inhabit the better it is for the human race.'[5] In this he succinctly expressed the credo which explains much of the motive power of the empire builders and the dedication which burned with so heroic and theatrical a glory and left such bitter ashes. His attitude to Britain, nonetheless, was complex. All southern Africa for him was divided into three parts: Imperial, Colonial and Republican. He was the great colonialist. He envisaged a vast territory of politically and economically federated, British protected but not directed, self-governing units under Cape Colony leadership, extending from the Cape to the Mediterranean and painted pink to the extent that it would be a part of the British

5. K. L. Roskam, *Apartheid and Discrimination*, p. 84.

dominions – probably also federated, and of the British global economic, political and defence system. More practically, they would offer opportunities for British emigrants, new markets for British industrial products, sources of raw materials for British industries and fields for British investment – prizes that other European powers were beginning to reach for. But, as he had no use for the divisiveness of the republics, he also had no place for imperial interference in the internal management of his projected federation.

In all of this he was soon to come up against his diametrically opposite number. Paul Kruger, about twice the age of Rhodes, became President of the Transvaal in 1883. For the next twenty years the history of South Africa was in a sense that of the war between these giant individualists, and they died within two years of each other at the turn of the century. The dust of their battle is not yet laid. Rhodes gave shape to the economic development of South Africa; Kruger set it on its political course. These nearly parallel lines have at last met in a conjunction that would have astonished and pleased both antagonists.

Kruger, the lad who went north in the Great Trek, had soon become the centre of a legend, performing fantastic exploits of courage as a hunter in mortal combat with wild animals and, later, feats of daring out on commando against African warriors. He threw in his lot with Pretorius and his weight through all the years of Boer dissension, quarrels and divisions in the Transvaal was on the side of unity, moderation and law. He had little education – the few months' schooling from an itinerant teacher that was customary for Voortrekker children – enough to enable him to read and write. His main reading was the Bible, read daily to the assembled household in Voortrekker fashion. Intensely conservative and religious, he was active in the religious disputes which disrupted the Transvaal in the 1850s. He helped to form the Dopper Kerk, a sect of extreme and fundamentalist faith – to his dying day he refused to accept that the earth was not flat. Dopper support won him succession to the liberal and unpopular Burgers in the presidency in 1883. Twice after the annexation of the Transvaal he travelled to London to plead for Transvaal independence and his lack of total success confirmed him as implacably anti-British.

This was the rock which Rhodes's ambitions struck. Kruger, who badly needed competent administrators, would have none of the liberal-tainted Cape Colonists or Free Staters qualified to serve. He imported Hollanders and Germans who brought with them current European anti-British feeling and concepts of national political divisions. These advisers fortified Kruger's opposition to proposals for a customs union with the south and to the extension into the Transvaal of the railway which Rhodes and his associates hoped to carry north of the Limpopo. With their encouragement, too, Kruger pursued his own dream of Boer independence and expansion into Central Africa, intensified his isolation from Britain and the Colony and pressed on with schemes for a line to Delagoa Bay, calling for support on continental powers jockeying for place in Africa. This Transvaal attitude, with the very real prospect of a rival rail connection with the east coast and an active German interest in the Republic's affairs, threatened Rhodes's plans.

The third figure of stature in South Africa at this moment of time stood by birth, by politics and by temperament between the headline-capturing British and Republican extremes. Jan Hendrik Hofmeyr, 'Onse Jan' as he was affectionately recalled in after years, came from an old Cape farming family. He had a liberal education in Cape Town, lived there in a largely English environment and as a vigorous practising journalist acquired a wide influence and a deeper insight into the White South African situation than many of his compatriots. He supported the Afrikaner cultural movements that were beginning to take life there but was not drawn to the parallel extreme political nationalism.

The annexation of Lesotho and of Griqualand West by Britain at the Orange Free State's expense had stirred in the Afrikaners of the Cape a sense of injustice and a feeling, for almost the first time, of solidarity with their kinsmen in the north. The long apathy which had inhibited them from any active part in the political affairs of the Colony – partly because of the difficulties of distance and isolation, but mostly because the progressive anglicization of Cape institutions raised a barrier to understanding, interest and participation – began to dispel. In this pervading sense of isolation the strength of the Church had been a reassuring and generally unifying force from which intense nationalism began naturally to develop. The nascent sense of unity and brotherhood was given further expression and direction by the development of Dutch journalism, and gradually these influences began to permeate all aspects of Afrikaner life.

The *Boeren Verenigingen*, associations of Dutch farmers, were formed in the Eastern Province from about 1873 to look after farmers' interests. At about the same time a cultural movement for the recognition of the Afrikaans language rather than Dutch got going at Paarl in the Western Cape. In 1875 *Die Genootskap van Regte Afrikaners*, the Fellowship of True Afrikaners, was formed by the Reverend S. F. du Toit, an extreme Calvinist, to encourage cultural and political patriotism and 'to stand for our Language, our Nation and our Country'.[6] In 1876 its journal, *Die Afrikaanse Patriot*, appeared and some few books in Afrikaans on Afrikaner history and Christian National Education made their contribution. These related movements were not without result. In 1882 the Constitution was amended to allow the use of Dutch (not yet Afrikaans) as well as English in the Cape Parliament; and two years later Dutch was introduced into the courts.

Hofmeyr, while he was fully conscious of the essential unity of the Afrikaners throughout South Africa, saw their development not as a separate national movement but in a slow evolving cooperation on equal terms with the English-speaking group. He formed the *Boeren Beschermings Vereniging*, the Farmers' Protection Association, ostensibly the protest of the wine farmers against a tax on brandy, but with more political than purely economic intent. With its backing he was elected to Parliament. Du Toit by now had formed the *Afrikaner Bond*, a fiercely pan-Afrikaner, anti-imperialist movement. Initially membership was to include all Whites who recognized Africa as the fatherland, but soon it narrowed to those of Dutch and Huguenot origin. It was based squarely on Calvinism, accepted that political authority was divinely ordained, aimed at a united republican South Africa (but under a British defence umbrella) and the development of the Afrikaans language, and was opposed to British-controlled financial and commercial interests. The Bond had strong affiliations in

6. T. R. H. Davenport, *The Afrikaner Bond*, p. 28.

the republics where the politically grounded Young Afrikaner movement hoped for a united South Africa 'under our own flag';[7] and where the President-to-be of the South African Republic, Paul Kruger, could write in 1881 to President Brand of the Orange Free State, 'Then it shall be from the Zambezi to Simon's Bay, Africa for the Afrikander.'[8] Du Toit joined Kruger's administration and the original ideals of the Bond lingered long after the withering away of its organization in the republics (where both Kruger and Brand discouraged the movement), and fertilized and stimulated by British mistakes, misjudgements, vacillation, economies, avarice and good intentions, were to grow into an indestructible edifice of a narrow exclusive nationalism.

This trend ran clean counter to Hofmeyr's aspirations – Rhodes's too on his different plane, though he, in the long run, was to make as large, if unwitting, a contribution as any to its realization. Hofmeyr set about capturing the Bond in the Cape and reshaping it to his own ideas; and in 1883 he was returned with its backing to Parliament, where Rhodes had represented Barkly West since 1881.

Hofmeyr at this stage was angered by Kruger's rejection of his attempts to woo him into railway and customs cooperation with the Colony, and so he was disposed to relax his opposition to Rhodes's schemes to extend the Colony's influence north into Central Africa. They found themselves in sympathy in many of their aims. Rhodes's wealth would be enormously beneficial to the Bond, the voting strength of the Bond, which Hofmeyr commanded, could give Rhodes enhanced political power. The backing of the Bond would gain Rhodes the premiership in 1890, which Hofmeyr refused, preferring to exercise power through the weight of the party. Their common ground was the ideal of cooperation between all the colonists, Dutch and British, on a basis of equality, an economic union of the Cape with the northern republics leading to a political federation free of internal imperial interference and with a single, agreed Native policy. Rhodes saw a united South Africa self-dependent within the empire; Hofmeyr envisaged eventual total independence but made no present issue

7. *Cambridge History of the British Empire*, Vol. VIII, p. 507.
8. ibid., p. 509.

of it. Rhodes agreed to defend Hofmeyr's protective economic policy in the Cape, and Hofmeyr undertook to make no obstacle to northward expansion or to the projected railway through Botswana and beyond. Hofmeyr, on behalf of the governor, used his influence to persuade Kruger to accept British concessions offered in Swaziland in return for renunciation of all interest in the lands north of the Transvaal.

The fertile land just over the Limpopo was rumoured to contain goldfields richer than the Rand (for King Solomon's mines were still dreamed of). Lobengula, son of Mzilikazi and Chief of the powerful Ndebele people, reigned at Bulawayo and at the royal kraal concession hunters, emissaries of many nations, including the expansionist Transvaal, were hotly competing. Rhodes had been able to persuade neither imperial nor colonial governments to take any interest in acquiring either territory that would advance Britain into Central Africa or minerals that would restore the Cape's financial lead over the Transvaal. He sent his own agents, led by C. D. Rudd, from Kimberley to Lobengula. On 30 October 1888, they secured from the chief all mineral rights within his domains and an undertaking that he would grant no land or mineral rights in future without their consent. In exchange for these concessions, the king was to receive £1,200 a year, 1,000 rifles, 100,000 cartridges and a steamboat on the Zambezi (which last did not materialize). Rhodesia was founded as a speculators' El Dorado and preserve.

Rhodes bought out all other claims and established the British South Africa (BSA) Company which, he could assure Hofmeyr, he intended should be controlled not from London but by a board of South Africans. The Company crushed the determined opposition to it both of its commercial rivals and of the Aborigines' Protection Society and the missionaries who were urging the government to protect African rights and in 1889 obtained its Royal Charter, saving the imperial authorities for the moment the complexities and expense of another settler community. The obstacles put in the way of the Charter and a British refusal to allow the annexation of British Bechuanaland to the Cape, stung Sir Hercules Robinson, Cape Governor and High Commissioner and Rhodes's friend, to a protest, then fast becoming familiar, against 'the amateur meddling of irresponsible and ill-advised persons in England . . . which converts many a colonist from an Imperialist into a Republican'.[9]

Effective settlement became urgent, both to forestall others and to accelerate the exploitation of the mineral rights. In 1890 Rhodes sent in a Pioneer Column of 700 settlers and police, many of them South African, guided by the famed elephant hunter Selous, to cut a road past the wary Ndebele to modern Mashonaland, whose people the Company regarded as Lobengula's vassals (though he only in fact controlled those near his borders) and thus included in his concessions. The Shona people were no longer under any uni- fying control, though a descendant of the Mutapa lived as a petty chief in the north-east, members of the Rozwi aristocracy were scattered amongst the people of the centre and west and memories of the days of power were strong. They still mined gold and traded with the Portuguese, while the wide pervasion of their old religion made them stony ground for missionaries. The Shona soon rea- lized the Whites were not temporary prospectors but were claim- ing each the promised 3,000 acres, were rounding them up as labour and seizing their cattle in fines. They regarded themselves as unconquered and resisted as they could. The rule imposed was unjust, oppressive and arbitrary in the extreme. If the Whites hated and despised the Shona for their inability to put up a united resistance, they hated and feared the Ndebele for their cohesion, pride and aggression. When Mashonaland turned out to be less richly rewarding than expected, hopes turned to Lobengula's fertile territory beneath which a rich vein of gold was thought to run. Despite Lobengula's long efforts for peace, a pretext for war was found in highly coloured accounts of cruel Ndebele raids on Shona (which interfered with the flow of labour). In 1893 Rhodes's close friend and colleague, Dr Starr Jameson, led a small com- mando-type force of settlers and troops in a hazardous offensive against 5,000 picked warriors; there was the usual story of fantas- tic courage on both sides, machine guns telling in the end. The king fled and was never captured. The British made a feeble assertion of authority, but, against a united Company-settler anti- imperial front, gave up. All they could do was insist on a land

9. *Cambridge History of the British Empire*, Vol. VIII, p. 533.

commission to make provision for Ndebele needs and on sufficient cattle for them, and these were ignored. Jameson was made administrator, the gate was opened to settlers; nothing was left to the Ndebele but reserves that were virtually desert and 'regarded', said Lord Grey, a later administrator, 'by the natives as *cemeteries*, not homes'.[10] Much of their cattle was confiscated, claimed as the king's by the Company; much was looted by settlers; drought, rinderpest and locusts completed the devastation. Their cattle was reduced from possibly some quarter-million head in Ndebele hands before the 1893 war to 14,000 in African possession in the whole of Rhodesia in 1897. The land was governed by a lawless administration and despotic and violent police.

The Whites were to be taken completely unawares within three years of this rule. Jameson and most of the police force had gone into Botswana and then launched into the disastrous raid on the Transvaal which was, in a matter of days, to make most of them Kruger's prisoners. The defeated, broken and apparently leaderless and submissive Ndebele and their Shona neighbours seized their opportunity, rose and massacred all Whites within reach. They were joined by Shona in many parts of the country in an organized rebellion which for some months put the whole White settlement in jeopardy. Though the contemporary political leadership had been largely broken, unregarded by the Whites, the priests and the spirit mediums of the Shona retained their age-old religious influence across tribal boundaries and, like Nongqause's spirits, were foretelling the driving out of the Whites as a preliminary to a golden age. They made common cause with surviving temporal leaders, the Mutapa and some Rozwi asserting their latent influence, and were able to provide the intelligence network, and the unifying force behind the cohesive action of Ndebele and Shona, the aptly sardonic pretext for the assembling of the people being 'to get medicine for the locusts'.[11]

Settlers and imperial government demanded 'that spirit of submission which . . . it is essential that a defeated native race should show to their White conquerors'.[12] Rhodes, on the other hand,

10. T. O. Ranger, *Revolt in Southern Rhodesia*, p. 319.
11. ibid., p. 220.
12. ibid., p. 251.

realized that extended fighting and need for South African and imperial assistance would break the Company and lose it its Charter. He persuaded the Ndebele chiefs to attend a dramatically publicized peace *indaba* (conference) in the Matopo hills, and they accepted his promise of protection from retribution and a return to their old lands.

In contemporary reports an occasional lightning flash illuminates the generally unrecorded African viewpoint. There is the poignant exclamation of the old *induna* (headman): 'The happiest man in this country is the man who is dead for at least he died fighting for his country.'[13] A South African journalist, Vere Stent, like Pringle on the Eastern Frontier half a century before, was there with Rhodes, taking it all down. Somabulana, the senior induna's impassioned account of the whole history of the wanderings of the Ndebele from their rift with Shaka, and their relations with the Shona and the Whites, contains this lament:

> But we, the Amandabili, the sons of Kumalo, the Izulu, Children of the Stars we are no dogs! You came, you conquered. The strongest takes the land. We accepted your rule. We lived under you. But not as dogs . . . it is better to be dead . . . the Children of the Stars can never be dogs.[14]

And he spoke of the indignities and insults suffered under the Whites and their African police. Of quite different quality was the exchange with Rhodes of an 'insolent' young leader, looking forward rather than back.

> Where are we to live when it is over ? The White man claims all the land . . . You will give us land in our own country! That is good of you! . . . I find if I talk with my rifle in my hand the White man pays more attention to what I say. Once I put my rifle down I am nothing. I am just a dog to be killed.[15]

These were no doubt words to be carried in the hearts of men filtering south over the Zambezi to near certain death as guerillas some seventy-five years later.

However, the Ndebele kept their traditional chiefs and structure, though divisions were fostered deliberately by the White

13. ibid., p. 247.
14. ibid., p. 121.
15. ibid., p. 248.

authorities, and some returned to their lands – where they found
themselves rent-paying tenants of White owners. The Shona par-
ticipated in no indaba; they fought on into the next year, were
dynamited out of their fortress caves and into unconditional surrender. Most of their chiefs were executed, but their old religious
life continued to wax and wane, adapting to a changing world,
permeating or absorbing alien sects, mostly those which promised
a glorious millennium, and aspects of it reappearing in resistance
movements of a much later date. The Whites, after the terror of
one of the widest and most challenging risings in southern Africa,
tried to make very sure it could not happen again. An official of the
administration at the time, Marshall Hole, looking back in after
years, was to admit that in Rhodesia race prejudice and discrimination were 'more deeply seated than in the older colonies of
South Africa'.[16] In 1898 a legislative council was set up of nominated and elected representatives on which the settlers were in the
majority within ten years.

Rhodes's attitude to the Blacks was regarded by his South
African contemporaries as enlightened. In fact it was entirely em-
pirical, geared to political and financial requirements. The Rudd
Concession, in the view of his biographers,

was obtained nearly by false pretences ... If he (Lobengula) had
realized that Rhodes's purpose was not only or chiefly to dig for gold,
but to found a settlement, he would have refused to set his seal to the
concession ... In his dealings with the white men Lobengula never
really understood what he was doing. Rhodes, who knew very well
what he was doing, cannot be altogether exonerated.[17]

He had, of course, precedents of generations of White dealings
with Africans behind him. When the Africans resisted he was
merciless, as in his dealings with the Ndebele; but when he realized they could never be crushed and their resistance jeopardized
his Company, with considerable courage he negotiated a – somewhat hollow – settlement. Much earlier he had opposed Sprigg's
war to take away Sotho guns which he considered they had
honestly bought from their earnings working for Whites. Later, in
Opposition, he defended the Africans' rights against Schreiner's

16. T. O. Ranger, *Revolt in Southern Rhodesia*, p. 324.
17. J. G. Lockhart and C. M. Woodhouse, *Rhodes*, p. 266.

attempts to disfranchise them and in Rhodesia he advocated distributing cattle alike 'to natives and white people who will work',[18] maintained the Africans were as entitled as Whites to own land, and preached the treatment of European and African on equal terms according to their abilities.

Through his positions both as Director of the Chartered Company and as Prime Minister of the Cape Colony, Rhodes was assuming responsibility for increasing numbers of Black peoples at every stage of Westernization. The entry of the Bond into Cape politics when it fought its first election in 1884 had enhanced the significance of the Black vote. The franchise had remained as enacted when the Cape obtained Representative government in 1853, open to all male British subjects on a very low financial qualification. The Bond constitution contained no colour bar, but no Black member was accepted and on traditional grounds it disliked Black voters who generally favoured English-speaking candidates. But the Bond's opponents were quick to appreciate their value in offsetting the prospect of Afrikaner domination and to encourage their registration. The Bond had to walk warily not to further antagonize the Blacks nor by raising qualifications to disfranchise numbers of its poor white supporters. In 1887, however, after most of the Transkei had been annexed and there was a fear that the White electorate would be swamped by a large 'blanket'[19] vote, communal tenure by general agreement had been excluded as a qualification. In 1892 Rhodes raised the occupational qualification from £25 to £75 and included a simple literacy test, measures which caused a fall in African and Coloured registrations without much improving the electoral position of the Bond.

In 1893 Rhodes took over the Native Affairs portfolio. He began a systemization of native policy, partly in preparation for a federation. The Glen Grey Act of 1894, 'a Native Bill for Africa', he called it, was based on earlier recommendations for land tenure reform in the populous and once fertile Glen Grey valley of the Ciskei, now overcrowded and deteriorating. The Act confirmed African occupation of their lands which a section of Whites hankered after. It attempted to give as many Africans as possible a

18. ibid., p. 434.
19. A. Hepple, *South Africa*, p. 197.

home base on the land by introducing, under a slogan of one man one lot, quit-rent tenure of a maximum of four morgen for those who could afford the survey costs. There simply was not enough land for such a system; the size of the lots was wholly inadequate for profitable farming (and a far cry from the fifty-five morgen plots originally recommended): enough for a woman to cultivate by primitive methods, but not so much as not to force the men away to work. The rigid prohibitions on sales and transfers, intended to protect the holders but preventing a skilful and ambitious farmer from increasing his holding, made it unjust and uneconomic and impossible for a progressive agriculture to develop. A landless class was soon formed with no option but to sell their labour, as Rhodes had intended. You would not, argued Rhodes, speaking on this Bill, make the Natives worthy of the country they live in, 'if you allow them to sit in idleness and if you do not train them in the arts of civilization'.[20] Further, a 10s. labour tax was imposed; but this was never collected and within ten years was withdrawn. To preserve the Cape franchise position individual holdings under the Act were to be regarded as communal. In compensation the Act introduced, and extended over the whole of the Transkei as well, a considerable measure of local self-government in village and district councils under the chairmanship of White magistrates, with powers to collect taxes, administer funds and control such local activities as upkeep of roads, cattledipping, education and agricultural colleges. Associating more closely later, together the councils formed the Transkeian General Council, the *Bunga*. By this means a large number of Africans for the span of two or three generations were to acquire a parochial experience of Western political institutions and of handling small revenues; and it paved the way for the establishment of the first Bantu Homeland under the apartheid system some fifty years later.

In the Colony itself, however, Rhodes proclaimed in 1897 'equal rights for every white man south of the Zambezi'; but, when challenged on the eve of the 1899 election when he depended on the Kimberley Coloured vote, amended his principle: 'My motto is – Equal Rights for every civilized man south of the Zambezi.' Later he defined a civilized man: 'A man whether black or

20. In tribal dress, un-Westernized.

white who has sufficient education to write his name, has some property, or works. In fact, is not a loafer.'[21]

The Africans had fought tenaciously, often heroically, but finally unsuccessfully to preserve land and independence. Once brought under White control and largely disarmed they had to turn to other methods of struggle to regain vanished rights.

Monica Hunter quotes an African's acid capsule history of Africa: 'At first we had the land and the White man had the Bible: now we have the Bible and the White man has the land.'[22] But the Bible as a handbook to revolt had not served them too badly. In the increasing number of mission schools more children were getting better education. Colour barriers shut off skilled occupations and most white-collar jobs. But the abler students who could raise the funds were free to become teachers, parsons, doctors or lawyers, vocations in which the more privileged among the Whites did not feel threatened, and to settle into a niche of some prestige but few prospects on the fringe of the White intellectual world. Many of the early educated Africans, often from Christian families of two or three generations, were intensely grateful to the Whites who had given them their opportunity and with whom they were intellectually assimilated, for they had moved away from their own people.

The field widest open and requiring least financial and intellectual resources was the Church and many able youngsters entered one or other of the Christian denominations, possibly went overseas to one of the theological colleges in the United Kingdom or America and finally returned to the stultification of South African churches which, in line with South African tradition in other fields, held no opportunities for others than Whites. So the ambitious or those more sharply stung by the inequities when confronted with unveiled discrimination, despite such biblical pronouncements as: 'Where there is neither Greek nor Jew, circumcision nor uncircumcision, Barbarian, Scythian, bond nor free,' broke away. They had before them the example of European sectarianism and behind them a tradition of easy tribal hiving off when dissatisfied. Largely under American Negro influences

21. Lockhart, op. cit., pp. 195, 376; E. Roux, *Time Longer than Rope*, p. 62.
22. C. and M. Legum, *South Africa: Crisis for the West*, p. 147.

numbers of separatist or independent African Churches grew up in which White domination and authority was rejected and Black men of ability, to whom other paths were closed, came into their own as founding fathers and even bishops, some with large followings, much power, fervent adulation and sizeable incomes. Separatist sects rapidly proliferated, stimulated partly by restrictions on land: 96 by 1918, 320 by 1938, over 800 by the end of the Second World War and 2,600 by 1963 with 1,500,000 members. (Only seventy-eight of the Churches received government recognition for such purposes as the granting of building sites, marriage facilities and so on.)

Some of these Churches were primitive and revivalist, blended mysticism and magic, pentecostal speaking with tongues and faith healing. Many were millenarian and anti-White and some built on old spirit cults and traditions of resistance. Many were entirely free of White control and largely independent of doctrinal influence. Often the leaders did little to encourage the education and progress of their flock lest the emotional foundations of their influence be undermined. But others were nationalistic breakaways, from established White Churches whose administrative methods, doctrines and forms of worship were retained. Nearly all in greater or less degree believed in 'Africa for the Africans' and the transition from religious to political militancy could be made. Whites tended to label all these sects Ethiopian and some of them were regarded by many Whites as subversive.

One of the first African Christian leaders to emerge as a rebel was the Reverend Nehemiah Tile, a Wesleyan minister in Tembuland who, in 1884, fell foul of his superiors, was accused of 'taking part in political matters and stirring up a feeling of hostility against the magistrates . . . and donating an ox at the circumcision of Dinyebo (Dalindyebo), heir to the Paramount Chief of the Tembus'.[23] Tile seceded and set up the Tembu National Church, one of the first of a succession of defectors from various denominations. In 1892, African Wesleyan delegates found themselve excluded from the Board of a Congress in Pretoria; separate Black and White meetings were to be held, and though White might attend Black sessions, Black were barred from White meetings.

23. Roux, op. cit., p. 78.

Mangena Mokone led a Black walk-out and founded the Ethiopian Church. This sect made contact with the African Methodist Episcopal Church of America (AME) and formed close and lasting bonds, the Ethiopians drawing their bishops from America. The AME became the largest of the separatist Churches. With 100,000 members, 400 churches, some 30 schools and training and theological colleges, it became enormously influential.

It was inevitable that once people began to kick against the pricks of race discrimination in the religious field that some of them should soon turn to journalistic expostulation and to political organization and action. The early African political leaders were generally the brilliant products of Christian education, members of orthodox or of independent Churches and most of them remained devout Christians all their political lives; many of them were ordained. For fifty years the link between the Church and political protest remained strong and many of these leaders were to cooperate with purely secular, political and industrial movements and, if yogi and commissar did not exactly lie down together, many of their South African equivalents of all races and language groups were to stand together on the same platform and march shoulder to shoulder at the head of police-harassed demos.

The *Imbumba Yama Afrika* (Union of Africans), the first African political association, was formed in the Eastern Cape in the early 1880s (at about the same time as the Afrikaner Bond) and the Native Education Association in the Cape made one of the earliest protests against pass laws. Young men of talent (as had happened with the Afrikaners) were expressing their germinating nationalism in journalism, particularly in the Cape where the Black vote could be directed to bear upon White politics to some small advantage. John Tengo Jabavu and Walter Rubusana, both from families of Christian 'school people' in the Eastern Cape, both gifted above the average, were the first Africans to become prominent in political activity. Jabavu, a Mfengu, born in 1859, was educated at a Wesleyan mission and became a teacher and part-time journalist. In the early 1880s he became editor of *Isigidimi Sama Xhosa* (the Xhosa Express), the journal of Lovedale Mission, a Church of Scotland technical, teaching and theological training college with its own press and publishing house. At the same time he could also study and he was the first African to matriculate. Journalism aroused an interest in politics and he was appointed agent for Sir James Rose-Innes who, with J. W. Sauer and J. X. Merriman, was a leader of the Independents and had strong support from the Black vote. Jabavu then founded *Imvo Zabantsundu* (Native Opinion), the first Bantu political paper.

Because of the old special relationship with the Whites, forged in the course of the Frontier wars, the Mfengu of the Ciskei, though retaining a formal tribal structure, had advanced more rapidly in prosperity and familiarity with Western ways, a fortune sorely resented by the much-harried Xhosa and Thembu, at whose expense in part they had thrived. While the Afrikaner Bond was hostile to African political aspiration the Mfengu favoured their political opponents. But when, with shifting party allegiances in the 1890s men like Merriman and Sauer allied themselves with the Bond, Jabavu remained loyal to them and the Mfengu tended to follow with their support. Xhosa and Thembu came later to politics from a traditional structure ruptured by the long frontier warfare and after communal tenure had ceased to qualify the more conservative reserve-based among them. The others were inclined to be more independent, to attack the traditionalists, as they regarded Jabavu and his following, and to support the other side. Walter Rubusana, born in 1858, was one of these young men, educated at Lovedale and ordained into the London Missionary Society. Then, in America, he was awarded an honorary Ph.D. by McKinley University for *A History of South Africa from the Native Standpoint*. Back in the Cape, he was for a time agent among the Non-white electorate for Sprigg's Progressive Party.

John Dube, junior to the others, was born in 1871 in Natal, son of an American Zulu Mission pastor, his grandmother having been an early Zulu convert. He made his way to America, subsidized, it is said, by thirty gold sovereigns left by his father for his education. There he became first a teacher, then a minister. He fell deeply under the influence of the great Negro educationalists, Dr T. Booker Washington of Tuskegee and Dr John Hope of Atlanta. Inspired to found the much-needed Ohlange Institute at his birthplace Inanda, he raised funds in the States by lecturing and singing, for like so many Africans he had a fine voice. He went into journalism and established *Ilanga lase Natal* (The Sun of Natal – still appearing) in 1903. His trips to the States and association with American missionaries and his declaration of such views as that 'justice would only be done when the African ruled the country',[24] led the Natal Whites, extremely nervous of any sign of Black assertiveness, to label him an agitator, suspect him of sedition and have him carefully watched. When he campaigned for the sending of a deputation to the United Kingdom to get grievances redressed he was forced, in line with White official views that natives should learn to be more respectful, to make a public retraction. In fact, Dube's demands seem to a later age very modest: he cooperated with moderate Whites who thought political organization provided a safety-valve, but advised going slowly and would not hear of Black franchise nor any sort of equality with Whites. Dube's own political proposals included a separate roll for Africans voting for White candidates.

The Africans cut their political milk teeth on prayers, petitions and protests, on Exeter Hall methods under the tutelage of sympathetic White missionaries and liberal politicians who tended still on the whole to believe that the native should keep in his place, though this admittedly was several rungs higher than most of White South Africa was prepared to allow.

2. ANGLO–BOER WAR AND INTER–WHITE RACISM

The discoveries of the Witwatersrand were to revolutionize South African development and, as Sir Alfred (later Lord) Milner was soon to observe, 'Two wholly antagonistic systems, a medieval race oligarchy and a modern industrial state', could not exist permanently side by side.[25] The tragedy was that for the time being the boundaries of this conflict coincided with those of the other Boer-British, Republican-Imperial areas of tension to make the solution of each more intractable than they might singly have been. (The issues, too, were sometimes clouded or distorted, though not basically influenced, by the dust of the more fundamental Black–White contest staged in a separate arena.)

24. Shula Marks, *The Reluctant Rebellion*, p. 75.
25. *Cambridge History of the British Empire*, Vol. VIII, p. 613.

Rhodes now had political control over two of the places where his financial interests lay, but in the Transvaal where he was deeply involved in the gold industry he was impotent. He had hoped that its encircling by his settlement of Rhodesia and the commercial activity and development all around would bring the Transvaal into line. Time on the whole seemed on his side. The logic of his goal of a closer unity was unanswerable and he had strong backing of both English and Afrikaner moderates. He was powerful, but he was ill and he was impatient for success: his reputed last words, 'So little done, so much to do,' were totally in character. But Kruger remained uncooperative.

The Transvaal continued a frustrating stalling of railway development. When the goldfields were proclaimed in the 1880s the railway lines from the ports ended at Kimberley, Colesburg, Aliwal North and Ladysmith. All machinery and stores – everything for the industries and for the rapidly increasing populations – had to be transported from those rail-heads to the Reef by ox-wagon. The fastest method for passengers to travel from Kimberley to Johannesburg was by coach drawn by teams of ten or twelve horses or mules and reaching Pretoria in three days and three nights. Rhodes had pressed for customs unions with the republics and the continuation of the rail north and over the Zambezi, but when Kruger for a short time in 1886 had been ready for this the Colony, partly because of farming interests, had not. But some progress was bound to come. Between 1890 and 1892 the whole Reef, from Krugersdorp in the west to the coal mines of Benoni and Springs in the east, was linked. The Cape lines were extended to connect with Germiston and the Reef line in 1892. But the Transvaal had come to an agreement with Portugal and the rival line from Lourenço Marques was on its way and was completed in 1895, so there was no prospect that the Cape lines would be allowed to extend through the Northern Transvaal to Rhodesia; the line to Mafeking was completed in 1894 and reached Bulawayo by-passing the Transvaal, in 1897. In 1892 a line destined eventually for Salisbury was carried from Beira to Umtali on the Portuguese–Rhodesian border.

In the Transvaal itself the mining industry, despite ups and downs, in the long term prospered and with it other sections of the economy. Farmers were provided with a swelling market and land values soared. A rapidly rising revenue was derived from the punishing taxation which Kruger's mixture of mistrust and native shrewdness led him to impose on the mines. This caused great discontent in the mining community but had the beneficial side-effect of forcing the industry to the highest efficiency to keep going and was to remain the king-pin of taxation policy for long after.

There were three aggrieved parties opposing Kruger: Rhodes and the Rand magnates, the humbler members of the *uitlanders* (foreign residents of the Transvaal) and the British Government, all with different causes for discontent and various aims in view. Other aspects of the Kruger administration also penalized the mining industry, especially the deep level mines in which there was huge investment, and on whose development long-term prosperity depended. These included the Government's dynamite monopoly, difficulties in the recruiting and the high cost of labour, the high cost of coal and the high railway rates to Delagoa Bay. In 1894 the London share market collapsed, further holding up development, and no compensating move was made to lower taxes or control the cost of living.

Rhodes's position was more complex than that of his fellow magnates. He shared their general financial concern, but he had his own preoccupations and political responsibilities. Rail freight and customs were the main sources of revenue for the Cape and Natal. The Transvaal commerce, railway traffic and food market were essential for the continuing prosperity of the Cape and much of this was likely to be drained off by the Delagoa Bay line. To make them more competitive, rates to the Transvaal borders were slashed; Kruger responded, in breach of the Convention, by trebling rates in the Transvaal. The Cape then off-loaded its goods on to ox-wagons at the Vaal and trekked them up to the Reef. Kruger threatened to close the drifts (fords) through the river. Rhodes knew as much as any man the potential of the Rand gold mines and the political power their wealth could confer; and he was also becoming more aware than most that the Rhodesian mines would prove a poor second and would not redress the power balance for the Cape. He shared British fears of an independent South African Republic that might be the end of his federal dreams. The magnates began to argue that if Kruger were to be overthrown and replaced by an efficient administration all disabilities would fall away and profits both from mining and the share market would be enhanced.

By this time probably one-half of the population of the Transvaal were uitlanders, not only from Europe and America but from the Colonies and the Orange Free State, energetic go-ahead people, but men with whom the Transvaaler, an inveterate isolationist, had no intention of sharing his hard-won Republic and independence. The qualifications for Transvaal citizenship and the franchise were constantly made stiffer, even in contravention of the terms of the Convention and later promises of equal rights; at first any White owner of land with one year's residence qualified; then, in 1882, five years' residence was required; and by 1894 citizenship was virtually limited to White persons born in the republic and it was said to be more difficult for a foreigner to acquire Transvaal citizenship than for a Transkeian African the Cape franchise. The sort of grievances for which the uitlanders sought redress were bans on outdoor public meetings; refusal to allow the use of English language in the courts, in politics or in education; the high costs due to Government monopolies; abuses in the regulation of native labour; a judiciary dependent on the Executive; and juries composed entirely of burghers which were suspected of bias against foreigners. Probably their main complaints were against inefficient, unjust and corrupt government, but a greater public commotion could be raised by the fact that though they contributed five-sixths of taxation they had no voice in the disposal of revenue nor any share in law-making. The miners and middle classes associated with the new urban developments came from people with a tradition of political freedom and they resented their inferior status, although their preponderant numbers and wealth gave them, in fact, considerable influence even without the vote. A National Union was formed to demand the franchise. Kruger, foreseeing the Afrikaner swamped by foreigners with the loss of independence, refused redress. His fears were probably groundless: most of the uitlanders, and the Rand magnates too, would have been quite content with citizenship rights within the Republic, as are their descendants today. And exactly there lay

the British Government's fears: that by a slow and gradual enfranchisement of the uitlanders an anglicized republic – and eventually a Transvaal-dominated United States of South Africa –
would be created content to remain outside the Empire. Indeed
it was just this that both uitlanders and magnates wanted, for, dis-
liking the Cape liberals and their native policy, they were not
drawn to Rhodes's Cape-dominated federation. Nor did they find
British pro-African concern and interference more acceptable.
Discontent seethed. A petition signed by 38,000 uitlanders was
rejected, the petitioners denounced as rebels. There was wide talk
of a rising.

Rhodes and his colleagues, watching these events, decided to
turn the situation to advantage by providing the outside help that
would be necessary to ensure the success of a rebellion on the
Reef. He and his fellow magnate, Alfred Beit, financed the Johannesburg agitation and supplied the arms. They planned to
have troops ready on the Transvaal frontiers to go in at the request
of the leaders after the rising had begun. Then the Governor and
High Commissioner, Sir Hercules Robinson, would call a conference to settle outstanding issues; this would confirm the independence of the Transvaal, but only in return for redress of uitlander grievances, the long-sought customs and railway union and
a common Court of Appeal. These achieved, the final goal of
federation must follow. The plot was long discussed and was well
known – in broad outline if not in detail – to men in high places
in the Cape and in London. Sir Graham Bower, the Imperial
Secretary, and Robinson, an old confidant of Rhodes's, were well
aware of what was afoot and Joseph Chamberlain, the Colonial
Secretary, had given his approval, advised on the date and assisted
Rhodes to acquire land on the Transvaal border, though his
complicity was never publicly acknowledged. Rhodes's friend,
Jameson, was to carry through the armed intervention.

Rhodes laid his plans with extravagant care. Rhodesia was too
far from the Reef to provide a suitable springboard for Jameson
and his force, and the BSA Company had tried to obtain control
of the Bechuanaland Protectorate for this purpose. The chiefs
there, leader among them being the great Khama of the Ngwato,
had apprehensively watched trouble approaching from all quar-

ters. To the west of them, throughout the 1880s and 1890s the Germans pursued their subjugation of the South West African peoples. From the east and south they were aware of the slow mesmeric approach of the lumbering wagons of Voortrekker descendants; and beyond these, Rhodes with his expansive ambitions covetously eyed the road through their domains. The missionaries of the LMS, Moffat, his son-in-law Livingstone and others, had built up great influence in the region and Khama was a puritanical Christian. In his long life he had learned a good deal from trader, trekker and freebooter about Whites and their ways. He led a top-hatted deputation of fellow Chiefs, Sebele and Bathoen, to call on the colonial secretary in London and claim that British protection which was their treaty due. Aware of Rhodes's efforts, one of them asked: 'Shall we be given into the hands of a Company whose work is to hunt for gold and the wealth of the land only?' Another accused: 'The Company wants to impoverish us so that hunger may drive us to become the White man's servants who dig in his mines and gather his wealth.'[26] They succeeded in getting most of the country reserved to its inhabitants, but were persuaded to grant the Company a six-mile-wide land concession for a railway from the Colony to Rhodesia. Rhodes had his springboard. Jameson, appointed Resident Commissioner, moved in from Rhodesia with a force of 500 men (to guard the less than incipient railway) and in possession of an undated bogus appeal for help from the leaders of the uitlanders.

The scene was set but the cue was fluffed. In Johannesburg there were delays in smuggled arms deliveries, not yet nearly enough. The possibility of the rumoured revolt leading to a federation with the Transvaal and Rhodesia gave a great boost to Chartered shares and the Rand was prospering again; a number of concessions were even then being considered by the administration; revolutionary ardour cooled as the hour approached. There was no real leader for the malcontents and they were at loggerheads among themselves on minor issues which revealed the unreadiness. In particular they argued over whether they should rise under the *Vierkleur* (the flag of the Republic) or the Union Jack, on which Chamberlain insisted, having no intention of sanction-

26. Margery Perham, *The Times* (London, 5 July 1934).

ing an independent revolutionary republic which would absorb the whole of South Africa. Jameson, poised at Pitsani, was advised to delay, but reckoned a move from him would set alight the Rand. His message informing Rhodes of his intention to stick to the timetable was held up and Rhodes's reply ordering him not to move met cut telegraph wires at Mafeking. But Kruger by now was well aware of what must have become one of the widest known secrets in all conspiracy and waited with strong forces in the Transvaal. Jameson and his 500 men capitulated and were handed to the British for trial. The leaders of the uitlanders who put on a belated show of force were sentenced to heavy fines, which Rhodes paid for them.

Kruger handled the situation with some skill. He proclaimed that all complaints would be considered, made some minor concessions and forestalled a German move from Delagoa Bay by offering burghers to guard the German consulate in Pretoria. The Kaiser cabled him provocative congratulations which enraged the British and seemed to confirm suspicions that Kruger was using the wealth the Rand gave him to finance an anti-British conspiracy with the support of Germany.

The consequences of the abortive raid were fundamental and of long duration. For Rhodes it was political disaster. On hearing of the fiasco he cried, ' Jameson has ruined me and wrecked my life's work'.[27] He might have saved his political position by repudiating the raid but he remained loyal to Jameson. His fruitful partnership with Hofmeyr in the cause of White unity, however, was shattered and the influence he had acquired through the Bond among the Cape Afrikaners was gone. Rhodes became seen as the personification of ruthless financial imperialism. The complicity of British officials threw British policy into disrepute which was exacerbated when the Government inquiry, instead of unequivocally repudiating the Raid, exonerated most of those, including Chamberlain, believed to be implicated, and Chamberlain himself whitewashed Rhodes. Kruger was furious. The souring of relations between Dutch and English in the Cape was expressed politically in the crystallization of two parties out of the previously fluid political situation: the Afrikaner Bond, now led by Schreiner,

27. *Cambridge History of the British Empire*, Vol. VIII, p. 563.

Merriman and Sauer in Parliament and Hofmeyr outside it, and the Progressive Party, led by Rhodes and Sprigg and backed by the jingoist South African League, formed to oppose the Bond.

The parts of South Africa which had been by slow degrees moving inevitably in the direction of some sort of unity were thrown as far as ever apart. The Free State, drawing shyly into closer cooperation with the Cape, was frightened off and found new ties of sympathy and kinship with the Transvaal where Kruger's own position was immeasurably improved. He was re-elected President with greatly increased support. He at last achieved the agreement to cooperate from the Orange Free State which he had long worked for, and a defensive alliance. His administration was strengthened by an influx of disillusioned and able young Cape Afrikaners, J. C. Smuts, who cast off his British nationality, prominent among them.

Jan Christiaan Smuts was destined to dominate South African and imperial policies for half a century. Son of a prosperous farmer, he had grown up on the wide cornlands and pastures of the Western Cape, where, running wild and happy as a small boy, he developed a life-long and profound interest in the natural world. He is said to have been a delicate child, listless, untidy, shy and solitary. When he was twelve years old he was sent away to school and then he developed a passion for learning. Stuck in his books, he cut himself off from companions and became even more strange and alone. He continued unsociable, gauche and brilliant at Stellenbosch University. Even in the years he read law in England, he lived austerely, very short of cash, unattracted to lesser intellects, with little tact and few social graces; his contemporaries on the whole were not drawn to him; he formed few friendships, but those he did, mostly with liberals and Quakers, were warm and enduring. He worked on a study of Walt Whitman who deeply interested him and began to lay the foundations of the philosophical thought which he built upon in later life. He was extremely successful at Cambridge and the Middle Temple, but, homesick, he turned down a Cambridge appointment and returned to South Africa. There, while building up a legal practice he embarked on political journalism, joined the Bond and ranged himself fully behind Rhodes, for a time obsessed by his personality and his ideals. The Jameson Raid was a shattering disillusionment and he completely changed course, becoming implacably anti-British as had always been his talented young fellow-student at Stellenbosch, Isie Krige, whom he was soon to marry. They moved north to the Transvaal and Smuts, transferring his fealty from Britain and from Rhodes to the other contemporary giant, joined Kruger's administration just in time to back the old man in his current battle with the lawyers over the independence of the judiciary. At twenty-eight Smuts was State-Attorney of the Transvaal. Clever, tactless, arrogant and impatient, energetic, ruthless and immensely hard-working, he set about cleaning up the many abuses of the backward feudalistic state that Kruger kept. He made many enemies and few, but again devoted, friends, among them Kruger himself and Louis Botha. He was himself impregnably incorrupt and, too agile even at this early stage for his opponents to undermine, he acquired the tart nickname of *slim*, crafty or astute, Jannie, that remained with him through life.

The basic differences in the Transvaal had survived the Raid and proliferated. Kruger maintained that the enfranchisement of the uitlander would result in the loss of Boer political independence about which the Transvaal felt, if possible, more passionately than ever. The uitlanders still looked down on the Afrikaners and resented their dominance, protested against taxation without representation and demanded a part in making the laws they had to observe. Kruger responded by tightening press and immigration regulations and asserting the administration's authority over the courts. He confirmed suspicions that he threatened the British position in South Africa when he substantially strengthened the Transvaal's forces and fortifications and, by infringing the terms of the Convention in his negotiations with foreign powers, provoked the precautionary dispatch of a British squadron to Delagoa Bay to preserve the *status quo*. The Transvaal mines largely depended on foreign capital, foreign management and foreign labour; and Britain, taking up the cause of the uitlanders – of British origin and others – inevitably seemed to be fighting for the riches of the Rand and to be dominated by financial and commercial interests.

Sir Alfred Milner, sent out in 1897 as Governor and High Commissioner, was in the manner of his day a dedicated believer in the value to mankind of the British Empire; he was a confirmed imperialist, doctrinaire and rigid, but he was an efficient administrator with a flair for finance. He was a moderate man, initially anxious for compromise, and preferred semi-official and personal rather than strictly diplomatic approaches to tangled relationships. He was soon to develop a deep and fatal suspicion of the loyalty of Bond members, but to begin with some easing of tension followed on his arrival. Johannesburg was given municipal government and a promise of a right of appeal to the courts. But the Transvaal administration continued its negotiations for continental support. Britain, on her part, emerged from a bout of complex international horse-trading with a secret Anglo-German agreement which excluded the Transvaal from any future control of Delagoa Bay and of the railway to Pretoria, should Portugal at any time retire from that scene. Some hoped for a solution through the waxing influence in Transvaal policies of such Cape Afrikaners as F. W. Reitz and Smuts whose educational background at Cambridge and the Temple made them conversant with British thought and might enable them to appreciate the need for reform and the direction it should follow. Milner insisted: 'We don't want the Transvaal any more than the Orange Free State, but only fair treatment for British industry and capital in the Transvaal and an abstention . . . from intrigues with foreign powers.'[28]

But he and Chamberlain were getting tougher. The War Office in London took the tactically overdue precaution of alerting the Cape military authorities. New uitlander fury boiled up after the shooting of one of themselves by a policeman in self-defence. The South African League, prompted by Milner, intensified its demands for reform. The Queen was petitioned.

The anxious Cape ministers, particularly Hofmeyr and Merriman, working with President Steyn and his adviser, Abraham Fischer, strenuously attempted conciliation, urging Kruger to concessions. Kruger opened discussions with a group of magnates on some outstanding issues including the dynamite monopoly and a franchise proposal, but these 'capitalist' negotiations broke down, bringing Chamberlain and the magnates closer and deepen-

28. *Cambridge History of the British Empire*, Vol. VIII, p. 585.

ing distrust. Milner urged that the (White) 'helots' of the Rand should be freed from British nationality and enabled to work out their own salvation by becoming Transvaal burghers; he demanded of the Transvaal a constitution as liberal as that of the Free State. The Transvaal might well have been prepared at this stage to give way on all issues except that of independence, but Chamberlain and Milner now reasserted the contentious but moribund principle of suzerainty and paramountcy. This F. W. Reitz, now State Secretary, challenged, undermining the very basis of the Convention by declaring that the rights of the Republic derived from its own inherent nature as a sovereign state. The Bloemfontein Conference on the franchise issue, arranged by Schreiner, Hofmeyr and Steyn early in 1899 to bring Milner and Kruger together, soon reached deadlock. Many Afrikaners pressed Kruger to yield, but he was swayed by his own more intractable followers and had evidence that he had a good deal of uitlander political support. Smuts, too, deeply concerned about the impasse, was working unstintingly to arrive at an acceptable franchise. But whatever issues were wrangled over, whatever anxious mediation was undertaken, the fundamental issue was not affected. On the degree of independence of the Transvaal there could be no compromise. In Milner's view: 'The franchise and every other question have merged in one big issue: Is British paramountcy to be vindicated or let slide?'[29]

Each side now played for time. Kruger hoped British liberal opinion might modify Chamberlain's imperial attitude; Chamberlain hoped for a chance to build up the totally inadequate British forces in South Africa. Futile negotiations continued with acrimonious misunderstandings. Smuts, reacting to failure, produced a propaganda pamphlet of impassioned invective, *A Century of Wrong*, recapitulating all the festering Afrikaner grievances, to backfire on him in later years.

Britain, in an ultimatum which was in fact never delivered, demanded of the Transvaal the repeal of all franchise legislation since 1881, political equality for all European residents, recognition of British paramountcy, including the right to interfere in internal affairs where the welfare of South Africa was involved,

29. *Cambridge History of the British Empire*, Vol. VIII, p. 595.

and the dismantling of forts and reduction of armaments. The Republicans moved up to the frontiers, intending to strike first and, it was hoped, decisively while the British were still weak. Kruger's ultimatum, delivered on 11 October 1899, demanded the withdrawal of all British forces.

The war of 1899–1902 has been called the Boer War, the English War, the Anglo-Boer War, the South African War, and the Second War of Independence,[30] revealing the variety of attitudes towards it. Almost the whole world, and certainly Germany, France and Russia, was pro-Boer and anti-British, but while Britain remained supreme upon the seas they were powerless to intervene. The antagonists seemed hopelessly unevenly matched. In fact, the initial advantage in men, armament and experience available lay with the Republic and through poor leadership they failed to reap the benefit. Britain won the time necessary to bring her armies across the seas and to season them the hard way. Eventually it was might that told and by the end of 1900 both Republican capitals, Bloemfontein and Pretoria, had fallen, the Orange Free State and the Transvaal were under formal British occupation and Kruger, old and broken, was an exile in Holland. Lord Roberts, the British Commander-in-Chief, regarded the campaign at an end and went home.

The war had not ended but had changed its character. Some 60,000 burghers, abandoning all pretence of conventional warfare, took to the veld and waged a guerilla campaign against communications and detachments. Every farmhouse became a fortress and a supply depot. Life on commando was in the Afrikaner blood, tales of the Great Trek the substance of their being. A new generation of bold young men took over command, Botha, Smuts, and Hertzog leaders among them, and the encumbered British regulars were not their match. The war gave Smuts full scope for his administrative talent, relentless drive and courage. He devised the strategy that was followed and he led wild raids deep into British-held territory, and his life seemed charmed. The change to an active and open-air life of danger and dependence on his own resources well suited him and made him physically robust. Republican commandos invaded the Colony,

30. The First War of Independence was the Transvaal War of 1880.

putting the Cape leaders in a difficult position. Sympathize as many did with the Republican cause, the fact was that Transvaalers and Free Staters were enemy subjects but Colonists who joined them (and there were many) were rebels.

The small remote people's defiance of British imperial might stirred the sympathetic imagination not only of Britain's old continental enemies. The Liberal Party in England, with considerable public sympathy, opposed the war and favoured immediate self-government for the conquered republics when it should end. Botha, the most conciliatory of the Boer leaders, met Milner and Kitchener to talk terms. Milner, who did not want to be trammelled in his task of post-war reconstruction and unification, to which his mind was turning, favoured an unconditional surrender to be followed by the most generous treatment. He offered Crown Colony rule leading to self-government, £1m. to meet burgher claims against the Republican governments, a possible loan to farmers, rights for the Coloured people as in the Cape and, with total disregard for the rights of the African majority, no Native franchise before representative institutions were granted and then only on terms that would ensure 'the just predominance of the white race'.[31] But in the end Botha, either because he would not abandon the Cape rebels to whom Milner refused amnesty, or because he could not accept loss of independence and Milner was bent on unconditional surrender, broke off negotiations.

The war was resumed more venomously. The Boers were elusive and disciplined and, based on the farms, able to prolong hostilities indefinitely. Kitchener, the British Commander-in-Chief, decided, against the inclinations of Chamberlain and Milner but having little military alternative, to destroy the farms and follow a scorched earth policy. The families thus made homeless were gathered into the concentration camps (a term carrying in those days only its literal meaning) already being established for the care of refugees; many unprotected women and children came in from the countryside of their own accord. The camps became very large, very overcrowded and very insanitary. Many of them were on unsuitable sites; many inefficiently

31. *Cambridge History of the British Empire*, Vol. VIII, p. 606.

run; many inmates arrived in poor health. Epidemic diseases –
measles, enteric, pneumonia – swept through the camps, short as
they were of doctors and staff and medical supplies, and before
the war ended 26,000 women and children had died. That British
soldiers were also dying in thousands from the same diseases,
which carried off doctors and camp staff as well, was not at the
time taken into account in the wave of anger that rose against the
British authorities and gave wide circulation to fictions of poison-
ing by powdered glass. Exposure of the conditions in the camps
roused world-wide abhorrence and criticism. Policies were
violently criticized by English liberals: 'methods of barbarism'[32]
thundered Campbell-Bannerman in Opposition. Numbers of
individuals, the most famous being the pacifist Emily Hobhouse,
went out from England to South Africa to investigate and to try
to ameliorate conditions.

Paradoxically, the existence of the camps and the knowledge
that their dependants were being cared for by the enemy enabled
the Boer leaders to call their men to prolonged efforts; and the
women themselves urged the men on to further resistance.

Time can either sterilize or ferment the consequences of events.
The losses and suffering caused by the farm-burnings and the
concentration camps were indelibly impressed on the outlook of
the already embittered and mistrustful Afrikaners. A generation
of politicians who were Boer generals in the war has only just died
out, and many of their successors now in power were reared on the
accounts of what grandmothers and mothers themselves had
experienced. Before the war began Lord Salisbury had prophesied
that if the Boers submitted without fighting they would hate the
British for a generation; if they fought and were beaten they
would hate much longer. The imprint has not faded. Inevitably
the Boers succumbed. The leaders were given British terms and
time to consult their scattered followers. They had lost 4,000 men.
The war cost the British 22,000 men and £250m.

There was dissension among the Boer leaders. The Transvaalers were naturally unwilling to risk further destruction of
their newly founded industrial society by continued hostilities.
But the Free State leaders resented being drawn into a war which

32. H. A. L. Fisher, *A History of Europe*, p. 1076.

might have been avoided if their moderating advice had been heeded. As it was, with a completely rural economy they had little to lose but their independence and for this they would fight on. But it was clear they would have an inadequate following. The old Afrikaner tendency to fissure separated 'hands-uppers' from 'bitter-enders' in a long sour hostility. The Treaty of Vereeniging, beaten out by Generals Botha, de la Rey, Smuts, de Wet and Hertzog with Milner and Kitchener, was signed in Pretoria on 31 May 1902.

The terms were a modification of those earlier rejected by Botha. Responsible government was to be granted as soon as the country was settled. The equality of the Dutch language with English was recognized. £3m. was granted to assist the resettlement of the farmers and large loans were also made.

On the question of Native franchise, Smuts redrafted the original clause, changing 'the franchise will not be given until after the introduction of self-government', to 'the question of granting the franchise to Natives will not be decided until after the introduction of self-government'. Milner persuaded Chamberlain to give way, but later, tragically wise after the event, confessed to Selborne:

If I had known . . . the extravagance of the prejudice on the part of almost all Whites – not the Boer only – against any concession to any coloured man, however civilized, I should never have agreed to so absolute an exclusion not only of the raw native, but of the whole coloured population, from any rights of citizenship.[33]

So Britain began the formal abdication from the responsibility she had carried – mostly intermittently and half-heartedly, but acknowledged – during all the confused manoeuvrings of the seething century, for the interests of the Africans. In the moment of its military defeat the spirit of the Transvaal, of the Great Trek, triumphed.

3. UNION AND PATTERN OF POLITICAL ALIGNMENTS

Early in 1901, even before the war ended, Milner had given up as High Commissioner and Governor of the Cape and, as Governor of the new Colonies, had moved to the Transvaal to take up the

33. L. Thompson, *The Unification of South Africa*, p. 12.

formidable task of reconstruction and prepare the ground for eventual self-government. The whole country was now, for the first time, under the British flag; but it remained politically ambivalent, the ex-republics administered directly as Crown Colonies, the Cape and Natal retaining self-government and unwilling, except on their own terms, to join any closer union. Milner approved short-cut proposals of a temporary suspension of the obdurate Cape's constitution, thus bringing all the colonies under central control, but this was abortive. There was, in the British Government view, not sufficient local support for so controversial and unprecedented a regression and the premiers of Australia and Canada were loudly indignant. More laborious paths had to be followed.

Grants considerably in excess of the £3m. originally promised by Britain and a loan of £35m. (increased after Chamberlain's visit to the country) were made available for resettlement and the rehabilitation of the ex-republics. As Governor, Milner had these funds under his management in addition to control of the railways and their further expansion and of the joint South African Constabulary. Together these opened a large field for the introduction of unitary policies. He brought the old Republics' legislation into conformity with the Cape legal system and he established an Intercolonial Advisory Council. With the aid of an enthusiastic group of brilliant young Oxford men, the famous 'Milner Kindergarten',[34] who were to fill distinguished positions in later years, he built an administration of efficiency and integrity in the fine if narrow concept of public service of the time and laid a foundation able to carry the prosperity of a distant future.

The war-time affluence of the Cape and Natal had evaporated with the departure of the army. Their revenues still depended very largely on customs duties and railway freights, but Lourenço Marques was now once again serving the Transvaal and drawing off more than half the valuable Rand traffic. The question of

34. Among them had been Lord Brand, a distinguished financier; Lionel Curtis, an authority on imperial and international affairs; Geoffrey Dawson, editor of *The Times*, Sir Patrick Duncan, Governor-General of the Union of South Africa; Richard Feetham, Judge of the South African Appeal Court; and Philip Kerr, Lord Lothian, British Ambassador to Washington.

customs and railways was to remain a continual source of inter-colonial rivalry despite a series of agreements. Not only was the Transvaal reluctant to give up its old Delagoa Bay link, but the gold mines were heavily dependent on labour recruited in Portuguese East Africa. Milner made a *modus vivendi* with the Portuguese regulating tariffs, customs and truck allotments; this ensured the labour supply from the area but fomented further discontent in the Cape and Natal which the South African Customs Union of 1903 failed to erase.

Viewing the gold mines as an eventually wasting asset (a spectre to haunt successive administrations), Milner was anxious that they should be immediately exploited to the full to provide the financial and economic basis for the restoration and expansion of the country's economy. Accelerated gold production would boost agriculture and attract population and investment; this in turn would lead to further and diverse industrial development which would provide a viable economy as the gold production declined. He hoped a buoyant development would attract British settlers in a stream sufficient to reverse the racial and political preponderance of the Dutch and establish a British ascendancy, but in this he was to be disappointed.

Obstinately wedded to his belief that British was best, Milner gave a heavy English language bias to the educational system of the Colonies, and this stimulated a fierce and enduring nationalistic reaction. Even before the war was over schools had been started in the concentration camps to occupy the children and to teach them English; teachers, who were popular and got on well with the mothers, were brought from the United Kingdom and from Australia and Canada. At the war's end there were 42,000 children in school, more than ever before at one time.

The Treaty of Vereeniging provided that Dutch should be taught in the government schools where the parents required it, but the Educational Ordinance of 1903 limited instruction to five hours a week, which was considered wholly inadequate. Language teaching now became a bitter source of disagreement. Changes were made as soon as responsible government conferred powers to do so. In the Transvaal General Smuts enacted that home language must be the medium of instruction in the lower grades;

after standard III, the medium was to be English, with adequate provision for the teaching of Dutch unless the parents objected. General J. B. M. Hertzog, Minister of Education in the Orange Free State, on the other hand, introduced a system of compulsory bilingualism.

Hofmeyr, in the Cape, replied to increasing anglicization by reviving the *Taalbond*, formed in the 1880s to promote the use of High Dutch and raise educational standards. The identity of Cape Dutch culture was now well established, spreading and taking hold of the Afrikaners to the north as tides of sympathy and sense of kinship flowed over the boundaries. In the Transvaal the *Christelik-Nasionale Onderwys* (Christian National Education – CNE) movement was launched in 1904 with control of two hundred private schools in the ex-republics. These could not hold their own against the high quality of teaching in the State schools and most Afrikaner parents were too poor to subsidize them. The CNE movement had little immediate influence, but it disseminated and fostered the seeds of nationalist sentiment and solidarity which gave a heavy harvest in the years to follow.

The growing national consciousness, nurtured by the educational movement and perversely strengthened by British policy in the past years, began also to find coherent political expression. In the Cape Hofmeyr advocated conciliation, and he reorganized and broadened the Afrikaner Bond to increase its appeal to the English-speaking section of the Cape population. Its parliamentary wing, the South African Party, under Merriman defeated Jameson's British-angled Progressives. In the north, political interest revived with economic recovery.

Living near one another in Pretoria after the war, Botha and Smuts had become very close. The need of his complex personality for the reassurance of a leader now placed Smuts squarely behind the simpler, more straightforward Botha who was a born commander with an intuitive understanding of men which Smuts, of totally different calibre, knew himself to lack. They had both welcomed the signs of an early change to a liberal administration in Britain and meanwhile endured the reforming zeal of Milner and his English kindergarten, while their mood of reconciliation came under heavy fire from many of the defeated Dutch. None the less, they became the recognized political leaders of the Transvaal and together built up their political party, *Het Volk*, dedicated to reconciliation between Boer and Briton and working for full self-government. *Orangia Unie*, with similar ideals, was formed in the Orange Free State. 'Our constitution,' said Hertzog, its leader, 'must be broad and all-embracing, to receive into its fold all men of whatever nationality, who have come to South Africa to make this country their home.'[35] Both parties were deeply influenced by Merrimen and by Bond principles.

Once Campbell-Bannerman's Liberal Party had come to power, Smuts went to London to bargain for self-government. 'Do you want friends or enemies?' he asked. 'I pledge the friendship of my colleagues.' (But he could not pledge that of his countrymen in the years to come.) 'If you do believe in liberty, it is also their faith and religion.'[36] He was never to forget Campbell-Bannerman's 'magnanimity' in granting responsible government so soon to a conquered people, and came back with a new more tolerant view of the English. He was inspired again, as by Rhodes, to work with Botha for a united South Africa – this time within the Empire. 'There must be a blending of the White races ... There must be no more race feeling,'[37] he declared, though he was opposed by many in the country and by his still politically unreconciled wife. In the Transvaal election in 1906 Het Volk defeated the divided opposition (representing imperial, capitalist and White labour interests) and Botha became Premier. In the Free State the next year Abraham Fischer became Prime Minister with Hertzog his Minister of Justice. There were now four White self-governing states still with individual and diverse policies and the hoped-for unity seemed no nearer.

After land, cheap labour had always been the preoccupation of the Whites and the demand grew: diamond, gold, coal and copper mines competed with each other and with the farmer for workers. The later growth of secondary industry was to introduce yet another claimant. Botha had been so conscious of the pressures that in 1903 he said he 'would, if necessary, break up the reserves

35. Davenport, op. cit., p. 259.
36. Hancock, *Smuts*, Vol. I, p. 215.
37. H. L. Armstrong, *Grey Steel*, p. 129.

(including the Protectorates) in order to provide labour for the mines and farms'.[38] But this, in fact, was already an out-dated solution of the central economic issue. The reserves policy had been advocated by Philip as a necessary protection for the Blacks until they could hold their own in contemporary society, but this purpose had long since changed. The reserves had become, as Rhodes well understood, an essential reservoir in which labour surplus to White needs accumulated, to be released as required under such pressures as overcrowding and taxation.

In 1903 Milner appointed an intercolonial South African Native Affairs Commission. Its members were almost all of British origin, and it wove the main strands of the policies which had hitherto prevailed into a fabric out of which most politicians of the next sixty years were to fashion their native policies. The Commission recognized the basis of South African policy to be White domination and that this could only be maintained by racial and colour differentiation in political rights and the ending of African political equality. It accepted the principle of permanent territorial separation and proposed that land set aside for African occupation should be finally delimited, no more to be reserved thereafter. Other recommendations were calculated to improve the labour supply: the ending of African squatters on White farms except as labourers; charging of rents on Crown lands; enforcement of pass laws in urban areas; encouragement of elementary education; easing of travel for Africans – all designed to control and facilitate the flow of labour.

Meanwhile the mines, where the workers were cruelly underpaid, ill-housed, ill-fed and prey to disease, remained desperately short of labour, and on them the economic advancement of the whole country depended. Unsuccessful attempts to recruit were made as far afield as Uganda and even Nigeria. During Milner's administration an industrial colour bar was subtly introduced into the mines where there had been no rigid exclusion of qualified Blacks from skilled work. Under the Mines, Works and Machinery Ordinance of 1903 the more highly skilled jobs were defined in such a way as to reserve them for Whites. But this did not improve the labour situation.

38. *Cambridge History of the British Empire*, Vol. VIII, p. 491.

THE TRANSVAAL PIE

Sing a song of Gold Mines,
Labour running dry,
Lots of Chinese miners baked in a pie.

When the pie is opened
The Chinamen will crow –
This is not the sort of dish to set before King Joe!

A demand was made for the importation of indentured Chinese labour, in view of its success in other parts of the world. The Transvaal Afrikaners strongly opposed the introduction of another racial group, and suggested the break-up of the High Commission Territories and the reserves and the strict enforcement of the Squatters' Law to increase the labour flow. There was also a shout of protest from Britain, where trade unionists saw a precedent for similar alleviation of possible labour shortages in Britain, while liberals were naturally against such a solution. In South Africa Colonel F. H. P. Creswell, later leader of the South African Labour Party, pressed (for the first time since Dominique de Chavonnes had questioned the economic advantages of slavery) for the replacement of Black by White unskilled workers, arguing that cheap labour was not cheap in the long run. He opposed the dependence of Whites on the underpaid labour of another race, an attitude which soon degenerated into the 'White labour' policy and the colour bar. For a short time he proved his argument to be economically feasible on the mine he managed, but the White artisans, expected to undertake more work, walked out and other attempts were unsuccessful. Besides, the mine owners feared that White labour replacing Black would organize and get economic political power, so the attempt was dropped.

The Chamber of Mines policy, like Milner's, was to extract the maximum profit in the fastest time from the low-grade mines and they pressed for the Chinese labour. Milner came round to the Chinese solution because of his anxiety to get the mines producing and to create the conditions which he still hoped would attract White immigrants in numbers enough to free the South African economy from dependence on both reserve and imported African labour. The rural areas began to favour the scheme, expecting Africans to become more available for farm work. White miners were persuaded to accept it, once assured that the Chinese would undertake only unskilled work. They were to be employed on extremely harsh terms and at wages which undercut those of the Africans. The first Chinese came in 1904. By 1907 there were over 34,000 employed. The numbers of Whites and Africans in employment increased rapidly in consequence and the output of the mines soared. The hard core of opposition remained both in the Transvaal (where it contributed to the formation of Het Volk) and in Britain where it was partly responsible for the defeat of the Conservative government, whose Liberal successors soon ended the importation of Chinese and repatriated the workers.

Political and economic differences were aggravated by the existence in and on the edge of all the colonies of majorities of Black people towards whom each government held a different attitude. Little progress towards constructive Native policies had been made during the distracting years preceding and following the war; and indeed two more old-style wars against colonists remained to be waged by the African.

In German South West Africa, the arid territory with which Britain had been reluctant to become involved, a tragedy was shaping in a manner which presaged in vivid miniature the German destruction of another race in a later generation: even in the *personae* an augury, for Heinrich Goering, the father of Reichsmarschall Hermann Goering, was the first Imperial Commissioner.

The German subjugation of the peoples of South West Africa – perhaps because it is among the most fully documented and widely publicized – endures as one of the darker stains on the smutched record of 'civilization' in Africa. The German rule in Namaland and Damaraland had been one of absolute repression. At first the Germans had tried to persuade the quarrelling land-starved tribes to stay at peace. Then everything was done to provoke a rebellion in which they could be crushed. They were tricked of land by bogus concessions. Their cattle were stripped away, confiscated for trespass, taken in fines or stolen. Samuel Maharero, the Christian son of Kamaharero who had begged so long for British protection, was debased by rum. The people were ill-used, swindled in trade and degraded. Almost every means had been used to create dissension and fighting between the Nama and the Herero, who were then competing for grazing land, and between sections of each; and in these quarrels German forces occasionally and ruthlessly took a hand. Goering's successor, Major Theodor Leutwein, explained his policy:

I have used my best endeavours to make the native tribes serve our cause and play them off one against the other ... It was ... more serviceable to influence the natives to kill each other for us than to expect streams of blood and streams of money from the Old Fatherland for their suppression.[39]

Though German recognition of a paramount – Samuel Maharero, it so happened, and he for a time was their creature – went quite against Herero tradition, he was, in the circumstances, to become accepted by all and a symbol of their unity. Finally the leaders began to realize what was at stake. Samuel Maharero forswore drinking, made common cause with the Nama, declared war on Leutwein and ordered that no neutrals or their property and no women or children should be touched. General L. von Trotha, who took charge of operations, decreed the banishment of the Herero nation from German territory and made his extermination order that:

39. This account is mainly taken from *The Report on the Natives of South West Africa and their Treatment by Germany*, HMSO, 1918.

within the German frontier every Herero with or without a rifle, with or without cattle, will be shot. I will not take over any more women and children, but I will either drive them back to your people or have them fired on. These are my words to the nation of the Hereros. The great General of the Mighty Emperor.

The war began in January 1904 and by August their organized resistance was over. Samuel Maharero and a fragment of his people fled to find sanctuary in the scrub of Khama's country; more than the total number of the tribe alive today died in the desert; the remnant, a pauperized starving 15,000 of the 80,000 once 'cattle-rich' Herero were forced into service in South West Africa where Hosea Kutako, the son of a Herero Rhenish pastor, at the request of the chief renounced his own hopes of the ministry to shoulder and devotedly carry the responsibility of leadership which was to endure for the remaining sixty-five years of his life.[40] The Nama fought on until their valiant, octogenarian leader, Hendrick Witbooi, was killed on the battlefield. 'A born leader...' Leutwein admitted, 'a man who probably might have become world famous had it not been his fate to be born to a small African throne.'

Dr Paul Rohrbach of the German Colonial Office formulated a characteristic White attitude to colonization: an attitude that not every colonial held and which in British official circles was not so nakedly expressed, but which underlay much of individual and official attitude and action.

The decision [he wrote] to colonize in South West Africa could after all mean nothing else but this, namely that the native tribes would have to give up their lands on which they had previously grazed their stock in order that the white man might have the land for the grazing of his stock. When this attitude is questioned from the moral law standpoint, the answer is that for nations of the 'kulturposition' of the South African natives, the loss of their free national barbarism and their development into a class of labourers in service of and dependent on the white people is primarily a law of existence in the highest degree. It is applicable to a nation in the same way as to the individual, that the right of existence is justified primarily in the degree that such existence is useful for progress and general development. By no argument whatsoever can it be shown that the preservation of

40. He died in July 1970 at the age of 103.

any degree of national independence, national property and political organization by the races of South West Africa would be of a greater, or even of an equal, advantage for the development of mankind in general, or of the German people in particular, than the making of such races serviceable in the enjoyment of their former possessions by the white race.[41]

On the other side of the country, in Natal, where Africans out-numbered Whites by nine to one, there had been no progress in administration since Shepstone's time. With his going had gone contact and trust between authority and people which his personal approach had maintained. The Anglo-Boer War had helped to unsettle the Africans. There was rapid extension of land expropri-ation – to Crown lands in Natal and to White farms in Zululand. The people had not recovered from the rinderpest epidemic of 1898 in which six-sevenths of African cattle were lost, leaving them with nothing for lobola, for ploughing or for food. They were frequently accused of stock theft and penalties became stiffer. Land which they had previously occupied free they now had to pay for in often exorbitant rent or in work for the White owner. Labour laws were tightened and the people came increas-ingly into contact, and inevitably into conflict, with the law. The introduction in 1905, without consultation and on top of the existing 14s. hut tax on married men, of a £1 poll tax on all other males over the age of eighteen was a crushing imposition on the African who was liable also for pass fees, dog tax and customs duties and whose average income was about £5 a year. The re-action was strong and widespread and wild rumours of unrest spread through the nervous country; white animals were being slaughtered and European tools destroyed – common symbolic expressions of protest; there were some demonstrations and refusals to pay tax. Panic grew among the Whites. An attempt to enforce tax collection in the Richmond district early in 1906 brought police up against a recalcitrant group, members of a separatist Church. Two white policemen were killed, martial law imposed and twelve tribesmen sentenced to death. London, already made sensitive by parliamentary questions on an earlier

41. *Report on the Natives of South West Africa and their Treatment by Germany*, HMSO, 1918.

shooting of two Africans after court-martial, ordered a stay of execution. There was country-wide uproar; British and Dutch united in protest, the entire Natal Government resigned and Australia angrily demanded by what right the British interfered in the affairs of a self-governing territory. The British Government capitulated and the men were executed. African unrest persisted and attracted harsh reprisals for 'insulting' magistrates and 'defiant' behaviour. There were sweeps through African areas by police, hut burnings and stock confiscations.

About this time Chief Bambatha, recently deposed by the government for ignoring official instructions, returned from Zululand to his home in the Weenen district. He and his people were tenants on White farms where they paid high rent; he was deeply in debt and, unable to get any redress or reserve of his own, had a long record of fencing with the authorities. He now kidnapped his government-appointed replacement, fired on police sent to investigate, and took off into the mountains and dense virgin forests of Nkandla, where he began to build up an army of several thousands. He conducted a vigorous guerilla war against White troops, held out for a month and was at last defeated and killed with many of his followers. Trouble continued to flare up in places along the Natal–Zululand border and was eventually suppressed by the harshest – often lawless – official measures; huts were burned, cattle confiscated, possessions stolen. Nearly 4,000 Africans and 30 Whites were killed (though no White women or children were harmed.) Many families had lost their breadwinner killed or in prison; over 4,000 were sentenced to lashings and it was reported that several hundreds had their backs lashed to ribbons. Peace was restored in a reign of terror and this in Natal, then the most British colony of South Africa. A wealthy sugar planter – no negrophile extremist for sure – wrote of his area west of Stanger:

The native population is absolutely docile and quiet throughout the district, though how long they will remain so depends upon the government; if they are to be harried by irresponsible men who act as demi-Gods and who, armed with a kind of self-imposed authority, think it the correct thing to flog unoffending people . . . then the area will be drawn into the area of disaffected with the result that the [European] people [here] . . . will have to leave their homes, wives and

plantations to the mercy of an outraged foe ... Pray let us have a
level-headed man at the head of affairs [here] and put a stop to this
nonsense of having every man in uniform requiring every native to
conform to his idea of what salutation consists of. This ... people is
being driven into rebellion and it speaks volumes for [their] good
sense ... that they have not risen.[42]

The political leaders of the other Colonies were deeply disturbed by Natal's 'hysterical' handling of the situation. Merriman, in the Cape, wrote,

We have had a horrible business in Natal with the natives. I sup-
pose the whole truth will never be known, but enough comes out to
make us see how thin the crust is that keeps our Christian civilization
from the old-fashioned savagery – machine guns and modern rifles
against knobsticks and assegais are heavy odds and do not add much
to the glory of the superior races.[43]

The need for a unitary native policy was becoming ever clearer to
White leadership. Meanwhile White fear and mistrust of Blacks
grew enormously; and Blacks drew into a closer unity in their
hostility to Whites, seeking like Nongqause comfort in dreams
that dead leaders would return with armies of Black Americans to
rescue them; but none the less they were to turn increasingly to
Western education and political organization to equip themselves
to redress the balance. Unrest simmered all the time and the land
was filled with rumours, signs and portents.

Most of the rumours were associated with Dinuzulu's name and
the Bambatha rising had used the Royal emblem and war-cry to
gather support. All the mystique of his Zulu forbears, of the great
days of Shaka and Cetshwayo surrounded him; he had a loyal,
devoted and increasing following and the Whites hated and feared
this. It was widely believed by White and Black throughout Natal
that he was the fount of revolt. Many of the rebel leaders had been
to see him and he had sheltered Bambatha's wife and children, but
it is probable that he remained uncommitted and could not be
persuaded to give the lead to the still divided nation which would
have multiplied the size and seriousness of the rebellion. There

42. Marks, op. cit., p. 227.
43. ibid., p. 246.

had always been deep White suspicion and distrust of Dinuzulu as the son of Cetshwayo who might aspire to his father's power; he was generally snubbed, diminished and ignored. He was believed to be behind not only the rebellion but also a series of murders which gave pretext for his arrest at the end of 1907. He was put on trial on twenty-three charges of high treason. His defence was arranged by the Colensos and the Colonial Office (one official there commenting: 'In this country no judicial officer would commit Dinuzulu for trial on any of the evidence we have seen').[44] He was tried by a special court under a non-Natal judge and defended by W. P. Schreiner, one of the most brilliant advocates of the Cape. He was convicted on only three counts, and given a £100 fine and four years' imprisonment. One of the first acts of the Union Government would be to release him. He was never allowed back to Zululand, but banished with an allowance of £500 to a remote farm with one loyal companion, sixteen oxen, three cows, a cart and plough. There he died in 1913, aged forty-five.

The Indian 'problem', initially Natal's, was also seeping over intercolonial boundaries and demanding attention. In the first fifteen years after British annexation the Natal coasts promised to be a fruitful sugar production area if the planters could be supplied with sufficient labour. Despite the numbers of Africans in the territory they would not work on the plantations, Zulu men being traditionally debarred from agriculture. In 1860, following the success of the system in Mauritius, an agreement had been negotiated with the Indian Government for the importation of indentured labour. The workers, with a statutory proportion of women among them, were brought into Natal at the expense of the Colonial Government. They were indentured to planters for three years at wages of 10s. a month and food and lodging for the first year, rising to 12s. a month in the third year (a wage which helped to keep down the cost of African labour). They had to re-indenture with the same or a different employer for another year or, if they wished, two. At the end of five years the labourer was free to live and work as he could, and after a further five years he was entitled to a free passage home or to a grant of Crown lands to

44. Marks, op. cit., p. 271.

the value of the passage. After ten years most of them had broken their ties with their homeland and elected to remain. Most continued to work on the sugar and tea plantations, but others became independent. They formed a frugal and hardworking settler population of smallholders, fishermen, hawkers, servants and labourers. A more prosperous class of immigrant, merchants and traders, followed them, supplying their countrymen's needs and, increasingly, the needs of the Whites, particularly in remote country districts.

The Indian population of Natal took root and grew and by 1904 numbered 100,000 – rather more than the Europeans, and by 1911 a total of 142,000 indentured Indians had been brought to South Africa. They were entitled to the franchise on the same terms as the Whites, though few in fact got on the roll. None the less the White Natalians, mostly of British origin, feared the competition of the smallholder and resented the small but increasingly wealthy trader class; but the sugar-planters could not do without them. After Natal achieved responsible government in 1893 the policy of encouraging Indian settlement was reversed and pressure was put on them to persuade them to return to India (the Indian Government would not countenance forced repatriation). The law offering Crown Lands was repealed, an education test was applied to immigrants, the franchise was denied to all who, like Indians, came from states which had no representative institutions, trading licences were given only to those who kept their books in English, a tax of £3 a year (almost six months' wages for the average plantation worker) was levied on all 'coolies' who had completed their indenture and did not go back and was later extended to their children, and it was made a criminal offence for a White man to marry an Indian woman. This treatment so angered the Indian Government that it was later to refuse the Transvaal indentured labour for the gold mines.

The Orange Free State had long barred the entry of Indians and had no problem.

Indian traders, however, almost from the beginning had been flowing over the border into the Transvaal. The Republican Government, in order to restrict commercial competition but also in conformity with the old Transvaal principle of no equality between White and Black, had from 1885 denied Asians all civil and political rights including the right to own fixed property. They were liable to registration and to restrictions on areas of residence and trade. The British Government, as was required in terms of the Convention, had sanctioned the restrictions but prevented a total bar on Indian entry. Although the Treaty of Vereeniging imposed no such obligation, the British authorities, in submission to the strong public feeling against the Indians, did not repeal the restrictive legislation and only pre-war Indian residents were allowed to return to the Transvaal at the end of hostilities. In 1907, after long Indian opposition, General Smuts, Colonial Secretary in the new Transvaal Parliament, put through the Asiatic Law Amendment Act, the 'Black Act', requiring all Asians to pass an educational test and all over eight years old to register and to carry a certificate marked with their finger-prints, the purpose of the Act being to restrict Indian immigration.

This Act, one in a long series of routine, though often disputed legislation regulating race affairs, was to have a momentous influence on South Africa's later international relations. Its immediate effect was a confrontation between two young lawyers of an age, but of different colour, race origin, temperament, philosophy and understanding, whose common English legal education gave them only a common language to dispute in.

M. K. Gandhi had come from India to South Africa in 1893 to conduct a case for a South African–Indian client. On the rail journey from Durban to Johannesburg he first experienced the indignities to which his compatriots, whatever their financial, social or educational standing, were liable to be exposed. Later, walking by Paul Kruger's house in Pretoria, it is said, he was pushed off the pavement by a policeman. Back in Natal, he was asked to assist the Indian community in organizing a protest against a bill to disfranchise the Indians on grounds of colour. He postponed his return to India and helped to found the Natal Indian Congress. Gandhi's attitude to White differences at that time was equivocal. When the Anglo–Boer War broke out he believed justice to be with the Boers. But he argued, 'Our rulers profess to safeguard our rights because we are British subjects, and what little rights we still retain, we retain because we are British subjects.'[45] He organized the Indians into an ambulance corps which did invaluable work in the war and later again in the Bambatha rebellion, but did not modify the attitude of the Natal Colonist towards the Indians.

Gandhi was evolving his philosophy of *Satyagraha* (Force born of Truth and Love), influenced by ideas of Tolstoy and Ruskin, which he developed later in India into, at its most ideal, a way of life. In South Africa he worked out and put into practice a system of civil disobedience and passive resistance to laws felt to be unjust or to violate human dignity, the full penalties for the infringement being accepted.

In regard to the new Transvaal legislation, the Indians objected not so much to the finger-printing as to the compulsory carrying of a pass, to the discriminating element. At a mass meeting in Johannesburg the Indians took the Satyagraha oath that they would not apply for registration. Gandhi refused to register, was arrested with others and led handcuffed and in prison clothes through the streets of Johannesburg. He was to spend much of the next forty years in prison – mostly British prisons in India.

Smuts now had Gandhi brought to him and, (apparently at cross-purposes) as the latter understood, agreed to the repeal of the Act if the majority of Indians registered voluntarily. Gandhi, on this understanding, made his own registration as an example to many doubting followers. The Act was not repealed but those who had registered were offered exemption. Gandhi at the time believed Smuts to be guilty of a breach of faith, though he later questioned whether it had been deliberate.

Smuts then suggested bringing the question of registration under the Transvaal Immigrants' Restriction Bill, but this would have debarred the entry even of educated Indians and was clearly discriminatory and was rejected. At a public meeting in Johannesburg over 2,000 Indians cast their passes into cauldrons to burn. Then large numbers of others individually or in groups defied the immigration law and entered the Transvaal illegally, to be arrested, imprisoned, or deported to Natal to enter the Transvaal again, a form of passive resistance which was continued on and off for years.

45. Roux, op. cit., p. 104.

By this time Africans and Coloureds had begun to realize the worthlessness of British assurances that those who had supported them in the war would receive the same treatment as Whites when peace came. Existing discontent began to spread and coalesce. Protest was becoming more articulate, expressed by the growing number of African journalists, ministers, doctors and lawyers, many of whom had trained abroad and some of whom were active in White politics. Gandhi had formed the Natal Indian Congress in 1894. Then at the turn of the century the Natal Native Congress of Civilized and Christian Africans was established by such men as Martin Luthuli (a name to be made world famous by his nephew, Chief Albert Lutuli, a generation later), who had been secretary to Dinuzulu and was later elected Chief of the Groutville Mission Reserve, and Joshiah Gumede and John Dube. Their purpose was to create machinery for bringing grievances to the attention of the government; timidly and respectfully they checked that nothing in their aims and regulations was out of line with government policies. Their meetings were accompanied by prayers, hymns, anthems, loyal resolutions and votes of thanks, a gentle pattern that somehow survived the brutal shocks African politics sustained in succeeding generations. Two years later Dr Abdullah Abdurahman formed the African People's Organization (APO), not so much to defend the rights of the Coloureds in the Cape for they were not yet threatened, but to campaign for their extension to other parts. And in 1906, the year Gandhi launched his first passive resistance march, the Transvaal Natives' Congress protested to the House of Commons against the pass laws and claimed their right as British subjects to liberty, freedom and equality, a claim that was ignored.

During most of this time the young men of the 'kindergarten' had been thrashing out the ideas on various forms of closer union that were occupying the thoughts of many South Africans. The case they marshalled was issued by Lord Selborne who succeeded Milner in 1905. They argued that White South African disunity was due to lack of political independence in the Cape Colony during the first part of the nineteenth century rather than to differences of national or historical backgrounds and that only through closer union could South Africans gain control of their own affairs, solve the railway and customs problems, devise a unitary native policy and make effective use of the native and other labour resources, and give the necessary impetus to economic development. The damaging dissension over railway tariffs and customs gave urgency to these considerations. Members of the group undertook an intensive campaign throughout the country and gradually the idea of a single state – federal or unitary, opinion on this differed – began to take firmer root than ever before. Meantime, Merriman and Steyn, veteran leaders in the Cape and Free State, and Smuts in the Transvaal took up the idea; privately and exhaustively they clarified and aligned their own views, all anxious to prevent an imperial stranglehold over the eventual union.

At an inter-colonial conference called early in 1908 to prevent the break up of the Customs Union a decision was taken on a motion of General Smuts to call a National Convention to discuss the possibility of union.

The Convention met late in 1908 and painstakingly hammered out agreement on a draft constitution on which Smuts tirelessly worked. The four provinces (replacing the existing colonies) of the proposed Union were to be left a certain autonomy, each under an elected provincial council and government-appointed administrator and executive committee. They would retain powers of local taxation, and control of education (except higher education), health and public works (except railways). The Union Parliament would hold overriding powers. Provision was made for the eventual inclusion of Rhodesia and the High Commission Territories. To satisfy colonial rivalries, Pretoria was selected as administrative centre, Cape Town as seat of the legislature and Bloemfontein of the judiciary. The railways and harbours were put under a Board independent of party political interference. Dutch and English were both to be recognized as official languages with 'equal freedom, rights and privileges'.

Most sensitive issue of all was that of the franchise. The form of representation, the sort of qualifications required and the delimitation and size of constituencies all affected the relative strength of rural and urban areas and so of predominantly Afrikaner and British sections. Finally an adult White male suffrage was accepted with a 15 per cent margin each way as between rural and urban seats, according to size of constituency and density of population, although this could mean, in extreme cases, a difference of 30 per cent between the values of urban and rural votes. There was more general agreement on the question of non-white franchise. The great majority of delegates were adamantly opposed to its extension outside the Cape. It was agreed in the end that the Cape suffrage should be based on the adult White male population of the Province as it had been in the Transvaal and Free State. This meant that the Cape African and Coloured voters would no longer be assessed in the allotment of seats and that the Cape would lose seven seats from its parliamentary strength. More significant was the fact that, though these Cape voters would retain for the time being their vote – but for only White representatives – they would lose the right to sit in Parliament. Africans and Coloureds could still stand for provincial election in the Cape and Natal. The Africans of the other provinces were to be represented in a proposed Senate of forty elected members by four Whites nominated for their knowledge of 'the reasonable wants and wishes of the Coloured races in South Africa'.

Once Union had come under discussion a growing number of politically alert Africans followed the negotiations with mounting distrust. It became clear that Britain's great liberal gesture of generosity to the lately defeated Boers would by-pass the basic rights of the majority of the country's inhabitants. During the meetings of the Convention, which included no Blacks, the Africans constantly urged the White Cape representatives to remember their rights; but when the draft terms became known it was clear that the claims of Africans, Coloureds and their White allies were unheeded. Some of the Cape representatives fought stoutly against the curtailment of rights. Hofmeyr registered a protest on behalf of the Bond in Cape Town while Merriman, the Cape Premier, would not hear of the inclusion of a prayer to Almighty God in a Constitution that embodied a colour bar. 'Justice cannot be tampered with, with impunity,' J. W. Sauer told the Convention. 'Justice for the Natives would secure the position of the White man in South Africa for all time ... We cannot govern the Natives fairly unless they are represented by their own elected representatives.'[46] But he was soon himself to introduce into the new Union Parliament the crippling Natives' Land Act.

In the end the Cape delegates had to be satisfied and soon were, with the entrenchment of the existing Cape franchise together with the language clause in the Constitution, to be altered only by a two-thirds majority of both Houses – Assembly and Senate – sitting together.

Only W. P. Schreiner was not satisfied. A convert in middle life from strong opposition to Black emancipation to a powerful championship of full citizen rights, he did not take part in the Convention as he was engaged in Dinuzulu's defence. In the Cape Parliament he first forced a division on the colour bar in the draft constitution and then voted against the draft South Africa Act. He alone condemned the entrenchment clause, forecasting that if only a few Cape members betrayed their trust, Black parliamentary rights would entirely vanish. He accompanied their representatives, Jabavu, Rubusana, Dube and Abdurahman, to oppose the Bill at Westminster. 'We do not base our movement,' he claimed, 'upon the doctrine of the equality of all men, but upon the doctrine of the right to freedom of opportunity – equality of opportunity.'[47]

There was a morally strong but numerically small opposition within the Commons, led by Sir Charles Dilke and including Ramsay MacDonald who foresaw that White South Africans would never of their own accord adopt a more liberal policy. To leave the Africans unrepresented in the Union Parliament, said Keir Hardie, the Scottish miner, mystic and socialist, was like writing above the portals of the British Empire, 'Abandon hope all ye who enter here.'[48] Another Labour opponent, G. H. Roberts, saw half a century ahead with prophetic clarity that a constitutional colour bar would force Blacks to adopt unconstitutional methods and lead to a revival of Krugerism.

British officials sanguinely and persuasively argued that the Cape civilization franchise would never be lost and would be in

46. Legum, op. cit., pp. 9, 10.
47. Thompson, op. cit., p. 404.
48. Marquard, *The Story of South Africa*, p. 219.

the liberalizing flow of time extended to the rest of the country. The British Government was convinced that if African interests were insisted on at this stage it would disrupt Union, lose the goodwill of moderates like Botha and strengthen forces of Anglo- and negrophobia (though Hardie maintained that the strong economic and business forces standing to benefit from union would anyhow prevail). Fearing pressures from Australia and Canada, the Government stood firm on the doctrine of no inter- vention in the concerns of a self-governing colony: South African affairs must now be settled in South Africa itself. Britain had in any case let go its control of the fate of the Blacks in 1902 when the franchise question was shelved until the granting of self-govern- ment. The political colour bar in the Transvaal, Free State and then the Union Constitutions became inevitable. The opposition to the Constitution did, however, extract from His Majesty's Government the assurance that the Protectorates would not be transferred to the Union without consultation with their peoples and a debate in Westminster.

'The Union Constitution,' de Kiewiet, the historian, has com- mented, 'in native policy, at all events, represented the triumph of the frontier, and into the hands of the frontier was delivered the future of the native peoples. It was the conviction of the frontier that the foundations of society were race and the privileges of race.'[49]

Looking back some fifty years on the South Africa Act, Chief Albert Lutuli said: 'This was the big divide, the great Segregation Act . . . [It] set the pattern for subsequent discrimination and un- just laws that have tormented non-whites since, and have made them political and social outcasts in their fatherland.'[50]

49. de Kiewiet, *A History of South Africa*, p. 150.
50. Legum, op. cit., p. 10.

5 The Nation (1910–48)

1. RECONCILIATION, RECONSTRUCTION AND WAR

On 31 May 1910, South Africa was united: the provincial quarterings in her coat-of-arms, supported by springbok rampant, included the anchor of Good Hope and the Voortrekker wagon above the wry motto *Ex Unitate Vires* or in the *taal*, the mother-tongue, *Eendrag Maak Mag*. Union was accomplished in an Act of Parliament, defined in a Constitution, symbolized in a coat-of-arms, and soon to be possessed of a fine administrative parthenon in Pretoria on which Smuts spent the Transvaal's £1¼m. surplus. But its White population, which alone was concerned, remained divided in language, religion, attitudes to imperialism and racial orientation, each sector secretly hoping to come out on top. The great mass of the people was unconsulted and unconsidered.

Lord Gladstone, the new Governor-General, in a first gesture of reconciliation summoned General Botha, the modest, genial and well-loved Boer War hero, to form a Cabinet, rather than Merriman who was abler and more experienced but was not a member of the Bond and lacked strong political following. This established a precedent for Afrikaner political leadership. Botha clearly recognized the overriding need for internal peace to launch the new nation successfully; he acknowledged British liberality to his defeated people and, commanding the total devotion of his followers, he decided that, possessing independence, his country could work with Britain within the imperial framework. The grail he followed was that of reconciliation between the White races, the dissolving of past bitterness; *hereniging*, unity, was his watchword. He aimed at the establishment of the two languages, English and Hollands (or Afrikaans – there was as yet no agreement amongst Afrikaners about this), in complete equality; a non-party solution based on segregation to the native problem; and an end to Asian immigration. In his determination to build White unity he was backed to the full by Smuts. They did not see it as (in their lifetime) a lost cause. But the fissures papered over by Union would soon begin to reappear.

The political parties which contributed members to South Africa's first Parliament were Botha's South African Party (SAP), a synthesis of the old Afrikaner Bond, Het Volk and Orangia Unie, of the Cape, Transvaal and Free State respectively; the Unionist Party, led by Jameson (whose political career survived the backlash of the Raid) and composed mainly of British people and in general supporting Botha's policies; the Independents, mostly Natalians; and a small Labour Party led by Creswell. Botha's ministry included General Smuts, as Minister of Interior, Mines and Defence; J. W. Sauer, the old Cape liberal, for Railways and Harbours; General J. B. Hertzog and F. S. Malan for Justice and Education respectively; and Abraham Fischer, last premier of the Orange Free State, for Lands.

Early on, following the Imperial Defence Conference in 1911, the Defence Act laid the foundations for a national South African defence force to replace the imperial troops. The system, based on the Swiss citizen army and familiar to the descendants of Voortrekkers, required every White citizen between seventeen and sixty to serve in time of war in any part of Africa, inside or outside the Union. A small permanent force of mounted police and artillery was supplemented by a Defence Force of Citizens (UDF) between seventeen and twenty-five who underwent a four-year training and then joined rifle associations organized on commando lines. Blacks were debarred from military service except on conditions specially determined by Parliament.

Milner's 'anglicization' policy of a few years previously had not been forgotten and while the South Africa Act provided for and entrenched the equality of the two languages, the way in which this worked in practice was watched with critical concern. There was inevitably a shortage of experienced South African-born administrators to run the new Union and many Britons occupying high office were unilingual and disdainfully made no effort to acquire the other official language. Language, mother-tongue, in South Africa as elsewhere, has been a most potent nationalistic force. The spoken Afrikaans language for a century had formed one stable bond between quarrelling exiles in the wilderness and their countrymen left behind at the Cape. It readily became a rallying point, a symbol of identity, for the Afrikaner who felt his young language severely handicapped by the prevalence of the stronger, more flexible English. The language controversy crystallized out in the education policy. Almost immediately, following on Opposition criticism of Hertzog's compulsory bilingualism in the Free State, a Select Committee was appointed to inquire into language inequalities and compulsory provisions in the laws of the four provinces. It recommended that teachers should qualify in either language and that up to standard IV (twelve years) there should be mother-tongue instruction, but parents could claim the other language to be taught as a subject and gradually introduced as a second medium of instruction. Above standard IV the parents could choose one medium or both and if this choice were not exercised the child would be educated in the language in which he was more at home. Parliament accepted the recommendations, but Hertzog opposed them, convinced that the weaker Afrikaans culture would be at great disadvantage, particularly, if the two groups of children met and spent their days together.

Although acceptance of the British parliamentary system was implicit in the Constitution, few in the Cabinet, except the Cape members, had any experience of working it. The concept of collective Cabinet responsibility was quite foreign to most of them, used to the Republican non-party executive whose members not only held but had freely expressed their personal views, and they frequently and openly disagreed. In a speech at de Wildt in December 1912, Hertzog forcefully advanced his doctrine of nationalism and advocated two separate medium educational streams with fully bilingual teachers throughout the whole educational life. He attacked Botha's entire policy of conciliation as being premature, supported the imperial connection only in so far as it benefited South Africa and maintained that the Union should be ruled only by Afrikaners. By Afrikaner, it is claimed, he always meant to include those of British origin who put South Africa first, but this was never made clear and the English minority was jittery. Botha expected Hertzog to resign on the issue. When he did not, Botha himself resigned and, after being asked again by the governor-general, re-formed his ministry without Hertzog. Hertzog remained a member of the South African Party, openly and bitterly attacking Botha, until the end of 1913 when he was expelled. He then formed the Nationalist (National) Party, taking with him most of Botha's Free State supporters, Tielman Roos in the Transvaal and Dr D. F. Malan in the Cape.

Trade unionism had been slow developing in South Africa. White skilled labour was an aristocracy and for some time saw no need to seek strength and protection in cooperation. From the 1880s, however, experienced British organizers had been building up White craft and mining unions, although these received no recognition and there was no machinery for dealing with industrial disputes before 1913. Members of Parliament, mostly of rural origin, were unfamiliar with industrial problems and out of sympathy with the difficulties of urban workers. A strike in 1907 against the mining companies' early attempts to increase profits by raising production and lowering labour costs had failed because of the flood of impoverished rural Afrikaners ready to accept low wages. The South African Labour Party had grown out of the trade union movement in 1909 and had gradually built up strength; but it was deeply imbued with the White workers' sense of privilege and fully accepted traditional attitudes to Indian and African workers, though Coloureds (with a vote in Cape) were accepted as members. Skilled jobs were jealously guarded by White workers against any sort of infiltration by Blacks.

Once Union had been accomplished and the very limited franchise rights of the Non-whites entrenched in the South Africa Act, the brief spot-lighting from Westminster was switched off; in self-governing seclusion successive South African administrations settled down to deal with the 'native problem' in ways designed to protect White civilization and White privilege. The South African Act vested the control and administration of Native Affairs in the Governor-General-in-Council. The Native

Affairs Department (NAD) was created to exercise executive authority and was given wide powers of government by proclamation. Thus from the Union's very inception the administration of every aspect of the lives of what was then more than three-quarters of its population was reserved, separated from the ordinary processes of democratic government and kept in the hands of a bureaucracy over which the governed had no choice and no control. In the old days of extending physical frontiers and rural economy the African had been excluded from good land and water, had been driven from the land to labour; now that there was industrial expansion he was to be barred from good jobs and wages and the machinery was set up which was to preclude him from work except in its most restricted form and drive him back to the land where there would be no place for him.

Under White rule the old African life, for better or worse, was crumbling, in some places with great speed, in others too slowly to be noticed; tribalism had collided with the West, and past ways could never be restored in the ferment of a new age. By the time of Union, the broad outline of existence as it was to be for fifty years was roughed in and it was to change only in degree. The African people were distributed among White farms on what had often been their tribal lands, in the scattered reserves which might have been in tribal occupation for many generations, and in the squalid locations of the urban areas. The Voortrekkers had fanned out over seemingly unoccupied areas, engulfing earlier occupants, who were forced to settle in some sort of serfdom to the Whites in possession. 'My grandfather,' said a petty chief in the Transvaal, 'woke one morning at his own kraal and found a white man who said: "You are living on my farm and you must work for me." '[1]

Four main kinds of labour servitude developed on South African farms, the details of which varied from area to area and from farm to farm. By one arrangement the tenant worked for a regular monthly cash wage plus payment in kind, which might include rations – maize, skimmed milk, occasional meat – as well as land to cultivate, pasturage for a few cattle and sites on which to build huts for himself and his family. Under another system, the

1. E. Hellmann, ed., *Handbook on Race Relations in South Africa*, p. 196.

labour tenancy found mostly in the Transvaal and Natal, the tenant would contract himself, and his wife and children when required, to work without cash wage, generally for 90 or 180 days a year, either continuously or for two or more days a week. In exchange he got the right to live on the farm, to build his huts, graze his cattle and cultivate maize and vegetables. He or members of his family could work elsewhere for a cash wage for the days not contracted to the farmer. (It has been calculated, for instance, that in an area of the Eastern Province in 1957, the monthly wage of a family in cash and kind, to which women and children contributed, was just under £9.) The restrictions on movement and urban employment virtually bound the labourers to the farms, bonds often tightened by the debts incurred to the farmer. The system was enormously wasteful as, on a ninety-day basis, the farmer had to keep on his land four times the labour he needed at one time. Squatters, that is rent-paying rather than labour tenants, were of two kinds. One sort paid rent for the right to live and to keep their family on the farm while employed elsewhere. The other category of squatter was kept as a part of a labour pool, often on a subsidiary farm in an area malarial or otherwise unsuitable for Whites from where the owner would get labour for his other farms. Kafir farming, this was called, and there were areas where the Whites were all absentees. Finally, especially in the Orange Free State after the Anglo–Boer War, there was the share-cropping system under which the African tenant farmed the land for the absentee White owner and shared with him the profits.

The traditional attitude of a farmer to his labour was similar to that of a man to his slaves and in practice was remarkably medieval. It was a highly paternalistic relationship where the farmer reserved the right to punish his workers which sometimes meant merciless floggings, but more often was a less extreme chastisement and disciplining. There was a current impression that the 'native' appreciated a 'just master' and accepted beating when he saw the justice and deservedness of it. A justice in which complainant, prosecutor, judge, executioner were all in the same person seemed seldom to be queried. On the other hand, on many Afrikaner farms where White and Black families may have lived for generations, there was often considerable kindness, care of the sick members of labourers' families by the farmer's household and interest in their welfare which drew a reciprocal devotion. There was also an understanding – a *rapport* – between Black and White who had commonly grown up in the same rural background as playmates (till the White children went off to school and traditional race attitudes prevailed), which made the often more distantly correct behaviour of English-speaking people to their Black subordinates seem cold, unfriendly and indifferent. These working arrangements, especially in the early days when the farmer had no cash to pay labour and the African's greatest need was land, had obvious advantages to both. But the system was as wide open to abuse as in the days when the allegations of van der Kemp and Read had led to the Black Circuit.

In the interests of what was regarded as traditional separation, the cruelly limiting Natives Land Act of 1913, drafted by Hertzog before he left office, was inherited and introduced by an embarrassed Sauer, once champion of African rights. The Act (closely following the recommendations of Milner's Commission) prevented Africans from buying any more land in 'White' areas, scheduled the 10,500,000 morgen then occupied by them as Native Reserves (to which another 1,500,000 morgen was shortly added) and thus confined over two-thirds of the population to one-seventh of the country's land area. At the same time Whites were debarred from acquiring land, except with government permission, in the Reserves. (The Act, when challenged, was found by the Supreme Court to be not applicable in the Cape where it would have conflicted with franchise qualifications entrenched in the Constitution.) This allocation of land was so manifestly inadequate that the Beaumont Commission recommended the addition of another 8,000,000 morgen, but nothing was done about it for over twenty years. The Act also attempted to stop share-cropping altogether in the Orange Free State and to eliminate rent-paying squatters or reduce them to the status of labour tenants. Farmers were now able to evict 'surplus natives' who had often been settled on the land (possibly land which their people had occupied for generations) before the White owner acquired it. Movement of Africans began from European rural areas to Reserves already overcrowded and to the towns. Thousands of families were driven off the farms, especially in the OFS, to wander homeless and starving until they were either absorbed on other farms as labour tenants or drifted into the towns as labourers.

Legislation on land and labour ran side by side. The old Masters and Servants Acts of the four territories remained in force and made breach of an employment contract by employer or employee a criminal offence. (This was to be rescinded in 1974 due to Union objections in the US to imports produced with forced labour.) The Native Labour Regulation Act controlled the recruitment of labour, provided minimum standards of accommodation and compensation for injuries. It also made breach of contract by Africans a criminal offence. The Mines and Works Act of 1911 regulated the working and inspection of mines, works and machinery and gave the governor-general power to frame regulations for the issue of certificates of competency. Largely as a result of trade union pressure a regulation was made to the effect that these certificates could not be granted to 'Coloured persons' in the Transvaal and Free State. With the increase in the numbers of White skilled workers and the rising powers of their unions, their determination grew to preserve their highly paid and privileged status. It was an easy transition to extend to other spheres restrictions no longer imposed to safeguard life but to protect White employment. The Labour Party was to oppose any replacement of skilled Whites by Blacks with their maxim of equal pay for equal work, which automatically eliminated Blacks from competition as long as the colour bar prevented their attainment of skills.

A colourful and talented young Zulu, Pixley Ka I. Seme, graduate of Columbia and Oxford Universities and called to the Bar at the Middle Temple in London, came home at about this time. Appalled at the humiliations Africans were subjected to, he attacked the bickering among their leaders. 'We are one people – these divisions, these jealousies are the cause of all our woes.'[2] Cooperating with other prominent Africans he called a meeting, in January 1912 in Bloemfontein, of representatives of all sections of Africans and of the existing three Provincial Congresses, in order to form an organization uniting all the African peoples of

2. Mary Benson, *The Struggle for a Birthright*, p. 24.

South Africa, to demand equal rights and justice and to put forward the political demands of the people on all occasions. Proceedings opened with a prayer and the singing of 'Nkosi Sikelel'i Afrika' ('God bless Africa') which became the African anthem, sung at great gatherings as far north as the shores of Lake Tanganyika; a pattern was set for many years to come during which Christianity indelibly coloured African politics.

The founding of the South African Native National Congress which later became the African National Congress (ANC) thus anticipated by two years the formation of the Nationalist Party. Dube was made the first President, in recognition of the sufferings the people of Natal had recently undergone and of the urgent sense of their need for unity that had spread in the aftermath of the Bambatha rebellion. Seme became one of the Treasurers, and a number of Royal Chiefs, including the exiled Dinuzulu, were appointed Vice-Presidents. Political action now became more coordinated and intense. 'We recognized that we were trying to find one another,' said one participant, 'and we felt wonderfully optimistic. To us freedom was just round the corner.'[3] *Abantu-Batho* was founded by Seme (financially backed by the Swazi Queen Regent) as a national African newspaper, with articles in English and Bantu languages. Rifts appeared immediately, for Jabavu could not work with the others and he formed the South African Races Congress. He also continued his association with White politicians, even to the extent of supporting the Native Land Act, which had aroused a storm of protest among Africans and was roundly condemned by their few White friends. The ANC sent another deputation to make unavailing representations in London. Later that year African women in the Free State, with ANC support, staged the first African passive resistance demonstration against the extension to them of the pass laws, and went to prison in great numbers (at a time when White suffragettes were active in England). They were to keep up their opposition until, in 1920, the laws were withdrawn.

Meanwhile, Jabavu was under fire from a younger and more politically minded generation for his loyalty – subservience some called it – to his White political mentors, for, like them, his narrow

3. Mary Benson, *The Struggle for a Birthright*, p. 25.

political vision could not encompass any African democratic power. His uncooperativeness in the ANC and his support for the Land Act gravely undermined his thirty-year-old position as leader of African opinion. When the next year Rubusana (who had exercised a right that still remained and became the first and only African provincial councillor) stood for re-election in Thembuland, Jabavu stood against him and fatally split the Black vote to let in the White candidate; then he toppled from influence and prestige. He lived, however, to see the establishment of the Fort Hare Native College for which he had long worked and was to die in 1921.

The growing Indian population was at this stage about 150,000 strong. The South Africa Act gave responsibility for Indian Affairs to the central government which began negotiations with Gandhi, then beginning to place his passive resistance campaign in the wider context of the independence movement in India. Regardless of Gandhi's demands for equal treatment for all, the Immigration Act of 1913, replacing the Transvaal Black Act (but still frankly aimed at the Indians), enabled the authorities to debar entry to South Africa on social or economic grounds, introduced an education test and limited movement from province to province. It naturally aroused vehement opposition among the Indians. At about the same time a court ruling against the sole wife of a marriage under a polygamous code nullified many marriages and roused the Indian women to militancy. Gandhi demanded the relaxation of the immigration laws, recognition of the position of married women and the abolition of the £3 tax. He led another famous passive resistance march initially of women and children, but supported by Natal Indian coal miners and workers and White sympathizers, over the Natal–Transvaal border at Volksrust to be arrested and gaoled. There was worldwide protest and the Viceroy publicly attacked South African policy – a precedent in imperial relationships. Gandhi was released and Smuts appointed a Commission of Inquiry (on which no Indian sat). On the recommendation of the Commission he passed the Indian Relief Act of 1914, which abolished the £3 tax, and restored the legal status of Indian women. Satisfied, in talks with Smuts, that more regard would be given to Indian rights and

1 Cattle raid
2 *below:* Kafirs surprising bushmen by adapting their tactics and disguising themselves with buck heads

3 *above:* Zulu
blacksmiths at work

4 *above right:* A Boosh-
Wannah hut

5 *right:* Boors
returning from
hunting

6 Slave riding

7 *right:* The Rev.
Moffat preaching to
the Bechuana

8 *left:* Gold crushing
at Eerstelling

9 Lobengula
reviewing his army

10 Commandant
Cronje surrenders
to Lord Roberts

that the question of Indian status could be later reopened, Gandhi advised the Indians to accept the Act, and soon after at the outbreak of war he returned to India.

After the initial excitement the newly formed Nationalist Party had languished. Botha was adroit in the fiscal and economic paths he followed and managed to reassure the British – mainly urban, financial, mining and professional – sector as well as the rural Afrikaner farming community, that he was not advancing the one at the expense of the other. For a short time Unionists and SAP followers worked together amicably while the growing Labour Party increased its influence and recruited to its ranks many Afrikaners who, leaving the *platteland* and flocking to the industrial centres, were eager to join battle for workers' rights against the big business interests. White racial distinctions were becoming blurred and were for the moment subservient to more conventional and universal lines of fission.

In 1914 the South African Federation of Trades called for a general strike on the mines and railways over wide issues of the relationships between industry and labour, skilled and unskilled workers and White and Black in industry. There was always the haunting spectre that unrest might spread to Black workers. The government declared Martial Law. Smuts was totally out of sympathy with the workers. 'I cannot agree to any socialism,' he once said, brushing off an appeal from unemployed for an increase on the 3s. 6d. a day relief. As Minister of Defence he called out the UDF and took control himself. He hi-jacked and illegally deported nine leaders and secured the passage through Parliament of the Riotous Assemblies and Criminal Laws Amendment Acts, giving the government authoritarian powers over freedom of speech and other civil liberties and laying foundations on which a great structure of repression would later be built. At the time these repressive measures led to a great strengthening of Labour at the polls, as well as of the party's support for White supremacist policies. During the war years that were to follow, however, a succession of Acts would be passed regulating labour conditions and considerably improving the lot of the White worker. But in 1915 the Labour Party's left wing was to hive off to form the 'War on War' group (later to develop into the South African Communist Party) and to begin to teach the African workers techniques of labour organization.

The fragile beginnings of White racial integration were soon to be shattered by the outbreak of the Great War. Botha and Smuts believed that South Africa as a part of the Empire was automatically at war with Germany once hostilities began, and a parliamentary majority supported Botha's contention. But twelve years had not been time enough to obliterate the resentments and distrust of generations which had culminated in the Anglo–Boer war. Botha argued the generosity of the Campbell-Bannerman ministry in so soon restoring responsible government to the defeated republics and pointed to the aggressive policies of Germany. But many among his countrymen believed responsible government only their just due and considered British action against the republics had been as aggressive as any German act. Many, including some of the Boer leaders then in high office, saw the war as another episode in the old struggle for independence and expected Botha and Smuts to seize the opportunity to declare the Union a Republic. Others would have been content with South Africa in a neutral role.

Turkey was an ally of Germany; an enemy lay once again across the Mediterranean, severing the Suez route to India and Australia. Once again the way to the East round the Cape became essential to Britain and its defence of vital military and commercial importance. Botha was asked to eliminate the menace to the route from the German ports and powerful wireless station in South West Africa. His arrangements for immediate invasion were interrupted by the outbreak of serious rebellion.

General Christiaan Beyers, a distinguished Boer General who since that war had held important official posts, was now first Commandant-General of the newly formed UDF. He declared himself opposed to the war and, when the decision to invade South West Africa was taken and a force dispatched to occupy Luderitzbucht, he resigned his commission. He joined the aged and much-loved General de la Rey who, swayed by an Afrikaner prophet's apocalyptic vision of England's downfall and the revival of the republics, had only been turned from his intention to urge a large meeting to rebellion by the passionate persuasion of Botha, his old comrade-in-arms. The two, Beyers and de la Rey, set off by car from Pretoria, making for the Defence Force camp at Potchefstroom. Their actual purpose has never been discovered. Passing through a road block set for a dangerous criminal, the car failed to stop when challenged and a police bullet fired at the tyre ricocheted off the road, killing de la Rey. At the huge and emotional funeral Botha and Smuts walked amongst the hostile crowds, Botha saying he would himself assume the Commandant-Generalship and take only volunteers into South West Africa. Meanwhile Colonel S. G. (Manie) Maritz, stationed at Upington in charge of one of the columns to invade South West Africa, had long been in contact with the Germans who promised the independence of South Africa and permission to annex Delagoa Bay. He defected with the bulk of his force to the Germans. Botha declared martial law and the Cape Dutch Reformed Church issued a warning against treason. Hopefully using only Afrikaner troops so as not to further exacerbate English–Afrikaner feeling, Botha defeated Maritz who fled into South West. He marched against Beyers and defeated him. Then he turned against de Wet, the renowned guerilla leader, heavily defeated him and wept on the battlefield as he offered pardon to all who surrendered. De Wet was at last captured and Beyers, to the sorrow of Botha and Smuts, was drowned trying to escape across the flooded Vaal. The rebels received lenient treatment; they were disqualified from public office for ten years and the leaders were also imprisoned and fined. Only one, Major Jopie Fourie, who had never resigned his UDF commission, was executed for treason. The total number of rebels had been fewer than 12,000, over half of these coming from the Free State, but Botha well knew that many more in the country were opposed to his policies. Armed rebellion was ended, but old discontents were brought again to the surface to remain and find, for the duration of the war, bitter political expression. New martyrs joined those of Slachter's Nek and the concentration camps.

Botha resumed the interrupted task of the occupation of South West Africa. In one of the swiftest and most efficient campaigns of the whole war he conquered a country three-quarters the size of the Union, of difficult terrain, barren and short of food and short of water for an invading army. He defeated a well-equipped enemy whom he treated with his natural leniency.

With the South West African danger to Allied communication lines and to the Union itself removed, Botha went home to fight a general election. The rebellion, the country's participation in 'England's war' and the prevalent belief, encouraged by her widespread successes, in Germany's ultimate victory had, in rural areas particularly, much increased the strength of the Nationalist Party under Hertzog's leadership in the Orange Free State and Dr D. F. Malan's, a DRC predikant turned politician, in the Cape. Botha's SAP was returned as the largest single party, but in a minority in the Assembly and dependent on the support of the ultra-British pro-war Unionists. The Nationalists, implacably opposed to the war, now formed the opposition. Botha continued to hold a middle course, checking the Unionists who cried out for conscription and resisting the Nationalists' demands for peace overtures.

From their position entrenched in Tanganyika the Germans commanded and were developing the considerable potential wealth and strategic advantage of Central Africa and had inflicted severe reverses on British forces. General Smuts, with a South African contingent, was sent to East Africa to take charge of operations in a long, costly and inconclusive campaign bedevilled by malaria, tsetse fly and drenching rains. His bold, impetuous guerilla tactics succeeded in bottling up the brilliant and seasoned German General von Lettow Vorbeck and preventing him from getting to the east coast.

Once South Africa itself was no longer immediately threatened, an infantry brigade could be sent to Europe where it served with distinction – and to near extinction at Delville Wood in France. Though Whites composed the bulk of the South African armed forces, an armed Cape Coloured Corps also served overseas with courage and loyalty. Africans too joined up in thousands in the Native Labour Corps to dig trenches and perform other noncombatant work in many distant battlefields (for they were not allowed to carry arms). Six hundred of them went down in the English Channel on the *Mendi* in 1917. 'Be quiet and calm, my countrymen,' exhorted the African chaplain, the Reverend Wan-

chope Dyobha, 'what is happening now is exactly what you came
to do . . . you are going to die. Brothers, we are drilling the Death
Drill. I, a Zulu, say you are all my brothers – Swazis, Pondos,
Basutos – so let us die like brothers.' From the chaos, concluded
the account, a great stillness descended over the bewildered men.
In due course Non-whites came back in their thousands, their
patriotism unhonoured and unsung; the Native Corps was disbanded on its return to South Africa without medals or ribbons
or even records of their awards. But they came with new ideas
about the colour bar, pass and liquor laws and with memories of
the promises (false, they turned out to be) made by enterprising
recruiters.

As the war dragged on Lloyd George invited the Dominion
premiers to join the Imperial War Commission. Botha, concentrating his attention on internal problems and divisions, sent
Smuts instead to London and so set him on his long road in international statesmanship. Arriving in England early in 1917 in the
trough of the war, Smuts, the one-time enemy now in the role of
conquering hero of the East African campaign, was widely ac-
claimed. His clear objective intellect and detachment (when far
from issues touching on South Africa) were found valuable in
discussion and planning. Surrounded by admiration and respect,
without personal responsibility, constantly rubbing shoulders
with his intellectual equals, welcomed by a growing circle of
liberal and Quaker friends, Smuts flowered as never before,
became more easy-tempered, less constrained, more assured. The
British Cabinet entrusted him with many responsibilities: he
played decisive parts in reorganizing British air power and forming the RAF, in ensuring the flow of war supplies, and in steering
the conduct of the war. He settled a Welsh miners' strike which
threatened industry after getting the angry crowd's temperature
down as, at his request, they sang 'Land of my Fathers'. He
refused the Palestine command, sat in on the British War Cabinet
and rejected the offer of a seat in the Commons. The Boer general
opposed suggestions of imperial federation which would put
limits on colonial independence, but the disciple of Rhodes had
visions, dreamed dreams of ever-greater unities of nations: of a
'British Commonwealth of Nations' – free states held together

by common allegiance on terms of freedom and equality; of a
'League of Nations' to keep the peace and build a new world. But
the great Non-white populations of this new world with rights to
freedom and equality simply did not exist for this visionary, any
more than they did for any of the more circumscribed statesmen
of the time. In one mission he failed. He was sent to Hungary
ostensibly to mediate in a frontier dispute but also to persuade
Bela Kun, the Communist head of government, to use his influence to get Russian representation at Versailles – if possible Lenin
himself. Sickened and indignant at the lavish hospitality offered
visiting VIP missions in starving Europe, he confined his staff to
the train and to army rations. He was distant and aloof, presented
his frontier proposals, and with agreement almost in sight was
angered by Kun's request for amendments, broke off discussions
and hurried away, leaving the Hungarians hurt and bewildered.
No Bolshevists appeared at the Peace Conference.

Botha joined Smuts for the peace treaty discussions at Versailles
and urged on the Allies a course of moderation and generosity.
'Peace you must know,' he said in a truism amply borne out since,
'is perhaps a hundred times more difficult to make than war. It
takes the wisdom of the world to make peace.'[4] He opposed the
humiliating terms: 'My soul has felt the harrow, I know what it
means.' When he found his counsel unavailing, he scribbled on
his agenda paper, 'God's justice will be meted out to all peoples
under the new sun. We shall persist in the prayer that it will be
meted out in love and peace and Christian charity.'[5]

Smuts had not the same religious scruples. But he opposed the
treaty even more urgently because, he argued, it was full of injustice to the Germans, particularly in the harsh reparations, and
would lead to dangerous resentment in the future. But he would
not countenance suggestions that South West Africa should be
restored to them. With most of the Allied leaders he believed
Bolshevik expansion was Europe's greatest danger and that
Germany, her only bulwark, must have armed forces to oppose it.
There would not be, he contended, a stable Europe without a
stable Germany. Towards Russia, however, he urged impartiality,

4. Earl Buxton, *General Botha*, p. 162.
5. Alan Paton, *J. H. Hofmeyer*, p. 85.

friendly neutrality and benevolence, and the lifting of the blockade. After great vacillation he backed Botha and signed the treaty
in the end, because it seemed the best way to make sure of South
Africa's place in the new Commonwealth and in the League of
Nations and he would not risk the loss of the South West African
mandate, which the peace terms gave to the Union. Botha and
Smuts both considered the possession of South West Africa,
which Smuts had never intended to be included in the Mandates
System, to be of the utmost importance to South Africa's security;
but they were disappointed in their hopes of a deal with the
Portuguese which would give them Delagoa Bay as well.

The Mandates System of the League of Nations, in final form
largely the brain-child of Smuts (who saw it as an extension of the
Commonwealth ideal) but crystallized from ideas that had long
been in the air, was devised for the administration and development of German ex-colonies until they were ready for independence. 'The crudity of conquest,' commented the historian,
H. A. L. Fisher, 'was draped in the veil of morality.' But he
allowed that this was a clear advance in international ethics.[6]

The Mandates were classified A, B and C, according to geographical situation and degree of advancement of the territories.
Smuts had declared: 'The Mandatory State should look upon its
position as one of great trust and honour, not as an office of profit
or a position of private advantage for it or its nationals.' But he
did not consider this ideal applicable to the German colonial
empire, 'inhabited by barbarians, who not only cannot possibly
govern themselves but to whom it would be impracticable to
apply any idea of self-determination in the European sense'.[7]

The Peace Conference did not go along with him in this. South
Africa was given the territory as a C Mandate, 'a sacred trust of
civilization', and was charged to administer it as an 'integral part
of the Union', to 'promote to the utmost the material and moral
well-being and social progress of the inhabitants of the territory',
and to report annually to the Permanent Mandates Commission
of the League of Nations.[8] South Africa, though ruffled that the

6. H. A. L. Fisher, *A History of Europe*, p. 1174.
7. Ruth First, *South West Africa*, p. 95.
8. Article 2 of the Mandate.

territory was not made over to her outright, accepted that, once administered as an integral part, it would soon become so in fact.

Made bold by apparent international concern over the fate of subject peoples and by peace treaty promises of self-determination, the ANC sent a deputation to Versailles to plead for extended rights and to oppose the South West African Mandate (there they found ahead of them a group of Nationalists led by Hertzog seeking a republic). They got no hearing. In Britain Lloyd George said he 'could not interfere in the internal affairs' of South Africa and suggested 'they humbly submit the grievances of the Black man to the Union Government'.[9] One member, Sol Plaatje, did not return with the rest of the deputation. He attended a Pan-African Congress in Paris organized by the American Negro Leader, Dr W. E. B. Du Bois, to influence the Peace Conference, and widened political contacts with Black leaders from other parts of Africa and from America.

Soon after Botha and Smuts returned to South Africa in 1919 Botha died.

2. RACE, COLOUR AND ECONOMICS

Smuts, divested of twenty years of friendship, guidance and restraint, took up his lonely task of government, shouldering not only the premiership but taking control also of the portfolios of Defence and Native Affairs (although in nine years in Parliament he had never spoken one word on native affairs). In a moment of truth he admitted: 'I have neither tact nor patience.'[10] He could have done with both. In power he was seldom to have the reassurance of spontaneous trust and affection from his colleagues or from the people at large, and for this his own aloof nature and autocratic disinclination to brook divergent views were largely responsible. He was subjected to bitter attack by Hertzog who belittled his international schemes and activity and lost no opportunity to needle and jibe.

Smuts had returned to problems as numerous and adamant as any politician had to face. World post-war economic difficulties

9. Roux, *Time Longer than Rope*, p. 111.
10. H. C. Armstrong, *Grey Steel*, p. 243.

could not pass South Africa by, and in addition her own idiosyncratic economic, political, social and racial complexities were boiling up into dangerous areas of conflict: Boer versus Briton, workers versus bosses, Black workers versus White workers, for example. They were years of seething activity, group conflicts and growing in-fighting. In the end the most disciplined and narrowly single-visioned came out on top.

The war years had been a great economic stimulus to the country. Gold output was maintained, agriculture thrived and secondary industries protected by war conditions sprang up to fill the imports vacuum. But beneath the hectic war boom taxation, particularly on gold, and customs duties rose steeply and with them prices; profiteering was rife; rents were uncontrolled, the cost of living soared. In the succeeding post-war depression the price of gold fell and with it profits and wages. Rising costs began to threaten the life of the low-grade mines and the jobs of many of the miners. Mines closed, agriculture slumped; there was bankruptcy, unemployment and labour unrest. Whites and Blacks streamed in droves from under-populated rural depression and from penury in the overpeopled reserves. The two streams of impoverished peasants met in the towns in competition for work. The situation was aggravated by the inevitable and successful seeping, during the war years while many of the White miners were on active service, of Black workers into semi-skilled jobs – and at lower wages than Whites: a trend the mine owners, faced with rising costs and falling gold prices, naturally wished to maintain. The Whites, returning from the war to high living costs, little economic planning and a prospect of collapse in living standards, resented the undermining of their economic privilege and demanded a return to the *status quo*, the agreement on conventional colour discrimination which was being eroded.

The influx of Africans into the towns and into the young war-stimulated industries accelerated the growth of labour organization. In 1917 the International Socialist League (ISL), a breakaway from the (White) South African Labour Party, formed the Industrial Workers of Africa, hoping to make of it a Union of all unskilled workers. The post-war rise in the cost of living hit all races but, while Whites were well organized in unions and could strike with impunity and often with success, Non-White trade unionism was in its infancy and under the Masters and Servants Act strikes were for them illegal. However, the 'Bucket' strike took place on the Rand in 1918. The most menial of all workers, those who in the weird lantern-lit, mule-drawn wagon processions known as the 'Kimberley Mail' at dead of night emptied the city's earth closets, struck for an extra 6d. a day. One hundred and fifty-two of them were arrested, sentenced to six months' imprisonment and told they would be shot or beaten if they tried to escape.

In the meantime, the ANC had extended the women's pass law protest to men in the Transvaal. Huge crowds gathered and were urged to non-violence and all sticks and *sjamboks* (whips) were collected. The demonstrators handed in their passes and with incongruous and irrepressible African amiability, sang 'Rule Britannia' and cheered the king, the governor-general and President Wilson of the Fourteen Points. There were 700 arrests; White civilians took a hand and inevitably it ended in brutality.

Clements Kadalie, a clerk from Malawi, a man of great energy and organizing ability and a captivating orator, founded the Industrial and Commercial Workers' Union (ICU) in Cape Town in 1919, initially as a union of dock workers. With promises of higher wages and improved conditions he attracted thousands and the union soon became a general organization for Black workers and remained the dominant one in South Africa for the next ten years. Its power at its zenith has not been surpassed. It was even to draw a letter of good wishes and a subscription from Hertzog in 1921 when political parties were beginning to prepare for the next election. The ICU's first industrial action was at the end of 1919 when 2,000 dock workers went on strike, refusing to load foodstuffs. They demanded a wage increase of between 4s. and 8s. 6d. a day to offset steeply rising food costs and a reduction in food exports to make more food available locally at lower prices. Scabbing by White workers ended the strike, but the stevedores in the end got their pay rise.

Early the next year some 70,000 African miners in twenty-two mines came out on strike, putting 8,000 White miners out of work in the process. Conditions were such that, in 1921, 21,000 White miners' wages were nearly double the total for 180,000 Black miners. The Africans were asking for wages of between 5s. and 10s. a day and for more responsible work; they succeeded in getting an increase of 3d. on their basic wage of 2s. 2d. a day plus food and accommodation. S. P. Bunting of the ISL described their action as 'an instinctive mass revolt against their whole status and pig level of existence'.[11] The strike was well planned and disciplined but it was put down when the police isolated each compound and persuaded the miners there (not without violence) that all the others had gone back to work; its main effect was to alarm Whites at the possibilities of African power in future industrial action.

The Communist Party of South Africa was founded in 1921 as a mainly White party and, though it repudiated the colour bar, it was largely preoccupied with the White workers' interests and divided in attitude to Blacks. However, its members began to work more and more with the Blacks, starting the first night school for Africans where literacy was taught along with Marxist doctrine.

In circumstances of economic slump, labour disturbances and sectional strife Smuts fought two general elections, in 1920 and 1921, largely on White political issues and with little regard for the Black population of the country. Through the war years Botha had kept in power by cooperation with the Unionist Party (successor to the Progressive Party); post-war attempts to reunite the SAP and the Nationalists broke down over the issue of the British connection and in the 1920 election Nationalists and Labour made great gains at the expense of the other parties. The support of Unionists and Independents gave Smuts a small majority for the next eleven months, a period of economic stability in which the Unionists agreed to absorption by the SAP. Smuts gained a large overall majority in a second election the next year, but the Nationalists had made significant gains in rural areas.

Further ammunition for attack on Smuts soon fell to Nationalists and all his other vociferous opponents in the industrial centres. A thousand Black 'Israelites', men, women and children, members of a separatist messianic sect, were encamped on their

11. Roux, op. cit., p. 132.

leader's land and overflowing on to commonage at Bulhoek on the slopes of the 'Mountain of the Rising Sun' near Queenstown. Accustomed to gather there annually for their passover, they had on this last occasion remained three years expecting the coming of the Lord. They were unpopular because they had mostly consumed their substance over this time and their religion forbade their working for wages, so many were destitute and some had taken to pilfering. The leader had visions of two white goats fighting, watched by a black baboon which then broke both of them, symbols readily interpreted. Their neighbours, Black and White, wished they would go and government repeatedly ordered them to disperse. They were entirely non-cooperative, taking orders only from Jehovah and afraid of offending him; they were impervious to all official persuasion and blandishments. All of White South African and sections of African opinion thought it was time the law was enforced, but the manner of its enforcement was deeply shocking. Eight hundred armed police were sent with a machine-gun and were charged by 500 Israelites armed with assegais and sticks who believed 'the time of Jehovah has now arrived' and they themselves to be impervious to White bullets. They were mown down, 163 dead, and 129 wounded. Smuts, as Minister of Defence and of Native Affairs, was widely held responsible for the Bulhoek massacre.

The 'Rand Revolution' of 1922 rocked the whole country, its economic foundations resting as they did upon the gold mines. In an attempt to save mines threatened by rising costs, the Chamber of Mines reduced wages and threatened an alteration in the accepted *status quo* ratio of White and Black by proposing the replacement of 2,000 unskilled White miners by cheaper Black labour. This would have eroded not the colour bar regulations under the Mines and Works Act protecting 2,000 White artisans, which remained sacrosanct, but other customary discrimination preferring unskilled Whites to Blacks. White armed violence flamed the length of the Reef. The groups most prominently active in the strike included the unions crying that White civilization was in danger and clamouring for reforms; a small number of leading communists who in fact had little influence on the course of events though the revolt was widely believed to be communist inspired and controlled; and a virulently anti-Black section of Nationalist Afrikaners, organized on commando lines and demanding a republic. These last were responsible for sporadic attacks on Africans who were mostly objective onlookers, unaware of their central though passive role. (It was the haunting spectre that the Black masses might turn to an active part in this labour dispute that disseminated throughout White South Africa the atmosphere of peril.) These assorted allies were combined under the oddly un-Marxist war-cry of 'Workers of the world fight and unite for a White South Africa.' Nationalists and Labour combined in calling for the replacement of Smuts by a government calculated to promote the interests of the White race. Smuts, to begin with, worked tirelessly for a compromise but every proposal was wrecked by one or other side. Finally acknowledging an impasse, and although he agreed the Chamber was dictatorial and uncompromising and promised that Parliament would decide terms for a settlement, he ordered a back-to-work with police protection for scabs. The disorders spread and a general strike was called for.

By openly taking the part of the mine-owners, Smuts had disqualified himself as a negotiator. He was forced to rely on tough measures. He proclaimed martial law, dashed to Johannesburg, then almost totally in the hands of the revolutionaries, and with olympian disregard for personal danger, took command of operations. With 20,000 troops, machine-guns and aeroplanes he crushed the revolt with the loss of 230 lives (more than had been lost in the whole South West Africa campaign). Four men were hanged for murder, adding new names to the Nationalist roll of martyrs. The results of the strike were far-reaching. Many of the new Afrikaner recruits to industry were given their first introduction to union organization and strike action. Though the strike was mercilessly quelled, it had made clear that White workers would never in any circumstance tolerate replacement by Blacks at lower wages and the mining companies never again pushed this to an issue. The colour bar would be carried over from mining to industry and become entrenched; capital and labour would find themselves allied against Black advancement. But immediately, White wages were reduced and machinery installed to prune labour costs further. The next year the colour bar regulations under the Mines and Works Act were challenged by a mine management employing African artisans, found 'unreasonable and even capricious and arbitrary'[12] and declared to be *ultra vires* by the same judge as had framed them a decade earlier. Skilled occupations were now open to qualified Blacks but the strength of public opinion prevented much advantage being gained. In any event, the Apprenticeship Act of 1922 ensured that few would be qualified. By stipulating minimum educational qualifications (eight years' schooling) for apprentices, it prevented Africans, and to a lesser extent Coloured boys and Indians, from obtaining apprenticeships.

Hertzog and his party made great capital among the workers out of Smuts's intemperate and insensitive handling of the revolt and his other errors of judgement and of the African threat to White jobs. Among the Afrikaners flowing into the towns from the poverty of the platteland were many who had been utterly unable to hold their own. Some were failed farmers; others, in the prevailing land shortage, were landless and had for generations subsisted as *bijwoners*, or squatters, on the farms of others; many were the victims of excessive sub-divisions of land under the Roman-Dutch inheritance laws. Without education or skills, used to extreme poverty, half-starved and undermined by disease, they had no ability for skilled jobs but were disqualified by their white skins from unskilled labour, 'kafir work'. By 1923 there were perhaps 160,000 of these 'poor Whites', 10 per cent of the White population. They were political tinder: as Whites living on a social and economic level as low or lower by White standards than many Blacks, an issue with a high emotional charge; as Afrikaners, allegedly neglected or exploited victims of capitalism, they were a great accretion to the political strength the Nationalists had been steadily working to build up.

As far back as 1914 the *Helpmekaar* Fund had been formed by Afrikaner sympathizers to pay the fines of those involved in the rebellion, the surplus being devoted to cultural activities. In 1915 *Die Nasionale Pers* was launched to establish a chain of Afrikaans language newspapers; the Reverend Dr D. F. Malan left the pulpit to become editor of one, *Die Burger*, in Cape Town. In 1918

12. H. J. and R. E. Simons, *Class and Colour in South Africa*, p. 301.

two insurance companies, SANLAM and SANTAM, were founded to encourage Afrikaners to 'invest in their own institutions'. Gradually the importance of economic power as a preliminary to political power was realized. The *Volkskas*, a bank to mobilize Afrikaner finance, was formed with capital of £700 and high Afrikaner backing to become one of the country's largest financial institutions.

The rising status of the Afrikaners' language and culture was the outward and visible sign of a growing internal unity and cohesion which was not achieved without a deliberate effort of organization. The *Afrikaner Broederbond* (Afrikaner Brotherhood) took care of this and was to become the most powerful and least revealed organization in South Africa, permeating the whole of Afrikaner political, economic and social life. Formed in 1918 as *Jong Suid-Afrika* with fourteen members, it was an open, purely cultural movement attempting to end Afrikaner apathy after the divisions and confusion of the war years. In 1924 the movement went underground and became a Freemason type of private association of the élite, the names of its members and its proceedings being confidential though individuals might disclose their own membership. Its aims were to establish unity amongst all who wished to promote the welfare of Afrikaners, to arouse a national self-consciousness and to promote the interests of the Afrikaner nation. Membership was open to Afrikaans-speaking Protestants over twenty-five years old who were influential in their particular field. Ignorant of their nomination, nominees were watched for several years and their acceptance for membership was on an almost unanimous vote of the whole Bond. There was said to be a dramatic enrolment ritual with a 'body' transfixed with a dagger on a bier and embroidered in blood-red on the winding sheet was the word 'Verraad', treason. The chaplain intoned 'He who betrays the Bond will be destroyed by the Bond. The Bond never forgets. Its vengeance is swift and sure. Never yet has a traitor escaped his just punishment.'[13] At the head of the Broederbond was a Supreme Chief and two assessors, the Trinity. There was a nominated executive council, the Twelve Apostles. The organization was divided into cells of from five to ten members. A vigi-

13. Colin and Margaret Legum, *South Africa: Crisis for the West*, p. 24.

lance committee operated an intelligence system throughout the whole movement.

Statements made from time to time by leading members have suggested the ardent purpose of the Bond. In a circular issued in 1934 the Chairman, Professor J. C. van Rooy, of Potchefstroom University, and I. M. Lombaard, the General-Secretary were to say: '... the primary consideration is: whether Afrikanerdom will reach its ultimate destiny of domination (*baasskap*) in South Africa. Brothers, our solution of South Africa's ailments is not whether one party or another shall obtain the whip hand, but that the Afrikaner Broederbond shall govern South Africa.'[14] Twelve years later, Lombaard was to describe the Broederbond ideal which included full independence for South Africa, the ending of Afrikaners' inferiority in the State, their economic advancement, Christian-National education and the full separation of Blacks under White guardianship. 'The Afrikaner Broederbond is born from a deep conviction that the Afrikaner nation has been planted in this country by God's hand and is destined to remain here as a nation with its own character and its own mission.'[15] There was no point of contact between these aims and Smuts's pursuit of independence within a far-flung and loosely knit Commonwealth, nor even his flexible expediency in Non-European affairs.

In any case, the time when South Africa's Non-European affairs could be kept an internal matter into which Britian might sometimes poke an uninvited and unwelcome nose was past. Having failed to get the Mandate of South West Africa outright, Smuts still confidently assumed that South Africa would eventually be allowed to incorporate the territory; it was administered in accordance with that assumption, and in the meantime the obligatory reports on its administration were submitted annually to the Mandates Commission. The Commission took its task seriously, carefully scrutinized the reports and, as it was constantly critical of the situation they revealed, South Africa's race policies were brought to the attention of the world and kept there. Year after year members remarked on such aspects as the 'complete stagnation of social work, the inadequate provision for

14. Brian Bunting, *The Rise of the South African Reich*, p. 48.
15. ibid., p. 49.

health and education, the general practice of colour discrimination', and the apparent assumption by the White population that 'Natives exist chiefly for the purpose of labour for the Whites'.[16] But, though it could uncover and condemn abuses, neither the Mandates Commission nor the League itself had powers to enforce reform.

An Advisory Council had been set up in South West Africa on which the German section of the population, about 8,000 people, had equal representation with the 10,000 British subjects consisting mostly of officially sponsored settlers from South Africa. A certain number of Germans had been deported at the war's end, but those remaining were generously treated and retained full civil rights. The African population of the Mandated territory was represented by one White official versed in Native Affairs. In due course the Germans became British nationals and the German language was freely allowed. In the first election for the eighteen-member Legislative Assembly in 1926 the Germans, then numbering just under half the White population, were to win seven of the twelve elected seats. Native Affairs was one of the departments reserved to the South African Government.

More than half the Black population of the territory, the Ovambo and related tribes, lived in the remote north, beyond the German colonizing reach and came late into contact with the Whites. The rest, remnants of the Herero, Nama and Berg Damara peoples and Coloured Rehobothers, were gathered in scattered reserves or lived in mean urban locations, generally very overcrowded and very poor. South West Africa being administered as an integral part of the Union, the Union's Native policy was generally applied and the people were subjected to pass laws, segregation, employment colour bars and all the miseries these involved exaggerated by the poverty of the territory.

Clashes between tribes and authority gave rise to further criticism from the Mandates Commission before the people reluctantly accepted their new masters. When an Ovambo border tribe appealed for protection from the Portuguese authorities in Angola it was pacified by a joint South West Africa–Portuguese

16. Leo Marquard, *The People and Policies of South Africa* (3rd edn), p. 253.

expedition. More notorious was the disciplining in 1924 of the Bondelswarts, one of the Nama groups which had moved from the Cape across the Orange River at the end of the eighteenth century. They had fought fiercely against the Germans in the Herero War and suffered much at their hands, losing a large part of their tribal land. Some of their leaders, including the Kaptein, Jakobus Christiaan, and Abram Morris who later had worked as a scout with Botha, fled back over the Orange. Homesick now, and with the defeat of the Germans, they hoped to return. But under the Mandate life seemed to the Bondels but marginally better than under the Germans and their miserable poverty grew. Their land was not restored as they had hoped in return for their support of Botha against the Germans. Many worked on White farms and were often in dispute over wages; they resented a government-nominated headman and the administration's refusal to allow the return of Christiaan, Morris and the rest. Finally Christiaan returned without leave and soon was in trouble with the police. His arms were confiscated, but he was allowed to remain though not reinstated. Now a punishing tax was imposed on the hunting dogs, which together with guns were necessary for the defence of the herds against predators and essential to the people's livelihood; many could not pay it. Then Morris and his followers also returned and the people refused to hand them over to the police. The Administrator, who considered them insolent, made no attempt to sort out the differences; he led a strong punitive expedition in person and supported by two aeroplanes which dropped bombs on people and animals, and extracted submission after 115 of the Bondels, men, women and children, had been killed.

The Rehobothers or Basters, a Coloured people from the Cape and proud of their origin, had long been set on independence for their tiny republic which they believed Botha had promised. When the majority refused a government compromise offer to recognize their council as an official administrative organ, they were surrounded by police and 600 prisoners taken. Other tribes, too, were bitter when the lands (often the best) they had lost to the Germans were not returned but instead were made over to White settlers while they themselves were restricted to generally

barren and overcrowded reserves, and they resented being dicta-
torially removed from areas they had long occupied, apparently
to accommodate White settlers.

Blame for all the bloodshed and unrest was piled on to Smuts by
his opponents at home and, though from a quite different standpoint, by his critics abroad.

Smuts never wavered in his pursuit of Rhodes's vision of a
White African dominion stretching far to the north. The first step
was to try to absorb southern Rhodesia. After the Shona and
Ndebele inhabitants had been defeated, disarmed and brought
under administrative control the territory had settled down under
Company rule to a period of general prosperity, a good flow of
settlers and steady development. There was a White legislative
assembly which achieved an elected majority in 1907, increased in
1913. Provision had been made in the Act of Union for Rhodesia
to join as a fifth province, but by 1915 the country was beginning
to pay its own way and was looking for closer relations rather to
the north than south. When, in 1921, Smuts made his bid for
incorporation it was widely believed that he also calculated on the
Rhodesians' loyalty to Britain, once in the Union, to support him
and offset the strengthening Nationalist electoral position which
would follow the expected integration (despite the League of
Nations) of South West Africa: 'to break the back of Afrikanerdom', was how the Nationalists saw his purpose. But the tide was
already against him. The Rhodesians had been thoroughly
alarmed by South Africa's sectional disputes; they wanted no
truck with republicanism or bilingualism and they suspected the
Rand would draw off their labour supply. The Chartered Company gave up its rule and the Rhodesians rejected the Union,
voted for independence and became a self-governing colony in
1923, Native Affairs being one of the matters over which the
British Government retained nominal control.

In South Africa itself there was a growing need to bring some
order into Non-European affairs in the White areas. The first
official recognition of the existence of the rapidly increasing
African urban population living in deplorable poverty and squalor
was made in the Native Urban Areas Act of 1923. The Act, in a
real attempt to improve conditions, gave each local authority

responsibility for the housing of Africans in its area, but in segregated locations; and it also made them virtually perpetual migrants by providing for the control of their movements into the towns and for the removal of 'surplus' persons not employed in the area, quite regardless of the economic forces driving them from the reserves. This was in keeping with the hardening of White opinion as expressed by an Under-Secretary for Native Affairs, 'that the urban area is to be regarded as an enclave where the European interest is paramount and within which the native may only be permitted more or less on sufferance'.[17]

It was not the state of the African people alone that called for attention. At successive post-war imperial conferences Smuts was faced with demands for better treatment of the Indians. Indians at that time formed about 30 per cent of the population of Durban but only $2\frac{1}{2}$ per cent of the Union's total numbers. But the Whites of Natal complained bitterly of the increasing Indian population, living in overcrowded slums and causing property values to drop. Smuts was urged to take stronger action against them: segregation or repatriation. In 1924 the government introduced the Class Areas Bill which would have restricted residential and trading rights. But his move to meet White prejudice was politically sterile, for his ministry was not to live to enact the measure.

Throughout 1923 the economic doldrums had persisted. The national income was catastrophically low, though skilled wages for Whites were as high as anywhere. Unemployment was increasing; farmers battled against a three-year drought and falling prices; trade was sluggish. Rural Afrikaners poured into the towns and came increasingly into industry and into the organized labour movement in which they were beginning to preponderate; they brought their own traditional race attitudes to reinforce labour's economic nervousness. The government strengthened White labour with the Industrial Conciliation Act of 1924; by excluding African men (but not women) from the definition of 'employee', it excluded them from membership of recognized trade unions. African unions received no official recognition and under other legislation strikes by Africans could be criminal offences.

17. E. Hellmann, ed., *Handbook on Race Relations*, p. 233.

In the prevailing slump conditions Nationalist politicians could readily play on fears of Black competition in industry. His strengthening of White labour's position did nothing to help Smuts shake off the widespread hatred and distrust engendered by his handling of the workers in past disorders. Nationalist and Labour parties drew together making a political pact; they cold-stored their respective secessionist and socialist objectives, united in branding Smuts and the SAP as the creatures of imperialist and capitalist interests and conjured up the background shadow of the huge Black masses, ready to take jobs and spread ruin.

In the heated electioneering that followed the SAP lost the initiative. Hertzog in the Orange Free State and Creswell in Durban promised solutions to the Native and Indian problems. In 1924, five years after Botha's death, Smuts was defeated by the Nationalist-Labour Pact by a majority of twenty-seven and lost his own seat in Pretoria West. In the next years of semi-retirement on the Opposition benches, he was to devote much of his time to his widening scientific interests and to the formulation of his complex and controversial philosophy of Holism in which he attempted to 'devise some simpler scheme to explain the unitary character of time, space, matter and all physical appearances and activities', to which he later added mind and personality.[18]

General Hertzog became Prime Minister, pledged to an all-out economic defence of White South Africa alike against under-cutting by the work-starved Black influx and exploitation by profit-hungry financial powers. He found strong support in both White groups. The Pact Government took over just as a period of world economic recovery began and in which South Africa was to share. The pursuit of its aims of economic nationalism, protection of the farmers (on whose votes the Nationalists depended) and solution of the Native problem were consequently much facili-tated. Easy loans were given to farmers, the Cape fruit export was expanded and reorganized and taxation was reduced. The output of gold and diamonds rose and imports and exports increased. To replace the eventually waning gold industry, incentives were given to the development of secondary industries for which there were raw materials and primary products in abundance, and the neces-

18. W. K. Hancock, *Smuts: The Fields of Force*, Vol. II, p. 176.

sary fuel and labour. The difficulties faced were huge. Distances were enormous, transport was expensive and the internal market – for consumer goods consisting virtually only of Whites – was depressingly small. But industry, encouraged by protective tariffs and subsidies, made great strides. By 1928 the iron and steel public corporation I S C O R was founded at Pretoria, on the site of iron deposits and very near to coal.

The protection of the disturbingly large substratum of poor whites against the competition of the Blacks was a matter of early concern for the Government. Government and municipal departments were instructed and industry pressurized to replace Black workers with Whites paid at rates appropriate to 'civilized labour', that is above market rates, which would maintain 'the standard generally recognized as tolerable from the usual European standpoint' (as opposed to 'uncivilized' requiring 'the bare ... necessities of life as understood among barbarous and underdeveloped peoples');[19] and this labour was often incompetent and expensive. It was hoped that in the growth of secondary industry, too, would be found an employment solution to the poor white problem, though many doubted the suitability of the rural recruits for skilled work. The scheme did, however, a good deal to reduce the old White aversion to manual labour and 'kafir work'; in time skills were acquired and a sort of self-respect discovered.

Alongside the economic advance were other outward and visible signs of national independence. The various cultural societies that had sprung up were having effect. Afrikaans was now developing a literature and becoming stabilized; it had replaced Dutch in 1914 as mother-tongue in the primary schools and in 1925 it ousted High Dutch as an official language and bilingualism became compulsory in the public service. With the publication of the Afrikaans bible in 1934 the language would be secure. After bitter Afrikaner–English dispute, which for an anxious moment teetered on the brink of civil war but was resolved by private negotiations between Hertzog and Smuts, South Africa acquired her own flag of compromise design. The Nationalists never ceased chafing under what, despite self-government, they supposed to be their political subordination to Britain. Hertzog persistently mis-

19. W. K. Hancock, *Smuts: The Fields of Force*, Vol. II, p. 207.

interpreted Smuts in his attitude to the Commonwealth as wanting a super-authority, though Smuts had in fact drawn up proposals for a statement on the status of the dominions which had been rejected by an earlier imperial conference. Hertzog, at the 1926 Conference where his charm and ability made him popular, got agreement on similar proposals. The Balfour Declaration recognized the dominions as 'autonomous communities within the British Empire, equal in status and in no way subordinate to one another in external affairs, united by a common allegiance to the Crown'. Hertzog returned home with a mellowed attitude to the Commonwealth and said that with the Declaration the Nationalists had achieved all they had striven for and were absolutely content. In 1931 the Statute of Westminster would formally recognize the legislative independence of the dominions.

While phenomenal industrial and economic progress was made during this period the submerged Black three-quarters of the national iceberg remained a major political preoccupation. Under competent and sometimes flamboyant leadership the Africans were becoming articulate. Throughout the 1920s they were organizing politically and industrially and struggling to achieve recognition. Black men of ability and stature were formulating the people's complaints while socialists and an increasingly active Communist Party, associating itself with the interests of Black rather than White workers, brought experienced and dedicated Whites to the tasks of education and organization. With the aid of the Communist Party a branch of the Industrial and Commercial Workers' Union was opened in Johannesburg in 1925 and, notwithstanding the frequent arrests and harassment of the leaders, its influence spread rapidly. Clements Kadalie, the founder of the ICU, moved his headquarters to Johannesburg the next year and attracted the allegiance of leaders of other organizations, including a son of Jabavu (also an editor of *Imvo*) and A. W. G. Champion, secretary of the Native Mine Clerks' Association. Kadalie was brought under the pass laws and refused a permit to go to Natal. He defied the ban and addressed huge meetings in Durban. At its Seventh Annual Congress in Durban the ICU called for more direct strike action, condemned pass laws and proposed a passive resistance movement if protests to the Government had no result.

African workers began to make international contacts when Kadalie was sent to represent the 'real workers' of the country at the International Labour Conference at Geneva to which only White representatives had previously gone, and 'to submit the claims of the Non-European workers who are the victims of merciless exploitation, of both capitalism and the White labour policy of the Pact Government'.[20] Afterwards he made a triumphal tour of Europe and England. The English trade unions promised to send a prominent leader to South Africa to advise.

The ICU soon began to run into internal trouble. Internecine conflict amongst the ICU, the Communist Party and the White liberal associates and factions within all of these, distracted the leaders. The union lacked experienced organizers and bookkeepers able to cope with the rapid rise in membership; financial irregularities occurred, while a whole series of commercial enterprises the union had rashly undertaken proved beyond its capacity and seriously strained its resources. For all the great organizational activity and expenditure, members saw small improvement in their working conditions and little industrial or political improvement was taking place. Two main factions developed: the left wing, with communist support, pressed for action – strikes, pass burnings, refusal to pay taxes and so on; the right wing pursued a policy of *hamba kahle* – go carefully, confined to old and unrewarding methods of deputations and protests. The left wing opposed the dictatorial methods of the leaders and demanded a better control of finances. European liberals, on the other hand, alarmed by the communist influence, were backing the *hamba kahle* party and devitalizing the movement. Police spy infiltration also increased division and suspicion. Kadalie, at the 1926 National Council meeting, forced the expulsion of the communist members and caused further disruption. Pressing the need for unity among the workers and rejecting racial animosity, and itself badly needing support, the ICU appealed for recognition by the White trade unions and offered assistance in an action planned by the TUC, but both proposals were rejected on the grounds that the Whites would be swamped. The Natal Indians too, ignored Kadalie's offer of closer cooperation. Meanwhile

20. Roux, op. cit., p. 172.

Champion, now leader of the flourishing Natal branch which had strong Zulu support, began to rival Kadalie and a showdown resulted in secession of the former with the bulk of the Natal paying members. Some of the Orange Free State branches also broke away.

The Communists expelled from the ICU concentrated on organizing the African workers and particularly on the building up of non-racial trade unions on the Rand. Many young Blacks came into the unions or night-schools at this time and the fact that the Communists were (apart from some individual missionaries) virtually the only Whites who worked with Blacks without any sense of colour bar made an indelible impression, more lasting often than any doctrine taught, and fostered through all the later stresses on confidence persistent multi-racial attitudes.

Throughout the 1920s, while the ICU gained in size and influence as industrialization increased, the ANC and its political effectiveness declined. A visit in the early twenties of the West African educationist, Dr J. E. K. Aggrey, who advocated racial cooperation (with his simile of the white and black keys of the piano which must both be played to produce a tune), had resulted in the formation of the Joint Councils of Europeans and Natives to discuss and make representations to Parliament on African affairs. The mission-educated Africans, including many Congress leaders, and the White liberals worked easily together but they were out of touch with the mass of the people.

As their recommendations went unheeded and as the methods of better education, moderation and patience advocated by some as the means to win White sympathy made no impression, African militancy was blunted and the partnership was politically un-fruitful. The ANC itself was hobbled by the nature of its leader-ship. The President-General, the Reverend Zaccheus Mahabane, a kindly and conscientious Methodist, was quite unable to attract an urban following in competition with a passionate demagogue like Kadalie. Congress lacked funds, many branches were in total confusion and the more able leaders had to devote much of their time to earning a living and could not stump the country rallying a widely scattered membership. The Native Administration Act of 1927 gave the government total powers of appointment and dismissal of chiefs (scaring many of them and their followers into withdrawing from Congress), and of banning meetings in tribal areas, thus further weakening the organization.

Mahabane was succeeded in 1927 by Joshiah Gumede, a Roman Catholic, who along with James La Guma, the Coloured secretary of the Cape branch, attended a conference of the League against Imperialism in Brussels and discussed problems of the national struggle in South Africa with leaders from other colonial countries. From there he went on to tour the Soviet Union where he was tremendously impressed by the freedom and equality he saw extended to the Asian populations. 'I have been to the new Jerusalem,' he said. At these meetings self-determination for South Africa was accepted as the goal with a call for a democratic independent Native republic. This was to give rise to serious dissension in the Communist Party in South Africa over whether the elimination of class distinction or of race discrimination should have priority. Gumede returned home to devote himself to trying to build up Congress strength and finances and a greater cooperation between races and organizations. 'Others are persuaded to be Communists. The Bantu has been a Communist since time immemorial.'[21] But Congress too was now sharply divided into right and left wings, ruptured by clashing personalities, by frictions with the I C U and the Communist Party and undermined by government bannings and banishments. The financial crisis that followed the Wall Street crash had serious consequences for the low-paid African workers and the A N C was in no shape to take action on their behalf. The right ousted Gumede in 1930 and substituted a now elderly and domineering Seme.

Hertzog it was who, mindful of his mandate from the electorate and against this background of rising angry rebelliousness and increasing ability to express and exploit it, gave a resolute shape and direction to the hitherto drifting trend of segregation. Van Riebeeck's unsuccessful thorn-hedge had been the first expression of White–Black separation; but before long this had changed from a purely administrative expedient to become the stark principle of *wit baasskap* – White supremacy, though with changing times and fashions and permissiveness it wore many dresses,

21. Simons, op. cit., p. 402.

more or less revealing, more or less constraining: separation, trusteeship and separate development would be some of them.

The assumption that the Blacks were the labouring class had spread across the land with the trekkers. Only in the Cape, where Malay slaves had from early days formed an important section of the artisan community, had the colour line between skilled and unskilled worker largely been smudged and ignored. Some form of firm social, economic and physical barrier had generally been believed necessary to preserve the small White minority from the hostility and the competition of the huge Black majority. Philip had in a sense fathered the segregation policy when he supported the institutions for Khoikhoi living within White territory. But his purpose had been the temporary one of protection of the Blacks until they were advanced enough and equipped to compete with Whites in a Western community. 'The day will arrive', he had declared, 'when Hottentot Institutions will be unknown . . . and unnecessary when the magical power of caste will be broken and all classes of the inhabitants blended into one community.'[22] Shepstone, too, in introducing his reserve policy in Natal, had acknowledged that 'humanity and especially the injunctions of our religion . . . compels us to recognize in the Natives the capability of being elevated to perfect equality, social and political with the White man'.[23]

However, the conflict of interests, the demand for land and labour, the growing complexity of White economic progress, the intolerable pressures on the rural African and the inherent attitudes of the Boer republics, and of Natal, transformed the purpose of segregation from the temporary sheltering of Blacks to the permanent protection of White interests. This interpretation was built into the Union in the South Africa Act, and all governments thereafter were agreed on it. The difference between British and Afrikaner-backed administrations was of degree and method. The mainly rural Afrikaners with long memories of frontier terrors and wars and with a traditional rigid race attitude stiffened by religious sanctions, were inflexibly doctrinaire: total separation, once labour requirements were assured. The English-speaking

22. Roskam, *Apartheid and Discrimination*, p. 89.
23. ibid., p. 90.

section was more pliable, empirical and unpredictable; it embraced many shades of attitude and lacked the Afrikaner's unanimity. In general the English were townsfolk, occupied with mining, industry and commerce, and they, too, demanded cheap labour. Slowly, as the manufacturing and commercial side of the economy expanded a dawning realization grew of the economic advantages of a stable, well-trained labour force to replace the wasteful inefficiency of the migratory system in a twentieth-century economy; but this was to come too late to be implemented as a contrary official policy hardened. The economic dissidents, along with a handful of heretical intellectuals and politicians crying in the wilderness, were too few to liberalize policies but enough to cause alarm and brace reactionary opinion.

All major White groups, though differing perhaps in emphasis, fully believed in race separation. The Local Government Commission, headed by Colonel C. F. Stallard of Natal, epitome of the diehard British imperialist faction, reported in 1922 that the urban areas were 'essentially the White man's creation'; the African would only be allowed in 'when he is willing to enter and to minister to the needs of the White man and should depart therefrom when he ceases so to minister'.[24] Smuts himself, Afrikaner by birth and environment, British by education and assimilation, was torn between his role of South African political leader and his aspiration to world statesmanship, making wildly contradictory statements in different circumstances. In London in 1917 he expounded the essence of what would later become the orthodox South African doctrine on race relations.

We have gained a great deal of experience [he said] ... political ideas which apply to our white civilization do not apply to the administration of our Native Affairs ... so a practice has grown up of creating parallel institutions ... Instead of mixing up black and white in the old haphazard way ... we are trying now to lay down a policy of keeping them apart as much as possible ... which it may take a hundred years to work out ... This is the South Africa you will have, large areas cultivated by blacks and governed by blacks where they will look after themselves in all their forms of living and development ... The Blacks will of course be free to go and work in the white areas,

24. Alex Hepple, *South Africa*, p. 187 and Roskam, op. cit., p. 97.

but as far as possible the administration of white and black areas will be separated and such that each community will be satisfied and develop according to its own proper lines.[25]

At the 1923 Imperial Conference (before his defeat by the Pact) and in 1929 in his Rhodes lectures at Oxford he gave full support to segregation as it was then understood. But when he opposed Hertzog in Parliament on the Mines and Works Amendment Bill in 1926, he criticized the introduction of a statutory colour bar as being 'sheer repression . . . I think we are building the future of South Africa on quicksands if we go in for this policy'.[26]

Hertzog, back in 1911, had advocated territorial segregation as the only permanent solution to racial problems, pointing out that without early implementation 'the conditions necessary for its realization will . . . vanish'. The Labour Party had come to a similar conclusion: 'European Civilization [and] the permanent maintenance of the White community in a position of political and economic supremacy' could only be preserved by segregation which would reduce race contacts.[27]

Once Nationalists and Labour with closely similar ideas on race matters were in political alliance, Hertzog was in a position to present and begin to implement an overall policy of segregation for the preservation of White South Africa. Almost immediately he prepared the Areas Reservation, Immigration and Registration Bill of 1925 (a more drastic version of Smuts's earlier one) which would have subjected Indians to compulsory segregation. The Bill did not go through. It caused great outcry in South Africa and abroad. An appeal by South African Indians to the Government of India led to the Round Table Conference between representatives of the two governments and the Cape Town Agreement of 1927. In terms of the agreement the segregation clauses would be dropped, repatriation would be encouraged by both governments, while the living standards of those who remained were to be improved; an Agent-General (later High Commissioner) for India was appointed. White antagonism continued, acerbated by the fact that wealthy Indians, with only limited investment opportu-

25. Hancock, op. cit., p. 113.
26. Roskam, op. cit., p. 93.
27. ibid., p. 92.

nities, were buying properties in White residential areas in Durban. The Mines and Works Amendment Act of 1926 – the Colour Bar Act – closed the loopholes in the original Act of 1911 by specifically excluding Africans and Asians from obtaining certificates of competency; it gave wide satisfaction to the White workers, but was opposed in Parliament by Smuts who thought the statutory enactment of colour bar disabilities was not the wisest way of entrenching White civilization.

Hertzog then laid before the House a clutch of four bills which made up the core of his segregation policy. 'Disproportion in numbers, differences in national character, development and civilization with consequent difference in interest and need demand that . . . each race should be treated as a separate unit . . . and possessing separate dominions.'[28] The Representation of Natives in Parliament Bill would take the Cape Africans off the Common roll on which they had been since 1853 and give them instead communal rights to vote through chiefs and headmen for Europeans with limited parliamentary rights. The complementary and compensatory Native Council Bill would set up as a substitute the Native Representative Council, part nominated, part elected, with very restricted legislative powers affecting Natives only. The third, the Natives Land Act (Amendment) Bill provided for the acquisition of more land as pledged in 1913. Fourthly, the Coloured Persons Rights Bill confirmed the franchise rights of the Cape Coloureds and extended a qualified franchise to Coloureds elsewhere, leaving open the possibility of full franchise seven years later. In effect this bill acknowledged the traditional acceptance of the Coloured people as socially subsidiary but otherwise equal and allied to the Whites and not on a par with the other non-white people, a view which Hertzog strongly held. These bills were submitted to a Select Committee and in 1929 the first and fourth bills both failed to get the constitutionally required two-thirds majority of both Houses in joint session.

Meanwhile the Native Administration Act of 1927, passed to the accompaniment of mounting political activity among the African workers, authorized the governor-general to govern all

28. Roskam, op. cit., p. 95.

African areas by proclamation, gave sweeping powers of banning and punishment and of control of meetings and made it an offence to do anything likely to promote hostility between the races (the 'hostility' clause). Champion was banished from Natal for three years.

The organizer the British TUC had promised Kadalie, William Ballinger, arrived and set about clearing up the financial confusion of the ICU. The weight of White anti-ICU feeling fell on him and, in his conciliatory speeches to White audiences, he tended to make derogatory statements about the union leaders which were deeply resented by Kadalie who, contrariwise, now moved sharply towards the left. He pulled out of the union and set up the splinter Independent ICU in East London where his last important action was to bring out 90 per cent of the railways' and harbours' labour force for a wage increase from 3s. to 6s. 6d. a day, but with little result. Kadalie was imprisoned and fined for incitement. Ballinger was left with the rump of the ICU and its debts, and as a great mass movement it petered out in the early 1930s.

Before its final eclipse, however, the ICU caused a serious rift in the Pact Government. Walter Madeley, the Labour Party Minister of Posts and Telegraphs agreed, against Hertzog's wishes, to meet representatives of the ICU (which was not recognized as a trade union) together with one from the TUC to discuss the wages and conditions of postal workers. This issue precipitated a Cabinet crisis, ended the Pact and divided the Labour Party. A general election was due and the Nationalists, capitalizing on Black discontent and unrest and White fears, issued their 'Black Manifesto'. They twisted Smuts's call: 'Let us cultivate feelings of friendship over this African continent so that one day we may have a British Confederation of African States . . . a great African Dominion stretching unbroken throughout Africa . . .' They denounced him as the 'apostle of a black Kafir state . . . extending from the Cape to Egypt . . . and he foretells the day when even the name of South Africa will vanish in smoke on the altar of the Kafir state he so ardently desires'.[29]

Playing on the electorate's inherent traditions and prejudices

29. Hancock, op. cit., p. 218.

and on the slogan, *Stem wit vir 'n witmansland !* (Vote White for a White South Africa!) the Nationalists swept back into office, in June 1929, with an overall majority and were able to dispense with the support of a seriously weakened Labour Party which played little part in the new administration. Political divisions once again followed familiar racial lines: the Nationalist Party composed almost entirely of Afrikaners, the SAP mostly English-speaking but with a persistent core of loyal Botha and Smuts followers.

3. POLITICAL PARTIES AND SEGREGATION

Hertzog was apparently stronger than before and clearly empowered by the electorate to press on with segregation. Of the African population about 50 per cent, it was estimated, lived still in reserves or on Native Trust farms, largely in the traditional tribal way; 30 per cent lived on White farms as tenants, labour tenants or squatters; 14 per cent were urban dwellers in the townships, locations and shanty-towns on the outskirts of the White towns where they worked.

The reserves were the basis of all segregation policies. They consisted of 264 separated blocks of land, totalling 33,000,000 acres and carrying over 4,750,000 people, who spoke different Bantu tongues and whose income per family of six (according to the Tomlinson Commission Report of 1954) averaged £43 per annum. Instead of the reserves developing as their founders intended, as refuges until the inhabitants were sufficiently advanced to be able to hold their own on equal terms with Whites, discrimination increased and the Africans' prospects of advancement became always more remote. While the extension of White authority had put an end to tribal migration, Western medicine and the basic vigour of the African increased the chronic overcrowding of the reserves and it became apparent that they were not nearly big enough.

Although the reserve Africans retained traditional social structure and custom, there was almost nowhere where some Western influences had not penetrated and tribal patterns were not being eroded. Almost everywhere the presence of missionary, storekeeper, magistrate and policeman was familiar. Young men had to pay their taxes and had to provide their families with cash for commodities essential in the new world they moved into: paraffin, clothing, tea, maize when the harvest failed, schooling and so on. So they went off, recruited either officially in batches or by traders to whom they were in debt, or making their independent way to the mines, to make their fortunes and see something of the world. While the mines were the biggest and most organized drain on the manhood of the reserves, secondary industry and other occupations took their quota; but these last, however little it might be acknowledged, for the most part required a labour force of workers stable enough to develop some technical skill.

The mines and the reserves were complementary – neither could exist without the other. The whole mining industry of South Africa, the basis of South African economy, depended on the inexhaustible supply of cheap labour. The people of the reserves depended on the filtering away of their young men to channel back money that would fend off starvation. There developed a constant coming and going between urban areas and even the remoter reserves. The numbers in the reserves grew; so did over-stocking, impoverishment of the soil, erosion, drought, starvation, chronic malnutrition and susceptibility to diseases. The reserves became vast rural slums whose chief export was manpower. It was always acknowledged and was often specifically stated (for instance, by the Social and Economic Planning Council in 1945) that: 'One of the main objectives of Native taxation, is, or was, to exert pressure on the Natives to seek work in agriculture, mining or manufacture. In this object it is probably very successful.'[30] In 1925 the Native Taxation and Development Act had imposed a poll tax (which had contributed to the rebellion of Bambatha's people twenty years before) on all African males between the ages of eighteen and sixty-five and a tax of 10s. on every male occupier of a hut in the reserves.

The agencies recruiting for the mines had set up their offices in all rural areas and bands of apprehensive young men in patched clothing, bright patterned blankets and carrying their bundles of possessions became a familiar sight as they were herded through the streets of Johannesburg from railway station to mines. The

30. *Handbook on Race Relations,* p. 233.

mines employed over 400,000 Africans, about one-third of them from South Africa and the rest from Portuguese and Central Africa (and about 65,000 Whites). Those recruited from abroad by the Witwatersrand Native Labour Association contracted for a minimum period of 180 days to whatever mine they were allotted. The majority of South African miners contracted themselves individually for either one month or six to the mine of their choice. Some 25 per cent failed the medical test because of malnutrition and their families tended to 'fatten' them up for some months beforehand. They were housed in mine compounds in barracks containing between sixteen and forty concrete bunks. Medical attention was good and food consisted of 4,500 nutritionally calculated calories. The minimum wage on the mines in 1890 was £3 3s. 0d. a month plus keep. Later it fell and fluctuated below that level. The Lansdowne Commission, appointed in 1943, found that wages had not risen in twenty years and then stood at 2s. a shift (£2 19s. 6d. a month) for underground and 1s. 9d. for surface workers. By 1961 these rates would have risen to 2s. 9d. (£44 a year) and 2s. 5d. respectively (probably in terms of real wages lower than in 1890), a White miner's wage being £566 a year. From his wage the African paid for clothing and two blankets, his tax and the cost of repatriation. The price of gold, however, rose from 85s. per fine oz in 1932 (when South Africa was to go off the Gold Standard) to 250s. in 1949. Trade unions were not allowed on the mines and strikes were illegal for Africans.

The basing of the whole South African economy on the gold mines, and so on migratory labour and on cheap labour, set a pattern of labour and a standard which depressed wages in all fields of employment. The mines paid on the assumption that the man's basic living and that of his dependants was derived from his holding in the reserves. If that were ever true it did not remain so for long and was to become a disastrously false foundation for South African society.

An investigation in the Belgian Congo in 1928 found that a maximum of 5 per cent of adult males could be away from their rural homes at any one time without detriment to agriculture and social life. In parts of the Union and Protectorates up to 50 per cent of the men were often absent, which aggravated a thousand-fold the consequences of chronic overcrowding and overstocking of the reserves and accelerated their economic collapse. The absence of most of the able-bodied men left agriculture in the hands of the over-burdened women and children. The men in their months of rest and recuperation had no incentive or opportunity at home to learn improved farming methods. No professional farming class could develop in these circumstances. As soil impoverishment and erosion increased, drought became more devastating and poverty and starvation more prevalent. The social consequences of the migratory labour system were far reaching. Frequent and protracted absences of the men meant broken homes, fatherless undisciplined children and lonely women harassed by too much work and responsibility; meant the rapid spread of tuberculosis and of venereal, nutritional and other diseases, of homosexuality, crime and all the evils of a poverty-stricken disintegrating society.

There were, of course, no hard and fast occupational divisions. Migrants from the reserves went away to farms, to mines or to towns, often graduating from one to another. They tended to stay longer periods, to return home less frequently. Some of those who reached the towns took their families; some never returned to the reserves; others took a town wife, established a second family.

The rapid urban influx brought great housing problems. In the early days those who were not accommodated either in mining or industrial compounds or as domestic servants on their employers' premises, built themselves houses or some sort of shelter on vacant land on the outskirts of the towns; or African, Indian or European landowners built huts to rent, which soon became pullulating slums.

Old standing liquor laws forbade the selling to Africans or the possession by them of wines and spirits, also the brewing by them (except in some circumstances for domestic use) of traditional millet 'kafir beer' or more potent concoctions for sale. Their extreme poverty made the brewing and sale of beer the obvious and often the only way women could augment a family income that might be far below the bread line. So brewing and illicit liquor-dealing were big business. The constant and often brutally conducted police raids in search of contraventions of the regulations made the liquor laws second only to pass laws as a source of resentment against the Government and of bitter hostility between Africans, particularly the women, and the police; tinder which easily could and frequently did flare into rioting.[31] An attempt was made in Natal in 1928 to make beer readily and legally available and stem the excessive drunkenness and disorder consequent on prohibition. Municipal canteens were opened to supply locations with 'Kafir beer', the profits to be devoted to social welfare in the location (thus relieving the White tax-payer) and all home brewing was even more rigorously penalized. This usurping of a valued source of income in Durban where wages, for many £3 a month, had not risen since 1914 enraged the women who, backed by the ICU, insisted the men boycott the beer halls. Demonstrations spread and grew out of hand and out of context, until the desecration of a European cemetery led to White retaliation and the trouble escalated, causing some deaths. As the boycott and disturbances continued there were reports that the Africans were not paying their poll tax. This enabled Oswald Pirow, the new Minister of Defence, to follow the Smuts precedent of tough dealing with insubordination. He melodramatically flew down to Durban and took charge. He led police armed with bayonets and machine-guns in an experimental tear-gas attack on crowds of curious African onlookers assembled to watch proceedings. The strike was quelled and poll tax defaulters rounded up. Protest meetings against the Riotous Assemblies Amendment Act, Pirow's 'Law of Oppression', took place in many areas often under the joint aegis of the ICU, the Communist Party and the ANC, and when armed police and, sometimes, White civilians took a hand the gatherings generally ended in bloodshed.

Hertzog pressed on with his task of creating segregation at all levels of national life. Whatever his vagaries and personal animosities, however, he remained strictly constitutional and resisted pressure from his right wing to reverse the parliamentary rejections of his attempt to disfranchise the Cape African by amending the entrenched clauses of the Constitution. However, in 1931, the

31. In the first six months of 1962, 78,000 people were to be sentenced under the liquor laws. Restrictions were then removed and there was a startling drop in the number of convictions.

franchise was extended to White women and the next year educational and financial qualifications were abolished for Whites. The letter of the law was observed, but by doubling the size of the White electorate the value of the Black vote was correspondingly reduced.

The Native Urban Areas Amendment Act of 1931 and the Native Service Contract Act of 1932 further eroded the rights of Africans to move into and live freely in the towns and accelerated the removal of squatters from White farms to reserves or reduced them to labour tenants, working for their White masters for 90 or 180 days a year. On the other hand, the old Transkei system of limited local authority, begun by Rhodes in the Glen Grey Act, was extended by the amalgamation of the Transkei and Pondoland Authorities into the Transkeian Territories General Council, the Bunga, with advisory and very limited executive and legislative powers. It was to become a pilot scheme for separate development in later years.

The great depression of 1929 hit America and Europe and spread to South Africa. The collapse of the diamond market and a drop in agricultural prices coincided with a devastating combination of locusts and drought. When Britain went off the gold standard in 1931, Hertzog and N. C. Havenga, his Finance Minister, tenaciously refused to do the same, in order to demonstrate to the electorate and to the world South Africa's independence of Britian. Immediately £12m. of capital left the country and the inflow of development capital all but ceased. Fall in revenue, increased taxation and slump in exports relentlessly followed and the country faced stark ruin. The most bitter political controversy raged.

Tielman Roos, a corpulent, genial Nationalist with a great Transvaal following, had been Hertzog's Minister of Justice until his elevation to the Appeal Court Bench and he still retained a hankering after power. Forsaking his judgeship, this capricious character acted as a catalyst in the financial impasse and for a brief moment was the bright hope of the nation. He declared it madness to stay on the gold standard and called for a National (as distinct from Nationalist) government which he hoped to lead. At this the outflow of capital became a speculators' flood. The total cost to the country was thought to be about £50m. On bankers' insistence Havenga precipitately abandoned the gold standard, leaving a stubborn Hertzog forever bitter about the power of money. There was an immediate spectacular reversal: money poured back along with investment capital. The gold mines rapidly recovered, the working profit rising in a month from 8s. 6d. to 18s. 7d. a ton and South Africa was set on the verge of an era of fabulous prosperity.

But Hertzog's support had ebbed with the country's fortunes and did not return. He could not win an early election. Smuts, for his part, was well aware that an election victory for himself would be hollow and would not eliminate the abiding dissensions. Roos's ideas of a strong National administration had captivated the shaken electorate, but Roos himself was a political lightweight. The obvious course was a coalition between Nationalist and South African Parties and the Whites, sated with years of political acrimony, anxiously watched the drama of reconciliation between bitter irreconcilables.

After attacking Smuts who sat silent in Parliament with searing insult, vicious even by the standards of democratic debate, Hertzog consented to a coalition. Smuts, persuaded that there could be no effective coalition unless he led his party, checked his impulse to resign. In a stunning gesture of abnegation the arrogant, internationally lauded statesman agreed to serve under his old politically petty and venomous rival. Undoubtedly he was still as dedicated to the ideal of White unity as he had been when under the spell of Rhodes. Perhaps too, the seer behind those ice-blue eyes had decided to bide his time. Hertzog, satisfied that dominion status had given South Africa effective independence, accepted her place in the Commonwealth and shelved his aim of a republic. Smuts, on his side, relaxed opposition to Hertzog's segregation policy. The Coalition without difficulty won the general election of 1933 (fought in an internationally darkly overcast period as Hitler's Brownshirts beat up the Jews and rattled collection boxes of the 'winterhilfe' tribute through the towns and villages of the Reich).

Two years later the parties fused, forming the United Party (UP). For two sets of bitter-enders this was too much to bear. Colonel C. F. Stallard led off a group of ultra-British – mostly

Natalians – and formed the Dominion Party. On the other side, and far more significantly, Dr D. F. Malan, the intransigent republican ex-predikant, defected with a small body of followers to form the 'Purified' National Party and do his best to wreck the Hertzog–Smuts *rapprochement*. At Hertzog's insistence the sovereign independence of South Africa under the Crown and in the Commonwealth, as already acknowledged in the Balfour Declaration, was constitutionally enshrined in the Status Act of 1934, creating an innovation and precedent for the Commonwealth. But the one issue still outstanding between Hertzog and Smuts, to remain at the time of fusion unresolved and dividing the electorate, was left by consent of both party leaders to be decided later in Parliament. This was the question of South Africa's neutrality in the event of Britain being involved in war. As the years of fusion passed, Hitler ruled more intemperately and the moment for a decision, which everyone knew must come, drew nearer.

Once the country's economy was set again on stable paths of progress, and fusion had for the time being taken much of the acrimony out of White politics, the legislature could return to Non-European affairs. Race relations was the national preoccupation. Hertzog had recast his four long-incubated Segregation Bills of the late 1920s. The first of these – the most contentious, affecting the entrenched clauses – the Representation of Natives Act, he introduced in 1936, and it now obtained the two-thirds majority of both Houses sitting together demanded by the Constitution. The Act provided that Africans on the Common roll in the Cape should be put on a separate roll enabling them to elect three White representatives to the Assembly and two to the Cape Provincial Council. Africans throughout the rest of the country would elect four Whites to the Senate. As a sop to world opinion and to South African critics of all races, a Native Representative Council (NRC) with advisory powers only was set up, to consist of elected and nominated African members and some White officials. An additional effect of ending the Cape franchise was to make the Natives Land Act applicable in the Cape and open the way to a uniform segregation policy. This legislation was desperately and unavailingly contested by Africans, supported by a handful of White liberals. The easy optimists at Westminster responsible twenty-five years before for the South Africa Act were proved wrong. The African voice never had much resonance in the nation's discussions but until now it did have its place which might always get greater. But this sleight-of-hand legislation politically emasculated the great majority of the people. It was regarded as the greatest betrayal; it destroyed Black reliance on White contracts throughout the continent; and, in a final analysis, it may take more blame than any other measure in the crisis of confidence which lies beneath present confusion in Africa.

The great partisan boost given to local Black political aspirations by African Abyssinian resistance to White Italian invasion of their country had turned to apathy with European victory, so no organizations were ready to lead a coherent opposition to Hertzog's bills. The I C U was defunct and its old membership disillusioned by its fate. The A N C under the ageing Seme was weak and collaboratory and the Communist Party had lost much of its influence. However, at the end of the year the All-African Convention (AAC) was called at Bloemfontein. With Indian, Coloured and African delegates, it was the largest all-race gathering yet. Opening proceedings, Professor D. D. Jabavu declared they had been brought together by *Madimo*, the ancestral spirits that guided the children of Makanda, Sekhukhune, Cetshwayo and Moshweshwe. Moderate counsels overruled the militants; a deputation led by Jabavu was cozened into accepting the compromise of Native representation by three elected Whites (initially the Malan–Natal view looked like prevailing – that no individual African should vote for the Assembly), which had been framed by the Eastern Province Members of Parliament who needed to save face with their Black constituents and accepted by Hertzog in order to gain the necessary two-thirds majority. The proposal was to be presented as 'what Natives themselves asked for'[32] and so disarm the critics. Dr James Moroka and Dr A. B. Xuma, overseas-trained, shrewd and representative of the younger men, hurried to Cape Town to put up a fight, backed by some of the old White liberals, against this path of 'honourable trusteeship'.[33]

32. Benson, *The Struggle for a Birthright*, p. 67.
33. Hancock, op. cit., p. 265.

Hofmeyr said that White civilization had no future save with the consent and goodwill of the Non-European people. But the more prevalent view was put by Heaton Nicholls, representing the arch-British of Natal:

The House of Assembly [he said] is the House of Democracy, the mere right to vote is the recognition of the existence of democratic institutions . . . [which] . . . are alien to the Bantu race . . . To ensure European dominance it is essential there should be no vote . . . cast except by Europeans.[34]

If the Hertzog conception of segregation was to be at all feasible additional land for African occupation remained a first essential. The second of his Acts, the Native Trust and Land Act of 1936, was passed without much opposition. This provided for an additional maximum of 7,250,000 morgen of land (the released areas) – still not the 8m. morgen the Beaumont Commission had recommended – to be added, at a cost of £10m. over ten years, to the existing reserves (established under the Natives' Land Act of 1913) in which population had risen to eighty-two per square mile compared with twenty-one in the Union as a whole. The African three-quarters of the total population would then be entitled to occupy under 14 per cent of the country's total area, leaving the rest to the Whites (but by 1961 only 4¾m. morgen would have been acquired, bringing the total area in the reserves up to 17½m. morgen). The Act also gave powers to eliminate squatters and to allow as labour tenants only those who would work at least half the year for the farmer. But the Whites were so reluctant to part with the additional land promised in the Act to accommodate the many families that would be turned off the farms that much of the Act proved unworkable.

The following year, Hertzog's third Act, the Native Laws Amendment Act, gave the Government powers to compel urban authorities to apply segregation by setting aside townships and providing houses for Africans. Magistrates and Native Commissioners must now grant or refuse permits for rural Africans to go to town to seek work. Africans could be excluded from townships unless they were in employment or *bona fide* visitors. Those 'in

34. ibid., p. 69.

excess of reasonable labour requirements' could be returned to the reserves. Smuts, speaking on the provisions, said, '. . . the proper way to deal with this influx is to cut it off at its source and to say that our towns are full, the requirements met [and] we cannot accommodate more Natives . . .'[35]

With more repressive laws to be enforced, relations between Africans and police, many of them raw young Afrikaners from the platteland with no understanding of urban workers, steadily worsened and a pattern of rioting and violence was laid. Politicians were quick to blame communism and 'the liberal doctrine of equality between black and white'. Others opposed the general repressive trend. They worked to make themselves heard, in Parliament and in such bodies as the Institute of Race Relations, the Joint Councils and in some missionary organizations. They were supported more militantly by Africans themselves, often guided and helped by a handful of White communists.

The liberal, Professor Alfred Hoernlé, however, pointed out how far the current practice of segregation – concentrated on the preservation of White blood purity, exclusive political power, control of the African and monopoly of skilled occupations – had moved from the original intention. He proposed instead a policy of separation, 'a sundering or dissociation so complete as to destroy the very possibility of effective domination', and 'the mending [of] the multiracial society by ending it'. But, defeated from the start, he acknowledged that 'the will to realize it is not there nor is there any power on earth which can bring it into being'.[36]

Meanwhile other events abroad were impinging on the south. Half-hearted sanctions against Italy's invasion of Abyssinia were proved ineffective. The Japanese (equated both legally and emotionally in South Africa with Whites) were launched on a long war of devastation against non-white China. The Spanish Civil War bred more bitter disillusionment with the failure of international peace-keeping machinery. South West Africa, as elsewhere, had been hit by the world slump of the early 1930s. Cattle prices fell, diamond mines closed down and the great distress caused amongst

35. *Handbook on Race Relations*, p. 234.
36. Roskam, op. cit., pp. 96, 97.

the Whites was of course magnified as it reached the Blacks. Among the German community there was a growth of pro-Nazi activity: the formation of a German political party, the movement of young Germans in large numbers to Germany for military training, the organization of Brown Shirts, Hitler Youth and Winter Help; all increasingly controlled from a Reich vociferously demanding the return of colonies, a demand with which some South African politicians, Hertzog and Pirow among them, expressed sympathy, though they jibbed at the suggestion that an example should be set with the return of South West Africa.

In the new sovereign independence of dominion status South Africa was increasingly touchy over any seeming infringement of her spheres of influence. Not only was South West Africa, whatever financial burden had to be carried, held in a tight grasp, but the High Commission Territories (Botswana, Lesotho and Swaziland), geographically embedded in South Africa and economically dependent on her but in relative political independence, remained a constant unendurable irritation and humiliation. British administration in general was firm, just according to its lights, uncorrupt and often dedicated. But, apart from a high proportion of the small tax actually raised, woefully little was spent by the British Exchequer on the social and economic advancement of these territories. Left to stagnate, they became almost entirely dependent on South Africa: as controller of postal, currency, banking and customs services; as the chief supplier of their imports, especially food; as their main export market and educational centre; and, above all, as the main source of employment. At any time 43 per cent of all adult males in Lesotho, 20 per cent in Botswana and 8 per cent of Swazi were away from home working on the farms, down the mines or in the towns of South Africa. Their total remittances home amounted to some £2m. Hertzog raised the issue with Britain in 1935, asking for their incorporation as provided for in the Act of Union – and this at a time when the Fusion government was openly tightening its native policy. Stout opposition in the United Kingdom forced the British Government into an undertaking that there would be no transfer until the wishes of the inhabitants had been consulted.

The elections of 1938 returned the United Party, still with a large majority although it had lost 6 seats; Labour and Independents had been hard hit, but the Nationalists had gained 7 seats, 27 to the UP's 111, and observant analysts noted they had a greatly increased number of votes cast for them, especially in the platteland.

The doubts and suspicions about their partners in fusion that were harboured in the minds of most members of both sections were fanned to a furnace glow by the centenary commemoration of the Great Trek, organized by the *Federasie van Afrikaanse Kultuur Verenigings* (FAK), established in 1936 with a network of cultural and educational institutions to organize intensively every aspect of Afrikaner life. The celebrations, which were dominated by Malan (for Hertzog retired to his farm for the duration and Smuts was present purely as an Afrikaner), took place in a fervour of religious patriotism and hero-worship. Companies in Voortrekker dress travelling by ox-wagon along the old trek routes converged on Pretoria, to camp on the hills outside, to lay the foundations of the monument which would dominate landscape and emotions, and to rededicate themselves to Voortrekker ideals. The followers of Malan, and many of Hertzog's, were brought to a ferment of chauvinism by their exclusive projection back into the pageantry of those perilous days and by the revelations thundered out by predikant and politician of the dangers besetting the latter-day Voortrekkers – from the same tough troops of Midian, Black and British. And hearing the reverberations, the followers of Smuts in the offices, shops and mining houses complained at his toleration and still followed him.

In the passion of the celebrations some £500,000 was raised in response to an appeal for something to be done for the 'sunken' descendants of the Voortrekkers, the swelling number of poor whites. The *Reddingsdaadbond* (RDB – the Rescue Action Society) was formed under the chairmanship of Dr N. J. Diederichs, a leading Broeder. Amongst its aims was to make the Afrikaner labourer 'part and parcel of Nationalist life', to keep the Afrikaner worker within the Church and his Nationalist and cultural heritage, to purge the trade unions of liberal and socialist

266

ideas, and to use Afrikaner resources to develop an Afrikaner capitalist class. During the next decade there was a great increase in the Afrikaner share of small business undertakings – such as shops, wine cooperatives and undertakers – and many young Afrikaners were enabled to rise to positions of power and wealth in commerce, industry and mining.

The Afrikaner workers were looked after by a subsidiary, the *Blankewerkersbeskermingsbond* (White Workers' Protection Society), into which a large part of RDB funds was directed. It was founded on the 'Christian-National traditions of the people of South Africa', to campaign for 'job reservation' (the detailing of certain classes of employment to certain racial groups), the separation of races in employment and the segregation of trade unions. Existing trade unions, many of which had a Non-white membership, were disrupted either by the formation of alternative exclusively Afrikaner unions or by discrediting the leadership by accusations of communist affiliations. Under the aegis of the FAK purely Afrikaner organizations were formed parallel with existing ones in almost every sphere: a student organization, the *Afrikaner Nasionale Studentebond*, in opposition to the old-established National Union of Students; and so on with boy-scout, first-aid, and teachers' associations and chambers of commerce and industry. Even in sport the revival of exclusive Voortrekker games and folk-dancing was encouraged.

Also conceived in the fevered days and nights of Voortrekker rededication, the *Ossewabrandwag* (OB – the Ox-wagon Sentinel) was founded in Bloemfontein late in 1938 to embody and perpetuate the idealism aroused, to foster patriotism by the celebration of national festivals and heroes, to establish memorials and keep up places of historic interest. It organized gatherings, processions, sport, drama, historical lectures, and camps and target practice for men and women. Though launched as a cultural movement, it was given a military form, shaped on commando lines, drew its first units from the ranks of the South African army, and had an élite arm, the *Stormjaers*, formed to defend political platforms and undertake sabotage. Its second and only significant Kommandant-Generaal, Dr J. F. B. van Rensburg, said: 'The OB regards itself as the soldiery of the republic . . . the OB is the political action front of Afrikanerdom.'[37] Whereas the Broederbond membership was highly select and its activities secret, the OB was an open mass movement which attracted wide support and had possibly almost half a million members at the time of its greatest appeal. In the beginning the Nationalist Party cooperated closely with the OB and many party leaders were prominent also in the movement – among them P. O. Sauer, F. C. Erasmus and Eric Louw (all to be Cabinet ministers), C. R. Swart (later Minister of Justice and then State President) and B. J. Vorster (later Minister of Justice and Prime Minister).

Continuing with his segregation policy and yielding to pressure to stop Indian penetration in the Transvaal, Hertzog introduced the Asiatics (Transvaal Land and Trading) Bill of 1939 to 'peg' the Indians to their existing residences and businesses. It caused strong protest; Hofmeyr resigned from the Party caucus; Gandhi protested to Smuts at the violation of the 1914 agreement and the Indians planned a new passive resistance campaign, which they called off because of the threatening war.

War came nearer with no decision taken on South Africa's position should Britain and Germany be in conflict. At the time of Munich the year before, a Cabinet memorandum was agreed on affirming that South Africa would not intervene in the event of war; her relations with the belligerents would remain unchanged and her obligations, to Britain in regard to the Simonstown naval base, and to the League of Nations, for example, would be maintained. Hertzog regarded the document as having continuing validity, but Smuts constantly declared that South Africa should take her stand with the Commonwealth. Suddenly war had begun. In a tense Assembly Hertzog pressed for neutrality based on the memorandum, but spoiled his case by his unrestrained sympathy with the German cause. Smuts more subtly argued that South Africa was directly threatened, especially in view of Germany's colonial ambitions; dissociated from the Commonwealth she would become vulnerably isolated. Hertzog was defeated by thirteen votes. He withdrew from the UP and sought reconciliation with Malan in a *Herenigde* (reunited) *Nasionale Party* (HNP).

37. Bunting, op. cit., p. 82.

4. WAR AND NATIONALISM

Smuts, now aged sixty-nine, after fifteen years' subordination, was again in command and with astonishing vigour, self-confidence and resilience he faced the problems of bringing a basically divided country into the war. He ruled that there would be no expeditionary force for overseas. Despite Pirow's frequent visits to Germany as Minister of Defence and his constant preoccupation with the subject, South Africa was sorely ill-prepared; she was equipped with a permanent force of under 1,400, the UDF at one-third its proper strength, almost no armaments except leftovers from the previous war and a notorious fleet of bush-carts built up by Pirow for some fantasy guerilla warfare he envisaged, possibly in defence of Whites some day beleaguered further north. There were, too, the large number of strident Nazis and German supporters of Hitler in South West Africa, hundreds of whom Smuts immediately interned, and the many bitter opponents of the war in the Union itself. The country, however, remained relatively calm, with no serious threat of rebellion, possibly mainly because the anti-war faction expected an early German victory. Volunteers flooded in, soon to build up two divisions and an airforce; the UDF grew to 137,000 by the end of the first year, the majority of the volunteers being young Afrikaners. Many other South Africans had already joined British units. Forty thousand Coloured and 80,000 Africans joined up, mostly as non-combatants. Blacks were urgently recruited not only for the army, but also for the mines and for war and other industries. Although it soon became clear that the law and White opinion still would not allow them to be armed, an ANC resolution to make recruitment conditional upon arms-bearing was shelved so as not to embarrass Smuts's government and in the hope that once overseas there would be some relaxation of the bar. Many served outside South African frontiers as seamen and gunners. At home they did police duty and, armed with assegais, were put to guard concentration or POW camps. But they were promised medals and pensions at the war's end.

In the wave of fraternal emotion engendered by the German invasion of Holland thousands of Whites volunteered for service anywhere in Africa, wearing the proud red flash that marked them for contumely and physical attack by Nationalist supporters in whose eyes they were traitors to the Volk. After Dunkirk, forces were sent to hold East Africa against Italian attack from Ethiopia. After the fall of France the Nationalists urged the making of peace but Smuts, remaining energetic and confident, hurled back at Hertzog, once long ago his brother-in-arms, the well-understood jibe, 'Hands-upper'.

Smuts, as Prime Minister, Minister for External Affairs and for Defence (and later as Commander-in-Chief), had concentrated political and military power in his own hands in a degree unique in the Commonwealth. For the first four months of the war, while he built up the armed forces and reorganized industry, he governed almost arbitrarily without Parliament. He was able to take immediate decisions and put them into effect. He had appointed as his Finance Minister, J. H. Hofmeyr, who, brilliant, prudent, financially conservative, was dedicated to the prosecution of the war.

For the next few years Hofmeyr was destined to occupy a central position in political affairs. He was a curious figure: a fragile child, born in Cape Town, in 1894, and bound for life by a dominant mother in a prison of mutual devotion. From early days his intellect and industry were remarkable. He matriculated first in his school, third in the Cape Colony and, at the age of thirteen and loaded with prizes, entered Cape Town University. At fifteen he graduated with First Class Honours and a Rhodes Scholarship, but he was considered too young for Oxford. At seventeen he was an MA of Cape Town University and was commissioned to write the biography of his famous cousin and namesake, 'Onze Jan', before he was permitted to go, accompanied by his mother, to take up his scholarship. Only now did she allow him into long trousers and in some way she kept his spirit in shorts for the whole of his life. Back in South Africa, at twenty-two he was Classics professor at the School of Mines (to become the University of the Witwatersrand) and at twenty-four its Principal. At thirty he was Administrator of the Transvaal. Such a prodigy inevitably lived his life in the glare of publicity and speculation both as to his public and private affairs. He was deeply religious, but because his mother had quarrelled with the local Dutch Reformed Church he had been brought up a Baptist – fundamentalist but without the race attitude of the D R C – and he became fluent in English while still very young. His worship of Onze Jan helped to liberalize his views and his education, friends and long years of Boys' Club work, begun at Oxford and kept up in later life, accelerated the process. He developed a great admiration for – almost subservience to – Smuts to whom his intellect and vast capacity for work were to prove invaluable. He could carry several portfolios and add to them the acting-premiership in Smuts's frequent absence abroad. He seldom took a holiday and was always there, 'dog's-body', ready to take on extra work or responsibility at Smuts's behest and with little overt appreciation. He was modest, unassuming and slow to push himself. It was often rumoured that he intended to start a liberal party, but in politics his loyalty to Smuts and to party interests inhibited his liberal tendencies. He expressed these wherever he had freedom to manoeuvre, but misleadingly, for in the end when challenged he would deny he advocated any doctrine of race equality to replace accepted official policy. He was always considered to be the logical successor to Smuts.

With Hofmeyr holding the finances steady, the country made great industrial strides and managed in large measure to keep itself supplied. Women moved increasingly into the factories and Blacks undertook more skilled work with the tacit acceptance of the White workers. In 1940 the ANC elected a vigorous new president, Dr A. B. Xuma, trained in Britain and the States, married to a Black American and possessed of the private means to enable him to begin an enthusiastic reorganization of Congress, based on a new, more democratic constitution. Xuma lamented the lack of training in skills which would have enabled the Africans to make a more effective contribution to industry. The Black workers, especially, were harassed by rising costs and wretched living conditions, and although War Measures made illegal 'all strikes by all Africans under all circumstances', and banned meetings of more than twenty on mine property, there was a great deal of industrial unrest.

The Hertzog–Malan alliance soon ended in one of those political vendettas so prevalent through Afrikaner history and on which English-speaking politicians tended to rely rather than on their own efficiency. Hertzog and the loyal Havenga formed the Afrikaner Party, while many other party leaders seeing in the war an opportunity of regaining the Afrikaners' lost freedom openly advocated totalitarianism. Oswald Pirow, of German origin and avowedly pro-German, formed within the Nationalist Party the secret New Order group of Hertzogites who had not followed their old leader into the Afrikaner Party. National-socialist ideals were spread with the old indestructible aim of a Christian-National Republic, anti-communist, anti-capitalist, anti-imperialist in which the British, being unassimilable, would have a lesser status. Great emphasis was laid on race and race purity. Van Rensburg, similarly inspired but for his part believing that fighting would be necessary to gain Afrikaner domination, led the OB along a path of hampering the war effort, by sabotage, by instigating riots between Stormjaers and soldiers and by a general creation of turbulence which deflected large forces from service abroad to security duties at home.

Between Hertzog and Malan themselves there were genuine policy differences. Firm in their opposition to the war, yet Hertzog and the Afrikaner Party advocated strict neutrality, maintaining that the decision to enter the war was a free decision of South Africa's Parliament. Malan, on the other hand, favoured early negotiations with Germany whose victory was confidently expected. The republic envisaged by him and his following would be achieved by a simple parliamentary majority. The English, they argued, would never cooperate, but no doubt would finally accept the *fait accompli*. But Hertzog, while supporting the Republican ideal, insisted, as he had done most of his parliamentary life, that it must come of English–Afrikaner cooperation and on the basis of full equality and must be representative of 'the broad will of the people'. At the end of 1941 Hertzog died in bitterness, discredited and broken by the vengeful Broederbond. Soon afterwards Havenga, his successor, and Malan made an election agreement, shelving the Republican issue for the present and agreeing to concentrate on native affairs.

As the East African campaign was concluded and South African troops were sent further afield to suffer the reverses and successes of the North African and Italian campaigns, dissension grew at home with various Nationalists' organizations – the 30,000 strong O B, Pirow's New Order, Greyshirts and Blackshirts – combining to undermine the war effort. A police raid revealed the extent of the subversive policies of the O B and police and civil servants were barred from membership. There was a good deal of generally ineffective dynamiting of cinemas, railway lines, telegraph poles and so on; more serious was the skirmishing between police and soldiers and civilians. There was much malicious rumourmongering. Nazi propaganda broadcasts from Zeesen, creating alarm and despondency, were received and believed and given wide currency by the Nationalist press, particularly *Die Transvaler* whose editor, the ex-Stellenbosch professor of social psychology, Dr H. F. Verwoerd, had then only a local notoriety.

At the back of these rowdy disturbances and behind its veil of secrecy lay the Broederbond. As long ago as the early 1930s the Bond had begun organizing in earnest to attain its republican goal and after 1933 it had shown considerable interest in the newly ascendant Nazi Party; a number of senior members, including Dr N. J. Diederichs and Dr van Rensburg, went to Germany to study its methods. In 1935 Hertzog had denounced the Bond as more political than cultural, as a wrecker of White unity, and as aspiring to rule South Africa. From then he began to be regarded as the enemy of the Afrikaner nation. But the Bond's influence rapidly extended until by 1944 its membership was estimated at over 2,500, 8·6 per cent of whom were public servants and 33 per cent teachers; in 1952 it was said that there were approximately 350 predikants, over 8,000 teachers, 900 farmers, 150 lawyers and 60 Members of Parliament; (by the mid-1960s its numbers might have been 7,000). Its members included most leading Nationalists, the editors of most Nationalist newspapers and the officers of most Afrikaner societies and organizations. The Manager of the *Volkskas*, a leading bank, the Chairman and Secretary of the *Transvaalse Onderwysers Vereninging* (Teachers' Association), the chief organizer of the *Reddingsdaadbond*, the Moderator of the D R C and the Editor-in-Chief of the *Die Transvaler*, Dr Verwoerd, were all members. There were members of the Bond in almost every town and every branch of public life, in church communities, educational institutions, provincial and municipal councils and cultural organizations.

Malan, who was a shrewd and capable tactician, recognized danger in diversity, and did not intend to brook, still less fall victim to, traditional Afrikaner divisiveness. His Cradock agreement with van Rensburg gave the OB freedom in the cultural and social spheres but reserved all political activity absolutely to the Nationalist Party. He called on all Afrikaner organizations to cooperate in achieving the Christian-National goal of a Kruger Republic. The HNP, preparing for the day of the Allies' defeat when they would take over, had appointed a Provisional Committee of Unity, Broederbond sponsored, on which in addition to the Nationalist Party were representatives of the OB, FAK, RDB and DRC. It was charged with the task of forming an Afrikaner Front and of defining the basis of 'a free, independent, republican, Christian-National state, based on the word of God, eschewing all foreign models . . . with a Christian-National educational system . . . and the strongest emphasis upon the effective disciplining of the people . . .'[38]

The Draft Constitution, accepted by the Nationalist Party in June 1941, was a highly significant document. The form of government which it advocated was to be Christian-National in character, with Afrikaans the official language, and English its equal when this was judged by the State to be in the interests of State and people. There was to be a selected citizenship of those deemed to be 'builders of the nation'; a wide censorship to prevent undermining of 'public order or good morals of the Republic internally or externally'; and the State President 'only responsible to God over and against the people . . . altogether independent of any vote in Parliament . . . decides on all laws . . .'[39] Segregation was to be established in residence and work, each race group to be given self-government in its own territories. Non-Europeans educated for the professions or trades were to be banned from practising them among Whites. Propaganda of any policy and the existence of any political organization in strife with

38. Bunting, op. cit., p. 94.
39. ibid., p. 97.

the fulfilling of the country's Christian-National vocation was forbidden. A great part of later Nationalist Government policies was closely foreshadowed in the Draft.

Malan himself was given wide powers as *Volksleier* and set about consolidating his position. Determined that the Nationalist Party alone should wield political power, he first limited the activities of Pirow's New Order, forcing them eventually out of the party, and Pirow was to have little political influence thereafter. Malan then attacked the OB, which had laid itself open by prematurely revealing the terms of the recently formulated Draft Constitution, thus breaking the Cradock agreement. The OB was banned to party members and as the influential Nationalist leaders withdrew the organization gradually withered away.

Smuts's main concern had to be with the prosecution of the war, and in his anxiety to keep a relatively united White community at his back he disregarded or was insensitive to the importance of winning the support of the Blacks. 'Politics,' he said over Hertzog's Bills, 'is the art of the possible and practicable, and one has to give in on small things to carry the bigger things.'[40] But his scale proved to be awry. Soon after the war began the Dominion Party started agitating against Indian penetration in Natal. (Though the Indians outnumbered the Whites in Natal, they formed only 2·5 per cent of the country's population as a whole.) Smuts was proposing to send South African troops across the Mediterranean and he was preparing for an election. To conciliate the electorate (but in the middle of a war for democratic rights) he introduced the Trading and Occupation of Land (Transvaal and Natal) Restriction Act of 1943, the 'Pegging Act', which bound Indians to the existing trading and land position for three years while a commission investigated all the difficulties of Natal Indians. It was a temporization neither side accepted, and it drew a threat of resignation from Hofmeyr, who had already warned of the possibility of a new passive resistance campaign, and unavailing protests from the Indian community.

Then in the Pretoria Agreement the Government, in an attempt to come to terms, accepted an Indian proposal of voluntary acceptance of urban residential restrictions, provided existing

40. Hancock, op. cit., p. 291.

rural, farming, trading and residence rights and urban land purchase rights remained. This was to be put in legal form by the
Natal Provincial Council; but the Council instead accepted an
Ordinance which extended the Pegging Act to all Natal and for
all time. Hopes of compromise died. The Indian militants took
over Congress and issued a ten-point programme based on the
Atlantic Charter.

The 1943 election was apparently a great victory for Smuts; he
gained fifteen more seats and 82,000 more votes. But Malan who,
with no prospect of winning, had made no election alliances and
had not to share the Opposition leadership, increased his representation from 27 seats to 43 seats and his total vote by nearly as
much as had the Government, while there was a notable drop in
the numbers of Afrikaners supporting Smuts. The Afrikaner
Party was almost eliminated.

Now, too, the tide of war turned and began to run well for the
Allies. There was a brief period of optimistic buoyancy among
the troops up north. The enlightened Army Education Units did
good work opening shutters of the mind and giving men a view of
the world as it was; and men of all races met and mixed on the
equal terms of war. In a very liberal gust of change, the men asked
that the National War Memorial should take the form of a Health
Service for the Blacks. Back in South Africa students were admit-
ting Blacks to their unions. There was an extension of social
services, which Hofmeyr insisted should include the Blacks,
particularly the educational services. A spate of reports of commissions inquiring into aspects of social and economic life highlighted the plight of the urban and rural Non-European,
especially of Africans. There was a sense of anticipation of a brave
new era in South Africa when Hitler should be defeated: possibly
to be introduced by Hofmeyr who as acting Prime Minister had
spoken generously of the new comradeship of war, of the need to
change old ideas on colour and even of a possible 'people's
charter'.

In the meantime there was also much cause for dissatisfaction.
Taxation was heavy. The control boards regulating distribution
were incompetent. Food costs were rising; food and goods were in
short supply. The Opposition, echoing Smuts at Versailles a

generation before, bitterly criticized the outcome of the war and the destruction by Britain and America of Germany, Europe's bastion against communism. The slowness of demobilization and reassimilation of the troops into civilian life and the tremendous housing shortage fermented discontent and gave Nationalist propaganda opportunity to dissipate what goodwill and brotherhood came out of the war. The Labour Party objected even to the training of Blacks to build houses for Blacks at lower wages than were paid to Whites, while Commissions of Inquiry urged they should be better trained and better paid. People soon slipped back into the old jealous sectionalism.

Although there was great war-time development, secondary industry suffered from shortage of skilled labour, bad siting, water shortage and uneconomical management. The whole economic structure was still too dependent on gold and diamonds and costs here were rising. Farming was backward, soil erosion menacing and many farmers only kept going by an increasing and inhibiting subsidization. The Blacks suffered severely from rising prices, static wages and a shocking housing situation. The country as a whole, despite the very high standard of living of a section of the Whites, remained poor. The average annual income for Whites was £125 and for Africans £10. Smuts was accused again of gallivanting too much abroad and devoting too little of his concern to his own country. It was not without some relevance; abroad the statesman-philosopher could spin a visionary web of increasing unities to captivate the squabbling nations of the world; back home the White politician was the victim of old conditioned reflexes.

Smuts's attitude to the Blacks was totally different from Hertzog's inflexibility. He had been purely expedient, moving with the strains of war, changing his approach with whatever considerations happened to bear most urgently on his divided personality. When Blacks were being sought for the forces and some sympathy with Japanese successes had slowed recruiting, he decided he would arm them if Japan attacked the Union. Early in 1942 speaking to the Institute of Race Relations in Cape Town, he had expressed the view that the policy of segregation had been a failure. He substituted the conception of trusteeship which sounded good in a world clamped in mortal struggle for human rights, and he stressed the responsibility of the European for his Non-European ward.

> When people ask what is the population of South Africa . . . I think it is an outrage to say two million. This country has a population of over ten million and that outlook which regards the natives as not worth counting is the ghastliest mistake possible . . . The native is carrying this country on his back . . . I think that if we were to . . . try out . . . this principle of trusteeship, we may build up that pattern of a new South Africa, variegated, unlike the pattern of any other country in the world . . . Isolation has gone and segregation has fallen on evil days, too.[41]

But no South African has been able to sound the clarion as Smuts could and the conception of trusteeship was to pass into the UNO with the difference that there it was envisaged that the ward would one day attain majority and pass from tutelage.

To speed up recruiting at this time administrative measures eased, pass laws were relaxed and arrests declined sharply. But the United States of America entered the war, Japan's advance to South Africa's shores was checked and the pass laws were tightened once again with the consequent thousands of arrests, convictions, gaol sentences, and by 1945 Smuts was asserting in the Assembly that 'all South Africans are agreed . . . except those who are quite mad . . . that it is a fixed policy to maintain white supremacy in South Africa'.[42]

The frustrations of the workers were expressed in a constant spluttering of strike actions and protest. Although such action by Africans was prohibited by War Measures of 1942 and 1943, some sixty illegal strikes took place between 1942 and 1944. The bus boycott of 1943 was a protest move more difficult to repress by legislation. Alexander Township was a festering, overcrowded, crime-ridden warren which at the same time pulsated with vitality and where rare and precious freehold rights existed. A penny on the bus fare – 2d. the double journey – was too much for the over-burdened budgets. In an almost spontaneous move-

41. 'The Basis of Trusteeship in African Native Policy', *New Africa Pamphlets*, No. 2, p. 42.

42. Roskam, op. cit., p. 94.

ment the people agreed to walk. Fifteen thousand men and women walked the nine or ten miles to their work in Johannesburg and wearily home in the evening for nine days. They won their point for the time being and displayed the power of their united resolve on a clear-cut economic issue affecting all. The battle had to be fought again the next year. Then they walked for seven weeks.

VE day came in 1945: Russia was briefly respectable and there was some inter-racial meeting at embassy parties and so on. An ANC delegation attended a Pan-African Conference in Manchester to meet leaders, such as Dr Nkrumah and Chief Kenyatta, of countries burning to shake off colonial restraints. In Cape Town a meeting of 8,000 people called for the implementation of the Atlantic Charter and suggested Smuts, when he returned from drafting the preamble to the charter, should follow it up by abolishing the pass laws. But in the rising social temperature violence everywhere was quick to break out. When, for example, the White driver of a tram serving the Black Western Areas knocked down and killed an African on a thronging Sunday afternoon, trams and passing cars were stoned and hooligans from the adjacent White suburbs seized the opportunity to burn down the nearby building of the *Bantu World*.

Throughout these confusing years the ANC, short of cash and disorganized, failed to give the people a strong, practical lead. Pass laws remained a constant irritant and sporadic anti-pass activities never entirely ceased. An ANC conference of six hundred delegates under Xuma issued a communist-backed call for one million signatures to a petition. The response was disappointing, but a deputation went to Cape Town where the acting-Prime Minister Hofmeyr, the most liberal of South Africa's Cabinet ministers, refused to see them.

A new generation was growing up of young African intellectuals, products of mission school education, who met and mixed at St Peter's Anglican Secondary School, at Fort Hare University and Wits University in the catalytic atmosphere of the war period. A group of them gathered under Z. K. Matthews, a teacher with a distinguished academic career at Yale University and the London School of Economics; he became Reader and then

Professor of African Law and Languages at Fort Hare, Vice-Chairman of its Senate in 1949 and was to be Acting-Principal when legislation for Bantu education forced his resignation. (Soon afterwards he joined the staff of the World Council of Churches in Geneva and after independence was Botswana's representative at the UN.) Together they had begun to formulate a Bill of Rights based on the Atlantic Charter. Some of the more able young men, among them Oliver Tambo and Nelson Mandela, lawyers, and Walter Sisulu from the ranks of the miners, frustrated by their elders' control, formed the Youth League within Congress, militant, nationalistic and fiercely opposed to all non-African influence.

The radical all-race Springbok Legion of ex-servicemen formed in 1941, anti-Nationalist and contemptuous of Smuts and Hofmeyr, clamoured for a reform of race relations. The Nationalists regarded the Legion and the newly proclaimed Declaration of Human Rights in the UNO as parts of the insidious liberal van of communism. The squalor of the Black shanty towns, swollen by the wartime influx of workers, cried to the heavens on the outskirts of all the larger towns. Growth of Black organizations and the strength of their various protests were alarming. Every political party except the Communists clung to the colour bar and in consequence all progressiveness in race attitudes was condemned as communist inspired.

The active promotion of trade unions by White ex-Communists and by African organizers, many trained by the Communist Party, was carried on with considerable success until in 1945 a Council of Non-European Trade Unions, formed in 1942, was able to claim to represent a membership of 150,000. Only in the largest fields of African labour were unions virtually impossible to establish. The million farm labourers were too scattered, too uneducated, too isolated for it to be possible to organize them significantly. In some areas there were sporadic attempts at protest against the agricultural worker's lot, set off by new variations introduced, particularly in the eastern Transvaal, into the farm labour pattern during the 1940s and 1950s with increasing production of crops, like potatoes, making heavy seasonal demands on labour. Men were recruited in numbers, housed in compounds for the length of their contract, often in conditions of pay, feeding, accommodation, supervision and restriction of movement as bad as anything ever reported under slavery, conditions which from time to time made press scandals. This form of labour was then augmented by farm gaols, first mooted by the United Party Minister of Justice, built by the farmers and managed by the Prisons Department, which hired out the workers at 9d. a day. By 1966 there were twenty-three of them holding 6,000 men. A further development was the 'voluntary' system (later suspended), which permitted the police to give Africans arrested for statutory offences the 'option' of contracting for a period of farm labour instead of being charged in the courts. Being 'sold to the farms' it was called, on account of the bribes given by farmers to police and pass official, and the men were virtually kidnapped. It was a dreaded fate, for men could vanish for months on end and, eventually discharged or escaped, would reappear half-starved and pitifully ill-used. (The system was to be suspended in 1959 after a public outcry.)

Among the 400,000 mine workers, however, there was some small success. The African Mine Workers Union (AMWU) was formed despite the formidable handicaps of the impermanence of the members, of their tribally orientated interests and above all of difficulties created by governments and mine owners: the War Measures banned meetings of more than twenty on mine property, while the Chamber of Mines forbade mine officials to meet or negotiate with representatives of the union and ignored all of its communications. Though the AMWU had not pressed its pay claims during the war, the Government had been repeatedly warned that a cost-of-living allowance was necessary to augment the average monthly cash wage of £3 11s. 8d. supplemented by a reserves income of £3 10s. 0d. The Lansdowne Commission had made a thorough investigation into conditions of employment but few of its recommendations were adopted. Seventy-five thousand miners in twenty-one mines came out on the biggest strike in South African history, demanding an average daily wage of 10s. to replace the current 2s. 5d. Using tried tactics the police cordoned off the individual mine compounds, isolating the mines from each other and the miners from their leaders and drove them down the mines back to work, often with batons and rifles. Thirteen strikers were killed and 1,200 injured, and fifty trade union officials and leading Communists were put on trial.

When the NRC next met under the chairmanship of the Under-Secretary of Native Affairs, members were shocked that he made no reference in his opening address to the strike, the matter uppermost in the minds of all of them. They attacked White government rule as the antithesis of the Charter and demanded the abolition of all discriminatory legislation. The impotency of the NRC was highlighted. They were asked, said a member with bitterness, 'to cooperate with a toy telephone, speaking into an apparatus which cannot transmit sound and at the end of which there is no one to receive messages'.[43] Hofmeyr, deputizing for Smuts who was still attending the UN, refused an appeal for concessions in a statement stigmatized by Matthews as oblivious of all the progressive forces at work and 'giving no hope for the future'.[44] The NRC presented its demands to the Government and adjourned to await a reply. (It was to adjourn finally in 1949 when a new administration rejected its demands and said it would be abolished.)

Through the war years the provision of houses for what were regarded as temporary workers was not only not generous, but had failed hopelessly to keep pace with the demand. Because of the colour bar insisted on by the White trade unions, building was done by Whites who were paid ten times the earnings of the Black occupiers of the houses. By the beginning of the war, African urban housing was in a disastrous state of neglect. During the war the locations, particularly those round the industrial centres, had been filling with Africans flooding in from rural areas to work in mines and industry. No houses were built during that time – no provision for natural increase let alone for the influx. Saturation point of overcrowding was reached. By the end of the war, during which the industry had greatly expanded, and influx control had been relaxed, the housing situation had become a dangerous scandal; by 1947 it was estimated that about 150,000 houses were needed. There were no more little rooms or screened stoeps into

43. Simons, op. cit., p. 495.
44. Benson, *The Struggle for a Birthright*, p. 109.

which a whole family could crowd, no more space in the yards in which leaky shacks could be set up by rent-hungry landlords. The first location to overflow was Orlando, near Johannesburg, from where thousands of people moved on to vacant municipal land and made shelters of old iron, tin cans, packing cases and sacks, without services or sanitation. Shanty towns grew up on vacant land adjacent to the locations round many major cities to accommodate their overspill. Disease, vice and lawlessness thrived in these conditions and encroached alarmingly on the exclusive well-ordered White areas. Gangs of Coloured *skolly-boys* in the Cape and young African *tsotsies* on the Rand terrorized Whites and, even more, the Blacks of the unlighted, unpoliced townships. Sixty per cent of the children knew no school but the streets. Very often both parents would be away at work all day, leaving before dawn and returning long after dark. Johannesburg and other municipalities were compelled to begin to provide accommodation for their workers at last.

It was unfortunate for South Africa's hopes that just at this time Smuts ran into further serious difficulties with his race legislation at home and so became embroiled once more with the government of India. In spite of the provisions of the Atlantic Charter, of world opinion and of the near emancipation of India and Pakistan with independent seats in the UN, Smuts, subjected to strong White pressures, followed the destruction of the Pretoria Agreement by introducing the Asiatic Land Tenure and Indian Representation Act of 1946, the 'Ghetto Act' to the despair of the Indian community. In its first part the Act barred Asians from acquiring fixed property from Whites (and *vice versa*) except in certain areas, unless by permit. The second part as a *quid pro quo* provided for Indians a qualified franchise to elect three Whites to the Assembly and one of two White senators, the other to be appointed. The first part of the Bill was the reverse of all the Indians had struggled for over the last forty years and they vehemently opposed it. The franchise offer, as they knew well from the practical ineffectiveness of the Native Representatives in Parliament elected on a similar basis, was an empty gesture and they rejected it. (The Nationalists and the Dominion Party in Parliament also condemned it for opposite reasons: they feared it to be the thin end of the wedge of effective Non-European representation). In Parliament the Bill as a whole was opposed only by the Native Representatives.

The passing of this 'Ghetto Act' reverberated ominously for South Africa. The South African Indian Congress, now led by Dr G. M. Naicker in Natal and Dr Y. Dadoo in the Transvaal, demanding the right to 'live as free citizens in a free society',[45] began a passive resistance campaign of protest. Groups of Indian men and women, and some Whites with them, gathered every night on a vacant municipal plot in Durban. They bore without retaliation the taunts and attacks of White hooligans. Each night they were arrested, charged in court with trespass and, pleading guilty and refusing fines, served their sentences and returned to trespass again. Nearly 2,000 participants served prison sentences and the protest action lasted well into 1948; then, although it had brought no direct concessions from the Government, it was suspended in order not to embarrass Smuts in the forthcoming election campaign. Although this Gandhian demonstration did nothing to relieve the lot of Indians, it attracted world-wide sympathy, indignation and condemnation of the Act, and focused international attention on the anomalous situation of Indians in South Africa and, past them, on the disabilities to which Africans were subjected. There were important indirect consequences of the passive resistance movement: Congress sent deputations to the Government of India which severed trade relations with South Africa, and to UNO. India, newly independent after decades of similar disobedience on an immensely magnified scale, was represented in the United Nations by Mrs Pandit, sister of Nehru, Gandhi's lieutenant and successor. The Trusteeship Committee was well aware of the Permanent Mandates Commission's old strictures on the administration of South West Africa. Now the Indian representative on the committee not only attacked the treatment of Indians in the Union but analysed and condemned the whole policy of discrimination against all Black inhabitants.

When Smuts was challenged by Mrs Pandit and by Mr Vyshinski of the USSR he was supported by representatives of

45. Simons, op. cit., p. 551.

Britain and other colonial powers, who maintained this was an internal matter and not within United Nations competence. A large majority of the General Assembly, however, demanded that Indians be treated in conformity with the 'gentlemen's agreements' made between representatives of South Africa and India. Smuts on his return home refused to negotiate with Delhi, but he appointed an Indian Advisory Board.

The 'Ghetto Act' marked an important turning point in South Africa's international relations. It caused the first overt rift between Commonwealth members with the breaking of Indian–South African trade relations. It brought South Africa's race relations under powerful UN scrutiny, which was intensified when the question of South West Africa came up soon after. It led to a long and often bitter conflict in the UN between, roughly, the old colonial powers and the lately colonial Afro-Asian territories which, increasing in numbers year by year, were set on destroying all remaining colonialism and were backed by many south and central American states and eastern Europe in this. In South Africa itself it hastened the joining of forces by the Black communities. The ANC had expressed support for the Indians during the campaign and had been impressed by passive resistance as a means of political struggle. A new generation of all races was introduced to the theory and practice of passive resistance. The provisions of the Act put Indians on a political footing with Africans, from whom they had previously held aloof, and so disposed a section of them to make common cause with the great mass of the South African people. Dr Xuma, Dr Dadoo and Dr Naicker, Presidents respectively of the ANC and the Transvaal and Natal Indian Congresses, made an agreement in 1947 to work together for full enfranchisement and for equal rights in economic, industrial and other fields. Early in 1948, just before White elections were due, the ANC called a People's Assembly for Votes for all, at which 322 delegates adopted a People's Charter – proclaiming 'a burning belief in the ideals of democracy', and containing an amalgam of the American Declaration of Rights, the Atlantic Charter and undertones of Marxism.

The United Nations Organization had succeeded the League of Nations, one of the war's casualties, and to its formation, as to the

League's twenty-five years earlier but less dominatingly, Smuts had contributed. In particular an early draft of the preamble to the Atlantic Charter had been his; his too the idea of Trusteeship replacing the Mandates System (also his) of the League. But again the apprentice was to escape the sorcerer's control. For it was expected that the Mandated territories would be made over to the Trusteeship Council, and this was done in every case except those of Palestine, which Britain intended soon to be independent, and of South West Africa. For South Africa it was more than ever of vital importance to retain control of South West Africa. There was by then a substantial White settler population, linked to the Union by the bonds of kith and kin and, despite the territory's overall poverty, beginning to prosper on the white diamonds of the alluvial fields and the black diamonds, the karakul lambs, of the parched farms. (The full extent was not then apparent of the rich mineral potential which, by 1966, was to give South West Africa one of the highest rates of development in the world.) The Blacks formed a large labour reservoir for the farms and mines of South West and for recruitment to the Union. Though the territory's old strategic value gradually faded in the modern world, it was a valuable buffer, a *cordon sanitaire*, along with Rhodesia and the Portuguese colonies (as the more far-seeing realized), against the African states to the north whose emancipation was to come even more quickly than feared.

South Africa's first application for the incorporation of South West Africa was made in 1945 to a United Nations Organization still in gestation. In November 1946 General Smuts appeared before the Trusteeship Committee of UNO formally to request the termination of the Mandate and the incorporation of South West Africa with the Union.

South Africa argued that South West, for twenty-five years administered as an integral part of the Union, was in fact now firmly integrated, that there was no prospect of its ever becoming an independent state and that uncertainty as to its future status was holding back development. Smuts claimed correctly that the large majority of the Whites of South Africa and South West Africa demanded incorporation. He also produced the results of a recent referendum which showed an overwhelming majority of

Blacks also in favour. South Africa claimed that 240,000 of the Black people of South West Africa had been consulted in the referendum and only 33,000 of them had opposed incorporation; but it was pointed out that the numbers were based on block votes of the chiefs mostly in remote Ovamboland, who were government-paid officials and that the minority included Herero, Nama and Berg Damara, all with long experience of rule by Germans and South Africans. The aged Herero chief, Hosea Kutako, asked to be allowed to send his representatives to the United Nations to explain his opposition and, when the administration refused this request, he sent cables of protest to the secretary-general. A petition from the ANC against incorporation was delivered at the UN by Dr A. B. Xuma. Further, six chiefs of the Bechuanaland Protectorate, under the leadership of the able and independent-minded regent of the Ngwato, Tshekedi Khama, also expressed their concern that the incorporation of South West Africa would be the first step to annexation by South Africa of the High Commission Territories and that it would threaten their own communications, particularly a hoped-for outlet through Walvis Bay. The South African administration had blocked the Herero spokesman; now the British Government refused Tshekedi Khama facilities to go to the United Kingdom, nor would it undertake to make the full documents available to the United Nations.

Smuts was invited to place South West Africa under the Trusteeship Committee (as all the other ex-German mandates had been). This he declined to do, but he agreed to continue to submit annual reports. The debate was already bitter, but Smuts at the end of the war had a considerable international reputation. He was a skilled diplomat and negotiator, accomplished in compromise and prevarication. He might have pulled off another of his political balancing feats, found some formula which would have attracted sufficient support for his policy in the United Nations. But events took an unexpected turn.

Frederick Maharero, Paramount Chief of the Herero, had lived since their defeat by the Germans, with a large part of the tribe in exile in the Bechuanaland Protectorate. There he was receiving frantic appeals from South West Africa: 'The heritage of your father's orphans is about to be taken away from them.' He summoned an Anglican missionary, Michael Scott, who, in the Philip tradition, had been campaigning for Black rights in the Union and who had just become interested in a report by the *New York Times* correspondent drawing attention to questionable aspects of the referendum. The Herero deputed Scott to represent them at the United Nations, where he presented their petitions and protests and a great deal of background material he had assembled. There was a drama about the White man's intervention on behalf of an obscure African tribe and a pathos in the appeals he conveyed that caught the imagination of delegates, press and public. (Scott was to stick to his brief and keep the issue alive for the next decade, until South West Africans capable of presenting their own case were to slip out of Africa and into New York.)

Another general election was in the offing in South Africa. In anticipation, Malan had made an election agreement with Havenga who had succeeded Hertzog as leader of the now diminutive and reputedly moderate Afrikaner Party. As a matter of tactics he soft-pedalled the Republican campaign, doused the anti-Semitism that had flourished during the war and dropped his anti-British propaganda. He reassured war veterans as to the treatment they might expect from a Nationalist regime. He cherished the new young generation of Afrikaners grown up on the platteland in thrall to dominie and predikant. He concentrated his attacks on the UN and Russia, whom the Nationalists feared, on India and other non-white nations whom they despised and feared, and these fears drew White South Africans closer. Nationalists maintained that the country was no longer bound by the Mandates system and attacked Smuts for approaching the UN at all. In Hofmeyr, the uneasy United Party liberal, Malan gave the country a scapegoat. He set his professors to find a formula to rally the Whites against the liberal advocacy of equal opportunities for all races.

It was in this setting – of widespread economic and social confusion, strikes, riots and violence, overcrowding, poverty and disease, an internal mass protest sophisticated and articulate as never before and a louring background of international condemnation – that the Nationalists found their formula; its name was *apartheid* and in that name Malan prepared to go to the polls. Smuts, versatile as ever, declared as the election campaign raged: 'Room must be made for them (Non-whites) on the principle of apartheid. It is neither a new word nor a new thing.'[46] But he had private misgivings:

Of course the Natives are not without a cause ... [he wrote to a friend]. But I dare not do anything that will outpace public opinion too much. On the eve of an election I shall do as much of the right thing as possible, but always keep before me the paramount necessity of winning the election ... What will it profit this country if justice is done to the under-dog and the whole caboodle then, including that under-dog, is handed over to the wreckers.[47]

The day of 26 May 1948 closed for Smuts, a giant in world reputation and at the zenith of his fame, in confidence of electoral success. Night brought a landslide and dawn defeat and with it a new era in South African affairs. Malan, in his moment of victory, exulted: 'Today South Africa belongs to us once more. For the first time since Union, South Africa is our own. May God grant that it will always remain so.'[48]

46. Roskam, op. cit., p. 94.
47. Legum, op. cit., p. 17.
48. Hancock, op. cit., II, p. 488.

6 The Volk (1948–58)

1. APARTHEID THE PANACEA

In coalition with the Afrikaner Party the Nationalists had obtained a precarious majority of five, but had polled in all 150,000 votes *fewer* than the Opposition (which would have had a *majority* of twenty if all votes had equal value). This anomaly was due to the weighting of rural seats where Nationalist strength had always lain, while the United Party gained huge but useless majorities in urban constituencies. For Smuts, when he had the right and the power, had obstinately refused to accede to those who pressed for delimitation reforms, who argued that the original need for heavy weighting in rural areas had long disappeared as the rapid flow of Afrikaners to the towns in recent decades had evened up the distribution of Afrikaans and English-speaking voters in the constituencies, and the once vast rural distances were shrunk to size by modern transport. Whether he was unwilling to antagonize his few platteland supporters or felt he must observe aspects, however outdated, of the spirit of the Constitution, he, his party and the country paid dearly for his scruples.

The next twenty years, years of Afrikaner power, was an era of international revolution, not always violent, not always Marxist, but one in which national postures of four centuries' acceptance were turned over. Just before it opened in 1947, India and Pakistan had gained independent status, the first of the British colonial countries of Asia and Africa to do so; they also acquired seats – and as vital, voices – in the United Nations. In 1957 the old West African colony of the Gold Coast, the 'White Man's Grave', became the new nation of Ghana. Before 1957 the only independent countries in Africa had been Ethiopia, Egypt, Liberia and

290

White South Africa. Ten years later only Portuguese Guiné, Angola, Mozambique, Rhodesia and some small Spanish colonies remained as European dependencies and the number of African countries in the United Nations had risen to thirty-eight.

These were years of gnawing anxiety for Whites, Afrikaners particularly, who were innately aware of being out-numbered four to one by Blacks within their own boundaries and of being a small and lonely White outpost of Western civilization. They knew they had no line of retreat such as generally lay open to other colonists if things went wrong; they had no motherland outside the harsh reality of Africa. But these were also years of dedicated purpose, growing cohesion and determination to safeguard for Afrikaner descendants their inherited way of life in its entirety. The efforts, in a time of world-wide reassessment, to impose the will of the White Volk on three-quarters of the country's inhabitants, the refusal to compromise and the resultant strains, tensions and conflicts which permeated these years of destiny for South Africa and brimmed over beyond her borders were knotted into the web of laws which enmeshed peoples and events.

When the Nationalist Party so unexpectedly found itself victorious, it was surprised but not unprepared. Power was seized with the determination that it would never be relinquished. Thanks to Malan's foresight and competence the party was strong and united, and two potentially dangerous challengers of its dominance, the New Order and the OB, had been emasculated. Through the leaders' behind-the-scenes connections with the Broederbond and its political, social, economic, religious, educational and press agencies, the party was in complete control of the Afrikaner people. There were ready a Draft Constitution to work on, an educational system to introduce and a systemization of the relationships between Church and State in the making. There was also a new formulation of traditional policy, apartheid, ready to apply.

A statement on the relations of State and Church was published by the Dutch Reformed Church soon after the Nationalists took office. This supplied a philosophic foundation for political practice and a reconciliation of Calvinism and Nationalism, in which the authority of the Broederbond was implicit.[1] The State, the authors declared, had been created by God and exists independently of its citizens, its authority over the individual being ordained by God. It is distinguished from other creations by possessing a monopoly of might, and its duty is to organize this power by means of a police force and army.

In every State, the authors went on, God is the fountain of authority. The Christian State acknowledges God's authority, while the non-Christian acknowledges the sovereignty of the people or of those in authority. Strongly opposed to the Calvinist conception are the humanist theories of individualism and universalism which regard the State as something created by man for his own use; no Christian may regard the State merely as a necessary evil. The authority of ruler over subject is not a human invention but a gracious gift of God to a fallen generation and must be exercised according to God's will; it is not unlimited; it cannot be replaced by another authority; and it is indivisible. Therefore there can be no division of power between legislature, executive and judiciary. The State has the authority to integrate harmoniously the various interests of its subjects. This doctrine is opposed both to liberal democracy and to totalitarianism. The State has definite territorial limits, part of God's plan, and attempts to wipe them out are of the devil. The humanistic idea of a world state is contrary to Scripture and an attempt to achieve world peace outside the Kingdom of Heaven. The individual has a voice in political matters and a Christian people has the right to get rid of a government that is not acting in accordance with God's will.

Applying these principles specifically to the South African situation, the D R C condemns the ideas of the school of Rousseau that all men are equal and so all, White and Black, must participate in law making. On that basis the mass of individuals become the source of State authority, the government becomes the servant of the people and is unseated when it no longer serves the wishes and needs of the people. The Christian does not regard

1. *Fundamental Principles of Calvinist Political Science* N.G.K. (1951) summarized by Leo Marquard in *The Peoples and Policies of South Africa* from which this account is largely drawn.

the vote as qualifying him to make laws which is a function of the State, but as a symbol of God's sovereignty authorizing him to apply a religious test to authority. The franchise is a treasure for those who are of age politically and able to use it responsibly before God, and those who do not have it are not slaves or suppressed peoples. Not only undeveloped groups, but all those in open rebellion against God, such as communists, should not be given it. Political parties are necessary, for where doctrines of unbelief – in Liberalism, in Democracy, in Communism – are powerful it is the duty of the Christian to try to become the strongest political force and establish a Christian government. Only the Christian political faith is valid and no anti-Christian philosophy should be given the right to form political parties nor any group who aim at a dictatorship allowed the right of organization.

This interpretation of Calvinist doctrine and its application to modern statecraft should be borne in mind if Nationalist government policies are to be understood. And if these policies were to receive the support needed to carry them out, the background thinking had to shape the attitudes of the ordinary people; this was done by a system of education so rigidly controlled as to amount to indoctrination.

Two educational systems for White children had developed, grown out of old pre-Union disputes when Smuts and Hertzog were responsible for education in the Transvaal and Free State respectively, and the medium of instruction carried strong political overtones and tensions.

Under Smuts parallel or dual medium schools had been established in which children were taught in English or in Afrikaans in parallel classes or else some subjects in each language. In either case the children grew up in one institution, living much of their day together, getting to know each other and acquiring, it was hoped, a fluent bilingualism. Hertzog, however, had strongly supported single medium schools in which children received mother-tongue instruction in separate institutions, were taught the second language as a subject and did not meet or mix. It was essential, he argued, to protect the still fragile Afrikaans language and culture from extinction by the more robust, broadly based

English. This was a real possibility as the English language exerted a strong pull in political, international, cultural and economic fields which Afrikaans as yet could not. When the United Party won the election of 1943, it had begun to extend the principle of dual medium in the Transvaal. The Nationalists were to reverse the trend when they in turn were successful. Throughout the 1940s the medium of education gave rise to bitter dispute between White South Africans.

At the beginning of 1948 a group of professors of Potchefstroom University (headquarters of the conservative Gereformeerde Kerk and of the Broederbond) and Nationalist politicians issued a programme of Christian National Education which went much further than the advocates of Christian National Education after the Anglo-Boer War had gone. Extreme Calvinist and fundamentalist doctrines were advanced as basic educational principles. The word Christian in this context was defined as 'according to the creed of the three Afrikaner Churches'; Nationalist as 'imbued with the love of one's own, especially one's own language, history and culture'.[2] The key subject should be religion (study of the Bible and the three South African creeds). All teaching should be nationalist.

Owing to the Fall [the programme stated], all children are born sinful, but the children of believers have inherited God's promise through Christ's redemption ... It is God's will that man should master the earth and rule over it and He has given to each nation its own particular national task in bringing about His will. Education should enable the young to take over from their cultural heritage everything that is good and beautiful and noble and develop it in accordance with their own gifts ... This only a CN school can teach them to do.

In content, the statement insisted, all teaching must be CN and in no subject might anti-Christian or non-Christian or anti-national or non-national propaganda be made. Mother-tongue should be the most important secular subject and the only medium of instruction. Bilingualism should not be aimed at, and the second language should be taught only when mother-tongue

2. Summary contained in *Blueprint for Blackout*, Education League.

is mastered. Every nation was rooted in a country allotted to it by God, and geography should give the child a thorough knowledge of his own country so that he would love it when compared and contrasted with others and be prepared to defend it. History should be seen as the fulfilment of God's plan for humanity, and its teaching must include such facts as the Creation, the Fall, the Incarnation, Life and Death of Christ, the Second Coming and the End of the World. Next to the mother-tongue, the history of the Fatherland was the best channel for 'cultivating the love of one's own which is nationalism'. Single medium schools were provided for. Parents must appoint teachers and keep a watch on the teaching and through parents Church vigilance over the doctrine and lives of the teachers must be exercised; 'unless the teacher was a Christian he was a deadly danger to us'. The secular sciences should be taught according to the Christian and National view of life and science should be expounded in a positively Christian light and contrasted with non-Christian science. There should be no attempt 'to reconcile or abolish the fundamental opposition, for Creator and created, man and beast, individual and community, authority and freedom remain in principle insoluble in each other'.

The education of other race groups (which should not be financed at the expense of Whites) must make them also nationalist, according to the CNE exponents.

The welfare and happiness of the Coloured lies in his understanding that he belongs to a separate racial group . . . Native education should be based on the principles of trusteeship, non-equality and segregation; its aim should be to inculcate the White man's view of life, especially the Boer nation which is the senior trustee . . . Nationalist education should lead to the development of an independent self-supporting Christian Nationalist Native community.

The notion that 'Bantu education' must be different from standard education, designed for a different sort of human being, goes far back in Afrikaner thought. Dr P. S. J. de Klerk, in 1923, wrote: 'The Bantu, after all, belong to a lower race which cannot be put on an equal footing with White, whether in the family or in politics or in the Church. No, here are lines drawn by the Creator himself which man may not wipe out on his own accord without it having evil effects.'³ Although a DRC Missionary conference three years later laid down that the Native was created in the image of God with rights as a human being and a Christian which may not be denied (the idea behind the 'total apartheid' of some of the intellectuals), the cruder beliefs of the mass of the Afrikaner people were not changed. Some twenty-five years after de Klerk, Professor Chris Coetzee, of Potchefstroom University, a member of the Institute which formulated the CNE Policy, wrote:

> God brought forth the kinds ... Man is a 'Genesis-kind'. He did not evolve out of other kinds, but ... all human races developed out of Adam – 'developed' here is regarded both as progress and as retrogression. The so-called Neanderthal man – if indeed this being was a man – is an example of degeneration after the flood.⁴

(From there it is a short step to the widely held popular belief in the curse of Ham.)

Professor Coetzee, again, commented on an exhibition of pre-history in 1952:

> As regards the place of pre-history in schools: I claim that my child ... shall not be taught evolution as a truth in school. This is why I send my child to a Christian school and expect that he shall be taught the creationist view ... At the university level my grown-up child will naturally learn about the evolutionist point of view ... He would then be old enough to understand this point of view. What he is going to accept as his own scientific conviction is his own choice.⁵

This is an unexpected statement to come from the educational heart of the land in which man – *homo sapiens* – is believed to have evolved and where exciting research on the subject was even then in progress.

That line of thought was specifically disavowed by Dr Eiselen and others of the intellectual framers of apartheid, but it has conditioned the mental reflexes of generations and clearly underlies such statements as: 'Equality of the White and Coloured races in university lecture rooms was a serious development because it caused the White man to lose his sense of colour. When that hap-

---

3. W. J. van der Merwe, *Development of Missionary Attitudes in the DRC of South Africa*, p. 140.
4. *A Twentieth-Century Inquisition*, Educational League.
5. *The Star* (Johannesburg, 15 July 1952).

pened it was the end of White civilization' (S. P. le Roux, Minister of Agriculture).[6] And: 'South Africa can only remain a white country if we continue to see that the Europeans remain the dominant nation; and we can only remain the dominant nation if we have power to govern the country, and if the Europeans by means of their vote remain the dominant section' (J. G. Strydom, later Prime Minister).[7]

Politicians, predikants, farmers, workers had always been certain there should be no equality anywhere between Black and White. But two world wars, the advance of biological sciences and changing conditions and attitudes in many countries made old definitions unacceptable to many of the more thoughtful Whites in South Africa and repellent to many people in the post-war world.

The task had fallen to the University of Stellenbosch (the old serenely gabled Cape town with its oak-shaded and stream-edged streets, which had mothered so many leading intellectuals and politicians) to formulate a comprehensive and modern race policy in harmony with a Calvinist form of State; a policy to replace such vague and empirical concepts as segregation, separation, White domination, parallelism and trusteeship, which had all in turn been extolled but none of which had been within any South African government's vision or capacity to apply; a policy to discipline the confusion in race affairs which had become chaotic in war years and was now thoroughly alarming. In Stellenbosch the South African Bureau of Race Affairs (SABRA) had been set up in 1947 to study race matters in the light of Afrikaner thought and policy. SABRA was founded by a group which included Donges, Jansen, Diederichs, Eiselen and Stallard, to run parallel with and be rival and antidote to the twenty-year-old liberal South African Institute of Race Relations.

The word apartheid had been used before – even by Smuts; it was no more than the Afrikaans of Professor Hoernlé's 'separation'. It went into general circulation in the election campaign of 1948, was taken abroad in the vocabularies of politicians and

6. S. P. le Roux, Minister of Agriculture, *The Star* (5 March 1949).

7. J. G. C. Strydom, Minister of Lands and later Prime Minister, quoted by John Hatch in *The Dilemma of South Africa*, p. 97.

journalists, soon was currency for any sort of discriminatory separation, made its way into dictionaries before the decade was out and by 1961 was sadly described by an Afrikaans newspaper as 'one of the ugliest swear words in the world'.[8] But apartheid, it was pointed out, was not a dogma but a policy and as such would be altered, expanded and redefined many times.

In presenting its policy the Nationalist Party emphasized that, 'The choice before us is one of two divergent courses: either that of integration, which would in the long run amount to national suicide on the part of the Whites, or that of apartheid.'[9] The party adopted the findings of a committee of prominent Afrikaners which defined apartheid as

a policy which sets itself the task of preserving and safeguarding the racial identity of the White population of the country; of likewise preserving and safeguarding the identity of the indigenous peoples as separate racial groups, with opportunities to develop in self-governing units; of fostering the inculcation of national consciousness, self-esteem and mutual regard among the various races of the country.[10]

The double goal was set. The first older than the Trek and nearly as old as White settlement in South Africa, the second a very new idea necessitated by modern pressures.

The haunting and galvanizing fears, especially of loss of identity, were variously expressed, but in essence were the same at this period as in the early days when the settler was out on his own. As recently as 1952 Dr N. Diederichs (soon to be Minister of Economic Development) wrote of the nature of the Afrikaner that he carried his Bible with him and what he read became actuality; he saw himself as 'part of the Creation, but separate . . . in that he carried with him a divine element . . . something . . . unique with its own reality and value'. Among the foreign influences threatening the people, he continued, is the drive towards equality.

The Trekker observed and maintained differences and lines of division. The division of day and night, summer and winter, rain and drought, black and white. But the world of today is the world of the

8. C. & M. Legum, *South Africa: Crisis for the West*, p. 49.
9. ibid., p. 50.
10. ibid., p. 49.

masses and from this arises liberalism and internationalism ... It is a wonder that we have managed to exist as we have so far, as the smallest people in the world, the only real people in South Africa, and the only white people in the whole of Africa.[11]

W. van Heerden, editor of *Dagbreek*, writing in *Optima*, a journal produced by the Oppenheimer Anglo-American Mining Group and circulating internationally among shareholders, said: 'To disappear as a White race in the quicksands of African Native blood is, of course, a solution. Suicide may not be an attractive way out of one's problems but it is a way out.'[12]

Dr W. W. M. Eiselen, once Professor of Social Anthropology and then Secretary for Native Affairs, writing for the same public, put the same idea more academically: 'White South Africa is numerically not strong enough to absorb and can therefore only choose between being absorbed or surviving by maintenance of separate communities.'[13]

Dr H. F. Verwoerd, who with Eiselen was the main architect of the apartheid structure, said in his 1963 New Year message (after he became Prime Minister) that the White people of South Africa 'refuse to commit national suicide – they are determined to survive and to rule this country'.[14]

Speaking in the Assembly soon after Harold Macmillan, the visiting British Prime Minister, made his controversial 'Wind of Change' speech, Verwoerd said:

The White man of Africa is not going to be told that, because he is outnumbered by the Black peoples, he must allow his rights to be swallowed up and be prepared to lose his say ... We do not accept ... that the White inhabitants must be satisfied as a minority in a multi-racial country to compete with the Black masses on an equal basis which in the long run can only mean a Black government.[15]

In 1948 immediately on taking office, Malan, conscious not only of the discontented Black masses within his country's borders but of the millions beyond in Africa and many millions of all

11. *The Weltanschauung of the Afrikaner* (Inspan, April 1952).
12. *Optima* (December 1960), p. 185.
13. *ibid* (March 1959), p. 3.
14. *The Times* (London, 3 January 1963).
15. *Survey of Race Relations* (1959–60), p. 280.

colours beyond them, had said that it was only under apartheid that Non-Europeans could enjoy 'a greater independence and feeling of self-respect . . . as well as . . . better opportunities for free development in accordance with their natures and abilities', and that the Europeans would feel sure that their identity and their future were protected.[16]

Here was where the policy of apartheid differed from its fore-runners: it laid a theoretical stress on the need for giving Blacks the opportunity to preserve and to develop their own national identities. The bare bones of the apartheid theory (or, some might say, the window dressing, to sell it to its critics) – as opposed to the hustings versions of it – were that despite the proven fact that there was no correlation between mental ability and skin pig-mentation nor any inherent Black inferiority, in a multi-racial society the Black man would always find his freedom of move-ment and of economic, social and political progress blocked by the White man who claimed permanent superiority by virtue of his colour.

'If,' said Eiselen, first outlining the policy to the Institute of Race Relations in 1948, 'the White man would retain national security for his own progeny, he must earn it by making just provision for the Native and Coloured communities whom he cannot with impunity regard as a permanently subordinate class of men.'[17] To make this just provision requires first of all the cordoning of White and Black into 'separate, self-sufficient socio-economic units', a slow process enabling both gradually to adapt to the new circumstances. The area of the reserves would have to be increased by much more than the 4,000,000 morgen still to be purchased under the Native Land Act of 1936. (It is clear that Eiselen then, and later other apartheid theorists, envisaged that the eventual incorporation of the High Com-mission Territories would provide much of this land.) The reserves would have to be rehabilitated, an African farmer class developed, and chiefs and headmen trained as leaders. Towns would be established in the reserves, linked to the existing railway system. Industrial development would initially be financed by

16. E. A. Walker, *A History of Southern Africa*, p. 775.
17. *The Meaning of Apartheid*, Race Relations, XV (3 January 1948), p. 70.

the government, later attracting capital in the usual way. A system of extensive Native education would be needed, 'supplemented by the training of adults in various directions to make them useful members of society', the scope and standard of education being determined by the capacity of the society to produce more wealth. As more trained men and women were produced they would replace Whites staffing their services. Local and regional government would be in Native hands and Natives would, like the inhabitants of the High Commission Territories now, be content to remain in their own countries away from the White urban centres. The withdrawal of African labour in pursuance of this policy, it was emphasized, would greatly affect White economy. But the labour problems of the mining industry would disappear as the mines were worked out, farmers would overcome their difficulties by increased mechanization, immigration of Europeans, reduction in farm size and so on.

The first roughing out of the apartheid policy was a good deal modified and reinterpreted as the years passed. In 1948 Eiselen did not commit himself on the key question of the exact amount of land it was intended to allot to the Bantu Homelands nor on the exact relationship envisaged between the administrations of the Homelands and the Union or foreign governments. As Prime Minister in 1951 Dr Malan said:

Now a Senator wants to know whether the series of self-governing areas would be sovereign. The answer is obvious. It stands to reason that White South Africa must remain their guardian. We are spending all the money on these developments. How could small scattered states arise? The areas will be economically dependent on the Union. It stands to reason where we talk of Natives' right of Self-Government in those areas we cannot mean that we intend to cut large slices out of South Africa and turn them into independent states.[18]

And in 1956 the South African Ambassador to the United States, the economist J. E. Holloway, pointed out that two Prime Ministers had said that total apartheid was an ideal but not realizable in practice.[19]

18. Senate (1 May 1951).
19. J. E. Holloway on Apartheid in *Annals of the American Academy of Political and Social Studies* (July 1956).

'Nice Pussy . . .!'

'Our policy of Apartheid has often been misunderstood. It can best be described as a policy of good neighbourliness.'

Dr Verwoerd

Commonwealth Indignation Meeting

Picked Audience

Multi-facial Commonwealth.

'I simply mind my own business.'

'I won't have politics in sport. Where do you think you are—Wimbledon?'

By the end of the 1950s, however, as criticism of South Africa's policies was hardening almost everywhere abroad, boycott movements were gaining support and resistance inside the country was mounting, views on the degree of 'totality' intended in apartheid broadened.

In 1959 Eiselen took the Commonwealth as an analogy:

> White South Africa would eventually become a Mother Country to the Bantu Countries . . . [But he added] It seems to the writer and to most members of the European electorate, as well as to many enlightened representatives of the Bantu and other groups, that the maintenance of white political supremacy over the country as a whole is a *sine qua non* for racial peace and economic prosperity in South Africa . . . The utmost degree of autonomy which the Union Parliament is likely to be prepared to concede to these areas will still stop short of actual surrender of sovereignty by the European Trustee, and there is therefore no prospect of a federal system with eventual equality among members taking the place of the South African Commonwealth . . . [20]

Verwoerd similarly updated the concept in the Assembly.

> We are giving the Bantu as our wards every opportunity in their areas to move along a road of development by which they can progress in accordance with ability. And if it should happen in the future they should progress to a very advanced level, the people of those future times will have to consider in what further way their relationships must be reorganized . . . I take as a comparison . . . the British Commonwealth of Nations, where the various constituent members . . . are not represented in the Mother Parliament, but within which organization there are still links – economic and otherwise – by which cooperation is possible without a mixed Parliament or government, whether of the country itself or of the federation, ever being established. [21]

This was interpreted by van Heerden, writing for overseas, as the proposal of possible eventual independence:

> On that day the present Prime Minister, in what may justly be called a historic speech, uplifted [apartheid] and made it a blue print for the future development, equal in worth, of the White and Black

20. *Optima* (March 1959), pp. 7–8.
21. Assembly *Hansard* (27 January 1959), cols 62, 63.

peoples of the Union and possibly – no, we cherish the thought hope-fully – for the whole of the sub-continent of Africa . . . In his declara-tion of policy, the fundamental and final objective of apartheid was for the first time officially defined as having in view for the Native people in their areas the same benefits in every respect as for the Whites in their areas – including eventual sovereign independence.²²

2. PRESERVING THE VOLK

The Nationalists were now in a position to create the sort of society they believed to be necessary and they approached the task on four well-assessed levels. Above all they had to ensure a permanent majority in Parliament. They had to maintain a financial stability. They had to implement the apartheid policy. Finally, they had to prevent the growth of an opposition strong enough to frustrate them. They believed that the State, under God, was the supreme authority but also that it should be based on the broad will of the people – the *Volkswil*. The leaders differed only as to who were the Volk. Hertzog had regarded all Whites who put South Africa first as Afrikaners, while Malan considered the English-speaking people could not be assimilated into Afrikanerdom. But, whatever drastic actions were advocated by wild men on election platforms or in Parliament, the leader-ship, sensitive to reaction at home and abroad, was careful to appear to observe the established democratic processes, though these were very much stretched from time to time.

Backed by a ministry wholly united in purpose, Malan tackled the matter of augmenting the Nationalists' small parliamentary strength in two ways: by increasing their own representation and by eroding the strength of the Opposition. Almost immediately they were in office they forced through Parliament, narrowly and against fierce opposition, the South African Citizenship Act of 1949 which, besides substituting South African for British citizenship, raised from 2 years to 5 years the time qualification for citizenship, and ensured that recent British immigrants who might have opposed the Government were disqualified from the next election. On the other hand Malan restored freedom and

22. *Optima* (December 1960), p. 189.

civil rights to men who had been imprisoned and penalized by the Smuts government for active opposition during the war. Many thousands of South West African Germans similarly were enfranchised.

Although an International Court of Justice opinion was awaited on the international status of South West Africa, Malan, in the South West African Affairs Amendment Act of 1949, took the first step towards incorporation of the mandated territory as a fifth province. South Africa had always been set on this despite international opposition and despite the fact that it was then still a poor country and constantly in heavy debt to the Union. The main considerations were the importance of precluding control by a hostile state of a country so close to the Union's borders, and the fact that as time passed increasing numbers of South Africans had settled in the territory. But, more immediately significant, the Act gave South West Africa extremely generous representation in the Union Parliament: four Senators and six members to represent the 24,000 White voters; this was one member for 4,000 voters compared with one for 9,000 in the Union itself. All the six seats were won by Nationalist candidates who at a stroke more than doubled their majority. The interests of the 300,000 Blacks of South West Africa were in the hands of one White senator, nominated for his acquaintance with the reasonable wants and wishes of the coloured races.

The International Court of Justice delivered its opinion in 1950, that the League of Nations' supervisory function had passed to the United Nations, that obligations continued to be binding and that South West Africa's international status could be modified only with UN consent. South Africa was now launched on a long, acrimonious encounter with the rest of the world. The Whites, blinkered by archaic race attitudes and economic interests, were quite unable to grasp the hostility their policies were engendering in a world in which nations, with recollections of a colonial tutelage still fresh, exercised increasing collective influence, while her own traditional friends trimmed their sails to the winds of change. The government just pushed doggedly on with its plans.

Its most formidable opponent was removed from the scene in

this year. At the age of eighty Smuts died: revered, reviled; romantic rebel, loyal imperialist; Commonwealth statesman, 'slim' politician; the philosopher of holism, seer of the mountain top; 'slaughterer' of Bulhoek, of the Bondelswarts, of the Rand miners; yet his life-work by no means entirely summed up in Roy Campbell's cruel epigram on the publication of *Holism and Evolution:*

> The love of nature burning in his heart,
> Our new St Francis offers us his book.
> The saint who fed the birds at Bondelswart
> And fattened up the vultures at Bulhoek.

Whatever the image one carried, the *Ou Baas* in his later days had been loved by many and had for sixty years dominated South African lives and fortunes for better or worse: their fate was now unequivocally in other hands.

Hofmeyr's untimely death, worn out by work, at the end of 1948, had removed the heir apparent. J. G. N. Strauss, once Smuts's secretary, succeeded him as leader of the United Party with tepid party backing, but supported by Harry Oppenheimer (MP for Kimberley and son of gold and diamond millionaire, Sir Ernest Oppenheimer) and some of the younger party men who were opposed to apartheid largely because they feared its effects on the economy. Strauss himself was not politically robust and was quite unable to give a vigorous lead either in outbidding the Nationalists or in withstanding them steadfastly. Under his leadership the United Party began seriously to disintegrate.

A possible focus for future Afrikaner electoral division was removed when the Nationalist Party absorbed the Afrikaner Party in 1951. In 1958 it was to gain further strength by the Electoral Laws Amendment Act which enfranchised the eighteen-year-olds. (The Afrikaner section of the population was increasing more rapidly than the English.)

It was a fundamental of apartheid that there should be no racial mixing on the roll and that Blacks should not be represented at all, not even by Whites, in the central Parliament which must be free of all Black political pressures. This was tactically important too, because the elected representatives of the Blacks had sometimes held the balance between the parties in the Assembly and, as the most outspoken opponents of the government, their strictures tended to resound outside South African frontiers; further, if Blacks on the Common roll should prosper and sur-mount the educational qualification their representatives must inevitably one distant day outnumber the Whites.

Another of Malan's early actions, therefore, was to withdraw the franchise offered to the Indians in Smuts's 'Pegging Act'. Next the Electoral Law Amendment Act of 1949 made it more complicated for Coloureds to get on the roll and this, allied to their inherent apathy towards White politics, kept the actual enrol-ment to under 50,000 of 120,000 who qualified, in spite of the efforts of White candidates to enrol the *stemvee*, voting cattle, as they were often contemptuously regarded.

This law went through with little opposition. In 1951, however, the government introduced a Separate Representation of Voters Bill to remove the Coloured voters of the fifty-five Cape con-stituencies from the Common roll. They would be placed on a separate roll (as had been the Africans in 1936) to elect four Whites to the Assembly and one to the Senate, and a Board of Coloured Affairs would be set up to advise the government on matters affecting the Coloured people. The Bill provoked a major political rumpus. The stubborn opposition to the Act was not only because the Coloured vote, such as it was, significantly favoured the United Party in half, and was decisive in seven, of the Cape constituencies. A minority also saw this reduction in the rights of the Coloured people as a betrayal; but above all it was resented as a violation of the Constitution and a threat to the still entrenched English language rights.

In addition to conventional constitutional opposition the War Veterans' Torch Commando was formed to be the spearhead of extra-parliamentary action in defence of the Constitution against the initial threat of the Bill. Under the appealing leadership of 'Sailor' A. G. Malan, a Battle of Britain hero, and the more prosaic financial sponsorship of Harry Oppenheimer, thousands of returned soldiers rallied and exaltedly pledged 'undying opposition to those who would bind the free spirit of men with chains of bigotry and ignorance and who would prostitute the spirit of democratic government in South Africa'.[23] They organized a 100,000-signature petition against the Bill, massive public demonstrations, spectacular torchlight processions and often rowdy mass meetings. There were inevitable street battles with civilians and police. The government managed to keep public attention focused on the racial aspects of its policy and the Torch's position as a radical movement became equivocal – after all, the majority of its members felt strongly their affiliations with White South Africa – when, caught in the old South African paradox, it refused to open its ranks to ex-servicemen among the Nonwhites whose liberties it was defending.

The Bill was carried separately in Assembly and Senate, instead of by a two-thirds majority of both Houses sitting together as required by the entrenched clauses of the Constitution. Tested in the courts on these grounds, the Act was declared invalid. Arguing that this decision interfered with the legislative supremacy of Parliament, Malan then introduced the High Court of Parliament Bill 'to vest in the democratically elected representatives of the electors, as representing the will of the people, the power to adjudicate finally on the validity of the laws'. The High Court of Parliament (boycotted by the Opposition) obediently reversed the Appeal Court decision, only to be itself invalidated by the Appeal Court.

Despite the United Party's conciliatory wooing of the electorate and agreement with the Labour Party and the Torch to join forces to fight the 1953 election, the Nationalists came in again with increased parliamentary strength and confidence (though it still had a minority of votes).

As a result, two other more lasting militant White anti-Nationalist groups were formed. The Liberal Movement (later Party) declared that race harmony would only be established by abolishing the economic colour bar and throwing open the franchise to all races. It first advocated a qualified franchise and later decided it should be open to all adults. Mrs Margaret Ballinger (wife of William Ballinger), an old liberal and one of the Cape Native Representatives, became the party leader and, until Native representation was abolished, its only voice in Parliament, though for

23. Alexander Hepple, *South Africa*, p. 128.

some years longer the Liberal Party formed a vocal and (for the establishment) tiresomely active extra-parliamentary irritant. Soon after the founding of the Liberal Movement, a group of radical Whites, including many ex-members of the disbanded Communist Party, formed the Congress of Democrats (COD), pledged from the start to total support of the various Black Congresses and to press for fully equal rights for all Blacks. While these forces with their sharply defined objectives came into action, intrigue amongst the Torch's United Party leaders, who feared the effect on the party if the strength of the Torch increased, sapped the movement's momentum and after the election it began to disintegrate.

Other consequences of the long-drawn but arguably constitutional manoeuvrings were the fracturing of the United Party, six members forming a more right-wing but short-lived Conservative Party and one moving to the left, later to join a new Progressive Party; the weakening of the United Party's election prospects in the Western Cape; and a demonstration that no constitutional safeguards can endure in the face of a determination that they shall not.

Throughout this period too there had been a steady elimination of individuals in positions of authority in the public service who were known to have United Party or moderate sympathies and their replacement by trusted Nationalist Party members. When elections were in the offing, public works projects on railways and roads frequently became necessary in the vicinity of marginal seats and required the moving into the area of large numbers of White labourers (poor whites on 'civilized' wages) who would certainly inflate electoral support for the government. At election times, too, politicians all over the country would lay great emphasis in their speeches on the 'Black Peril' and the apartheid plans to contain this. From time to time rumours circulated that Non-whites were going to poison the milk or water supplies or blow up the electricity works. All of these devices, as well as United Party ineffectiveness and uncertainty, against a background of augmenting Non-white resistance, played their part in ensuring the steady rise in support for the government election after election.

The Prime Minister, Dr Malan, after winning the 1953 election, changed his approach to the Coloured vote and submitted a South Africa Act Amendment Bill to validate the Separate Representation of Voters Act to a joint session of both Houses correctly in terms of the Constitution, but he failed to get his two-thirds majority. An Appellate Division Bill to transfer final authority on Acts of Parliament from the Appeal Court to a new court of Constitutional Appeal was introduced and, on second thoughts, withdrawn. Another attempt in 1954, with the Separate Representation of Voters Act Validation and Amendment Bill also failed to get a two-thirds majority.

Malan, now eighty and feeling his years, resigned from office in 1954. The able but also ageing Havenga, last link with Hertzog and his policy of unity of true Afrikaners whichever their language background, was ousted and he too retired, all three of them to acquire retrospective reputations as moderates in later, tougher years.

Malan's successor as premier J. G. Strydom, 'lion of the North', leader of the party in the Transvaal, was supported by Afrikaner power groups. He was a director of the *Voortrekkerpers*, publishers of the party newspaper *Die Transvaler*, had been a farmer, rugby player and lawyer before he turned politician. He was a loyal follower of Malan whose rejection of coalition and fusion he had supported. Before the war he had backed Germany's campaign for the return of the colonies. He was regarded as a sincere and straightforward politician, but he was uncompromising, limited in his knowledge of the world beyond South Africa, and a zealous republican, convinced that English and Afrikaners could not cooperate except in a republic. He was a devout 'Dopper', fond of quoting the scriptures and certain of the divine mission of the Afrikaner Volk to defend White civilization. 'If the White man is to retain the effective political control in his hands by means of legislation, then it means the White man must remain the master.'[24] He took office at a time of great political and industrial unrest in South Africa, and the rebellious (mostly Black) sectors were attracting much attention and support abroad. He was to prove himself to be altogether the strong man the party sought.

24. Brian Bunting, *The Rise of the South African Reich*, p. 134.

The lawyer Strydom immediately justified his appointment by finding the way round the constitutional blocks to getting the Coloured voters off the roll. He approached the problem more deviously than had his predecessor by way of two Acts neither of which required a two-thirds majority. The first was the Appellate Division Quorum Act of 1955, which raised the quorum of the court to eleven when the validity of any Act of Parliament was in question, while the appointment of another five judges of Appeal brought the total bench to eleven. The second was the Senate Act which enlarged the senate from forty-eight to eighty-nine members and altered the basis of their election to give the government a certain majority of two-thirds in any joint session, while the previous Act would prevent any frustration by the courts. After five years of obsessional strife the South Africa Act Amendment Act of 1956 was at last passed in a joint sitting of Assembly and 'enlarged' Senate with an ample majority of 173 to 68. It validated the Separate Representation of Voters Act, abolished entrenched franchise rights, and ensured that no court of law was competent to pronounce on the validity of a law passed by Parliament. The last scene was played in the long charade which spelt White political supremacy or Baasskap.

The Black Sash (Women's Defence of the Constitution League) was founded in 1955, as tensions rose over the Coloured vote, to oppose Strydom's attempts to circumvent the Constitution, and the movement grew rapidly. With notable courage in the face of oral and sometimes physical assault the women demonstrated by 'vigils' when they stood in black sashes, heads bowed, outside Parliament or some public buildings, and 'haunts' when, at stations or airports with heads held high, they met ministers arriving or departing. The ministers, embarrassed by this silent accusation, were forced to all sorts of back-door subterfuges to avoid it. When these more picturesque and internationally newsworthy activities ceased, protests against discrimination continued and the women began to try through lectures, investigation, and attendance at magistrates' courts or pass offices, to get a deeper insight into the meaning of discrimination. The movement was confined to women voters, and to begin with excluded Blacks, for no Black women had ever had the vote. (In 1963, however, it was to open its membership to all the women of South Africa, partly influenced by the enfranchisement of the women of the Transkei.)

Nor did all Afrikaners give the Nationalist Government unqualified support. There were the many – mostly business and professional people, successors to the 'loyal Dutch' followers of Botha and Smuts – in the United Party who favoured White supremacy but in some less unequivocal form than apartheid. There were others, too, who faced their compatriots' unforgiving hostility to moderates and deviants – 'traitors'. From time to time a brave and individual voice was raised in the heart of intellectual and Calvinist Afrikanerdom: Dr Ben Marais and Professor P. V. Pistorius, Professor B. B. Keet and Professor L. J. du Plessis, theologians of Pretoria, Stellenbosch and Potchefstroom, were four, who during the 1950s, denied any scriptural justification for apartheid and urged, some of them, a relaxation in its application and cooperation at least with Westernized Africans, or, others, its total extension to give full political freedoms to independent states. They advocated the holding of discussions, not with salaried government-supporting chiefs, but with the chosen leaders, 'the rebels and the agitators . . . They represent the strivings of the Bantu'.[25] These viewpoints attracted wide attention but exerted small influence on political direction. However, the government was temporarily shaken by the challenges to authority by White and Black organizations and individuals over a wide area of country and in a broad sphere of activity. The laws had to be further tightened. But other Afrikaners were to find self-emancipation in the early 1960s. Professor A. S. Geyser would be convicted of heresy, and the Reverend Beyers Naude lose his job and facing ostracism in founding the inter-racial Christian Institute. There were other, not many and less exalted, Afrikaner names in the trade unions and radical political movements who worked tirelessly and made great sacrifice in the struggle against discrimination and for the extension of opportunities to the Black peoples.

In 1956 the enfeebled United Party replaced Strauss as leader by the equally weak Sir de Villiers Graaff, a rich Cape farmer. Its

25. *Survey of Race Relations* (1957–8), p. 17.

policy remained basically unchanged but gradually revealed a strong rightist look. It opposed apartheid but firmly believed in 'the maintenance of White supremacy for the foreseeable future'. It proposed a 'race federation' with a central federal Parliament uniting races rather than territorial units. Each group would have a defined share in government, the Coloureds ranking as equal with the Whites. The basic rights of individual groups and areas would be entrenched constitutionally. But this did not win the party any greater national support, and the government pressed on along its way with general United Party acquiescence and ever increasing White approval.

No amount of skilful manipulation of franchise rights, however, would keep a government in power if it had not adequate funds behind it. When the Nationalists found themselves in office, they had already built up considerable financial power in Afrikaner hands; but the great bulk of interests in finance, mining, industry and commerce remained in the hands of British and Jewish magnates, who had useful outside connections and were by no means well disposed to the Volk ideology.

The Nationalists had by good fortune taken over at a time of considerable post-war prosperity. Although large contributions by the Smuts administration to new international agencies and prodigal post-war importation, on top of the expense of a grain subsidy during a long drought, had reversed the balance of payments and drained the gold reserves, Smuts had still been able to make the British Government a shrewdly calculated loan of £80m. repayable in three years and much of it to be spent on South African foodstuffs, wine and fruit. Much 'hot' money from post-war Europe at the same time had been pouring into the country; share and property markets were active; immigrants and refugees from heavy British taxation were bringing in capital. But the Nationalists' victory in 1948, while the memory of their war-time activity was still fresh, and the defeat of the tried and trusty Smuts caused immediate loss of confidence and money began to pour out. About £200m. was soon withdrawn and the heavy import costs resulted in the largest adverse trade balance in the country's history.

Havenga, who had succeeded Hofmeyr as Finance Minister,

was fortunate in inheriting £8½m. in tax arrears. He imposed severe import controls on luxury goods, recalled the balance of Smuts's loan to Britain and followed the British move in devaluing the pound in relation to the dollar. He managed to borrow £26m. abroad. His luck held further, for the New Gold Fields of the Orange Free State began to come into production in 1951 and helped to offset his financial problems. Though he failed in a campaign for a higher gold price, he managed in the next year to raise a substantial Swiss loan and the United Kingdom and United States made large advances towards the development of important uranium deposits associated with the gold fields.

Big business interests had undoubtedly been shaken by the fall in confidence, by the increasingly inefficient use of labour, inevitable as apartheid was stepped up, and by acutely deteriorating race relations. Sporadic and ineffectual protests were made, in chairmen's annual reports or in statements by the Chambers of Mines, Industry and Commerce, on specific issues. But such was the economic potential of the country that these concerns recovered an equilibrium and came to some accommodation with the government of the day, arguing that if apartheid could not be defeated politically, it would be made economically unworkable by industrial expansion. And indeed as the years passed the sheer buoyancy of the economy slowed down the processes of racial separation because the withdrawal of increasing numbers of African workers would have caused economic collapse and without a sound economic basis the government could not have survived. As it was the budget expenditure began to soar. Money had to be found to increase subsidies for farmers, to allow small increases in White wages, to finance the machinery of apartheid, to subsidize the industries planned for the borders of Bantu territory, to increase the police and defence forces and to meet the rising expenditure on arms. Big business supported the government in all this, fearing above all an increase in African militancy and interference from outside.

All this did not happen in a vacuum but against rising protests and civil disturbances. The demonstrable economic and political stability, however, did much to retain international confidence, and foreign investment continued its flow back, in its turn to strengthen the government's position and further expand the economy. There was, however, constant attack abroad, and not only in the United Nations, on the policy of apartheid and the means of implementing it. Campaigns for economic and cultural boycotts had only marginal effects, but South Africa was beginning to find herself more and more isolated under these attacks.

Parallel with the steps taken to ensure parliamentary security and financial stability, the Nationalists pressed on with the overall measures to establish apartheid, and the right man for the job was there – the man who had been largely responsible for its formulation, the Minister of Native Affairs. Hendrick Frensch Verwoerd had been born in 1901 in Amsterdam, the son of Hollander parents who had emigrated to South Africa when he was three months old, not long before the Anglo-Boer War ended with the Treaty of Vereeniging. For a few years he had gone to an English medium school in Cape Town and then at the age of nine, when his father became a DRC missionary in Rhodesia, he moved to Milton High School in Bulawayo. Verwoerd senior returned five years later to settle in Brandfort, Orange Free State, where his son matriculated.

Verwoerd, according to his father, was a brilliant scholar, but 'strongwilled and obstinate, obdurate ... restless ... not interested in sport'.[26] His fellows found him 'lonely and aloof'. He had no traditional Boer upbringing nor, unlike many of his future rivals and colleagues, did he bear the familiar Boer War scars. There was no early emotional involvement with White or with Black, which in the case of so many South Africans turned friendship to bitterness without always eradicating all trace of the early underlying warmth. The blood of martyred Voortrekkers did not run in his veins, he was not bereft of mother or infant sisters by enteric in the English concentration camps. He could look at the South African scene with detachment and make his objective choice, uninfluenced by the deep race memories and childhood conditioning of the average Afrikaner. And so, presumably, he did. He won a scholarship to Stellenbosch University, then the hot-house of the new nationalism producing many political, cultural and theological leaders of the future, as it had

26. Garry Allinghan, *Verwoerd, The End*, p. xiv.

done of the past. There he was considered to be one of the most brilliant students to have passed through the university. Work for a master's degree in philosophy and psychology on a thesis entitled *Thought Processes and the Problem of Values* undermined his orthodox DRC concepts and he abandoned an intention to become a predikant (though he later reverted to orthodoxy). He refused a scholarship to Oxford and in 1923, at the age of twenty-two, he became a lecturer in logic at Stellenbosch and worked for his Doctorate in Philosophy; the subject of his thesis was *An Experimental Study of the Blunting of the Emotions*. Then, in the mid-twenties, when Nazism was in its sturdy infancy, Verwoerd won a scholarship to Germany and studied at the Universities of Hamburg, Leipzig and Berlin.

By this time strongly racist and anti-Semitic, he returned to Stellenbosch in 1928, became Professor of Applied Psychology and then of Sociology. He was active in various welfare projects in Cape Town and was giving much thought to the political significance of social policy. He had long since acquired the intensely nationalistic and anti-British attitude prevalent at Stellenbosch, was strongly attracted to the secret organization of the Broederbond and dedicated to the goal of Afrikaner domination in South Africa. He particularly advocated the harnessing of the mass of poor white Afrikaners in a struggle for a 'Christian-National, disciplined republican State'. In 1936 he joined a delegation of protest against the admittance to South Africa of Jewish refugees from Hitler's Germany.

At the time of the Great Trek centenary Verwoerd abandoned academic life to become editor of *Die Transvaler*, founded by Strydom and the organ of extreme nationalism. Through the paper he gave ardent support to the Nazis during the war and wide publicity to Nazi propaganda broadcast from Zeesen; he exploited racial sentiment and did much to mould Afrikaner public opinion in conformity with party thinking. In 1942 he published the Draft Constitution and two years later a defence of the Broederbond. He gave up the editorship in 1948 to fight the election and was defeated. Strydom pressed Malan to appoint his protégé to the Senate and from there, and not as an elected Member of Parliament, he had become Minister of Native Affairs.

Though not particularly liked in the party he was respected in the House for his brisk efficiency, meticulous attention to detail and his firm control of the new members of Strydom's 'enlarged' Senate. He created an impression of great sincerity, confidence and inflexibility and compelled attention by his stubborn adherence to principles and his prolix exposition of practical apartheid. He was undeterred as Black resistance rose against the measures he, as Minister for Native Affairs, had introduced. An able propagandist and convinced believer, he indefatigably laid the unpopular legislative foundations for total apartheid, expounding his plans in endless, involved, repetitive speeches. His smoothly youthful, cherubic appearance was curiously unnatural at an age when life has generally etched some lines of experience, painted some shadows of wisdom. Not until 1958 was Verwoerd elected – to a safe seat in Assembly, where he was to sit as a Member of Parliament for only four and a half months.

Essential to the whole apartheid policy was the disentangling of individuals. European, African and Indian were in general clearly distinguished both in physical appearance and in way of life. But the more amorphous group of Coloured people overlapped the others, blurring distinctions. An amalgam of all the races in South Africa, they had a sizeable inheritance of White blood and until now had been treated as an appendage to the Whites – a poor relation, it is true, and something of a responsibility, but possessing a useful voting power. The Coloureds varied very much in physical appearance, and some individuals of all races could 'pass' into more privileged groups giving rise to a seepage upwards – Africans infiltrating the Coloured ranks and Coloureds 'passing' as Whites. This slow, sure process of hybridization had to be ended.

The Population Registration Act of 1950 aimed at a rigid system of classification, the compilation of a racial register and the issue of identity cards. It defined and froze into immutable categories White, Coloured and Native people. Later the Coloureds were sub-divided into Cape Coloured, Cape Malay, Griqua, Chinese, Indian, other Asiatic and other Coloured. Classification was based on appearance and general acceptance and repute and 99 per cent of the population presented no problem. Official investigation of the borderline cases, however, causes untold humiliation and misery. Down-grading, in existing South African conditions, meant total devaluation, including change of employment and consequent drop in income, change of residence to a more unattractive area, drop in social status, and a change of children's schools. In one family three children went to three different racial schools. In another a child hanged himself when he alone of his family was classified as Coloured. A leading boxer, reclassified as Coloured, could see no future but to leave the country with his family.

The Prohibition of Mixed Marriages Act of 1949 had made marriages between White and Black illegal. Now the earlier Immorality Act of 1927 prohibiting extra-marital intercourse between Whites and Africans was extended to Blacks in general. In ten years 3,890 people were convicted and many families of long-standing unions broken up. These three Acts caused personal suffering, humiliation and degradation to many Whites as well as Blacks, but the country had been warned that if White civilization was to be preserved in Africa, much sacrifice would be required.

Territorial separation of the races was the foundation on which apartheid was to be built. In 1951 Malan's administration appointed a commission under the chairmanship of Professor F. R. Tomlinson to devise a 'comprehensive scheme for rehabilitation of the Native Areas with a view to developing them within a social structure in keeping with the culture of the Native and based upon effective socio-economic planning'. The commission did its work thoroughly and submitted a seventeen-volume report in 1954. Having examined broad policy it echoed the conclusions of a Committee on Race Relations in 1947 that: 'A choice will have to be made by the people of South Africa between two ultimate poles, namely, that of complete integration and that of separate development of the racial groups', and favoured separate development.[27]

The commission's drastic recommendations included proposals, valuable in any circumstances, for the rehabilitation of the

27. Summaries in *Survey of Race Relations* (1955–6), pp. 139 ff., and D. Hobart Houghton in *Africa South*, Vol. I, No. 2.

reserves, the prior task to be accomplished. But it by no means
planned for total apartheid. The commission estimated that by
the year 2000, the African population of South Africa would be
21,500,000. The most the rehabilitated reserves would accommodate (without much further acquisition of White-owned land
but with the eventual inclusion of the High Commission Territories) would be 15,000,000 people. 6,500,000 Africans and
5,500,000 others would remain without rights in the White areas,
still living with a White population by then grown almost to
6,000,000. The Whites, in their own areas, would be outnumbered 2:1 instead of the current 5:1 which, said the critics, if the
Bantustans should gain a real degree of autonomy, might prove a
considerable Trojan horse.

The Bantu Homelands, developed in accordance with the commission's proposals, should support a farming population of just
over 2,000,000 people, 357,000 families. The gross incomes
necessary to satisfy the basic requirements of African peasant
families were estimated at between £60 and £110 a year according
to the type of farming and the benefit derived in kind. To achieve
this would require freehold tenure of farm units of a uniform
value of £400. A further 2,500,000 people could find a living in
mining and forestry, and 20,000 jobs in secondary and 30,000 in
tertiary activity would have to be created each year to absorb 70
per cent of the population. More than 100 new towns and villages
would be needed for people moved off the land and who would
find work in White-owned border industries to be set up outside
the reserves, or in new industries within the reserves and developed initially with White capital. The commission recommended a twenty-five- to thirty-year plan and considered that in
the first ten-year period £104m. would have to be provided,
£9m. being required in the first year. The government, however,
was reluctant to accept any definite financial commitment.
(Indeed the average sum spent on the reserves in the seven years
following the publication of the report was £4m.) Other important recommendations also proved unacceptable. The suggested
changeover from communally-held land to freehold tenure to
enable the land to carry the largest possible professional
agricultural community was at total variance with the apartheid

concept of the African developing along his own lines and would, according to the Minister of Native Affairs, 'undermine the whole tribal structure. The entire order and cohesion of the tribe is bound up with the fact that the community is a communal unit'. What moral right, he demanded, has the White state to take land from the tribe and to sub-divide it amongst a small section?

The High Commission Territories were envisaged by Tomlinson and many of the policy makers as being, one not-distant day, in some sort of association with South Africa and helping out with her territorial segregation problems. They had enormous space to offer – almost 300,000 square miles and much impoverished labour which in any case served South Africa, and very little else. They had remained barren, drought-ridden (Botswana), mountainous (Lesotho and Swaziland), undeveloped and with minimal primitive production. They held Britain's undertaking that they would not be handed over without prior consultation, but after generations of stagnation there was still little adequate British effort to set them on sound economic foundations. Lesotho, with a sheep-grazing and water-power potential, was overpopulated, overgrazed and searingly eroded on its lower pastures; besides man-power it exported some wool, mohair, cattle, beans, and wheat. Old established missionary contacts had provided some higher education, small industries such as printing and an active political awareness. The young chief, Mosheshwe, went to Oxford to study before succeeding to the paramountcy, while a number of political parties grew up and argued their differences in the part-elected Basutoland National Council, the Pitso. Botswana was huge in size with limited habitable area in the eastern part where an eighteen inch rainfall made good ranching country. A few hundred yards between Rhodesia and the Caprivi strip of South West Africa gave it a small common frontier with Zambia which was becoming an increasingly used escape route for South African political fugitives; and in the late 1960s it was to be a source of serious contention with South Africa when Botswana began to construct a modern highway to follow the old missionary road and recent refugee route. In 1950 the territory had made news when Seretse Khama, the young Oxford educated chief of the Ngwato, by marrying an English woman fell foul of his uncle, Tshekedi Khama, and of the tribe, mainly because he had omitted the customary pre-marriage consultations; the tribe at a push was prepared to accept the mixed marriage, but the South African Government was not and (under strong pressure it was believed) the British authorities exiled both Khamas. In 1956 Seretse renounced the chieftainship, was allowed to return and threw himself into local politics.

Swaziland was by nature best endowed of the three, with well-watered, fertile grass slopes for stock and agriculture, rain-soaked mountain sides for afforestation and a pulping industry, substantial deposits of asbestos, iron, copper, cobalt and so on. Its relative wealth and long association with the Transvaal had brought it (unlike the others in which White settlement had been barred) a large settler population to advance its economic development but slow its social and political progress. Under the British administration was the Paramount Chief Sobhuza II, a conservative, powerful and very astute ruler. All the territories were totally opposed to any closer administrative association with their powerful neighbour whose internal policies and practices they disliked more and more.

Long before the Tomlinson Commission reported, however, the government had begun to introduce a series of laws destined to establish and maintain territorial separation. The Group Area Acts of 1950 and 1957, often amended, went much further than earlier legislation in controlling the ownership, occupation and disposal of land. Separate Group Areas could be declared for Africans, Asians, Coloureds or Whites in which property might not be occupied by members of another group, nor could they attend any place of entertainment in such areas. Whole populations could be removed from homes and businesses and resettled, and land could be expropriated. Housing of generally a better standard might be provided, but any advantage here was offset by higher rents and transport costs. Many thousand people were removed from their homes and often their livelihood. Under the Natives Resettlement Act of 1954, a Board was set up to undertake the removal of more than 10,000 African families from townships (notably Sophiatown) in the Western Areas of Johannesburg where many of them owned land in freehold and to resettle them at Meadowlands, much further away, where no freehold rights were available. Similar mass removals of Africans and Indians were made in many areas.

The Abolition of Passes and Coordination of Documents Act of 1952 obliged all Africans (even those then exempted) over the age of sixteen, women as well as men, to carry reference books containing detailed information about themselves (photograph, identity card, registration number, particulars of tribal connections, ethnic grouping, authorization by the labour bureau and influx control, tax receipt and employer's name and address and monthly signature), to be produced on demand by the police. The official equating of the reference book with a passport was rejected, for Whites were not expected to carry on their persons any documents such as passports, driving licence or tax receipt, nor were they liable to summary arrest and prosecution if unable to produce them on demand by any policeman. The Africans were thus in check at every move; their tribal connections were known and whether they were in legal employment or were entitled to be in the urban area; and the identity card established, if there might be any doubt, their race.

The Native Laws Amendment Act the same year extended the system of influx control to all urban areas and to women. African workseekers were to register at labour bureaux and no one might go from country to town unless suitable vacancies existed, nor, under the highly controversial 'church clause', attend a religious service or a meeting in a White area if the minister thought they created a nuisance or were present in undesirable numbers. He could also prohibit the holding of any meeting in a White area attended by an African. Under Smuts's Native (Urban Areas) Consolidation Act of 1945 no African had been allowed to remain more than seventy-two hours in an urban area unless he (or she) continuously had resided there since birth, had worked there for one employer ten years, or lived there for fifteen years and had no criminal conviction, or was the wife or unmarried daughter or under eighteen-years-old son of one qualified to live there, or had special permission such as a pass to seek work. The Native (Urban Areas) Amendment Act of 1956 now enabled local authorities to order an African out if his presence was considered detrimental to the maintenance of peace and order, and to move his dependants to his new place of residence. A later amendment in 1964 made it obligatory for wives and children to have entered the area *lawfully* before they would be permitted to live with their husbands and fathers. As there was almost no lawful entry for women into urban areas very few men were able to bring their families with them. So influx control legislation finally pinned families to their rural homes and returned 'surplus' – unemployed or undesirable – men there.

If apartheid was to work it was essential that its acceptance by the mass of the Africans should be won and to achieve this African education was completely reorganized. Hitherto, education for Africans had been a hotch-potch of State, State-aided missionary and individual enterprise. Unlike White education it was not universal, nor compulsory, nor free, and it was grossly underfinanced. Education was keenly desired by Blacks and parents made great sacrifices to find the costs; children, often ill-fed, walked many miles to school; students accomplished examination triumphs, working by candlelight in overcrowded shacks. Everywhere there was acute shortage of places and extreme overcrowding. By 1967 the State was spending £70 per annum on each White child and providing free text and exercise books and materials, while on each African child in school it spent £7 and they paid for their own books, materials and secondary education.

It had already been laid down in the CNE statement that African education should be based on principles of trusteeship, non-equality and segregation, its aim to inculcate the White man's view of life, especially that of the Boer nation. This had, of course, long been the practice. The following problems appeared in the same exercise in a *Longman's Arithmetic Book* widely used at the end of the 1940s: 'Twenty persons each earn £15 a week. How much would they earn etc . . . ?' 'If a Kaffir earns £3 a month, how much would six Kaffirs earn?' The uses of maize were taught the African child, too, in some engaging verses:

> 'What is it you live on,
>   Kaffir in the Kraal?'
> 'Mealies, missis, mealies,
>   And they make us strong and tall.'

> 'What is it you grind, boy,
>   For horses and for kine?'
> 'Cobs and mealies, missis,
>   And they make them fat and fine.'[28]

The CNE statement had also advocated mother-tongue medium, a knowledge of both official languages and the fitting of the Native to undertake his own education under control and guidance of the State.

The Bantu Education Act of 1953 transferred control of African education from the provinces which had hitherto controlled all education to the Native Affairs Department and later to the Bantu Education Department. All schools had to be registered; the State would continue the existing subsidy of £6½m. a year, additional costs to be met by the African taxpayer. Grants to mission schools and training colleges were ended and unsubsidized mission schools had to be registered. School boards and committees of Africans nominated by chiefs and headmen were set up to give more experience in management and to reinforce the Tribal Authorities which were strictly controlled by the Bantu Administration and Development Department (BAD, successor to NAD). The form and content of education was much altered by the stress laid on Bantu languages, by the introduction of a second official language and by the separation of the Junior Certificate examination from that written by Whites.

Speaking to the Bill in the Senate, Verwoerd said that mission schools could not serve the communities, were unsympathetic to the country's policy and that

by blindly producing pupils trained on a European model the vain hope was created among Natives that they could occupy posts within the European community ... This is what is meant by the creation of unhealthy 'white-collar ideals' and the causation of widespread frustration among the so-called educated Natives ... The general aims [he continued] of the [Act] are to remedy [these] difficulties by transforming education for *Natives* into *Bantu* education, to transform a service which benefits only a section of the Bantu population and

28. *The Forum* (21 November 1949). *Longman's Arithmetic for South African Schools*, std. 2 (1947 edn) and *Longman's English Reading Book for Native Schools*.

consequently results in alienation and division in their community
into a general service which will help the community as a whole ...
[He concluded] My department's policy is that education should
stand with both feet in the reserves and have its roots in the spirit and
being of Bantu Society ... There is no place for [the Bantu] in the
European community above the level of certain forms of labour ...
Until now he has been subjected to a school system which drew him
away from his own community and misled him by showing him the
green pastures of European Society in which he was not allowed to
graze.[29]

A vast amount of work and law-making by now had been put
into establishing apartheid. Whites and Blacks were permanently
classified and separated in personal relationships, in economic
and residential spheres and in education. Any rudimentary mixing for sporting and social purposes was ended by the Group
Areas Act and pressure was put on cultural bodies to observe
strict apartheid by the withdrawal of subsidies from those which
did not comply. But the situation remained chaotic. Critics of the
government claimed that only *klein apartheid*, 'negative' or petty
apartheid, was being applied and that, in spite of it all, integration
in economic life was actually increasing.

3. DESTROYING THE ENEMY – THE CLASH OF NATIONALISMS

All the active reshaping of the South African structure to fit the
pattern of apartheid hardly touched the consciousness or convenience of the White population, and only on issues likely
adversely to affect economic or political interests did the parliamentary Opposition take any stand. In fact, however, the
economy, despite ups and downs, strengthened. The Whites
were increasingly relieved at having a government with a positive policy pledged to safeguard White interests and, as the stormy
years went by, showing itself able to stand firmly against civil
commotion inside the country and threats and pressures from
outside. They expressed appreciation by giving the Nationalists
increased support at every election.

29. *Bantu Education Policy for the Immediate Future*, Dept of Native
Affairs (7 June 1954).

Once the new regime was in power issues became clear cut. White fears of Black Nationalism had been spelled out with the apartheid policy in the election campaigning. The Blacks, no longer mesmerized by Smuts's versatility and the promise always dangling of a better world, were released from bonds that had held them despite themselves to the United Party: perhaps the lingering aura of Cape liberalism had kept the elders captive and half-hopeful, unduly careful not to embarrass in the time of crisis. With the Nationalists all this dissolved.

The Nationalists indeed had inherited a chaotic situation. Apartheid was to be the means of reducing it to order and the Blacks did not want apartheid: they wanted homes and land, enough to eat, less conflict with the police, better wages, more vocational opportunities, their due share in government and above all the freedom to develop as human beings. Apartheid would not give them these things and they would reject it. Attempts to put it into practice in a context of rising living costs and static wages enormously increased the social and economic burdens the Africans were already bent under. Quite naturally the active opposition inside South Africa came from the Black people to most of whom apartheid brought such untold hardship with so little gain. Their very strong and necessarily extra-parliamentary opposition, the support of groups of liberal and radical Whites, and their appeal to international bodies seriously threatened the basis of apartheid and the whole South African racial and economic structure. The State responded with a system of legislation designed to protect itself in accordance with the Christian National conception of its duty, and which provoked other demonstrations of resistance which in turn called forth further disciplinary laws.

The election campaign of 1948, the wildly virulent, provocative statements on race matters that were often made in electioneering speeches, the pervasive atmosphere of inter-White friction as well as unveiled White hostility to Blacks unsettled and alarmed the Non-whites; anger already smouldering against discrimination began to blaze. The Coloureds of the Cape were embittered by their disfranchisement. The Indians were appalled at the threats to home and livelihood implicit in the Group Areas

Act. The Africans, even more than the others captive in abysmal
poverty, had long been protesting over segregation and pass laws
and were furious at the extension of these to the women. Resentment found expression not only in protests by leaders but also in
continual eruptions in the teeming slums of riots and strikes and
demonstrations of all kinds, triggered off by a variety of actual
flash points.

For the first ten years the Nationalists ruled to an accompaniment of almost continual disturbances, taking place against a
background of rapidly increasing urbanization and industrialization and a growing familiarity with political and industrial
methods of reaction. Many of these disturbances sprang spon-
taneously from the particular circumstances and grievances of the
locality; others were planned mass protests intended to force a
change in policy; often the two merged. The sudden Durban race
riots at the beginning of 1949 were one of the ugliest, most
ominous of such outbreaks. Inflamed by what had begun as a
trivial quarrel in which an Indian injured an African child,
African mobs rampaged through the Indian quarters, clubbing,
burning and looting. There were 142 deaths, over a thousand
injured and great destruction of property. The riot, probably due
to a welling-up of old resentment and bitterness, focused on the
Indians at first (particularly the traders), as exploiters. Election
candidates in Natal had made speeches of vindictive racialism
directed largely against the Indian community which frustrated
Africans could interpret as a green light. There was also evidence
that some Whites were egging on rampant gangs in the actual
course of the riot. On the other hand many African households
at great risk gave shelter and succour to terrified Indian refugees.
Shocked Indian and African Congress leaders joined forces to
calm the frenzied people and in a remarkably short time the outbreak was seen not as a pattern for the future but a ghastly
aberration. The Indians showed an impressive maturity and
absence of rancour and revengefulness and budding understanding between leaders of all races was not impaired, but rather began
to seep to the politically aware of the rank and file. The Youth
League of the ANC, whose members had been forging personal
friendships with young Indians and White radicals, were begin-

ning to abandon their exclusive Africanist stand and acknowledge that it was possible, and even desirable, that the races should cooperate to fight discrimination. They took control of Congress and replaced the now too cautious Xuma by their own more vigorous presidential candidate, Dr James Moroka, a successful general practitioner and wealthy landowner of the Orange Free State and a great-grandson of Chief Moroka who had befriended the early Voortrekkers. Walter Sisulu, one of the Youth League founders, became secretary.

Towards the end of 1949 and early in 1950 there was serious rioting along the reef – Krugersdorp, Randfontein, Newlands, Newclare, Benoni; the underlying causes, according to a government commission of inquiry, were widespread resentment at pass and liquor raiding directed against the police, and the absence of adequate amenities. A 'Freedom Day' call by the ANC to stay away from work on 1 May ended at half a dozen places in scuffles with the police who escorted home those who had gone to work.

The Nationalists had long regarded communism, with its egalitarian doctrine which undermined 'traditional' standpoints and recognized no distinction of colour or race, as the greatest danger to the Christian Nationalist State. The attitudes of various liberal and religious bodies to race relations, Black franchise and the colour bar seemed very near to communism – or at least fellow-travelling – and to justify the severest measures. The Suppression of Communism Act of 1950 (amended 1954) was a legislative landmark, the basis of the elaborate machinery designed to destroy opposition to apartheid. 'Communism' was very widely defined to include not only the doctrine of Marxian Socialism but also any doctrine or scheme which aimed at the bringing about of any political, industrial, social or economic change within South Africa by the promotion of disturbance or disorder or by unlawful acts or omissions, or which aimed at the encouragement of feelings of hostility between Black and White, the consequences of which were calculated to further the achievement of doctrines or schemes such as those mentioned. The Communist Party of South Africa was declared unlawful and the governor-general was empowered to outlaw any other organization if he felt satisfied that it was furthering any of the aims of communism as described. The

Minister of Justice was authorized to list members of a banned organization and could prohibit those listed and those he 'deemed' to be promoting the aims of communism or anyone convicted under the Act, from holding public office or belonging to specified organizations, from attending gatherings or from leaving defined areas. He could ban publications or prohibit meetings if he considered those were likely to further the aims of communism. There was no appeal either for organization or individuals. The Bill was rushed through Parliament at the end of the session and the United Party, always very sensitive to allegations of fellow-travelling, put up little opposition except to suggest a postponement while the government tried to remove the evil conditions in which communism flourished.

Under the Act the government was enabled to exclude from Parliament the elected (White) Native representative, Sam Kahn, and his successors, Brian Bunting and Ray Alexander, who was also excluded from the Cape Provincial Council. By 1956 the Minister of Justice could announce that 604 persons (including 75 trade union officials) had been listed, 98 (56 of them trade unionists) ordered to resign from their organizations, 71 banned from attending gatherings or confined to a specified area, and 51 convicted under the Act. Many of the government's leading opponents were stripped of all political power, most of their liberty and much of their earning ability. The net was spread far beyond the communism it purported to check, to hamstring almost any criticism of or opposition to the government. The congresses called for a day of mourning and stay-at-home in protest against the Act, on 26 June, in future to be called Freedom Day.

On 6 April 1952 it was 300 years since van Riebeeck's three small ships had sailed into Table Bay to plant there the Company's refreshment station. The authorities decreed national celebration in which a subsidiary place was made for the Non-whites with suitably traditional feasting on slaughtered oxen. The leaders of African, Coloured and Indian peoples, however, for the first time had begun to plan joint political action against all discriminatory legislation. A year earlier the SAIC, the ANC and the APO elected a Franchise Action Committee and pledged themselves to resist oppressive policies. In December 1951 the

ANC wrote to the Prime Minister reiterating the old pleas for direct parliamentary representation. In an ultimatum threatening a mass civil disobedience movement they called for the repeal by 29 February of six 'unjust laws': the Pass Laws, the Group Areas Act, the Separate Representation of Voters Act, the Suppression of Communism Act, the Bantu Authorities Act and the Stock Limitation Regulations. 'The struggle which our people are about to begin is not directed against any race or national group but against the unjust laws which keep in perpetual subjection and misery vast sections of the population,' they declared. In a not unexpected dusty answer, Malan refused to alter any of the long-existing laws differentiating between European and Bantu, 'especially when it is borne in mind that these differences are permanent and not man-made'.[30]

The Defiance Campaign began on 26 June 1952. Volunteers were asked to commit technical offences, such as contraventions of the pass laws, apartheid regulations at railway stations and in post offices and the curfew regulations. Those arrested would plead guilty and serve a prison sentence rather than pay a fine. By the end of 1952 over 8,000 volunteers had been to jail and served the increasingly heavy sentences that were imposed. The government increased the maximum penalties for incitement to a fine of £500 or five years' imprisonment or ten lashes or a combination of any two of these. These were penalties heavier than people could be asked to court and the campaign ended after two multiracial demonstrations, one in Cape Town and one in Germiston, near Johannesburg. The latter was led by Patrick Duncan, son of a past governor-general of South Africa, and Manilal Gandhi, son of the Mahatma who, in South Africa half a century before, had created this form of protest over the same issues.

Eight thousand was far too small a number to block the processes of the law or compel a government to rethink (a hundred times that number might have succeeded), but it demonstrated the understanding the African had of such forms of protest and the increasing movement towards cooperation between the racial groups; both factors, hitherto discounted by Whites, now gave cause for consternation.

30. Mary Benson, *The Struggle for a Birthright*, p. 141.

But while 8,000 politically mature Africans were getting themselves arrested and serving prison sentences without one recorded act of violence or retaliation, other unplanned explosions took place in widely different places. In Port Elizabeth serious rioting began when police arrested a man accused of theft. There was a flare-up in a Johannesburg municipal hostel when rents were raised. Then a row in the Kimberley beer-hall. Then in East London police tried to break up a meeting and the crowd ran amok. Rage seemed to centre on White influence – cinemas, churches, municipal offices, schools were looted and burnt down – even where these were only of benefit to local Black inhabitants. Cape Town, Krugersdorp and Durban – disorder could not have been more widespread and both Whites and Blacks were victims. The government blamed the organizers of the Defiance Campaign, though they had showed themselves in complete control of their followers; but the general temper of the times, the intolerable conditions and lack of hope of improvement laid the frustrated people open to exploitation by malcontents and tsotsies – delinquents and young criminals, as well as, it was often alleged, *agents provocateurs*.

The government reacted fiercely to the campaign and other demonstrations. The Public Safety Act of 1953 gave the governor-general powers to proclaim a state of emergency during which any law, except those concerning defence and the operation of the legislatures and of industrial conciliation, might be suspended. The Criminal Laws Amendment Act of the same year made it an offence to advise, encourage or incite anyone to commit an offence by way of protest against a law or to solicit or accept financial assistance for organized protest or resistance against the laws of the country, the maximum penalties being those which brought the Defiance Campaign to a close. The United Party with an election three months away supported both bills.

In addition to tightening up the law, nineteen leaders of the congresses were charged under the Suppression of Communism Act, found guilty of 'statutory communism' which, the judge remarked, had 'nothing to do with communism as it is commonly known' and given suspended sentences.

Moroka, afraid of the taint of communism, had separated his

defence from that of his fellow accused and kept aloof. When the office of president-general next fell vacant, a fresh and more resolute candidate was found in A. J. M. Lutuli. Lutuli, a profound Christian, was grandson of a Christian, son of John Bunyan Luthuli, and nephew of Martin Luthuli. He had been educated at Dube's Ohlange Institution and trained as a teacher. He joined the staff of Adams Mission in Natal, becoming a colleague of Z. K. Matthews. After fifteen contented years there he felt compelled to respond to a call in 1935 from his small tribe at the Groutville Mission to become their chief as his forbears had been. Deeply committed by temperament and background to a multi-racial ideal, he associated a good deal with Whites in Natal, joined many mixed associations and was elected to the executive of the SA Christian Council. This led him in 1938 to an International Missionary Conference in Madras with opportunities to meet delegates from other parts of Africa and Asia. He joined the Natal ANC in 1945 and the next year was elected to the NRC, taking his seat just before it adjourned indefinitely. In 1948 he visited the United States as a guest of the Congregational American Board of Missions. With the opportunity of addressing a variety of audiences in many places, he warned that whether Africa became noble and progressive or dominated by anger and revenge would depend largely on how government, industry and commerce behaved towards Africa. He returned home to find the Nationalist regime in charge. When as a member of the ANC he supported the Defiance Campaign and actively recruited volunteers, the Native Affairs Department gave him the choice of resigning either from Congress or from the chieftainship on the grounds that activities in the two spheres were incompatible. Lutuli maintained that his Congress activities were part of his chiefly duties to advance his people's welfare and refused to relinquish either function. So in November 1952 he was deposed.

In a statement issued immediately afterwards he gave a short résumé of his public life and asked: 'Who will deny that thirty years of my life have been spent knocking in vain, patiently, moderately and modestly at a closed and barred door?'[31] Elsewhere in the statement he said:

31. A. J. Lutuli, *Let My People Go*, Appendix A.

It is ... with a full sense of responsibility that, under the auspices of the ANC, I have joined my people in the new spirit that moves them today, the spirit that revolts openly and boldly against injustice and expresses itself in a determined and non-violent manner ... Laws and conditions that tend to debase human personality – a God-given force – be they brought about by the State or other individuals, must be relentlessly opposed in the spirit of defiance shown by St Peter when he said to the rulers of his day: 'Shall we obey God or man?' ... I have embraced the non-violent Passive Resistance technique in fighting for freedom because I am convinced it is the only non-revolutionary legitimate and humane way that could be used by people denied effective constitutional means to further aspirations ... What the future has in store for me I do not know. It might be ridicule, imprisonment, concentration camp, flogging, banishment and even death ... It is inevitable that in working for Freedom some individuals and some families must take the lead and suffer: The Road to Freedom is via the cross.

Lutuli undertook a tour of South Africa, addressing huge meetings of Blacks and Whites, his theme being:

World progress has been achieved by revolutionary action. In France the people fought for liberty, equality and fraternity. In America they did the same. Now the process has reached South Africa itself. We do not want to drive the Europeans away, we wish to share equally as partners in this country.[32]

He was soon banned from the main centres and from addressing meetings, as were a great many other leaders, and this made the effective organization and control of demonstrations extremely difficult. The people too were falling into apathy, resignation and hopelessness which attached them to whatever material advantages they possessed. These conditions and the great show of force the government could mount ensured that most of the planned demonstrations at this time went off at half-cock.

Meanwhile, the authorities were occupied with the implementation of territorial apartheid. Dr Eiselen announced the government's intention to remove all Africans from the Western Cape, considered to be rightfully a Coloured sphere, and began a strict application of influx control there. At the same time the

32. Mary Benson, *Chief Albert Lutuli of South Africa*, p. 25.

Indian community was beginning to feel the effects of the enforcement of Group Areas which was moving them out of the cities.

When the Nationalist Party came to power in 1948 it had begun a direct attack on the chaos of urban housing. By 1950 the Site-and-Service Scheme had been devised, by which the water, light and sewerage were provided on municipal land. Sites were then rented to people who could either build their own houses or obtain government loans for the building. Africans were trained and employed on building schemes for Africans much more cheaply than Whites. A levy was imposed on employers to pay the additional transport costs from these more distant areas. Between 1951 and 1959, it could be claimed, 100,000 houses had been built and half a million Africans rehoused. In deference to apartheid the new areas were ethnically zoned to facilitate mother-tongue education, help newcomers to feel more at home and enable chiefs to keep better control. Zoning also tended to revive tribal differences and antagonism and inhibit the growing urban trend to replace tribal solidarity by neighbourhood, employment, recreational or political friendships. The general breakdown of tribal and language barriers had allowed the beginning of a growth of class and national unity, a cohesion which was even becoming inter-racial and, used against apartheid, was threatening the White established order.

Under the Group Areas Act a Resettlement Board was set up to remove 10,000 African families from the Western Areas of Johannesburg. A dismayed clamour arose from Africans and many White liberals because in areas such as Sophiatown not only was much vile slum property to be cleared, but it was decided to turn this old established African township into a White residential zone. The entire population was to be moved, lock, stock and barrel, despite its vehement protests; an entire vibrant community would be broken up, the people stripped of rare and valued freehold rights of long standing (which they could never get again outside the reserves, with which many of them no longer had any links) and houses into which life savings had gone would be bulldozed into the ground without adequate compensation. The opposition to these measures was given additional emphasis and direction when Father Trevor Huddleston, whose Order, the Community of the Resurrection, ran a mission and a fine church there, took part and ensured wide publicity of events. Congress planned passive resistance to the move. The Minister of Justice, C. R. Swart, made his customary chilling but imaginary revelations to the country that the removals were to be opposed by

attacks with firearms; explosive in old motor tyres that would be rolled towards the police; old cars loaded with explosives which would be crashed into the police cars and lorries. [He continued] The police had reliable information that the natives of Sophiatown were in possession of a few machine-guns and revolvers and pistols, hand-grenades and home-made bombs.[33]

In the tense foreboding that built up, the police struck first. Two days ahead of the published date, 2,000 armed police arrived in a dawn of pouring rain to remove 110 dismal families and their possessions to new homes, lines of little boxes erected in a distant waste, misleadingly called Meadowlands. There was a legacy of intense and bitter frustration.

A formidable body of legislation existed by this time governing every aspect of African life. For this the government and co-operating White opposition were held responsible and against the government rather than the White public the mass resistance of those years was directed. The web of laws and statutory regulations concerning the Blacks was of baffling complexity, and few of a largely semi-literate population of peasants and labourers were not in some unwitting breach of it most of the time. The law was administered by White policemen with Black policemen under their command, and they were constantly in an antagonistic contact with the people. The conflict between police and people exerted a singularly malign influence in race relationships. There was difficulty in recruiting for the force. The police were poorly paid, ill-educated, generally drawn from poorer types of platteland families; they had generally grown up with the most pernicious of race prejudice and in deep irrational fear of the Blacks. Sometimes a policeman charged with a crime was found too young for the ordinary courts and would appear in the juvenile court, his name withheld. The police went armed and with extremely wide powers to attend meetings, even private ones,

33. Mary Benson, *The Struggle for a Birthright*, p. 169.

searched without warrant and made arrests. On the whole among Whites it was only those suspected of political or Immorality Act offences who were likely to have the police break in on them without notice. Africans, however, were always liable to have their pass demanded at any time of night or day or their homes invaded at dead of night by police who could throw them and their children out of bed in a search for illegal liquor, visitors or literature. Police methods were extremely harsh, often without regard for individual dignity. In order to extort confessions and get evidence which would lead to arrests, gross ill-treatment often amounting to torture was used, occasionally exposed but seldom adequately punished; generations of Blacks lived under a police reign of terror. Up to half a million Africans a year were being imprisoned for statutory offences which were no crime for other sections of the population and so bore no stigma among the Blacks, who would generally elect to serve sentences, because they could not afford to pay the fine. In this way prison itself ceased to carry any moral sanction. While a great deal of police energy was dissipated on infringements of the law, big-time crime and gangsterism spread rapidly and flourished, and the people lived under the twin terror of police and gangsters.

The overall result was a burning sense of injustice among the Blacks, and hostility towards the government, which made the laws, the Whites who supported them and benefited from them and the police who enforced them. All the police (and a great many White civilians) were armed and were filled with a great inherent distrust and often an implacable hostility towards the African and, when face to face in crowds, they feared him. These circumstances made them quick on the trigger and all too commonly what might have begun as peaceable demonstrations quickly broke down into tragic riots, not infrequently, as down the years, because of shooting by the police.

Although justice was supposed to be the same for Black and White, penalties were often unequal, glaringly so in such cases as under the Immorality Act where Black and White had committed the same offence. A quite impartial administration of justice in so distorted a society became inequable in operation. The same fines imposed could represent a day's pay for White, a week's pay for

Black. The White paid; the Black, unable to, was jailed, with the
evil cycle of social consequences that must follow. Magistrates, as
members of the White community, tended to support White
against Black and hesitated to jeopardize their promotion by finding contrary to the government's wishes. Their verdicts, however,
were frequently criticized and their sentences reduced by higher
courts. The judges, more independent of government control,
better educated and less narrowly orientated than magistrates, administered a much more impartial justice in so far as the lop-sided
law allowed; but they, too, were White and, with the best will in
the world, imbued with the attitudes and prejudices of their upbringing and associates.

In these circumstances inevitably many people, representing all
shades of opposition, were giving great publicity overseas to South
Africa's race problems, were attending international assemblies
and soliciting support for anti-government activities. Many
Africans going unobtrusively abroad had at last found an acceptable use for the 'dompas' – the stupid pass – as travel document.
The Departure from the Union Regulation Act of 1955 banned
travel without a valid passport. This effectively immobilized,
though did not silence, many of the regime's most plangent White
critics; Mrs Jessie MacPherson and the author Alan Paton,
Labour and Liberal leaders respectively, and a young African
scholarship winner to an American university, were among the
Act's early assorted victims.

The Criminal Procedure and Evidence Amendment Act and
the Criminal Procedure Act of 1955 widened authority for the
issue of search warrants and police attendance at private and public
meetings and permitted search without warrant in some circumstances. Extensive police raiding and search was taking place
and huge collections of documents and paper were taken from the
homes of individuals and the offices of organizations known to be
hostile to government policies. Reports of widespread treason
were alarmingly discussed in Parliament.

After the stamping out of the Defiance Campaign the Congress
leaders had been casting around for another legal form of mass
protest and means of making their voices heard. The executive
committees of the Congress Alliance had begun in 1953 to plan a

mass gathering at which the people would say how they would like to be governed in a democratic South Africa. At hundreds of meetings held throughout the country grievances against the existing system of government and demands for the future were gathered. Their proposals were sent to a national action committee which then drafted a Freedom Charter. In June 1955, 3,000 delegates from all over the country (whom the authorities proved powerless to stop) sent by local committees and representing all race groups including Whites, gathered at Kliptown outside Johannesburg to discuss the charter. The meeting was raided by 200 armed police who took names and addresses of those present and seized documents. Nevertheless, the meeting went on and the Freedom Charter, based largely on the United Nations' Declaration of Human Rights, was adopted.[34] The charter (which was to become central evidence in the Treason Trial) declared that South Africa belonged to all who lived in it, Black and White, and only a government based on the will of all the people could justly claim authority. Many of its demands, such as those for bringing the country's natural wealth, basic industry and land into national or communal ownership and establishing social services, were in line with general revolutionary aspirations. Others clearly reflected the particular restrictions, impositions and discriminations suffered by Blacks for generations. These demands included: rights for all to vote, to stand for election and to take part in administration, to speak, gather, organize, worship, educate their children and travel freely and to choose where to live; the ending of race discrimination in land ownership, of compulsory culling, of imprisonment and deportation without fair trial, of police raids on homes, and of ghettos and of laws dividing families; and the reform of police and prisons.

The Federation of South African Women had been formed in 1953, chiefly to resist the extension of the pass laws to women. This had been feared and fought as far back as 1913 in the Free State because the raiding and arrests put the women particularly at the mercy of the police and physical and sexual assaults were not unknown. It also promised chaos in the home if women were liable

34. For the full text see, e.g., *Africa South*, Vol. I, No. 3, or Helen Joseph, *If this be Treason*, pp. 188–92.

to summary arrest and small children and invalid relatives left unattended. Huge demonstrations by women and pass burnings took place in many areas. The impressive culmination, after repeated refusals by the Prime Minister, Strydom, to meet their representatives, came in August 1956, when 10,000 women of all races made their way to the Union Buildings in Pretoria with 7,000 independently signed petitions which were left in the Prime Minister's deserted office. The petitions were handed on to the Security Branch police without the Prime Minister ever seeing them.

These events took place accompanied by a vigorous exercise by the government of all its powers of banning, banishment, restriction and prohibition which made orderly protest almost impossible. The police continued their raids of homes and offices and they confiscated a vast accumulation of material in the course of an investigation, the minister made known, of treason. The application of pass laws and of influx control regulations were all the time tightened. The (Natives) Prohibition of Interdicts Act of 1956 prevented legal interference with removal orders until they had been carried out. Africans in rural areas could be served banishment orders without prior notice. The presence of Africans at church services, schools, hospitals, clubs and places of entertainment outside African townships and on White private property was controlled. Apartheid was introduced into the nursing services and into the 'open' universities. Job reservation was enforced. Taxation increased for Africans. The rise in the cost of living far outstripped wage increases. Rents and transport costs were relatively high and numbers of people in arrears were prosecuted or ejected. The application of Group Areas forged ahead and tens of thousands of Indians and Coloureds were moved away from areas they had occupied for generations. Meetings attended by Africans were ever more stringently controlled and it became an offence to divulge information about prisoners or prison conditions.

Then, in the dawn of 5 December 1956 and with all the dramatic trappings appropriate in a Minister of Justice who had been a Hollywood extra in his time, arrests began of 156 people: men and women of all races, many bearing well-known names, many

leaders of the Congress Alliance. They were flown to Johannesburg to stand trial on allegations of treason. They included Lutuli,
Sisulu, Matthews; Tambo and Mandela of the Youth League;
Dadoo and Naicker of the S A I C; Helen Joseph, Lilian Ngoyi and
others of the Women's Federation; trade unionists, among them
the Levy brothers, Morrison and September; clergymen Calata
and Thompson. At the end of the year-long preparatory examination ninety-one were committed for trial on charges under the
Suppression of Communism Act and of high treason. The charges
against all were eventually withdrawn and thirty were reindicted
on the high treason charge only, the allegations under the Suppression of Communism Act being dropped. The trial was to last
for over four years until, in March 1961, the court found all thirty
accused not guilty and they were technically free to resume their
interrupted lives. The trial was a watershed in South African legal
and political history. The case attracted extraordinary interest. It
was attentively followed by the International Commission of
Jurists, who sent observers from time to time to report on particular aspects, and by other prominent lawyers such as Professor
E. N. Griswold, Dean of the Harvard Law School. Religious and
other bodies in South Africa and in many countries abroad, in a
remarkable fund-raising effort, provided a first-rate legal team for
the defence and basic welfare to keep the families of those accused
from actual starvation.

At this time, however, the end of the Treason Trial was still far
in the future and disturbances, protests and rioting continued in
one or another part of the country almost without abatement.
Once again the people of Alexandra successfully resisted a rise in
bus fares. '*Azikwelwa* – they are not to be boarded'; and they
walked in great numbers and without flagging for three months.
The women were particularly determined, sending deputations
of protests to the officials or burning their passes. Demonstrations
often ended in violence. Hundreds of women in the Eastern
Transvaal were arrested for taking part in an illegal procession
and the local Whites were reduced to near panic. The women of
the Hurutsi Reserve near Zeerust in the Western Transvaal, too,
were incensed by the issue of reference books in September 1957.
Books by the hundred were burnt, large numbers of women ar-

rested. Anxious menfolk at work on the Reef hurried home; factions developed with violence between supporters of the chiefs who were helping to implement government policy and those who opposed it. Tribal courts and police took severe disciplinary action, aeroplanes were used to terrorize one procession of furious women. Five hundred people fled across the border to take refuge in Botswana. The unrest lasted about a year before harsh government measures brought the reserve under control. Similar events took place in 1958 in the Sekhukhune Reserve in the Central Transvaal, sparked off in this case by the introduction of Bantu Authorities and of cattle culling schemes under the Stock Limitation Regulations. The latter were sensibly intended to reduce the devastating overstocking and consequent erosion and impoverishment of the reserves; but they were not properly understood by the people and took no proper account of traditional tribal attachment to cattle, nor of the extreme poverty of people whose only property was their scrawny beasts and they highlighted the desperate shortage of land in the reserves. So they were fought tooth and nail. Again there were hundreds of arrests, fiercely punitive sentences and a build-up of resentment checked only by draconian control. The introduction of Bantu Authorities in the Transkei again set off dissension between chiefs who supported the government's apartheid policies and others who did not, which rapidly burgeoned into faction and tribal fighting. This was aggravated by the harsh authoritarianism of some chiefs supported by the police, and was kept at only simmering point by the ostentatious use of sten guns and armoured cars and the proclaiming of a state of emergency (to be still in force at the end of 1975).

In 1958 Strydom died. His four years in power had been years of great political activity and extremely repressive law-making, during which a highly explosive racial situation both internally and abroad built up. As for apartheid – the strictures of its critics were only too apparently justified: that so far only the repressive and negative aspects had been introduced; the promised benefits were as remote as ever. For, although the Nationalists had put forward the intellectuals' apartheid conception as an election platform and as a progressive policy when under foreign criticism, very few actually believed in it as a practical proposition and the findings of the Tomlinson Commission in 1954 confirmed the doubts. Even Malan himself, within two years of attaining the premiership on the wave of the electors' enthusiasm for apartheid, had said: 'If one could attain total territorial apartheid ... it would be an ideal state of affairs ... but that is not the policy of our party ... I clearly stated ... that total territorial apartheid, was impractical under present circumstances in South Africa, where our whole economic structure is to a large extent based on Native labour.' During his term of office the approach did not change. In 1956 Mr M. N. de Wet Nel said, 'The idea of Bantu states must be rejected because it is dangerous.'[35] But two years later he was the minister responsible for creating the first Bantustan.

Strydom's death gave the opportunity to one man of single vision, the total believer in the rightness and practicability of apartheid, to justify his faith. After a short, sharp struggle among party factions behind the scenes (no outward signs of rift were permitted), Verwoerd, who had been an elected Member of Parliament for only four-and-a-half months, emerged as party leader and Prime Minister, the party's choice as the only man able to impose an order on the apartheid confusion.

Hertzog, the gentle general and irritable, narrow patriot, had patiently built up the Afrikaner's sense of nationalism; the dour and determined predikant-pressman, Malan, had forged from many elements the weapon of the Nationalist Party. But it was to be the triumph of the alien Verwoerd to attain the old Afrikaner goal of an independent republic. They all used the same tool; the unifying antagonism that can be called up by the fear of being worsted in the struggle for survival.

Verwoerd appeared never to question that he was divinely guided: 'I believe the will of God was revealed in the ballot,' he said on his election, and a few days later repeated: 'In accordance with His will it was determined who should assume the leadership ... in the new period.'[36] 'I do not have the nagging doubt of ever wondering whether perhaps I am wrong.'[37] Under his granite rule a new era began for South Africa.

35. Legum, op. cit., pp. 50, 51. 36. *The Times* (London, 3 January 1963).
37. *Observer* (London, 11 September 1966).

7 The Republic (1958-74)

1. THE ERA OF VERWOERD

Hendrick Frensch Verwoerd took up his responsibilities not only in a sure faith of divine appointment but with superb self-assurance. 'Sincere conviction and firm action command the confidence and esteem of friends and foe,'[1] he said, and at the end of the next seven years he was oddly, perversely proved right.

He set about completing the cardinal task of differentiating the education of the race groups by means of two Acts, the Extension of University Education and the University College of Fort Hare Transfer Acts of 1959. These provided for the establishment of a number of separate university colleges (ethnic or tribal colleges they came to be called) for Africans, Coloureds, and Asians. The government retained complete control over appointment of rector, managerial council and staff, over registration and grants to students and over curriculum. The conscience clause, the constitutional guarantee of religious freedom to staff and students in all White universities except Potchefstroom, was omitted. Hitherto there had been no legal colour bar in university education, although in practice only two, the 'open' universities of Cape Town and the Witwatersrand, admitted Blacks to the same lectures as Whites, while Natal had separate colleges. In all three residential, recreational and social segregation was maintained. Now, except by ministerial consent, the attendance of Blacks at the open universities was to be ended because, according to the majority report of a commission of inquiry, its continuance would

give students a background which does not fit in with their national character and will give them an alien and contemptuous attitude towards their own culture . . . Each [college] should serve an ethnic

1. Stanley Uys, *Africa South*, Vol. III, No. 2, p. 9.

group . . . as well as promoting the broader interests of South Africa . . . The product of the University should seek and find its highest fulfilment in the enrichment of its own social group . . .[2]

Two new colleges were set up in isolated and insulated rural areas in the Northern Transvaal and Zululand; Fort Hare was converted into an ethnic college for the Xhosa, its autonomy and conscience clause abolished and its administration brought under the control of the NAD, its principal and many of the African and English-speaking staff were dismissed or resigned. A side-effect of the changes was an unusual reversal of the pattern of expenditure. It was reported in 1965 that the university education of 33,000 White students out of a White population of three million cost the state annually £250 each: that of the 946 African students from a total of eleven million, £900 each. The United Party, the universities and many other bodies strongly but uselessly opposed both Acts. Educationists condemned the whole policy of segregated education because of the reduction in fluency in the official languages, the absence of suitable textbooks and terminology in African and Indian languages, multiplication of libraries, laboratories and other services, and shortage of money which would inevitably add up to an inferior educational standard for the Blacks.

Verwoerd was becoming very sensitive to the derogatory connotations acquired by the word apartheid which by this time was commonly used abroad to denote any form of discriminatory separation. He increasingly substituted 'separate development' and then 'separate freedom' to describe his vision for the future, a vision which had now to be translated from theory into practice. The educational system would induce a suitable acquiescence while the infra-structure had been prepared with the establishment of Bantu Authorities.

The Promotion of Bantu Self-Government Act of 1959 was as revolutionary a piece of legislation as any in the Union's history. It set up machinery to create the separate 'homelands' where the various African peoples would have their independent states. De Wet Nel, Verwoerd's successor as Minister of Native Affairs, was responsible for establishing them. The Act provided for the

2. *Survey of Race Relations (SRR)* (1957–8), p. 199.

W.Bromage

RHODESIA
(ZIMBABWE)

BOTSWANA

MOZAMBIQUE

TRANSVAAL

Pietersburg

Nelspruit

Pretoria

Johannesburg

SWAZI-
LAND

Vaal

ORANGE

Harrismith

NATAL

Kuruman

FREE

Bloemfontein

Vaal

STATE

LESOTHO

Orange

Durban

CAPE

PROVINCE

Indian Ocean

line indicating scattered
areas comprising
individual homelands

East London

Port
Elizabeth

WHITE SOUTH AFRICA ☐
BANTU HOMELANDS ■
1 VENDA   6 SWAZI
2 GAZANKULU   7 CISKEI
3 LEBOWA   8 TRANSKEI
4 BOPHUTATSWANA 9 KWAZULU
5 SOUTH NDEBELE 10 BASOTHOQUAQUA

Miles

0   100   200

Map IX The Distribution of the Homelands

creation of eight separate African units: Northern Sotho, Southern Sotho, Tswana, Zulu, Swazi, Xhosa, Tsonga and Venda. Each would have its own territory, based on the existing native reserves, and its own government, limited in power and subject to the veto of the Union Parliament; each a White commissioner-general appointed to guide, advise and liaise between the central government and respective Bantu Authority. A White Paper explained that the purpose was to return to the basic principle formulated by the governments of 1913 and 1936 of identifying each of the African communities with its own land and to ensure that the Africans entered the White areas as migratory labourers only. All African representation in the Union Parliament was at last abolished by this Act. Africans would have civic rights only in their ethnic homelands (although many had long lost contact with these) and 'diplomats' would be exchanged with the central government. Traditional forms of self-government must be developed by Africans in accordance with the demands of modern civilization, said Verwoerd, who foresaw, 'that there will arise what I call a Commonwealth, founded on a common interest and linked together by common interest'.[3]

But the obvious immediate results of this sort of legislation for ethnic grouping, which was also being imposed in the towns, was once again to build up a divisive and rival tribalism among the Africans who, with urbanization and the adoption of Western ways and of English as a *lingua franca*, were beginning to find a common nationhood. The unity which is strength of South Africa's motto was for Whites only. M. C. Botha, who was Minister in 1966 when South Africa was justifying her policies to the world and especially in Africa, could – in an access of scrupulosity – then say:

I want to bring a most interesting point to the attention of all of us. As regards the various nations we have here, the White nation, the Coloured nation, the Indian nation, the various Bantu nations, something to which we have given too little regard is the fact that numerically the White nation is superior to all other nations in South Africa ... It has very wide implications for us all. Firstly, it demonstrates our duty as guardians ... It also demonstrates the utter folly

3. South African *Hansard* (Assembly, 20 May 1959).

of saying a minority government is ruling others in South Africa . . . In the final instance our work is directed at eventual geographic partition.[4]

The United Party expressed its alarm at what it forecast would be the Balkanization of South Africa, but, in the main, party opposition to government measures was by this time little more than formal. Its own policies were framed to try to keep the allegiance of its right-wingers and to attract the adherence of fringe Nationalists – a forlorn hope. In consequence its programme seemed a weak copy of the Nationalists' and was not attractive to anyone. The Nationalists could always bring the core of the United Party to heel by accusing it of wanting racial integration and of travelling with communism.

A section of the party, however, was dismayed at its increasingly reactionary policy and poor showing on issues of Non-white affairs, in particular the decision to oppose Bantustans by resisting any government move to acquire more land in terms of the 1936 pledge to augment the Bantu areas. Eleven of the more independent members splintered off and formed the Progressive Party, under the leadership of Dr Jan Steytler, to campaign for the opening of a dialogue between Whites and the recognized Black leadership. The party advocated a non-racial qualified franchise of all adults on a Common roll, a federal parliament with an entrenched constitution embodying a Bill of Rights, and an Upper House of Representatives supported by all races with power to block discriminatory legislation. The Progressive Party attracted many intellectuals in the professions and business, both English and Afrikaans, the most substantial being Harry Oppenheimer. But it was considered too liberal by Whites in general and too conservative by Blacks and therefore its following, though distinguished, was small. Its members, together with the Native Representation, made a formidable White liberal conscience in Parliament, although they could not affect the eventual passage of the bills they opposed. In later elections all but one lost their seats to the United Party and, with the abolition of the Native Representatives from the Assembly, only Mrs Helen Suzman, representing the wealthy and cosmopolitan Johannesburg constituency of

4. *SRR* (1966), p. 146 (in the Assembly, 13 October 1966).

Houghton and largely through the influence of Oppenheimer, remained a lonely Horatio holding a frail bridge of a mild liberalism.

While the Whites were engaged in acrimonious legalistic but strictly constitutional wrangle, outside Parliament there was turbulent Black protest throughout South Africa. Whatever the theoretical progress towards separate development, the poverty and frustrations of Black life were only felt more keenly and almost every constitutional vent for the expression of opinions, desires or dissent was closed. The ANC remained the only organized political channel of expression and lack of success in recent demonstrations had lost it support. A strong Africanist group challenged the leadership and its policies of non-violence, alleged domination in the Congress Alliance by non-Africans and finally in 1959, with the slogan 'Africa for the Africans', broke away to form the Pan-Africanist Congress (PAC), led by Mr Robert Sobukwe, lecturer in Zulu at the Witwatersrand University. PAC aimed at 'Government of the Africans by the Africans and for the Africans, with everybody who owes his only loyalty to Africa and is prepared to accept the democratic rule of an African majority being regarded as an African'[5] (curiously recalling Hertzog's conception of a Nationalist). PAC proposed universal franchise; but Africans, they argued (again not unlike Hertzog), must build up their bargaining power before attempting to cooperate with other races.

The ANC reasserted its multi-racial ideals, its willingness to cooperate with any who shared them and its policy of non-violence. It initiated a boycott of the products of certain firms believed to be Nationalist controlled or where treatment of Black employees was unsatisfactory, and also a boycott of potatoes in protest against the barbaric working conditions on some farms; it appealed for the boycott overseas of South African products.

Concurrent with these organized movements, disorders, large and small, were still flaring all over the country in which women, more quickly sensitive to the many consequences of poverty, continued to play a leading part. Furthermore, the government, pressing on with population registration, was extending the pass system in earnest to women. Police used batons to disperse an anti-

5. *SRR* (1958–9), p. 15.

pass meeting of women near Pretoria. In days of rioting, led by women angered by police raids for illicit liquor in the Cato Manor location near Durban, the people boycotted the municipal beer-halls, destroyed beer and attacked municipal property. Trade union troubles reached a head in Paarl, in the Cape, when a banishment order led to the flight to Lesotho of Mrs Mafeteng, a prominent trade unionist and a mother of eleven. Banishment orders (there were eventually twenty-five different kinds) fell as softly, stifling as volcanic ash on individuals of all races, mostly those connected with the congress movements. The most significant was the banning of Lutuli who was confined to his home in northern Natal for five years. In the middle of all this came the news that he had been awarded the Nobel Peace prize and, despite the government's bewildered disapproval, he was granted ten days in which to receive it in Oslo. Ironically, the award marked the virtual end of passive mass protest. Leaders dedicated to non-violence, experienced in handling mass demonstrations, trusted and obeyed by rank and file, were now in fetters, unable to do more than issue directions: the way was open to hardliners.

All the same, there was a feeling that the tide was running with the liberation movement, that white baasskap was reaching its climacteric. All across Africa people were shaking free of colonial tutelage – peoples in the main less advanced and with less intimate experience in the ways of Western civilization than the Non-white peoples of South Africa. It seemed their progress could not be long delayed. The power of the developing states was mounting at the United Nations. But the disastrous civil war in the Congo (later to be called Zaire), newly independent under an African government, was a set-back to liberal views and did much to reinforce the Nationalists.

In February 1960, Mr Harold Macmillan, the British Prime Minister, came into Cape Town fresh from a tour of Africa to make his startling 'wind of change' speech. He commented on the strength of African national consciousness and said that, like it or not, it was a political fact which national policies must take account of and come to terms with. He expressed British distaste for South African race policies; her desire to raise material standards and to create societies which gave an increasing share in political power and responsibility and in which individual merit was the criterion for advancement. He placed the issue squarely into the context of the cold war struggle and suggested that if it came to a choice between the friendship of 200,000,000 Blacks or 4,000,000 Whites in Africa there was no doubt where Britain would stand.

This speech hardened Nationalist attitudes. In Parliament on 9 March Verwoerd complained:

It appears to me that the White nations are prepared to abandon the Whites in Africa . . . The White man of Africa is not going to be told that, because he is outnumbered by the Black peoples, he must allow his rights to be swallowed up and be prepared to lose his say . . . We do not accept . . . that the White inhabitants must be satisfied as a minority in a multiracial country to compete with the Black masses on an equal basis, which in the long run can only mean a Black government.

He amplified this a fortnight later: 'We will see to it that we remain in power in this White South Africa . . . [The Bantu] should really be rooted in the areas inhabited by their forefathers.'[6]

As White politicians argued and fulminated, the peculiarly explosive mixture of anger, poverty, frustration and sheer misery brewing among the Blacks gained some extra potency from the hope engendered by Macmillan's remarks. African protests against the pass laws mounted. (Published figures showed nearly 400,000 convictions for offences against control regulations in 1958.) The ANC had agreed on a major campaign to include deputations to local and government authorities urging the abolition of passes to lead up to a meeting to plan mass demonstrations in May and June. In February the Congress, supported by a number of Whites led by Bishop Reeves of Johannesburg, staged a silent anti-pass demonstration. In March, Mrs Ballinger (still a Native Representative in Parliament) introduced a motion condemning the pass laws.

The PAC, too, had resolved on 'decisive and final positive action' against the pass laws as a first step in achieving freedom and independence by 1963. A campaign was planned to begin on

6. *SRR* (1959–60), pp. 280–81.

21 March when members would leave their passes at home and surrender at local police stations for arrest. The slogan would be 'no bail, no defence, no fine',[7] and in the spirit of non-violence they would disperse in orderly fashion if ordered by the police to do so. They informed the police of the intention. The ANC regarded the PAC campaign as sensational and insufficiently prepared and declined to cooperate, but the PAC went ahead. In many areas the demonstration went to plan, but in the tense atmosphere of the time hundreds, not PAC members, joined in and built up into excited throngs. The shocking culmination came when the police fired on a wrought-up but not hostile crowd at Sharpeville, near Vereeniging, killing 67 and wounding 186, mostly in the back as they fled.

Sobukwe and Lutuli then called for the observance of 28 March as a stay-at-home day of mourning. This had considerable success in the major centres. But throughout the tense week disturbances and rioting took place. On 30 March, a peaceable but alarmingly large column of 30,000 people marched on Cape Town. The government mounted a show of air and police strength but the people dispersed readily on the instruction of their young leader, Philip Kgosana, who accepted a hollow promise of a meeting with the Minister. The government had at once prohibited all meetings; it now banned the ANC and PAC organizations, declared a state of emergency and began the arrest and detention of nearly 2,000 of its militant opponents including those still on trial for treason, and 10,000 others. The state of emergency (except in the Transkei) ended on 13 August when the last of the detainees was released. Sobukwe received a three-year prison sentence for incitement.

Immediately after the Sharpeville event a temporary relaxation of the pass laws led to a short-lived belief that the system was about to be abolished. There followed a flood of statements by White political, commercial, industrial, financial, liberal, religious and even some nationalist organizations and individuals urging an inquiry into the underlying causes of the disturbances and a reassessment of policies. On 9 April, the day after the banning of the congresses, at the Rand Agricultural Show in Johannes-

7. *SRR* (1959–60), p. 55.

burg, David Pratt, a wealthy White farmer (found later to be deranged) shot and just failed to kill Verwoerd.

For a moment Nationalist single-mindedness faltered. P. O. Sauer (son of the Cape Liberal), who was Minister of Lands and acting-Prime Minister, said in a speech at Humansdorp in the Cape on 21 May: 'The old book of South African history was closed a month ago and, for the immediate future, South Africa would reconsider in earnest and honesty her whole approach to the Native question. We must create a new spirit which must restore overseas faith – both White and Non-white in South Africa.'[8]

But Verwoerd recovered. 'In this miraculous escape,' *Die Burger* declared, 'all the faithful will see the hand of God.'[9] He who at his accession had acknowledged: 'I do not ever have the nagging doubt of ever wondering whether, perhaps, I am wrong,' was confirmed the Lord's anointed and the Volkswil the will of God. Deviationists were called to order and (on the very day of Sauer's doubting) a statement from the premier was read in the Assembly. This reaffirmed the whole policy of separate development and rejected demands for an inquiry before existing commissions investigating related problems had reported and the Treason Trial was concluded, since this 'in part has the character of an inquiry into the causes of the disturbances'.[10]

However, the liquor laws were shortly abolished, not only on the recommendation of the police and many responsible persons but also under pressure from the powerful Cape wine farmers' lobby, and one source of friction between police and people was removed. Mitigation of the administration of the pass laws was promised, and the issuing of reference books to women was postponed until the date on which it would be compulsory for Whites to possess identity cards; but the pass-law system was by now but a part of the whole structure of control of the Africans.

Verwoerd, confidently in control again and unshaken in determination, pressed on with a previously announced intention to hold a referendum on 5 October on the latent but never entirely

8. Edward Roux, *Time Longer than Rope*, p. 413.
9. ibid., p. 411 (on 11 April 1964).
10. *SRR* (1959–60), p. 105.

dormant issue of a republic. The decision was to be by majority verdict, even if it were a majority of only one. 'If we do not succeed . . .,' he said, 'next time we will adopt the . . . method . . . of allowing [the] . . . decision to be taken by the majority in a Parliament elected for that purpose.'[11] In the event, by a majority of 74,000, or 4 per cent, the White electorate voted for a Republic. The 13,000,000 Blacks were not consulted.

At the next conference of Commonwealth Prime Ministers in London, in March 1961, Verwoerd formally applied for continued membership of the Commonwealth for South Africa as a republic. He explained his policy of separate development (or 'co-existence' as he was now calling it), giving figures to show that South Africa spent more on education, health and welfare services for Africans than other territories on the continent. For all his efforts South Africa's treatment of Blacks was so cogently criticized that he could only withdraw his application. 'I am sure that the great majority of the people of my country will appreciate that in the circumstances no other course was open to us. National pride and self-respect,' he said, 'are attributes of any sovereign independent state.'[12] On the 31 May 1961, the fifty-first anniversary of Union, South Africa became a Republic outside the Commonwealth. The constitutional connection between Britain and South Africa that had existed since 1806 was broken.

The constitutional changes made little difference to the Black population but the date, 31 May 1961, was used for further demonstration and protests.

The Treason Trial ended on 29 March with the abrupt acquittal of all the accused before the defence argument was concluded. The court found that the congresses had been working to replace the existing form of State with a radically different one based on the Freedom Charter, but that it had not been proved that this would be communist, nor that the accused had personal knowledge of the communist doctrine of violent revolution, nor that it was ANC policy to overthrow the State by violence. The twenty-eight thus absolved returned to the freedom struggle elated and with vigour. The verdict infused the political masses

11. *SRR* (1959–60), p. 5.
12. *SRR* (1961), p. 6.

with revived hope, despite the organizational disarray which followed upon the outlawing of the ANC and PAC and the banning or restriction orders imposed on so many of the leaders. Some of the more prominent men, unable to be effective at home any longer, were sent clandestinely abroad to set up as the congresses' official representatives.

The leaders still in the country, in a last non-violent bid, called for an 'All-in' African conference which was attended by more than a thousand delegates in Pietermaritzburg late in March. PAC did not participate because of objections to cooperation with other races, especially the COD and the Liberal Party. The meeting demanded that an all-race conference be held not later than 31 May, Republic Day, failing which mass demonstrations would be launched. All Africans were charged in no way to cooperate with the Republic, and Indians, Coloured and democratic Whites were urged to join forces with them to 'win a society in which all can enjoy freedom and security'. A call went out for world economic sanctions against the 'minority government whose continued disregard of all human rights and freedoms constitutes a threat to world peace'.[13] A National Action Council was appointed, and, as its secretary, Nelson Mandela. Mandela was a member of the family of the paramount chief of the Thembu, a graduate of the universities of Fort Hare and the Witwatersrand, who had abandoned a thriving legal practice for politics. With an impressive physical presence, great charm of personality and natural as well as intellectual authority, he rose rapidly to leadership and with his legal colleague, Oliver Tambo, who was by then in exile, stood next in succession to Lutuli. Mandela went 'underground' to organize a nation-wide African stay-at-home planned for the 29 May, 30 May and 31 May. As the 'Black Pimpernel', he dodged the police hunt for him for fifteen months.

The government took strong counter-measures. After its failure in the Treason Trial and other legal set-backs, the need of still further powers was felt and a great deal of amending legislation was rushed through Parliament during May. Most important was the General Laws Amendment Act of 1961 directed against

13. *Fighting Talk* (April 1961).

'agitators', which gave the police powers of detention for twelve days (instead of forty-eight hours) without bail and further restricted the holding of meetings. Amendments to Defence and Police Acts greatly increased the strength and powers of these bodies. As the end of the month approached police raids were multiplied. Five thousand troops and Saracen armoured cars were called out, helicopters flashed searchlights over the townships, dismissal of those who stayed at home was threatened, and scare stories and misleading accounts of a lack of response to the stay-at-home were circulated. The first day met with a good response, but the confusion of rumour and the leadership difficulties (added to by P A C opposition) and the show of official strength were too great and the protest – the last disciplined non-violent demonstration – spluttered out. A general election overwhelmingly affirmed White support for the unyielding strong arm of the Nationalists.

A total change in the South African situation became apparent with the first acts of sabotage. In the next two years many sabotage acts were committed, most of them rather inept. The existence of two new underground organizations was revealed. *Umkonto we Sizwe* (the spear of the Nation) consisted mainly of ex-members of the old Congress Alliance. Led by Mandela, it committed sabotage of installations selected with the express aim of doing material damage but causing no harm to people. *Poqo* was an offshoot of P A C, its name being variously defined as meaning pure – purely for Africans; we stand alone; only; completely; and with an old religious denominational usage implying a refusal to have anything to do with Whites. Poqo was formed in cells throughout urban and rural areas, was sworn to the murder of informers and was involved in many acts of violence. Hundreds of young men were being smuggled out of South Africa for training in sabotage and guerilla warfare, but as they filtered back many of them were to be soon picked up by the police.

Speaking in the Assembly in May 1961, Verwoerd had said: 'The state of the nation will remain healthy only so long as the policy of this government is supported *in all respects*,'[14] and more drastic measures were taken to ensure that it was. Amendments

14. *SRR* (1961), p. 12.

in the next years to general, criminal, police, defence and censorship laws, introduced, *inter alia*, the new crime of sabotage with a possible capital penalty; the system of house arrest; powers to detain suspects for ninety days without charge and *incommunicado* (directed especially against Poqo and the Spear); powers to detain witnesses in a range of criminal and political offences for 180 days *incommunicado*; powers to refuse bail before trial and to hold political offenders for further periods after the expiry of their sentences (which was repeatedly done in the case of the PAC leader, Sobukwe). The publishing of statements by banned persons became an offence and the importation or possession of a large range of political books was banned. The circulation of sketches or plans of military or police institutions or of information about troop or police movements or conditions inside gaols was forbidden.

At the same time, defence expenditure enormously increased, until it was £128m., 15 per cent of the budget in 1967 estimates. Extensive manufacture of armaments, increased oil from coal production, search for natural oil, creation of a national tanker fleet, and an increase in the size of the forces put the country virtually on a war footing. The defensive measures were ostensibly directed towards Soviet or communist quarters. But the true source of official fears was revealed in the training of three specialist forces: to defend the country's borders, to fight on the platteland, and for street fighting.

Once on strong legislative ground, the government moved against its remaining opponents. In 1962 the White Congress of Democrats was banned and a list issued of the names of over a hundred persons many of them well known, many of them professional writers, whose writings might not be published. Banning and house-arrest orders still came thick and fast. Protest meetings were banned, and *New Age* and *Spark*, journals of radical opposition, were closed down. What remnants of organization there were had been white-anted by informers. People held in detention and often solitary confinement for ninety-day periods acted (as was intended) unpredictably. Under the system of interrogation adopted by the special branch police (allegedly including, for Whites, long hours of standing, deprivation of rest and alternate threats and promises and, for Blacks, the much cruder measures of electric shock and other physical ill-treatment), many were induced to turn State's evidence or made statements which often later in court they repudiated. On evidence thus gleaned a series of mass trials in various parts of the country was staged, held often in obscure rural districts where it was difficult to arrange legal defence.

In August 1962 Mandela was arrested and put on trial in an atmosphere of great emotion, and sentenced to five years' imprisonment. In July 1963 an informer led the police to the hideout, on the outskirts of Johannesburg, of the High Command of the National Liberation Movement and *Umkonto*. Here they arrested seventeen people, including all the known leaders of the congress movement still at large in the country, and took a mass of documents which laid bare the whole underground strategy. The leaders were held in ninety-day detention and, joined with Mandela, were then charged with acting in concert with many others who had fled abroad with the object of causing a violent revolution in South Africa, with embarking on a campaign to overthrow the government by violent revolution and with causing 193 acts of sabotage. Sabotage was a capital offence and the men were aware that they were on trial for their lives. Mandela, from the dock, recalled the long history of the ANC and its demands for the African people.

It could not be denied [he said] that our policy to achieve a non-racial state by non-violence, had achieved nothing . . . The time comes when there remain only two choices – submit or fight . . . Our struggle is a truly national one . . . It is a struggle for the right to live . . . During my lifetime [he concluded] I dedicated myself to this struggle of the African people. I have fought against white domination and I have fought against black domination. I have cherished the ideal of a democratic and free society in which all persons live together in harmony, and with equal opportunities. It is an ideal which I hope to live for and to achieve. But, if need be, it is an ideal for which I am prepared to die.[15]

There were no death sentences (the trial had attracted tremendous

15. Nelson Mandela, *I am Prepared to Die* (Christian Action).

international concern). Mandela and seven others were sentenced to imprisonment for life on Robben Island.

In another mass trial under the Suppression of Communism Act the main accused was Mr Abram Fischer, QC. He was of impeccable Afrikaner stock, grandson of the Abraham Fischer, Prime Minister of the Orange Free State, son of its judge-president and married to a niece of Mrs Smuts. Fischer had long been a Communist, joining the party because of his hatred of traditional race attitudes, and as a distinguished lawyer he had defended many political cases with a great measure of success. He estreated bail and went underground for eleven months to oppose the policy of the government as long as he was able. He was finally arrested and sentenced to life imprisonment in 1966.

With mass trials still in progress and the Transkei still under a state of emergency imposed in 1960, Verwoerd gave further remarkable proof of an unassailable assurance. He introduced the Transkei Constitution Act of 1963. The Bantu Authorities Act of 1951 had set up Bantu Tribal, Regional and Territorial Authorities with limited executive and administrative powers; in spite of violent opposition, 454 tribal, community and district, 27 regional and 6 territorial authorities were functioning by 1963. The Promotion of Bantu Self-Government Act of 1959 had established eight national units. The Transkei Constitution Act was in a logical sequence and created the first of the promised Bantu homelands.

The Transkei was the largest of the reserve areas, 16,000 square miles, with a mainly Xhosa population of 1,500,000. It contained no large White towns or areas of great industrial development or potential; the White population numbered only some 13,000, most of them officials, farmers or traders. The Africans living in the Transkei were mostly peasants, but another 1,500,000 Xhosa kinsmen lived in the White areas, on farms or mines or in the towns, many of them having lost all contact with the tribal areas. Since the times of Lord Grey and of Rhodes, the Transkei had had experience of a measure of local self-government through the Bunga. In every way it was suitable as a pilot scheme for the next step in separate development. The Act provided for the creation of a separate Transkei Territory (excluding the 'White' areas: a number of small towns, some farm areas and Port St Johns, the only port in the territory). It would have its own government in the shape of a Legislative Assembly consisting of the four paramount chiefs and sixty salaried chiefs, *ex-officio*, and forty-five members elected on an adult franchise of all citizens, including all those tribesmen working and living in the White areas of South Africa who would have civic rights only in the Transkei Homeland. The Chief Minister and Cabinet would be elected by the Assembly from its ranks. However, the control of a number of important departments was reserved to the South African Government: defence, external affairs, internal security, postal communications, national roads, railways, harbours, aviation, immigration, currency, banking, customs and the Constitution. This left the new 'independent' state with powers of administration somewhat greater than those of the Bunga or than those possessed by the provincial administrations of the Republic.

The Bill was criticized in the South African Parliament by the United Party because it must lead to eventual sovereign independence and the fragmentation of South Africa. It was criticized by Mrs Suzman, the Progressive member, because the exclusion of the White economic centres made the territory too poor to be able to compete with industrialized South Africa and because the Republic's repressive laws, such as the pass laws and banishment without trial, would remain in force in the Transkei.

African reactions in the Transkei varied. Chief Kaiser Matanzima, a lawyer, a government-appointed chief and a supporter of apartheid, called it 'an honest offer of race separation'. But he soon caused consternation when he took apartheid at its face value and declared, in a speech to the Xhosa in the Cape, that the Whites had no claim to the land between the Fish River and Zululand. Verwoerd had quickly to reassure White South Africa: 'There can be no question whatsoever of the whole territory between the Fish River and Zululand becoming a Bantu Homeland. The existing division in White and Black areas will be maintained.'[16] Other chiefs, notably Paramount Chief Victor Poto, advocated an upper house of review composed of chiefs, a fully elected Assembly and votes for Black and White. Paramount

16. *SRR* (1963), p. 90.

Chief Sabata Dalindyebo opposed separate development altogether in favour of a multi-racial South African society. When elections took place Poto, supported by Dalindyebo, won at least thirty-five of the forty-five elected seats. However, the Assembly elected Matanzima as Chief Minister by a majority over Poto of fifty-four to forty-nine, revealing that many of the *ex-officio* chiefs in supporting Matanzima had not voted in accordance with the wishes of the people and so had acted contrary to traditional tribal democracy.

Complementary to the establishment of the first homeland were the provisions of the Bantu Laws Amendment Acts of 1963 and 1964. These complex Bills, described as 'the most ferocious apartheid measure yet devised',[17] when related to other legislation were punitive in effect. Earlier laws made it an offence for Africans to visit urban areas for more than seventy-two hours, except certain categories who had an automatic right of residence, and this was now abolished. Africans lost all security of employment or residence in White areas and a system of direction of labour was established. Any African could be 'endorsed out' of an area if the minister decided its labour requirements were met, or that no more labour was to be recruited from the area from which the African came, or deemed the African 'undesirable' or 'idle' or believed that it was not in the interests of employer, employee or the public that the contract of service should continue. The Deputy Minister of BAD, M. I. Botha, explained the paternal government purpose:

> The entire basis of the presence of the Bantu in the White areas depends on the labour he performs . . . we say very clearly to the Bantu in the whole of South Africa, 'You may be in the White areas in order to come and work there . . . We shall see to it that [while there] you are protected, that you will be able to live properly . . . that you will make such progress as you as worthy labourers are entitled to . . . If you misbehave as labourers, if you are unworthy labourers, you cannot remain here.'[18]

Graaff, for the United Party, clearly stated the objections. Africans outside the reserves 'must remain in a permanent state of

17. Christopher Kavanagh, *Sunday Times* (London, 3 March 1964).
18. *SRR* (1964), p. 186.

insecurity as long as they live. There is an almost total denial of individuality. Each one is becoming an interchangeable labour unit . . .' 'The whole justification for the Bill' (i.e. granting full rights in the reserves), he said, 'is a falsehood, but the inhumanity, the hurt and the invasions of dignity as a result of this policy are real.' The Bill 'mutilates and destroys the security of family life . . . [The Bantu] cannot offer their labour on the market for free negotiation as to the wage they are to be paid . . . [The Bantu in the reserves] can stay in the reserves where there are very often no jobs . . . or they may come into these areas [outside] with no hope whatsoever of getting a permanent place of abode or of being joined by their families.' To this Mrs Suzman added that the Bill 'strips the African of every basic pretension he has to being . . . a free being in the country of his birth and reduces him to the level of a chattel'.[19] The only Black criticism came from the African Chamber of Commerce and the Interdenominational African Ministers Association. There were no parties or politicians free to protest.

At a general election in March 1966 the White electorate again showed its approval of Verwoerd's policies by returning the Nationalist Party with 126 seats to the United Party's thirty-nine and the Progressive's one seat. The Nationalists won 776,766 votes and the UP 490,971, an estimated swing of 17 per cent. Verwoerd had won for the Nationalists an overall majority of votes for the first time.

2. APARTHEID AND THE WORLD

The South African Government, harassed by internal disturbances, now also faced constant international criticism of its policies, internal and external opponents aiding, abetting and reinforcing each other. Although her foreign relations worsened, South Africa had continued throughout the post-war years to co-operate with international and inter-African bodies, making valuable scientific and technological contributions. The government, with no diplomatic contacts in Africa, except with Rhodesia and the Portuguese colonies, was very conscious of the need for

19. *SRR* (1964), pp. 185–6.

some machinery for consultation and cooperation in matters of common interest, especially as trade prospects rapidly expanded with the emergent countries to the north. In a tentative political approach, a South African representative had attended Ghana's independence celebrations and a Ghanaian had been received at a conference in South Africa. The shift in outlook had been revealed when Eric Louw, in the Assembly in June 1957, welcomed the development of the continent of Africa as long as there was no impediment to South Africa's access to markets north of the Limpopo, 'the natural markets of our large and expanding industries'.[20] The next year he told SABRA that an exchange of diplomats was bound to come (though old conventions of segregation could not be changed overnight); international conferences which included Black delegates would be held in South Africa; an international guesthouse was to be built at the Johannesburg airport for Whites and Blacks in transit.

1958 brought a sharp change in the tempo of events. The first All-African Peoples' Conference (AAC) in Accra that year called on African states, the United Nations and all states professing democracy to take positive action against race discrimination and to impose economic sanctions against South Africa. This call, echoed at various African political and labour gatherings, began to be heeded and to snowball. Later inter-African meetings proposed diplomatic, political and oil sanctions and several West Indian, African and Asian countries responded with bans on many South African imports, while in Britain and Scandinavia token non-governmental boycotts were imposed. Labour and race organizations in the United States urged a government ban on South African gold and strategic raw materials where other sources were available, a consumer boycott and a ban on business investment. All of this was a forceful expression of disapproval, not a direct means of forcing change: psychological and moral rather than economic warfare with a negligible economic impact on South Africa. More serious was the legal action taken by the second All-African Peoples' Conference, authorizing Ethiopia and Liberia, as members of the defunct League of Nations, to approach the International Court of Justice for a judgement (similar

20. *SRR* (1956–7), p. 239.

to its previous opinions, but legally binding) on South Africa's administration of its mandate in South West Africa. (The country was increasingly to be referred to in international circles by its name of choice – Namibia.)

1960 was a critical year. No fewer than sixteen newly independent African countries were to take their seats in the United Nations. Flexing their political muscles, they dreamed of a giant strength in unity. Until now South Africa had been protected against the stronger United Nations resolutions by the Western nations – particularly the United States, Britain and France – which though critical of apartheid, had opposed interference in domestic affairs. This support was becoming less dependable. Race tensions within both the United States and Britain were blazing into riots and compelling modifications of domestic and international attitudes. When, in 1959, the General Assembly had again condemned South Africa's discriminatory policies as no mere domestic matter but a threat to international harmony, the United States was notable among the sixty-two nations voting for the motion (opposed by Britain, France and Portugal), her delegate declaring: 'Apartheid is a violation of human rights buttressed and sanctified by law.' The Netherlands (with which South Africa had old historical and religious affinities) found apartheid incompatible with the sense of justice of the Netherlands kingdom. Macmillan's 'wind of change' speech in the New Year seemed to herald at least a change of direction in Britain.

Then Sharpeville rocked South Africa and horrified the international community. The drastic emergency measures and detentions that ensued suggested strong internal elements of revolt. The attempt on Verwoerd's life and the momentary teetering of authority caused a flare of hope that now was the moment for pressure, the time for a great reversal. The Brazilian delegate to the United Nations tried to organize a collective stand by Latin American nations, 'born of a fusion and combination of efforts of different races' whose internal security was threatened by the propagation of doctrines aimed at destroying the relationship between people of different races and creeds.[21] The racial situation

21. *SRR* (1959–60), p. 283.

in South Africa and Namibia was now widely accepted as a threat to world peace. Britain, the United States and the Soviet Union with most Western nations supported the General Assembly resolution of 1962 which urged the establishment of a United Nations presence in South West Africa as a first step in preparing the territory for independence.

An African Summit meeting in Addis Ababa in May drew up the All-Africa Charter, its members (who controlled one-third of UN votes) pledging themselves, *inter alia*, to unity, to the eradication of colonialism in Africa (for which volunteers, arms, and guerilla training were offered), to contribute 1 per cent of national budgets to a liberation fund and to sever economic and diplomatic relations with South Africa and Portugal.

United Nations' resolutions continued to demand sanctions, especially arms and oil embargoes, and the release of political prisoners. The United States, Britain and France, all important distributors of oil, then in surplus, rejected any embargo but made some token limitation of arms sales, though Britain continued to supply the needs of the Simonstown naval base and France to sell Mirage jet fighters. The UN-appointed Myrdal Committee, reporting in 1964, foresaw 'a long ordeal of blood and hate for the people of South Africa', in which 'all Africa and the whole world must be involved'.[22] It proposed to South Africa an amnesty for political opponents and a National Convention to work out a new Constitution which might include a Declaration of Human Rights, a federal system of government, a revised social and economic structure, improved education and UN expert assistance. The committee saw international sanctions as the only peaceful means of achieving a rapid transformation with minimum suffering should South Africa refuse to cooperate. The call for sanctions, originally raised by the ANC, reverberated from meeting to meeting and country to country, amplified by the many scattered South African political refugees. Sporadic boycotting continued and was augmented by measures such as a ban on South African aircraft overflying African countries which enforced a re-routing of flights to Europe by way of friendly Portuguese airports or Spanish Las Palmas, and added 900 miles

22. *SRR* (1964), p. 108.

to the flight each way. But in sum all these measures had mainly an irritant value.

More acutely disturbing was South Africa's growing isolation. For a long time international organizations with Non-white members had hesitated to hold conferences in South Africa despite assurances of non-discrimination. Now there was increasing reluctance to accept South African (White) delegations at international conferences. She had withdrawn from UNESCO in 1956 because of objections to some publications on race matters. She later withdrew or was cold-shouldered from the International Labour Office, the World Health Organization, the Commission for Technical Cooperation in Africa, the Economic Commission for Africa, the Food and Agricultural Organization of the UN, and so on. Dissociation spread. A Netherlands parliamentarians' tour was cancelled because members might not meet Lutuli. The visit of a United States warship was called off because separated entertainment was arranged for the racially mixed crew. Many prominent playwrights refused performing rights, and musicians and actors performance, before segregated audiences. New Zealand's All-Blacks would not agree to drop their Maori players and cancelled their tour. Because South African teams were never representative of the whole population as the rules required but only of the White élite, they were barred from the Olympic Games in Tokyo in 1964 and the 1970 cricket tour in Britain would be called off. These gestures began to make sports-loving South Africans realize the extent of their ostracism. The sense of danger in the internal situation and the menace of international hostility had the result, converse to critics' intentions, of drawing the Whites of all political shades behind Verwoerd in a close and grateful unity such as had never existed before. Only with Rhodesia, with similar race policies, and Portugal, whose principles of slow assimilation were nullified by actual poverty and draconian administration, did South Africa retain openly cordial relations; and the renewal of agreements relating to trade, labour recruiting and defence consolidated their conjoined image in the rest of Africa as the last hateful enclave of colonialism.

Traditional friendly relations with South Africa became more difficult for Britain and the United States to sustain against domestic and foreign aversion, but any telling counter-action, beyond public stricture and private advices of moderation, was controlled by the huge extent of their financial commitment. The real harm South Africa suffered lay in lost opportunities of profit from an expansion of trade that could otherwise have developed with the countries to the north: South Africa was barred from contributing to, or benefiting from their progress, for all her scientific and technical ascendancy.

The feasibility of sanctions was being analysed by an assortment of organizations and the cost, implications and consequences studied by numbers of experts. A 250-delegate conference representative of forty nations met in London in 1964 and found intervention was justified because South Africa maintained a tyranny that was exclusively *racial*. 'It exacerbates and epitomizes the racial division of the world which both sides alike most dread.' The conference feared that South Africa's intransigence 'may lead to a breakdown of the UN, to alignments on a colour basis and to extreme crisis on a world scale'.[23] Studies by the British Council of Churches, a UN expert committee and the Carnegie Endowment for International Peace all expressed similar fears. All agreed that to succeed sanctions would need to be total, that participation by South Africa's main trading partners was essential, that a blockade would be necessary for enforcement. On one estimate this would require between 4 and 7 aircraft carriers and 30 to 100 other ships. It was recalled that the twenty-eight-day Cuba blockade needed 180 ships and cost £17m. It might cost the UN between £70m. and £130m. a year to sustain a naval blockade of South Africa and several hundred million pounds for air patrols. Another estimate put the cost of UN military intervention at £34m. a month and questioned whether, after a struggle on this scale, any eventual accommodation between the races would be possible. Britain, South Africa's main trading partner, estimated that participation would add £300m. to her balance of payments shortfall in the first year. The United States expected a drop in revenue of £105m. a year.

At this juncture an almost laboratory experiment in the application of sanctions could be made. In November 1965 the Govern-

23. *SRR* (1964), p. 115.

ment of Rhodesia, constitutionally a self-governing British colony, made a defiant unilateral declaration of independence (UDI). Rhodesia had demanded the independence already granted to the Black states of Malawi and Zambia, its partners in the ill-fated Central Africa Federation. Under pressure from the non-white members of the Commonwealth, Britain imposed her usual condition of no independence before majority rule – unacceptable to the Rhodesian White autocracy which controlled a quite ineffectively represented Black population twenty times its size under a regime resembling South Africa's apartheid. The British Labour Government, with a parliamentary majority of only three, could not see its way to use military force to subdue what it pronounced to be a rebellion, although this apparent tenderness for the errant but White 'kith and kin' enraged the non-white world, used as it was to firm, to say the least, British methods of disciplining rebellious Black colonials. Britain, however, outlawed Rhodesia and, with strong international support and an expensive blockade, consecutively imposed a variety of diplomatic, financial and economic sanctions, notably on oil and tobacco, which left Ian Smith, the Rhodesian Premier, unrepentant. Verwoerd, declaring his policy to maintain friendly relations with all neighbouring governments, White and Black, declined to participate in any boycott and promised to maintain normal trade, which in practice meant a greatly accelerated flow of oil and other necessities across the Limpopo to fill Rhodesia's needs. South African and Portuguese assistance kept Rhodesia afloat, and served grim economic notice to those nations expected to bear the brunt of any sanctions against the infinitely stronger South Africa.

For six years past the verdict of the International Court of Justice had been awaited in general expectation that it would go against South Africa. But, delivering judgement in 1966, the Court rejected the case on purely legal grounds that Ethiopia and Liberia had no standing in law to bring it. No ruling was given on substance: whether apartheid in Namibia was compatible with the 'sacred trust' of the mandate. The General Assembly, however, relying on earlier ICJ opinions resolved (114 votes to 2, Britain, France and Malawi abstaining) that the mandate was terminated. A fourteen-member committee, including the United States and

the Soviet Union, was set up to recommend practical steps by
which South West Africa should be administered. But there was
no agreement on the basic issue of how to get rid of South Africa,
which in twenty years disregarded seventy-two resolutions of the
General Assembly.[24]

Two decades of unrelenting foreign criticism had knit all
White South Africa (except the remnants of the disorganized left)
in close support of a government so clearly resolute and in command. Political convulsions, growing Black authoritarianism and
spreading Chinese influences in the independent states to the
north seemed to testify to the rightness of Verwoerd's rejection of
compromise in the United Nations. It was now amply and re-
assuringly clear that however much the African states fulminated
they could not, as they fell into greater political and economic disarray, mount an army against South Africa; while Britain, however much she deplored the explosive effect of South Africa's race
policies on the Commonwealth, could not afford to apply sanctions on a significant scale. The United Nations itself was made
impotent by differences between East and West and unaligned
states.

South Africa became more confidently positive in approach.
Verwoerd began to court the long-coveted Protectorates. Once
South Africa was declared a Republic the Schedule to the South
Africa Act, with the safeguards for their protection provided by
the King-in-Council, had become obsolete and by this time, in
any case, they were moving to their own individual independ-
encies, though a viable independence was not simple for any of
them to achieve. Lesotho had gained a limited autonomy in 1959
and Botswana in 1961 and by 1964 Swaziland would have agreed
on a Constitution. Verwoerd, uneasy at politically independent
and antagonistic African states in such an intimate geographic and
economic relationship, in 1963 offered them a South African
guardianship which would allow them to develop to independence

24. A further ICJ opinion, delivered in June 1971, found (by 13 to 2,
British and French judges against) that South Africa's presence in Namibia
was illegal since she had violated the Mandate which now vested in the UN,
and that all nations should refrain from giving any support or recognition
to the South African administration there.

along the lines of the Transkei. In the Assembly the next January he elaborated: 'The government has adopted the realistic attitude that South Africa no longer claims the incorporation of these territories . . . We want to have the best possible relations for the sake of our common safety and economic interests.'[25] By the end of the year he had begun to foresee the development of a multi-racial southern African 'common market'. While most African states were implacably hostile, there was a group, he claimed, 'who are opposed to our policy but willing to cooperate with us economically'.[26] As to the High Commission Territories, he said, 'It is important we give our friendship to such parties [those opposed to infiltration of Chinese money and influence] especially as now they are the ruling parties.'[27]

By 1965 a general election in Botswana under universal suffrage had returned Khama's Bechuana Democratic Party with a large majority over the more radical Bechuanaland People's Party. In September the next year the independent Republic of Botswana came into being with the Democratic Party in power and committed to a non-racial society, 'an example to other people'. Launched in one of the worst droughts in memory, the new state faced serious problems. However, by then, important iron, copper and diamond deposits had been located though as yet undeveloped, and there was a plan for a dam to irrigate 4,000 acres of arable land and provide a thermal power station. It was hoped that economic prospects were sufficient to attract foreign capital to finance a railway line to Zambia, Tanzania and the Indian Ocean and reduce dependence on South Africa. The President, now Sir Seretse Khama, took immediate precautionary steps towards establishing good relations with South Africa and no doubt was required to make political concessions including restrictions on the movements of political refugees. He said he aspired to create through tolerance and racial cooperation better understanding between northern and southern African communities. 'We fully appreciate that it is wholly in our interests to preserve as friendly and neighbourly relations with South Africa

25. *SRR* (1964), p. 126 (on 21 January 1964).
26. *SRR* (1964), p. 127.
27. *SRR* (1965), p. 102.

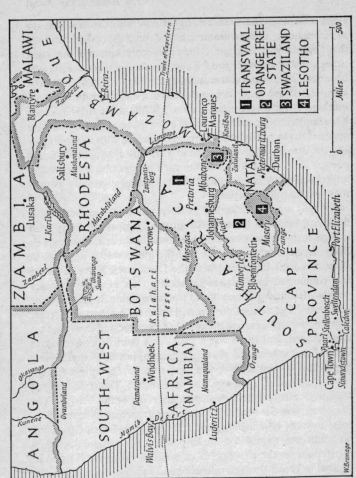

Map X Southern and Central Africa

as possible. Our economic links . . . are virtually indissoluble . . . While our race policies differ radically, I believe our approach is the right one.'[28]

In October 1966 Lesotho became independent. Paramount Chief Moshweshwe became a constitutional monarch; his Prime Minister, Chief Leabua Jonathan, with British support led a minority government with a strong radical opposition; this, the Basutoland Congress Party, was led by Ntsu Mokhele, who asked for a referendum before independence because his party feared that the British Government would allow the country to become in effect a South African dependency. Jonathan showed himself well aware of the country's total dependence on South Africa and made a pilgrimage of conciliation to Pretoria to meet Verwoerd and establish good neighbourly relations. The two purposefully genial premiers, defying South African protocol, allowed themselves to be photographed together in a diplomatic hand-clasp. Jonathan negotiated for South African cooperation in the Ox-bow scheme in the Lesotho mountains to supply water and power for both countries and acquired the services of Dr Anton Rupert as honorary industrial adviser, charged with persuading South Africa and other countries to finance Lesotho's development.

Swaziland, smallest and most prosperous of the three, was also nearing independence (which was to be gained in 1968). With nearly half its area in White ownership it had good prospects of development. The conservative policies of the traditionally minded Sobhuza II received the support of the great majority of tribesmen and, once independence and majority rule were accepted as inevitable, of an influential section of the Whites. A group of Europeans demanded separate White and Swazi rolls, but in the end a Constitution providing for a non-racial House of Assembly, mainly elected, and a Senate half nominated was accepted with a human rights code to guarantee against discrimination.

So the conciliatory courses upon which Britain set the territories erased the years of dispute over their future and fitted them, for the time being, neatly, if obliquely into the separate development scheme. In return for financial aid, South Africa was assured of

28. *SRR* (1966), p. 120.

her labour supply – if not of a huge territorial accretion – and of a check on local political development and the activities of political refugees in the territories.

Looking northward, in token of the new friendliness, Verwoerd sent an airload of medical supplies to right-wing Tshombe in Katanga, permitted the recruitment of White South African mercenaries and received Katanga envoys.

Dr Hilgard Muller, an urbane and persuasive diplomat who had succeeded the irascible Louw as Foreign Minister in 1964, predicted that a time would come when all the territories in southern Africa would work together for their mutual interests. He affirmed support for most of the principles of the Charter of the Organization of African Unity, particularly those relating to sovereign equality, non-interference in internal affairs, respect for

"Yessir, baas, I believes in independence, too."

territorial integrity and the inalienable right to independent existence; but not for those of non-alignment or acceptance of outside arbitration in domestic disputes.

South Africa had economic ties with Zambia and Malawi before the Federation was dismantled at the end of 1963. Then 40,000 White South Africans were working in Zambia, mostly in the copper mines; but Zambia stopped all further internal recruiting for South Africa's gold mines, sacrificing the £350,000 her 6,000 miners had sent home annually. Richly endowed with copper she could afford to begin to take an independent line, though her economy was still closely bound up with South Africa.

Malawi, underdeveloped and mainly agricultural, was ruled by Dr Hastings Banda, the able arch-opponent of Federation, but otherwise anglicized, conservative, grandiloquent and authoritarian. He retained Whites in the administration, reserved seats for Whites in Parliament and pursued 'a policy of discretional neutralism'.[29] He opposed colonialism but claimed that to cut ties with White neighbours would do Malawi irreparable damage. He was rewarded for his conciliatory approach and his support at the United Nations with considerable South African financial aid for industrial development; substantial help was also given for the building of a new capital at Lilongwe, in return for the use by the South African Air Force of its new up-to-date airport dominating Zambia, Rhodesia and northern Angola where guerilla movements were beginning to operate.

3. APARTHEID AND ECONOMICS

'Foreign investors look at the stability of the government rather than the policy of the government ... The simple fact that the White man is determined to maintain himself here is not a factor against investment but a factor in favour of investment,'[30] said Verwoerd in another of the coldly reasoned forecasts that proved so accurate. Throughout the 1950s South African economic expansion continued, but with some slowing of growth rate in the later years and increased unemployment, especially among Blacks, due largely to the fall in the world prices of some primary products and a contraction of many foreign markets. Increased gold production and government capital expenditure warded off a general recession. By 1960 the economy was reviving and exports were on the increase.

29. *SRR* (1964), p. 127.
30. *Fact Paper 98*, p. 5. Public Address, Pretoria, November 1961.

Then the shock of Sharpeville and the sense of crisis engendered by the state of emergency shattered the confidence of foreign investors and led to a rapid and augmenting drain away of capital. The reserves dropped by about £80m. between January 1960 and June 1961. Heavy selling abroad of South African shares brought down the market valuation, for instance, of the shares of the Anglo-American Corporation by 23 per cent and of the General Mining and Finance Corporation by 40 per cent or £12m. Unemployment rose to the highest level since 1948. The government acted with swift authority. It imposed severe import controls, particularly on textiles and motor vehicles, and raised the bank rate with all the associated curbs on the economy. Foreign exchange allowances for travellers and ex-patriates were stringently curtailed; foreign assets had to be declared; South Africans were barred from buying on stock exchanges abroad; repatriation of foreign funds invested in South Africa was prohibited. At the same time an International Monetary Fund loan of £26m. gave valuable external support.

These emergency measures trapped in South Africa a great deal of capital; banks, insurance companies, industrial concerns and private persons, however uneasily they viewed the country's prospects, could do nothing else with their money but invest in local enterprises and so refuel the economic machine. Government expenditure gave a further injection of vigour and rose to the record total of over £500m. in the estimates of 1964 (a year described by the Governor of the Reserve Bank as being 'from the economic and financial point of view one of the best ever experienced in South Africa').[31] The chief stimulus was the phenomenal escalation in defence expenditure as a consequence of both the recent internal unrest and the crescendo of criticism overseas and discussion of the possibility of imposing sanctions. The 1964 estimates included £105m. for defence (25 per cent of the budget and an increase of £25m.), 'to discourage foreign aggression',[32] said the Minister of Finance, Dr E. Donges. Expenditure included increased manufacture of munitions in which South Africa was made self-reliant, research in poison gases and the de-

31. *SRR* (1964), p. 230.
32. *The Times* (17 March 1964).

velopment of the nuclear potential. Other items in the estimates were a preliminary £10m. of the total £78m. recommended by the Odendaal Commission as necessary to make South West Africa a Bantu Homeland and £6½m. for the Transkei. £7m. was allocated to the Orange River project, a thirty-year irrigation and hydro-electric development which would divert some of the waters of the Orange River by way of a fifty-mile tunnel into the Great Fish-Sundays River system at a total cost of some £255m. There remained a record estimated surplus of £44m. The country's gross national product was £3,000m. with gold production at £344m. and a rise of 12·9 per cent in manufacturing product.

This return of buoyancy had been helped on by Harry Oppenheimer who personally had raised a £10m. loan in the United States of America for his companies, a substantial token of reviving confidence. The drift back of foreign investment soon became a flow. Britain and the United States especially, although loud in condemnation of apartheid, increased their trade and encouraged private investment in such degree that their economic fortunes were soon so bound with South Africa's that any economic pressures on South Africa could not be countenanced. By 1965 the United Kingdom took £181m. of South African products, one-third of the total export; South Africa, her third best market, imported £261m. In all, trade with South Africa gave Britain a balance of £145m.

Once the acceleration was steady the attraction for the overseas industrialist and investor was great, immediate rewards far outweighing fears of chaos to come. There was in South Africa an internationally rare industrial peace because effective conciliation machinery existed for White workers' disputes and African strikes were illegal. Tax was low on investment income. Dividends averaged 12 per cent compared with 6·6 per cent in western Europe, though doubters pointed out that such high returns could only mean short-term expectations. Over £1,500m. foreign money was invested in South Africa in 1963: £300m. was invested and 160 plants were established under licence as subsidiaries of American industries; £1,000m. invested and over 300 concerns, gave Britain a return of £65m. by 1965. The leading banks, and I C I, Courtaulds, Dunlop, Vickers, Ford, B M C and

Cyril Lord were a few of those taking advantage of the conditions. Garfield Weston, the biscuit manufacturer, seemed to speak for big business: 'South Africa is a great country, with a strong leadership. I believe in it.'[33]

All in all, Verwoerd's sanguine assessment of the country's position, in the Assembly in May 1964, was justified:

> I do not believe that sanctions of the kind threatened will ever be applied to South Africa . . . South Africa is fortunate in being blessed with a wealth of natural resources . . . We could keep going for a long time. We are busy building up our industries and diversifying them so that we are becoming self-supporting in many important respects . . . South Africa is of too much value to most of the countries of the world who count . . . as a provider of raw materials, of gold and other minerals and . . . as a market for other countries.[34]

The South Africa Foundation contributed much to this well-being. Formed at the end of 1959, when foreign criticism was high and the boycott movement gaining a momentum disturbing to the authorities, its purpose was to promote 'international understanding of South Africa, her people, their way of life, achievements and aspirations',[35] and to stimulate investment and export. Its members included Major-General Sir Francis de Guingand, Montgomery's wartime chief-of-staff and director of some twenty South African companies, and Oppenheimer, leader of the Progressive Party, who controlled the world's diamond markets and largest gold production group, half Zambia's copper, South Africa's main sources of uranium, lead, zinc, vanadium, coal and much besides – ninety world companies with capital of £500m. and annual profits between £15m. and £20m. Others were: Dr Anton Rupert, the Afrikaner tobacco emperor; Dr F. Meyer, Broeder and Chairman of the now frankly political South African Broadcasting Corporation; Dr J. B. Webb, a leading Methodist, and many DRC churchmen. But it contained no Blacks and so the Foundation in its own words presented more clearly than it intended, 'to the world a true picture of South Africa'.[36] With

33. Legum, *South Africa: Crisis for the West*, p. 129.
34. *SRR* (1964), p. 116.
35. *SRR* (1959–60), p. 177.
36. Legum, op. cit., p. 112.

branches in Britain and the United States and wherever members had strong economic connections, they rallied their foreign associates and created a powerful, persuasive propaganda machine. The Foundation was in being by the time of Sharpeville to cushion the economic shock, a steadying force in the difficult aftermath, and it contributed valuably to the remarkable economic advance.

South Africa was blessed with almost unlimited mineral wealth and fuel (except, so far, natural oil),[37] an industrial and commercial prosperity founded upon an abysmally low wage structure, and a potentially huge internal market when she chose to abandon her cheap labour policy. The economy was inherently strong and expansive; the brakes upon it were not directly economic, but were those of African poverty, 'South Africa's most haunting problem', preserved by a political system shoring up White privilege. This much was confirmed by Oppenheimer in his 1964 annual report: in the five years 1959–64 White wages had risen 3·7 per cent and Black wages 5·3 per cent, but the latter were still too low as was Black productivity. To maintain progress and avoid inflation the level of skills, particularly of Blacks, must be raised and opportunities given for those skills to be exercised, he said. The fact that 60 per cent of South African workers were classed as unskilled compared with 15 per cent in the United States, illustrated both the magnitude of the problem and the opportunity offered.[38]

White incomes averaged £476, African £43 10s. 0d. in 1960. The net national income of the African three-quarters of the population was 23 per cent of the total. The average unskilled wage in Johannesburg in 1963 was under £20 a month and nearly half the workers in commerce and industry earned less than £24. The bread-line was set at £26 6s. 9d., below which (despite the general prosperity and booming economy) it was estimated over half the African population lived. At the same time the Director of the National Institute for Personnel Research drew attention to the low educational standard of White skilled workers and of

37. Traces of oil were to be found in 1973 near Port Elizabeth.
38. *The Times* (4 June 1964). In 1971, with critical inflation, he reiterated these views.

people in managerial, professional and technical fields compared with the United States. By 1962 the paradox of separate development in a modern industrial context was apparent: a high level of unemployment, especially among the better educated Africans, existed alongside a rapidly developing (and artificial) shortage of skilled man-power. By 1964 development was curtailed by a lack of about 50,000 skilled workers while much Black unemployment persisted and the government intensively recruited White workers abroad.

Inevitably Blacks unofficially – job reservation and colour bar regardless – infiltrated traditional White spheres of employment: Coloured postmen, Indian railway workers, African drivers on African buses, Black clerks and typists. Especially were Blacks more and more to be found doing skilled and semi-skilled industrial work, generally at wages well below the White minimum. 'There is no doubt,' commented the Johannesburg Chamber of Commerce, 'that employers in general are keen to develop the skills of Bantu workers.'[39] The mines, the inner sanctuary of the colour bar, now short of 2,000 Whites, began to probe the possibility of officially introducing Africans into skilled sectors. With government and trade union sanction a limited experiment began, to train and promote 'boss-boys' to become 'competent non-scheduled persons', while the Whites they replaced were given supervisory and more responsible posts at higher wages. The scheme was working well, with falls in both accident rate and production costs, when certain White unions raised a cry and it was abandoned.

Meantime, however, the general level of prosperity continued to rise notwithstanding forebodings and sporadic overseas boycotts; the annual increase in the gross national product (9·5 per cent compared with Japan's 4·6 per cent and the United Kingdom's 1·7 per cent) was the highest in the world and the cost of living amongst the lowest. But as 1965 passed the rate of growth slowed, prices rose, the balance of payments worsened and the reserves fell. Inflationary tendencies, against which Oppenheimer had warned, strengthened. Clearly the human and material resources could not keep pace with the rate of development. The

39. *SRR* (1964), p. 241.

government cut capital expenditure, asking local government and business to follow suit, and tightened import control but the manpower shortage persisted. The more capable Whites were being held back because sufficient Blacks were not allowed to replace them. All the same, the Deputy Minister of Labour estimated that 39 per cent of economically active Africans were operatives or semi-skilled workers, and many of these on full wages. Many authorities urged the more effective use of manpower and concessions to encourage the productivity and skills of Blacks so as to lead to higher wages, a greater domestic market and more exports.

Big business ambivalence persisted. Oppenheimer, with a huge financial empire and great political experience, declared (in his role of a Progressive Party leader) in his 1964 annual report, his belief 'that race and colour discrimination were morally wrong and that race or colour partition were economically impossible'.[40] But (as a Foundation member, presumably) he asserted that within the limits of a Whites-only franchise a true parliamentary system operated, that the press though threatened was free, the judiciary independent, the civil service efficient and honest and the standard of living high by African standards. He opposed political pressure by sanctions as likely to lead to dictatorship or chaos. Rather, he urged (foreshadowing government policy), build bridges in fields of mutual interest between South Africa and other African territories and apply South Africa's available capital and special knowledge to help the economic development of the continent. The Anglo-American Corporation, he pointed out, had long been an international group working successfully under different political and social conditions. He set the tone for all big business which feared above everything revolutionary change and so were prepared to back a strong government, even one with restrictive policies contrary to immediate economic interests. If apartheid could not be defeated politically it must become unworkable economically.

Anton Rupert, with twenty-five factories in fifteen countries, and representative of the younger Afrikaner capitalist, conscious and mildly critical of the grosser aspects of apartheid, was of like

40. *The Times* (4 June 1964).

mind: 'However important politics may be, South Africa's racial problems are not going to be solved by political parties but by industry.'[41]

This insidious economic integration was, of course, totally out of line with separate development and its prevention was in essence what apartheid was about. But apartheid measures had so far been unable to check its growth which somehow had to be checked, even at the price of economic stagnation. Separate development had primarily to make the Bantu Homelands economically viable. First it must increase their agricultural potential and encourage the growth of a self-supporting class of professional farmers, no longer dependent on the migratory worker's wage; and, complementary to this, it must absorb into a new development of secondary and tertiary industry that half of the population which would be turned off the land. A five-year plan was launched in 1961 for the development of the reserves at an expenditure of £57m., of which two-thirds was directed to providing houses and villages and one-third to actual farming improvement. The Africans in many areas were deeply suspicious of changes suggested or often imposed by Whites and were only slowly to be won over as benefits became apparent and they were reassured there was no ulterior motive to dispossess them. Within the limits of funds available much progress was made, especially in establishing villages for the landless families, in combating menacing erosion by contouring, soil conservation and reclamation, in increasing water supplies and irrigation, in improving agricultural methods and stock quality and in introducing new crops. M. C. Botha, the Minister of BAD, told SABRA in 1963 that the department was spending more on the Bantu areas than the Tomlinson Commission had recommended. However, a scheme for 1,000 miles of irrigation canal on the Pongola River in northern Zululand, originally proposed by the Institute of Race Relations for the settlement of Africans on land largely State-owned and long in African occupation, was adopted by the government. By 1966 good progress was reported, but it was intended to settle an initial 3,700 White farmers there. Labour on the scheme and for the White plot-holders would give employment for Africans. Whether

41. Legum, op. cit., p. 110.

the existing reserves would be developed by Africans or given over to Whites was not made known.

The Tomlinson Commission in 1954 had estimated an expenditure of £60m. over ten years as necessary for the establishment of industries in the reserves and recommended that White industrialists should participate and so contribute capital and specialist know-how; but White participation was contrary to the tenets of apartheid and was rejected at the time. So in 1959 the Bantu Investment Corporation, with an all-White Board, was set up with funds provided by the Native Trust to further Bantu development in the reserves. Besides commercial enterprises it aided small industries – brickfields, furniture factories, small engineering works, bakeries, and the establishment in the Drakensburg mountains of a White tourist resort with museum, handicraft centre and model village. (Whites, tourists or others, were no longer allowed to move freely in reserve territory in the midst of African life or in real villages.) But this development was slow and provided a living for only a few of the 300,000 who needed it. Not until 1965 did the Bantu Homelands Development Corporation Act set up eight corporations to finance and accelerate development of the reserves, the first, with capital of £500,000, being in the Transkei. The boards were to be of Whites only, White capital was accepted and a reasonable profit was allowed until the various concerns should be handed over to the Africans. But restrictions on White entrepreneurs and foreign experts and technicians in the reserves discouraged foreign investment and assistance.

In another approach to the problem (while the ban on full White participation remained an article of faith) the Border Industries scheme was devised in 1960 with the triple purpose of providing employment in the rural areas, dispersing industrial development (growing water shortage, for instance, had put a stop to further industrialization of the huge Vaal area), and checking and eventually reversing the flow of labour to the White urban centres. This development on the reserve perimeters would remain under White initiative and control while African workers would maintain homes and families inside the reserves. To attract labour-intensive industries to remote sites substantial inducements were offered: assistance in the provision of power, water and transport, the construction and leasing of houses for Whites and large financial concessions. Above all, these industries were based on low wages; an agreed wage differential related to the lower productivity and cost of living, which in the long term would perpetuate the artificially limited communal purchasing power which already inhibited industrial progress. Employers (to the alarm of urban unions who feared the effects on wages and conditions in similar urban industries) had virtually a free hand in fixing wages as there could be no trade union action, strikes were illegal and influx control narrowed to vanishing the workers' choice of employment. The siting of many of the factories far from the reserve population centres meant workers were often accommodated on the premises during the week, returning home only at week-ends, so that the migratory labour system gained a new scale and direction and was not abolished.

By 1966, eighty-eight new factories and fifty-seven extensions had been set up with State aid, employing 40,000 Africans (increasing by 8,000 a year) and 11,000 of other races. £88m. was privately invested. All border industries employed nearly 100,000 Africans with a total investment of £100m.

But progress still loitered. In 1966 a further move in Tomlinson's direction and away from the pure apartheid goal was made when negotiations were opened by the Bantu Investment Corporation with certain White-owned companies prepared to finance factories, commercial undertakings or afforestation *in* the reserves. They would receive a reasonable profit on investment and would provide managers and technicians to train Africans to run the concerns which ultimately would become African property.

In sum, if the development of the Homelands dragged, South Africa's general economic situation at the close of 1966 matched the Swiss Professor D. W. Ropke's appraisement of two years earlier. Progress was, in his view,

based on the government's political stability that remains without parallel, not only in present day Africa ... but in the entire world. The government can rely not only on a strong and increasing majority in its own party but, at least as regards its economic policies, it can also count on the agreement of the opposition United Party and a small but intellectually influential Progressive Party.[42]

4. AFTER VERWOERD

In eight years of autocratic premiership Verwoerd, non-Afrikaner and ultra-nationalist, had realized for the *Boere Nasie* the primordial dream of freedom. What is more, he succeeded in uniting the whole White community – suspect British and resented Jews as well – in subservient political support of the Afrikaners in the laager of patriotism built to hold the world in check. He had laid firm legislative guide-lines for dealing with internal dissentients; and by the whole philosophy, structure and enforcement of 'separate development' he contained not only the threat of physical subversion in the presence of the Black under-privileged majority but the potentially, perhaps, more erosive danger of the questioning Afrikaner conscience.

Then, at the summit of this achievement, he was for the second time struck by an assassin. On 6 September 1966, Demetrio Tsafendas, a parliamentary messenger of Greek–Portuguese origin, listed for deportation (and later found like David Pratt to be insane), stabbed Verwoerd in the crowded Assembly minutes before he was due to make a major speech. Shocked by the violent drama and relieved that it omened no race revolt, the national press poured out eulogies to the man who had become a father figure, the soothing benevolent protector of all races. In columns of obituary tribute his pro-Nazi past and authoritarian arrogance were virtually forgotten.

After intense lobbying and a number of candidates having been persuaded to stand down, the Nationalist Party chose as the new *hoofleier* (party leader) and, automatically, Prime Minister, Balthazar Johannes (John) Vorster who had proved himself a man of iron over the years, when, as Verwoerd's Minister of Justice, Police and Prisons, he had devised the legislative machinery for separate development and the armament against those who opposed it.

Vorster was born in Jamestown in the north-east of the Cape (the area of the Xhosa wars) in 1915. The intelligent thirteenth

42. *Schweitzer Monatshafte* (May 1964).

child of a very poor family, he grew up, like so many a bitter Afrikaner, resentful of the slights and patronage of the English. He graduated at Stellenbosch University, the nursery of patriots and incubator of apartheid, and built up a successful legal practice in Port Elizabeth. An open admirer of Hitler, he was a founder of of the OB and a general in its terrorist Stormjaer branch which had been condemned by Malan and outlawed by the Nationalist Party; and he had always advocated authoritarian central control to replace local government. In 1942 he was interned without trial for two years and claimed to have been in solitary confinement for forty-two days. His personal experiences, on top of a natural atavism, deeply entrenched his frontier outlook and he was generally considered an extremist in race matters. He had an implacable hatred of communism and his brother Dr J. D. Vorster, high in the DRC ministry, later was Chairman of the Congress to Combat Communism. After the breach between OB and party was healed, Vorster was accepted as Nationalist Party candidate, defeated in 1948 and elected to Parliament in 1953. He became deputy Minister of Education in 1958 and Minister of Justice three years later when Swart became State President. In the national trauma that followed Sharpeville, the long state of emergency and the mass detentions, when the outlawed congresses turned to hopeless sabotage, he took control.

Each leader chosen by the Nationalist Party had been more uncompromisingly a White supremacist than the last and Vorster was no exception. He was a short burly man with a heavy deliberate walk: thick eyebrows over flinty eyes emphasized an unsmiling impassive expression. His brother declared him to be a man capable of 'great kindness', citing his intense interest in ex-prisoners, to the extent of employing almost exclusively ex-convicts. A skilled debater, with a wit suggesting undertones of sadism, he drew ironical amusement from the twist of history that had entrusted the ex-internee with a charge of security at the moment the State seemed in deepest jeopardy. His ominous presence was confirmed by his ruthlessness in power. He gave South Africa a supremely efficient security system, permeating every section of society with police spies and informers. His complex of laws stilled organized opposition to apartheid, crushed the underground of sabotage and stamped on the foreign-trained in-filtrating freedom fighters. He showered banning and banish-ment orders, introduced house-arrest, 90 days and 180 days detention *incommunicado* and seemed to shut his eyes to police use of third-degree methods of interrogation to attain his purpose. Significantly, on taking over the premiership he retained control of the police while relinquishing the Departments of Justice and Prisons to his successor, P. C. Pelser.

The choice of a strong man as successor to Verwoerd was re-ceived generally by White South Africa with relief.

In the Parliament which must decide the fate of the Republic of South Africa and its inhabitants [he said], the White man and the White man alone will have the right to sit. This is not because the Nationalist Party is hostile to any group, but because it is its God-given right to control what belongs to it ... because it believes that this nation must maintain its identity.[43]

Vorster repeatedly declared that he would follow the path laid out by Verwoerd. His initial statements were confident, con-servative and conciliatory. In the Assembly he affirmed his belief in Parliament as an institution, in the rights and privileges of mem-bers and in the rights of minorities in Parliament. In international affairs, he declared South Africa sought lasting friendship from all, would not interfere in the affairs of others and wished only to be left in peace to work out her own salvation. In internal matters he believed there should be unity of purpose between English-and Afrikaans-speaking people, expressed in service and love for the fatherland, and that the will to such unity existed. He be-lieved in the policy of the separate development of the White and the various Black groups in order to eliminate friction and do justice to every group and every member of every group. 'The best of service to humanity lies herein, whether one is capable of rendering service to one's own people ... There is more work for every leader among his own people than he can do in his lifetime.'[44]

As the intellectual theoretician was succeeded by the tough man of action there was almost at once an unexpected and para-

43. *Observer*, Profile (18 September 1966).
44. *SRR* (1966), p. 10.

doxical sense of relaxation among the opposition Whites, due to change in circumstance as well as change in personalities. Vorster had not the aloof, deific quality of Verwoerd. He was an Afrikaner among Afrikaners, born into the aggressive defensive frontier tradition, nurtured in the equivocal, fraternal quarrelsomeness of Boer–British brothers which is kept inside the family. In office he was genial, accessible and reasonable. The press found him approachable, the United Party found him much easier to work with than Verwoerd had been. There was an immediate easing of Nationalist–UP relations and he won more English-speaking support than any other Nationalist premier had done. Where Verwoerd had dominated, Vorster delegated, relied on teamwork and went out to meet his critics. Subtly race policies modified. The United Party replaced its scheme for a racial federation by one for territorial federation but without the ultimate sovereignty of the Homelands, the goal of Verwoerd's separate freedoms which, though still proclaimed by Nationalist spokesmen, was becoming obviously improbable. The more affable image of South Africa could be projected basically because of the grip the government had over the country, having routed or subdued all elements of overt opposition; at the same time it had become pretty clear that there was no likelihood of military intervention or effective economic sanctions in the near future. Greater flexibility was soon apparent, too, in foreign affairs. Vorster's sole experience of the world beyond South Africa's shores had been gained on a convalescence cruise to South America. The country's policies were explained abroad by the Foreign Minister, Hilgard Muller, with temperate and patient persuasiveness. This cut little ice among South Africa's traditional opponents in the United Nations, but made it no easier for them to raise effective majorities.

In particular Vorster and Muller threw themselves into the assignment set by Verwoerd of wooing Black Africa. Muller with his diplomatic experience in London, the United States and the United Nations, was strongly opposed to isolation and induced both Verwoerd and Vorster to move his way. In 1965 he had declared in the Assembly that the day would come when all African states would work together to secure their mutual interests. South Africa, he proclaimed, was in a particularly favourable position to contribute to the welfare of Africa and glad to do so on a basis of mutual respect. He said he welcomed signs of the rejection by African states of the new 'Red colonialism'. Again in the Assembly some two years later, he emphasized that, despite its political and economic preponderance, the Republic did not want to dominate in Africa. He believed the diminishing hostility of various African states would contribute to more countries accepting South Africa's proffered aid and friendship. It was South Africa's aim to construct an area of common interest, in which states would look to her for assistance, in return abandoning anti-South African hostility and even becoming actively associated with her in exploiting the resources of the sub-continent. 'The Republic,' he said, 'is inspired with only one desire as regards the rest of Africa. It is to live in peace and friendship with the Non-white states. The Republic will do nothing ... which might jeopardize this. But it demands at least two to live in peace and friendship with each other.' A Nationalist paper commented on this speech: 'Nairobi, Lusaka and Dar-es-Salaam are for us almost more important today than The Hague, or Bonn ... We are not an outpost of Europe ... We are not only in Africa, but also of Africa.'[45]

The government was well aware of the glittering prospect, the economical potential of South Africa's 'true hinterland': the nine countries of southern and central Africa with over 34,000,000 inhabitants; and beyond them the Congo and East Africa with 38,000,000 people: a market of 72,000,000 people in one of the potentially richest parts of the world.[46]

Ties with Portuguese territories and with Rhodesia had long been close and had reached a high level of military cooperation against freedom fighters and guerillas since UDI. The old High Commission Territories, in their new impoverished independence, were already economic dependencies and were, as Britain relinquished them, prototypes of what Bantustans were intended to be – virtually self-governing colonies in a new Southern African Empire.

Speaking near Oudtshoorn, in the Karroo, in March 1967,

45. *Press Digest (PD)* (5/67) from *Die Beeld* (5 February 1967).
46. *PD* 14/67.

Vorster declared it to be his duty to lead South Africa into participation with the international world, but, 'we don't want to be accepted only if we have first reformed'.[47] A few days later he said
that the Nationalists' struggle was no longer against the United
Party but was directed overseas to put South Africa's point of
view in perspective. She wanted to cooperate with White, Brown
and Black people but she must be accepted as she was: she would
not give up separate development for cooperation. South Africa's
attitude had always been that differences of internal policy did not
prevent cooperation with other states. Later, at the University of
the Orange Free State, he expounded South Africa's duty to
Africa.

We are not Settlers, we are part of Africa ... the most highly
developed country in Africa. The African states need leadership.
We ... not only have the knowledge but the experience for we understand the soul of Africa and its people and therefore I say we have a
vocation in Africa and the world.[48]

He reminded Africa that South Africa had been the first African
state to rebel against imperialism.

In this spirit Vorster followed up Verwoerd's interview with
Jonathan. The Prime Minister of Lesotho paid an official visit to
Cape Town in January, flown in an aircraft of the SAAF and
given VIP treatment. He interviewed Vorster and other Ministers
and was entertained at an official luncheon, a remarkable precedent. The South African Government promised to look into the
possibilities of economic and technical assistance in return for
guarantees of political stability and vigilance against dangers of
international communism. Jonathan duly hailed the occasion as a
'landmark in international cooperation'. He thanked the South
African Government for its

friendliness and understanding of my country's problems. Everyone
knows that I have come to ask South Africa to help my financially
embarrassed country. We in Lesotho ... realize that any help we may
now be given will be meaningful only to the extent that it enables the
establishment of a stable and prosperous African continent.[49]

47. *PD* 9/67.
48. *PD* 11/67.
49. *Africa Digest* (*AD*) (February 1967).

Shortly after, a ministerial delegation from Botswana came to sort out common problems with South African ministers.

A significant break-through to the north was marked by the visit, in March, of three ministers from Malawi to negotiate a two-way preferential trade agreement, specifically with no strings attached.[50] The accommodation of the visitors in a luxury hotel caused one commentator to recall that in the past contacts with the Black man were not unknown, and to cite 'a good Nationalist' whose parents 'made a regular habit of entertaining Basuto chiefs who came to do business on their farm near the border at the kitchen table'.[51]

So, away from the alarums and excursions of the United Nations, the Nationalist Government continued quietly to build its defences against sanctions. Many of the original radical governments of African independence were giving way to conservative and more narrowly nationalistic military regimes, beset by their own internal problems, and the OAU was having difficulty in pursuing a united policy, for the East-West detente in limiting competition for their support reduced the influence of the African states. The political and economic disarray of its African critics gave South Africa her opportunity. South African firms for a decade past had been investing an average of £5m. a year in foreign subsidiaries, mostly in African territories and often with African nationals on the boards. As the volume of her exports to these countries grew their economic dependence provided a basic buffer against sanctions.

In a gesture of conciliation, designed to reduce isolation at any rate in the sphere of international sport, Vorster announced that a mixed team would be allowed to take part in the Olympic Games and that the government would not prescribe to 'our traditional sporting opponents' the composition of their teams visiting South Africa. But he was quick to insist that separate development would be maintained internally.

Still intransigent in regard to the United Nations, Vorster declared he would not let the Special Committee into South Africa

50. In 1970, further headway was made in approaches to Madagascar and other French-speaking territories.

51. *PD* 12/67, Willem in *Die Volksblad* (17 March 1967).

and he had nothing to discuss with it. But obliquely the peace offensive was carried into the international organization when, in March, M. C. Botha, Minister for Bantu Affairs, made an offer to a meeting of Ovambo chiefs in Namibia of self-rule for the quarter million people of Ovamboland, nearly half the Namibian population. This was in line with the recommendations of the Odendaal report, which had been in cold storage while the International Court of Justice judgement was awaited and it anticipated the report of the UN Special Committee. Botha emphasized that the right of self-government was the policy of the government which would give financial assistance as long as it was necessary. He promised £15m. in aid over the next five years. The proposal was received with the heart-warming old-world phraseology of salaried chieftains: 'The government of the Republic is our government . . . We trust it like our father and therefore we do not want any other foreign government like the UN, the Damaras or the Hereros . . .'[52]

In the *South West African Survey 1967* South Africa's critics were rebuked for regarding apartheid as 'an evil thing'. Apartheid, they were told, was not an ideology or doctrine but a pragmatic approach: South Africa subscribed fully to the democratic principle and aimed to extend the franchise to all South West African groups as soon as possible. However, in the previous October the introduction of the omnibus General Laws Amendment Act 1966 had extended to South West Africa the security laws already in force in South Africa, giving the police greatly extended powers, making the Suppression of Communism Act retroactive to 1950, empowering the minister to ban political parties and introducing the Sabotage Laws with the death penalty. The relative political latitude enjoyed by Namibia in comparison with South Africa ended abruptly. Leaders of both the active African National movements were arrested and many guerilla fighters, filtering back from training abroad, were rounded up.

The change in approach to foreign and particularly to African affairs was not symptomatic of any relaxation or rethinking of apartheid. Rather was Vorster following the theory of apartheid into a wider context. In their fierce nationalism, ardent pursuit of

52. *AD* (June 1967).

Africanization and discrimination against Whites in land ownership, jobs and so on, many independent African states seemed to display the obverse of the apartheid coin, while their need for assistance in development made these areas the economic complement of South Africa.

In South Africa itself separate development legislation was extended under Vorster. The new parliamentary session promised to be largely devoted to the realization of the White homeland: to making ' South Africa a White man's land in the true sense of the word'.[53] In removing Africans from the urban areas, said Blaar Coetzee, Deputy Minister for Bantu Affairs, the government was looking two hundred or more years ahead. So the administration tackled with new zest the intractable task of *ontswarting* (unblackening) the cities.

First of all the Coloured Cadet Training Bill was introduced, designed to move the African labour from the whole of the Western Cape eastwards to Humansdorp, near Port Elizabeth, and north to the Orange River, leaving the area for Coloured and White workers whose sphere it was considered traditionally to be. This was regarded as something of a test case, for if the Western Cape could not be 'unblackened', what hope was there of turning the Black tide back to the Bantustans in the rest of the country? The Bill also provided for the establishment of compulsory labour training centres for all Coloured youths aged eighteen to twenty-four where they would be trained for any kind of employment and so provide the necessary labour force to replace the Africans. The 1,750,000 Coloured were also promised self-government through a Coloured People's Representative Council to be set up in 1969. But there was no Coloured Homeland where they would acquire separate freedom. Poor and demoralized, the Coloureds had abandoned resistance and most of their leaders were prepared to work with the authorities, not because they accepted apartheid status but because there seemed to be no alternative and they hoped to be able to build up the people's strength within the apartheid frame ready for a change in the future. Their isolation was completed early in Vorster's premiership by the Prohibition of Improper Interference Act, which forbade the participation of

53. PD 20/67, in *Die Transvaler* (22 May 1967).

the various races in the politics of other racial groups, with the immediate purpose of preventing Progressive Party candidates from standing for election in the Cape as Coloured representatives. It also banned racially mixed political parties and so would automatically put an end to the Liberal Party, and possibly to the Progressives, whose policies no legal stretching could bring under the Anti-Communism Act, but whose constitutions rested on multi-racialism.

The development of the Homelands so far was still on nothing like the scale, intensity or degree of subsidization required ever to create an economic magnetism stronger than the pull of the White urban areas on the rural Africans – or White industrialists. So the second line of attack in the 'unblackening' of the cities lay in the Physical Planning and Utilization of Resources Act. This stiffened the border industries policy by giving the government powers for the direction of new industries (with control of siting, zoning, town-planning and numbers of employees) to the border areas where they could absorb surplus reserve labour and intercept the flow to the White cities. The Bill was attacked by the Opposition as a declaration of martial law on the economy and even the government's Economic Commission advised against such measures.

Thirdly, acknowledging the overriding urgency of accelerating development enough to absorb the natural increase of the reserves, the government further relaxed its policy so as to encourage the investment of White capital and initiative in the Homelands to stimulate their development. This was to be strictly controlled on an agency basis, the White entrepreneurs obtaining no entrenched right in the Homelands and paying royalties to an appropriate Bantu body. The Minister also announced a £250m. development plan for the Homelands over the period 1966 to 1971, though without any time-table to indicate how much would be voted in any year. But when Matanzima, again literally interpreting 'separate freedoms', claimed the incorporation of the Ciskei, including East London and King Williamstown, as land belonging to the Blacks but where Whites could stay 'as long as we need their help',[54] BAD rejected it.

54. *AD* (February 1967).

Vorster's administration retained a firm grip on internal affairs. The National Education Bill of February 1967 gave the minister complete control of all White education in State and State-aided schools. The provinces, where responsibility for education had lain for fifty years, became the instruments of ministerial policy. School education was to have a Christian and 'broad national character', but the religious convictions of parents would be respected in regard to instruction and ceremonies. This was the final step in the plan, outlined in CNE, giving the moulding of young minds, White as well as Black, into the unfettered charge of a doctrinaire state. The Roman Catholic Church, which had evaded the implications of Bantu education and kept its schools open by refusing all State aid, had been forced to close over a hundred of them under the Group Areas Act.

The Population Registration Amendment Act, retrospective to 1950, closed loopholes found by Supreme Court decisions and, by making descent a criterion, forced many cruel reclassifications. The definition, 'In deciding whether any person is in appearance obviously a White person or not a White person, his habits, education, speech and deportment and demeanour in general shall be taken into account', had made many Blacks technically more South African White than many an immigrant. It still remained possible to be a member of different races under different laws depending on whether they affected employment, residence, occupation or sport.

The vigorous and closely allied defence and economic policies adopted were governed by the international threat of sanctions and by the lessons learned in the UN and from Rhodesia's experience. Still apparently without adequate powers for the control of internal subversion, the government introduced, against very little opposition, the Terrorism Act with a maximum death penalty for terrorism, defined as any act (not crime) committed with intent to endanger law and order. The commission of twelve categories of act was presumed terrorism unless no such intent was proved. Secret arrest and indefinite detention for questioning were permitted. The Defence Amendment Act provided for the call-up of 17,000 (White) young men a year between the ages of seventeen and twenty-five to form a citizen force of 100,000 and

395

imposed a blanket ban on the publication of any news relating to the Defence Force or any auxiliary service. The minister, P. W. Botha, announced that he proposed to equip Defence Force trainees spiritually to meet such dangers as communism but denied they would be brain-washed. The threat of sanctions made the build-up of naval strength imperative. £20m. was spent on acquiring three submarines from the Netherlands, £100m. on other ships and equipment and £3m. on the latest radar apparatus which could be used for coastal defence. By agreement with Britain (which retained some use of it), the Defence Ministry took over the Simonstown Naval Base and the last outward and visible sign of South Africa's colonial past was erased.

During 1966 there had been a drop in British exports to South Africa of £25m., while Britain's imports had risen and Britain's favourable trade balance of £40m. with South Africa disappeared. South Africa, on the other hand, had turned a balance of payments deficit of £61m. into a surplus of £13m. Exports, especially to beleaguered Rhodesia, rose steeply and reserves were high. South Africans became increasingly confident that their developing military preparedness and economic prosperity would make the cost of sanctions too high to be undertaken.

Great efforts were made all the same to offset her oil vulnerability. Two years' reserves were stockpiled and individual industries were also urged to stockpile a year's supplies. Negotiations were opened to acquire with government help six more new 50,000-ton tankers to make a fleet of nine able to carry 50 per cent of the oil requirements, much of it from the expanding production of the Angolan fields. A second oil-from-coal plant was expected to increase production from 10 per cent to 35 per cent of requirements, a £17½m. refinery was planned and an intensive search for local oil was initiated.

No pains were spared to increase South Africa's economic independence. In any case, after Sharpeville she had become a big capital debtor and so in a stronger position than Britain in any contest of financial sanctions. South African companies were encouraged to take over foreign shipping and airlines and financial interests, and insurance companies were compelled to keep 70 per cent of premium income in the country.

The only shadow over the generally encouraging prospect was that of inflation caused by the great influx of foreign capital, the unprecedented defence expenditure, the general call-up (which put an important section of the population on to unproductive work and set up a competition between defence and industry for workers), the public's increasing purchasing power and the recent good rains. The budget of 1967 tried to dispel this cloud and White South Africa was exhorted to work and save. This general well-being of the Whites was not of course communicated to the African section of the population. In the past five years the real rise in their wages was under 18 per cent and their average earnings remained about one-tenth of White incomes.

Nothing could have seemed more comfortably secure than the Nationalist rule in mid-1967, in its twentieth year in power. Vorster could look with satisfaction on the achievements of less than twelve months in office: the economy as resilient as any in the world, the White population prospering beyond their dreams, all sections of Whites united as never before, effective internal opposition eliminated, a new purposeful attack on the problems of separate development, the successes of the new relaxed approach to foreign affairs, some easing of social relationships between Nationalist Members of Parliament and foreign diplomats in South Africa, and all accompanied by a notable reduction in the perils that had threatened.

Fissures, however, began to appear unexpectedly within the regime itself. Two camps began to take shape: the *verligtes* (enlightened – liberals) and the *verkramptes* (narrow-minded – conservatives). The dissension was mostly obliquely political. The critical die-hards were shocked by the official unrolling of the red carpet for distinguished Black visitors; they deplored the prospect of visiting Black sportsmen and diplomats receiving White treatment. This was the thin end of a wedge which could extend to Black business men and professionals and from visitors to locals, especially with White money developing Bantu Homelands. Where could a new line be drawn ? They were uneasy, too, about the great influx of immigrants, particularly from Catholic southern Europe and South America, often less colour-sensitive, who tended not to learn Afrikaans but to swell the English-speaking section, so becoming a threat to Afrikaner culture and language.

Among the resurgent associations the anonymous Purified Nationalists strongly opposed the immigration policy. The old DRC Antikom body and a new National Council to Combat Communism, anti-Communist and anti-Semitic and led by such men as Dr Albert Hertzog, Minister of Posts and Telegraphs (son of the old premier who, years before, had rebuked him for his Broederbond affiliations) and Dr J. D. Vorster, brother of the Prime Minister, were in close touch with foreign organizations like Mosley's British Fascists and the John Birch Society in the United States. The *Rapportryers*, the dispatch riders, was an élite group challenging the Nationalist Party, as the OB and Pirow's New Order had done until Malan crushed them.

Cultural bodies proliferated, all basically agreed in fearing both the dilution of Afrikanerdom by immigration and the Afrikaner–English integration taking place. Already this had led, it was said, to the anglicization of some 200,000 Afrikaners, mainly of the upper and middle classes. The attacks were focused on the new school of Afrikaans writers of the sixties, the *Sestigers*, who were condemned as decadent neo-barbarians and destroyers of Christian values, who were playing into the hands of liberalists and communists. A spiritual slackening was observed among Afrikaners since the Republic had been achieved. The DRC, critical of the immigration policy and the strengthening of the Roman Catholic Church, made efforts to bring Afrikaners and immigrants together, increased its evangelical work and developed English-language congregations among immigrants. Professor J. Chris Coetzee, Head of the Department of Education at Potchefstroom University, called for a conservative Christian Afrikaans system of education. 'Many lesson books advocated the evolution idea,'[55] he accused, persistently eccentric in the country in which the evidence for evolution was persuasively accumulating.

On a superficial assessment this hydra-headed criticism suggested the existence of an underground movement prepared to challenge the government in its more latitudinarian policies. Vorster and his supporters, however, were not unduly concerned

55. *PD* 23/67.

about this trend. The Nationalist Party was now so strongly entrenched that the immemorial divisiveness of the Afrikaner no longer threatened the fundamental unity. Open debate, on means rather than purpose, was freely permitted among Nationalists in Parliament and in the press and the differences turned to advantage. The Verkramptes reassured the conservative platteland and the Rhodesian ally that liberalization would not be permitted, while the more relaxed policies were directed to winning toleration if not support in Black Africa and beyond. But when, as South Africa moved into the 1970s, Hertzog and his followers appeared to be making headway and offering an open political challenge, Vorster attacked. Using the security police and criminal charges, he curbed their freedom of speech and disrupted their organization. He called an early general election in 1970, routed his right-wing opponents and left himself free to pursue his 'enlightened' external policies in Africa, rewarded with promises of official visits from the Heads of State of Malawi and Ghana.

So it was that a nation of 3,500,000 White people had been forged by the interaction of genealogy and geography, economics and history into one as tenaciously obdurate as the world has known. In less than a century a poor and factious tribe of nomadic farmers under constant threat of annihilation has been transformed into a nation of substance and significance: its substance founded on a feudal-colonial exploitation of a subservient class in a natural El Dorado, its significance on a systemized manipulation of racial inequalities which spread like a contagion into the world inflaming latent *malaises* everywhere. Most of this took place under a British suzerainty inconstant in purpose and mainly governed by the fluctuating imperial, strategic and economic considerations of the moment.

A few clear-sighted and objective men in each century have warned of the dangers along the political path. There have been times – perhaps almost up until Sharpeville – when a spirit of White compromise would have met with Black cooperation. The early chiefs were for the most part conciliatory and often eager for the benefits of Western culture. The first mission-reared African politicians were far closer in outlook to their White mentors than to their Black compatriots. Indian leaders came mainly from a merchant class and shared a common commercial language with the Whites. The Coloureds had been, until quite lately, accepted as part White by origin and wholly White – Afrikaner – in culture and interests. But the chances of building a multi-racial policy, with possibly an eventual painless transfer to majority rule, were missed time and again. For the Afrikaners decided they had no line of retreat back to a mother-country. Their myopic preoccupation with establishing their livelihood in Africa and preserving White blood and culture against the expected tide of colour dictated their defences. These seemed justified by the upheavals in many territories newly freed from and resentful of White control, a view which took no account of completely different circumstances in South Africa where the leaders of a large and long-Westernized Black population acknowledged the right of the Whites to be there, declared a willingness to cooperate with them in responsibility and accepted the need for the White contribution. A multi-racial community might well have been possible: that does not mean South Africa would have escaped political conflict, but that, if it came, it could have been a conventional class struggle and not a race war.

In a hopeful misreading of recent events, changes of methods in South Africa have been hailed as reversals of policy. But the general direction has been entirely consistent, with minor disagreements along a road marked out with clear legislative milestones. While Smuts compromised, improvised, temporized, the Nationalists theorized, codified, justified. The objective was always the same: the entrenchment of White privilege.

Van Riebeeck, at the tip of the continent, planted the principle of segregation, a flowering hedge with hidden thorns. Rhodes, at Glen Grey, drew across the rolling hills and wooded valleys of the Transkei the hard line of separation. Hertzog's Land Acts of 1913 and 1936, completed and set legal seal upon the long process of dispossessing the African millions of title to all but a debilitated 13 per cent of their birthright. Hertzog's Colour Bar Act of 1926 completed and set legal seal upon the closing to Africans of all ways of advancement in modern technology. The franchise laws of 1936 stripped the Africans of their small constitutional voice and erased their little power to influence policies. The Indians, first imported to advance White fortunes, few in numbers, but industrious, frugal and intelligent, and so an obvious economic challenge, were likewise barred in social and economic advancement by the Pegging and Ghetto Acts of Smuts and Malan.

When, with the march of world events, Black refusal to accept eternal inferiority began to find forceful expression, the Whites, whatever their differences, drew close in the resolve to defend their racial purity and their vision of a Christian civilization – the emotive concepts which formed the bulwarks of the citadel of economic security within which White incomes averaged ten times those of Blacks. This purpose was accomplished in twenty years of unshaken Nationalist rule by building up a police-enforced legal system of pervasive intricacy. White people were screened from its devastations and generally protected from full realization of its abuses by barriers of privilege. The progression – apartheid separate development, separate freedoms in Bantu Homelands – was persuasively presented by scientific, economic and social experts directed by a master social-psychologist. It won almost unquestioning support in White South Africa and many adherents especially in those Western nations whose prosperity derived from colonial prerogative of one sort or another.

South Africa's economic strength, withstanding the shock of Sharpeville, attracted foreign capital which accelerated economic growth and entrenched the administration and so in turn invited further investment in a beneficent circle. This induced a schizophrenia into the attitude of Western nations to South Africa. While declaring their abhorrence of apartheid and its consequences, they mostly abstained in the United Nations from voting against South Africa in critical issues, continued to derive massive economic benefits from it, to supply South Africa's military requirements, and give unrestrained economic support to the White supremacists whose policies they castigated. The small nations, Afro-Asians and Latin Americans, backed by Scandinavians and eastern Europeans, condemned bitterly but were powerless. After the high hopes of independence the African and Asian states began to find themselves beset by their own problems. The first unity was often shattered by factional disputes.

Their rate of economic growth was a dismal disappointment. Their economic dependence on ex-colonial powers reduced their freedom of action and was humiliating. Some, even, were insolubly dependent on trade with South Africa. The OAU made its recommendations to sever all links with the Republic, but when it came to implementation each country had to act in accordance with its individual circumstances. With bitter disillusionment, fed by Rhodesia's successful defiance, came the realization of their impotence: to those economically involved with South Africa sanctions would do more harm than to South Africa, and for those without these ties sanctions were a meaningless gesture.

By 1967 the bonds of trade and dividends were ineluctable.

So South Africa could claim, and did, that far from being the danger to world peace she was accused of being, she was, in a continent disintegrating under economic failure and sectional conflict, a haven of peace, prosperity and order. This evaluation was widely accepted by her friends.

The threat to world peace remained, no longer localized in South Africa, but subtly distributed throughout the body of the world community, taking the sinister shape of race conflict and civil war. The absolute repression of the Black opposition in South Africa, the lack of more rapid success of revolutionary movements in Portuguese East and West Africa, White mercenaries acting in the Congo, British failure to call to heel White Rhodesia in contrast to her disciplining of Non-whites in Aden and Hong Kong, the United States' bombing in Vietnam, race riots in the States were all thrown increasingly into relief as White versus Non-white conflicts. The short, sharp war in the Middle East highlighted this. The Israelis, for all their contribution to African development, were widely identified in Africa with the White colonial powers, exploiters of the local population. More and more was South Africa symbolic of the crystallization of mankind into two irreconcilable equations: White equals advanced, privileged and rich; Black equals backward, exploited and poor. The consequences for the future are alarming.

The last word might be left with Smuts, the Afrikaner-Imperialist, whose achievements fell so far short of his moments of sharp perception; he said in 1934: 'Freedom is the most ineradicable craving of human nature; the denial of human rights must in the long run lead to a cataclysm.'[56]

POSTSCRIPT: 1969–74

In the six years that have passed, there have been significant movements in the evolving South African situation.

Primarily, the economy has continued to flourish. World currency crises brought a strong inflow of capital to a seemingly steady and developing economy; there was a sustained acceleration in the growth of secondary industry; and there was the unprecedented rise in the price of gold. But, following on this, the prospect of inflation, already gripping the rest of the industrial world, became threatening and apartheid restrictions created severe shortages of skilled labour. Blacks were penetrating increasingly into skilled jobs, in spite of White fears that this would erode apartheid and, probably, the wage structure.

The government would not yield to industrial pressures but intensified apartheid measures. The Bantu Laws Amendment Act of 1970 extended job reservation and gave absolute powers over what work an African could do and where he did it.

The anomalous coexistence of these conditions provoked a widespread reassessment of the situation of the Black, particularly the African worker. A majority of families lived below subsistence level; White incomes were found to average seven times African incomes; White gold-miners earned nearly twenty times what their African fellows earned. The wage gap in the main industrial sectors kept widening, and the plight of farm labourers, the unemployed, and those 'endorsed out' and dumped jobless in resettlement areas to survive on minuscule pensions was hopeless.

When the public in the United States and Britain suddenly became awakened to the meaning of these facts of Black labour, so often previously publicized without attracting concern, a considerable rumpus was created. Black Power in the States forced the Polaroid company, for instance, to pay better wages in South Africa and to reduce its technical cooperation in enforcing apartheid. In Britain, not only were arts and sports boycotts

56. *Christian Action* (Summer 1964), p. 17.

stimulated but, when the disturbing condition in British concerns operating in South Africa were disclosed, a parliamentary committee, after a year's investigation, drew up a code of practice for United Kingdom firms in South Africa. But the code was not binding; it set the wage target at only the minimum effective level (50 per cent above the PDL, and still far too low); and it received little attention in South Africa. There were, however, some economic withdrawals; local authorities, universities, trade unions, churches and individuals began to consider investment policies in relation to Black wages and their consciences. Some began to sell out.

Searching discussion was taking place in the South African community as well. Afrikaner intellectuals and others questioned the inferior situation of the Coloureds. A variety of interests, organizations and liberal individuals warned of impending catastrophe unless the White–Black wage gap was closed. White students at the English universities became more vociferously critical of official attitudes and policies than for long past and some staged vigorous demonstrations. There was a remarkable revival of unofficial, but overt, meetings and discussions between cordial Whites and conciliatory Black politicians, intellectuals and Homelands' leaders, such as had not taken place since Sharpeville. The debate developed in South Africa and abroad: some urged total dissociation, maintaining that cooperation would merely entrench the *status quo* and that, though economic conditions for the few in commerce and industry might improve, there could be no betterment for the Black masses – the essential structure of White supremacy would remain; others, South African and foreign industrialists, opposition policians, intellectual and Homelands' leaders, argued that it was by increased investment, along with equal treatment for all, that the position of the Blacks could be improved.

As a consequence of the latter line of thought, wages in some areas were promptly increased (often still remaining below the PDL), fringe benefits extended and educational grants made. Equal pay for equal work was widely proclaimed in these circles. Trade unionists urged the full rate for the job (aware that few could qualify). Many of the churches took a shocked look at

themselves and decided to raise salaries of Black ministers over a
ten-year period to the level of Whites. The Johannesburg City
Council put Black and White doctors on the same salaries. The
Chamber of Mines maintained that if wages were to be raised
many marginal mines would close and many thousands of Black
jobs vanish. However, the African miner's average wage was
raised by £1.90 a month (approx), but the White miner's wage
went up by £5. In the 1920s and 30s White miners had earned
about ten times what African miners earned; in 1970 it was seventeen times as much.[57] The Anglo-American Corporation, the
Oppenheimer group, raised African wages by about 26 per cent,
but with White increases the White–Black ratio changed from
thirteen to one to sixteen to one; pre-tax profits were nearly six
times the whole African wage bill and the free market price of
gold, the 'golden river', had more than doubled[58] (and by 1974
had doubled again).

Oppenheimer himself, in 1971, attributed the serious inflation
and resultant dearth of skilled labour to the lack of formal educational opportunities and technical training for most of the population and the positive prohibitions on their playing a full part in
national development. But not until the end of 1973 did the
government, turning dead against its long and loudly proclaimed
principles, announce a £2 million scheme for the industrial
training of Africans within the White areas.

In the meantime, pressing on with separate development, the
government catered for those who were to remain in, but never of,
the White communities. The South African Indian Council Act
of 1968 gave the Indians a purely advisory government-appointed
council, and the Coloured Persons Representative Act gave the
Coloureds a council consisting of 40 elected and 20 nominated
members with limited powers of local government. When the
first elections for the latter, in 1969, resulted in a large majority of
seats for the Labour Party,[59] outspokenly opposed to apartheid,
the government nominated eleven of the defeated (more co-
operative) Federal Party to give it a working majority and Mr Tom

57. Prof. Sheila van der Horst, *SRR* (1971) p. 228.
58. *Economist* 7/7/73.
59. Led by Mr D. Arendse, soon succeeded by Mr Sonny Leon.

Swarts, a roundly beaten candidate, the chairmanship of the council.

As for the six million Africans who, it was now tacitly accepted, could never be crammed into the Homelands, there was another great reversal of principle. At the end of 1973, plans were announced to set up twenty-two African Councils in the White areas, formed by Africans themselves, to work in consultative capacities with the existing twenty-two White Bantu administrative boards, with which all final decision would remain.

Insisting that South Africa was now ten nations, one White and nine Black, the government put further effort into irreversibly building the crazy pavement of the Homelands. The Bantu Homelands Citizenship Act of 1970 made all Africans citizens of the relevant Territorial Authority; though in international relations they would remain citizens of South Africa, they would have no civic rights in White areas.

The Bantu Homelands Constitution Act of 1971 followed on Acts of 1951 and 1959[60] and enabled the Homelands, other than the existing Transkei, to be set up with similar limited powers of self-government.[61]

Industrial decentralization was accelerated with increased inducements to move to the Homelands borders. In the decade from 1960 jobs (only a fraction of those needed) were thus created for some 87,000 people, three-quarters of them African. Much work and money went into the development of the Bantustans themselves; new capitals were built, personnel trained, scattered pieces of land consolidated, health services and police forces set up, and agricultural, economic and financial development, much

60. see p. 360.
61. The Homelands and their Chief Councillors were:
Ciskei: Paramount Chief of the AmaRarebe, Chief J. K. M. Mabandla.
Transkei: Paramount Chief K. Matanzima.
BophuthaTswana: Chief Lucas Mangope.
Lebowa (N. Sotho): Chief M. M. Matlala.
Gazankulu (Machangana): Professor H. W. E. Ntswanwise.
Venda: Chief Patrick Mpephu.
BasothoQuaQua: Captain Wessels Mota.
KwaZulu (a constitutional monarchy): King, Paramount Chief Z.G. KaCyprian Bhekuzulu; Chief Councillor, Chief Gatsha Buthelezi.

of it superficial, encouraged. Yet, where minerals were discovered, White developers were granted leases for from ten to
thirty-five years – by when possibly the mines might be ex-
hausted. The Mines and Works Act which restricted the training
of Blacks applied in the Homelands, and exemptions which could
be granted were mostly opposed by jealous White unions.

Throughout the sixties widespread changes were made with
only isolated protests. The Black communities seemed deep in
sullen, apathetic resentment, withdrawn from any communication with the Whites, intimidated by White power and the ubiqui-
tous police informer. At the end of the decade, as apartheid's silver
jubilee approached, there came a startling change in many areas.
The new leaders of the Homelands, presumed to be loyal disciples
of apartheid, and indeed generally subscribing to the official
political and economic line abroad, were turning out to be far from
compliant vassals in South Africa itself. Like Matanzima, taking
separate development at its face value, their voices all were now
raised in condemnation of the state of affairs. Primarily, they were
at one in demanding more land. By 1970, 12·95 per cent of the
total land area was in African possession, still almost 1,400,000
morgen short of the undertaking given in the Native Trust and
Land Act of 1936. Two decades earlier, Tomlinson had understood the impossibility of ever converting the existing reserves
into Homelands capable of accommodating the millions destined
by separate development to migrate to them. Despite the development effort of the intervening years this had not changed. For
example, the tiny homeland of BasothoQuaQua in the Orange
Free State had a current population density of 136 to the square
mile; were all its 'nationals' resident in White areas to be returned,
it would crowd 7,085 souls into every square mile of its extent.

Vorster stated unequivocally that there would be no more land
than the Act allotted. The Transkei and KwaZulu leaders, particularly, complained of land shortage and the difficulties caused
by resettlement and mass repatriations from the Republic; they
refused to regard the Act as binding since the Blacks had not been
consulted and, in any case, the proposals of 1936 were not realistic
in the radically changed circumstances of the seventies. A full
consolidation of the scattered portions of territory was essential;

the proposed consolidation of KwaZulu's 179 fragments would still leave it in ten separate blocks. The leaders all pressed for elimination of 'White spots' and the transfer, for instance, of Port St John's, East London and Richard's Bay. Matanzima envisaged the eventual linking of the Transkei and Ciskei, from Natal to the Fish River, into a Greater Xhosaland and advocated a federation of the Black Homelands.

Chief Gatsha Buthelezi, Chief Councillor of KwaZulu, cousin of the King and product of Adams Mission, Fort Hare and Natal University, was fast becoming one of the most outspoken and influential critics of government policy and its failure to consult the Blacks: 'The White government should be honest and rule as always instead of giving the world the illusionary impression we are a Black government in the making.'[62] His call for a National Convention to discuss a *modus vivendi* received considerable support from leaders of all race groups but was dismissed by the minister of BAD.

A series of Acts during 1969 had converted the existing Black university colleges into five universities for separate ethnic groups. All had White councils and Black advisory councils and were absolutely under White control. By 1972 the long simmering rebelliousness of Black students became articulate, finding a unity of purpose and an intellectual basis in the new Black Consciousness movement. Rejecting cooperation with White liberals, with NUSAS or with Black leaders working within the system, the newly formed South African Students Organization (SASO) sought to encourage Black independence and self-respect, the preservation of loyalty to universal standards of western tradition along with the rediscovery and proclamation of loyalty to the indigenous values of Black society. There was constant friction between students (often supported by parents) and White authorities. The expulsion in 1972 of 1,146 Turfloop students provoked widespread student demonstrations.

Plans for a national convention fell through, but the Black People's Convention (BPC) was formed to provide a political home for all Black people who could not be reconciled to working within the framework of separate development; to advance Black

62. *SRR* (1972), p. 36, 37.

Consciousness; and to work for appropriate economic, social, educational and theological changes.

Perhaps most unexpected of all, after their long political apathy and economic dejection, was the self-assertive revival of the Coloured people. A new generation had grown up and few had any but the most formal master–servant relationship with Whites or accepted the old poor-relation status. Although they differed as to the extent they should work within separate development, the majority, as the Labour Party's 1969 electoral success showed, rejected apartheid; for the first time they claimed absolute equality with the retention of separate identity and they rejected political rights at the expense of the African. There were vigorous, aggressive debates in the Coloured council, considerably embarrassing the government.

Elections in 1974 returned the Nationalists once again and, surprisingly, gave the Progressives six members to support Mrs Suzman, a success at the expense of the failing UP. The Labour Party, in separate Coloured polling, eclipsed the Federal Party and captured a Council now unanimously demanding a restoration of parliamentary representation. Vorster, on this occasion unable to pack the Council, prorogued it, so increasing the dissension on Coloured policy in his own party. Speculation was stimulated as to further White political realignments among the liberal and conservative wings of the UP and the verligtes and verkramptes of the Nationalists.

The government effort to construct the Homelands was duplicated in Namibia. In 1971 the ICJ gave a majority opinion that the termination of the Mandate in 1966 had been valid and South Africa's presence and acts in Namibia were illegal. But the Development of Self-government for Native Nations of South West Africa Act of 1968 had presented the UN with a *fait accompli*. A council for Ovamboland (Owambo) was created on the lines of those in South Africa. By 1972 the 'nations' had been set up.[63] The South West Africa Affairs Act of 1969 gave the South African government enormously increased centralized

63. The Homelands were: Owambo, Kavango, Eastern Caprivi, Damaraland, Hereroland, Namaland, Rehoboth, Kaokoveld, Tswanaland and Bushmanland.

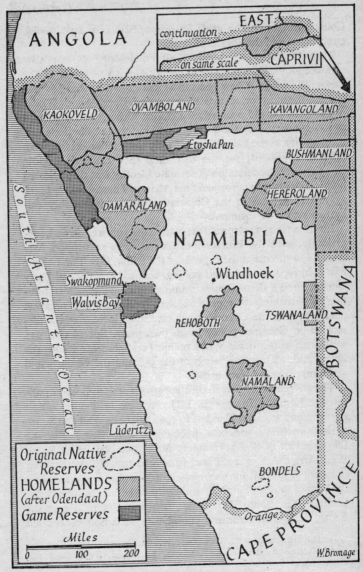

Map XI The Distribution of the Homelands in Namibia

powers over the territory. By 1972 Vorster was ready to receive a UN mission. There was a somewhat confused agreement between the parties on regional self-government under an overall territorial authority composed of nominated Africans and officials with purely advisory powers. This was promptly rejected as a tool of government by the broadly-based National Convention of Freedom, recently formed to press for an independent unitary Namibia.

Towards the end of 1971, Ovambo workers demanded improved labour conditions and by mid-January about 13,000 of them were on strike, paralysing mines, industry and administration. The strikers gained nominal concessions, but there was no consultation with them; outsiders, particularly churchmen and press, were banned; and police sealed off Ovamboland. The next year the Ovambo clearly showed their contempt for the homeland policy by an almost total boycott of the first elections for the Ovambo Assembly. Since then there has been a systematic programme of intimidation, terrorization, public floggings and brutal imprisonment of leaders, particularly those of the South West Africa People's Organization (SWAPO), the body recognized by the OAU.

In the Republic itself strikes, though illegal, occurred sporadically. But the series of stoppages in Natal early in 1973 was unexpected. At one stage 60,000 Zulus were out and industry after industry was forced to close. The situation was handled by the police peaceably and with a rare restraint. The strikers' eventual gains were marginal: Vorster conceded that in very restricted circumstances strikes were to be legal; workers' committees were instituted which proved unpopular and tended to stifle trade unionism. In fact strikes, despite the legal restrictions, became widespread and commonplace. Increasing numbers of Whites, both employers and workers, called for full trade unionism – either parallel or integrated – for Africans. Bad labour practices were acknowledged to be at the root of the miners' disturbances, at the Anglo-American mine at Cartonville in September 1973, over pay relativities, when eleven men were shot dead by the police. The event was likened to Sharpeville; it aroused outspoken anger in Lesotho and Botswana whose nationals were among the victims.

South Africa was encountering new difficulties abroad. Immediately to the north the Pearce Commission, in a revived British attempt to resolve the Rhodesian impasse and assess Black willingness to accept the old proposals, met with an overwhelming and utterly surprising 'No'. So South Africa had to remain with the consequences of that awkward constitutional situation.

Furthermore, the policy of dialogue with the Black states was turning sour. Botswana and Lesotho were both striving to reduce their economic dependence on the Republic and fall more in line with OAU attitudes. A change of government in the Malagasy Republic destroyed the close relationship South Africa had been nurturing and with it much of the hope of cooperation with the French African states.

In a number of Western countries governments and churches increased their financial aid to guerilla movements, and intermittent trade boycotts still took place. On the other hand the United States, Britain and France, in line with NATO policy, and Japan were adopting more sympathetic official attitudes to South Africa, cooperating in the building up of military supplies and bases and in naval exercises. Trade increased and financial backing for the Bantustans was promised. But for Britain a new significant trend in commercial patterns was emerging as trade with the Black African Commonwealth began to show a sizeable increase over that with South Africa.

Predictably, the South African official reaction to all internal and external pressures and trends towards a more open society was to tighten controls. In 1969 the Public Service Amendment Act was passed (with UP support) setting up the Bureau for State Security (BOSS) to coordinate the security activities of police and military; it was not subject to any public control. This was followed by the 'Boss Bill', the General Laws Amendment Act. The principal act banned the publication of any information relating to police or military matters. Now the ban was extended to security matters, including those relating to BOSS or the relationship between any person and BOSS. No one could be compelled to give evidence if BOSS certified it prejudicial to the security of the state. Only with the bulldozing through of the second bill did the

UP awaken to the sinister effect of the two Acts in conjunction.
There was strong but futile protest from politicians and lawyers.

These laws, along with others available, were used to the full.
An immediate end was made to public and judicial probing into
the unaccountable deaths of eleven political detainees and the
associated allegations of torture. Action against dissidents was
ferociously extended: bannings, banishments, house arrests, de-
portations, refusal of passports and visas, detentions and arrests.
Two distinguished journalists were convicted after publishing
reports about prison conditions. A number of mass trials, mostly
of Blacks, including the much persecuted wife of Nelson Mandela,
took place with a few acquittals when perjury was established
against State witnesses. There was a drive against the churches,
with action against at least fifty church workers, many of them in
Namibia. A priest who revealed appalling conditions in resettlement camps was severely banned; the Anglican Bishop of
Namibia was deported; the Dean of Johannesburg was convicted
under the Terrorism Act, but he won his appeal. Demonstrating
White students were harshly disciplined and some were banned.
In 1972 the Schlebusch Commission (of six NP and three UP
members) was appointed to probe into such organizations as
NUSAS, the Christian Institute and the Institute of Race Re-
lations; some individuals refused to testify and were prosecuted.

The banning, towards the end of 1973, of a great many Black
leaders suffocated the new growth of Black organizations, including SASO and the BPC; passports were withdrawn from
prominent members of White organizations, including the
Christian Institute and the Institute of Race Relations, and from
Sonny Leon, of the Labour party.

The silencing of intellectual opposition was to be completed
by the gagging of the press, the English sector of which had been
increasingly abandoning its conventional support of the UP, reflecting the demand for social and economic changes, and the
interaction of external criticism, student and progressive dissatisfaction, and the growth of Black Nationalism. The government regarded these developments as extremely dangerous. By
agreement with the Press Union the area of self-censorship was
greatly extended and heavy penalties imposed for such ill-defined

infringements of the revised press code as racial incitement. The agreement was condemned by civil rights experts and some lawyers and editors; it alarmed sectors of the Afrikaans press; it was totally rejected by the English language South African Society of Journalists which had not been consulted.

Other defensive measures were rushed through. The Affected Organizations Act of 1974 empowered the authorities to act against organizations (for example, the Christian Institute) which received money from abroad and which 'engage in politics'; they would be subject to searches, interrogation and stiff penalties. The Riotous Assemblies Amendment Act further crushed student protest and extended powers to ban gatherings to those on private property.

The continually rising guerilla activity in Rhodesia, the Portuguese territories and the Caprivi strip were taken very seriously. By this time, South Africa was making almost all the most up-to-date arms, nuclear and electronic equipment, vehicles and planes she needed and, arms embargoes notwithstanding, was able to acquire the rest. Large reserves of natural gas, one third of the total needed, were found near Plettenberg Bay, and traces of oil discovered off Port Elizabeth and in Namibia gave hope at long last of a near self-sufficiency.

The defence estimates were annually increased; in 1974 the overall military expenditure increased by 55 per cent over the previous year, the naval expenditure by 100 per cent. The Permanent Force was expanded, a Coloured unit was incorporated – a step never hitherto contemplated in peace time, and an Indian unit was envisaged. The arming of Africans had never before been acceptable, but, in a dramatic reversal of traditional Afrikaner policy, a college was set up to train 300 Blacks in the use of sophisticated weaponry; they were armed for para-military duties with the police in the Caprivi Strip where large South African army and air contingents were based. The Kariba Dam, the Cabora Bass Dam nearing completion, and the newly begun South African–Portuguese power project on the Kunene River between Namibia and Angola had all to be heavily protected. Large South African forces were patrolling the Namibia–Angola border, the Caprivi Strip, the Rhodesian frontier with Zambia along the

Zambezi to Mozambique (leaving Rhodesian troops free for internal anti-guerilla action) and working with 60,000 Portuguese troops, engaged against Frelimo forces in Mozambique. South Africa's defences were spread across the breadth of the continent. Furthermore, Rhodesian paratroops and South African and other mercenaries, according to a later Portuguese army report, were cooperating with the Portuguese in atrocities against Mozambique villagers suspected of harbouring guerillas; warfare chemicals were traced to South African sources.

The Minister of Defence said, 'I do not wish to spread alarm, but I must state unambiguously that for a long time already we have been engaged in a war of low intensity, and that this situation will probably continue for some considerable time to come.'[64]

Within a year of that acknowledgement the sudden collapse of the Caetano regime in Portugal led to an abrupt reversal of Portuguese policy in Africa. There was agreement on almost immediate independence with Black majority rule in Guiné - Bissau and in Mozambique (not without White resistance), after almost 500 years of Portuguese suzerainty. Whether the mineral-rich Angola with its 600,000 White colonists would be so readily relinquished had yet to be seen.

Rhodesia (Zimbabwe, as it was beginning to be called abroad), encircled by Black states except for the short 150 miles frontier with South Africa, was in a revolutionary context; South Africa too. Vorster put great pressure on Smith to come to terms with Black Rhodesian nationalists and extended his expressions of goodwill towards and offers of cooperation with Black Africa to include Mozambique's new rulers, Frelimo. The future of Angola must, in turn, influence the fate of Namibia. The area of physical White domination in Southern Africa radically diminished over the years 1968 to 1974. Political and economic influences persisted.

64. White Paper on Defence; quoted *Guardian* (London 11 April 1973).

Chronology

BC

2m.   (Dates highly conjectural)
    Australopithecus in E. and S. Africa using simple tools.

1½m.   Pre-sapient men of various types developing in Africa and elsewhere and making simple tools.

                                    200,000 Pekin man learns use of fire.

50,000   Making of improved tools and use of fire in Africa.

35,000   *Homo sapiens* developing in Africa.

10,000   *Homo sapiens* dominant in Africa

                                 12,000 Beginning of farming in western Asia.

8000   Ancestral Bush types predominate in South and East Africa

      Negroes evolving in West Africa forest margins.

                                  6000 Domestication and cultivation in Egypt.

5000   Sedentary fishing culture into West Africa and East African Lakes.

2500   Neolithic food cultivation moves into West and Central Africa.

                                  2600 Great Pyramid built.

                                  1600 Q. Hatsheput's voyage.

                                  800 Iron-Age Assyrians and Hittites overrun Lower Egypt.

500   Meroë becomes iron-working centre.

                                  600 Voyage of Necho's Phoenicians.

300   Iron-working skills spreading south of Sahara.

                                  500 First Greek navigators cross to India.

AD

1–100	Early Iron-Age people settle north of Zambezi. Indonesian voyagers introduce new crops to Central Africa.	1–100	Sailings between coasts of South-West Asia, India and East Africa.
	Ancestral Bantu iron-working groups moving from West to Central Africa mingling with Khoikhoi and other groups.	70	Dispersal of Jews.
300–399	Iron-Age farmers settle south of Zambezi.	360	Arabs, Abyssinians and Indians close Red Sea to Europeans.
c. 400	Site of Zimbabwe occupied.	622	Mohammed founds Islam. Muslims begin conquest of North Africa.
c. 770	Iron working in N. Transvaal.	770	Muslims found trading settlements on East African coast.
700–899	Stone building beginning in Transvaal.	900–1000	Arabs settle at Sofala.
1000–1099	Widespread Iron-Age occupation of Transvaal.	1020	Persians settle at Kilwa.
1100–1300	Mapungubwe occupied by Iron-Age groups.	1299	*The Travels of Marco Polo* published.
		1415	Birth of Henry the Navigator.
		1417	Chinese trading with East Coast.
		1453	Fall of Constantinople.
		1475	Caxton prints first book.
		1492	Columbus discovers America.
1487	Bartholomew Dias rounds Cape. First contacts between Khoikhoi and Whites.	1500	Chinese abandon maritime role. Portuguese capture Arab East Coast trade.
1497	Vasco da Gama reaches East Coast. First known Bantu-African and White contact near Delagoa Bay.	1536	Calvin in Geneva.

AD		
1552	Sao Jao wreck survivors meet Nguni cattle-herders near Port St Johns.	1571 Turkish Navy defeated by Spain at Battle of Lepanto.
1593	Nguni-speaking cattlemen near Umtata.	1642 English Civil War.
1652	Dutch settlement under van Riebeeck at the Cape.	
1657	First Free Burghers.	
1658	First slaves imported.	
1658–60	First Khoikhoi War.	
1673–7	Second Khoikhoi War.	1685 Repeal of Edict of Nantes.
1688	Arrival of French Huguenot Settlers.	1694 Bank of England founded.
		1701 War of Spanish Succession.
1702	Xhosa people and Boers first meet on Fish River.	
1706	Adam Tas memorandum.	1713 Treaty of Utrecht.
		c. 1730 Beginning of Industrial Revolution in Britain.
		1741 War of the Austrian Succession.
		1756 Seven Years War.
		1763 Peace of Paris.
1770	Xhosa and Boer settlers clash on Gamtoos River.	1772 Slavery in Britain declared illegal.
1775	Gamtoos made east boundary of Cape. Xhosa Chief Phalo dies.	1774 American War of Independence.
1779	Cape Patriot Movement. First Xhosa War.	1776 *Wealth of Nations* published.
1780	Great Fish River made boundary of Cape.	1778 Death of Rousseau.
		1780 Britain at war with the Dutch Republic (allied to France).
1789	Second Xhosa War.	1783 The Clapham sect founded.
1793	Xhosa occupy Suurveld.	1789 The French Revolution.
1795	First British occupation of Cape.	1795–1815 Napoleonic period.

AD		
1799	Third Xhosa War.	1802 Peace of Amiens.
1803	Dutch Batavian Republic at the Cape.	1805 French navy defeated at Trafalgar. Beginning of revolt of Spanish and Portuguese American Colonies.
1806	Second British Occupation.	
1807	Abolition of Slave Trade.	
1809	Hottentot Pass and Land Laws introduced.	
1811	First Circuit Court.	
1812	Fourth Xhosa War.	
1815	Slachter's Nek Rebellion.	1815 Battle of Waterloo, Congress of Vienna.
1818	Fifth Xhosa War. Makanda and Ndlambe defeat Ngqaika. Fish to Keiskamma declared neutral (Ceded). Shaka becomes Chief of Zulu.	
1819	Dr John Philip arrives at Cape.	
1820	5,000 British settlers at Port Elizabeth.	1821 Republic of Liberia founded in West Africa for ex-slaves.
1822–36	Mfecane	
1828	Shaka assassinated. Dingane succeeds. 50th Ordinance gives Non-whites full civil rights in Cape. Freedom of Press recognized.	1832 Reform Act in Britain.
		1833 Indian Charter; Britain declared native interests paramount, banned discrimination.
1834	Emancipation of slaves at the Cape. Sixth Xhosa War against Hintsa and Maqoma.	
1836	Beginning of Great Trek.	
1837	First Boer Republic. Boers defeat Ndebele.	
1838	Battle of Blood River. Boers defeat Dingane.	
1841	Masters and Servants Law gives legal equality to servants of all races in the Cape.	
1843	British annex Natal.	

AD

Year	South African events
1846	War of the Axe. British annex Kaffraria. Boundary carried to Kei.
1848	British annex OFS. Battle of Boomplaats.
1850	Lt-Gov. declared 'Supreme Chief' in Natal. Eighth Xhosa War. Sandile deposed.
1852	Sand River Convention gives Transvaal independence.
1853	Cape gets Representative Government.
1854	Bloemfontein Convention, gives OFS independence.
1857	Cattle killing among Xhosa.
1858	First Basuto War, OFS against Moshweshwe.
1860	Indian indentured labour brought into Natal.
1865	Second Basuto War
1867	Discovery of diamonds.
1868	Basutoland becomes British Protectorate.
1871	Keate Award. Britain annexes diamond fields.
1872	Cape granted Responsible Government.
1873	Langalibalele Rebellion.
1876	Sekhukhuni War with Transvaal.
1877	Britain annexes Transvaal.
1878	Ninth Xhosa War. Sandile killed. EP Boundary to Umtata.
1879	Formation of *Afrikaner Bond* in Cape.
1880	Britain defeats Zulu under Cetshwayo. Britain defeats Sekhukhuni. Basuto War of Disarmament with Cape. First Anglo-Boer War. British defeat at Majuba.
1881	Pretoria Convention.

Year	World events
1848	Communist Manifesto published.
1853	Livingstone's journeys begin.
1854	Crimean War begins.
1859	Darwin's *Origin of the Species* published.
1861	American Civil War begins.
1867	Marx's *Das Kapital* published.
1869	Opening of Suez Canal.
1870	Franco-Prussian War.
1871	Japan abolishes feudal system.
1879	Leopold II of Belgium annexes Congo.

AD

1882 Paul Kruger becomes President of South African Republic

1883 Germans annex Angra Pequena in South West Africa

1884 London Convention.

1884 Conference of Berlin.

1885 Northern Bechuanaland becomes British Protectorate.

1886 Gold found on Witwatersrand.

1887 Zululand annexed by Britain

1888 British South African Company founded by Rhodes.

1889 Fabian Society in Britain.

1890 Rhodes becomes Prime Minister of Cape.

1890 Mashonaland (Rhodesia) occupied by Rhodes's BSA Company.

1892 Ethiopian Church established on Rand.

1893 Responsible Government in Natal.

1893 Ndebele War in Rhodesia.

1894 Glen Grey Act. Pondoland annexed to Cape.

1895 Bechuanaland and Tongoland annexed.

1895 Jameson Raid.

1896 Ndebele-Shona Rebellion in Rhodesia.

1897 Zululand annexed to Natal.

1899 Second Anglo–Boer War. Transvaal and OFS annexed.

1902 Peace of Vereeniging.

1904 Chinese labour introduced in Gold Mines.

1905 African People's Organization formed at Cape.

1905 Japan defeats Russia.

1906 Gandhi begins passive resistance. Bambatha rebellion in Natal.

1907 Transvaal granted Responsible Government.

1908 OFS granted Responsible Government.

1908 South Africa Labour Party formed.

1910 Union of South Africa founded.

1911 Mines and Works Act regulates issues of certificates of competence in which colour bar is applied.

AD		South Africa
1912		African National Congress founded. Nationalist Party founded by Hertzog.
1913		Native Land Act schedule 10⅓m. morgen as native reserves.
1914	1914 Outbreak of War.	General strike on Rand. Smuts illegally deports nine Labour leaders. Rebellion in South Africa.
1915		Capture of South West Africa from Germans.
1918		Industrial and Commercial Workers' Union formed by Kadalie.
1919	1917 Russian Revolution. 1919 League of Nations formed.	South Africa given Mandate of South West Africa.
1920		South African Party formed under Smuts.
1922	1922 Mussolini comes to power.	'Rand Revolt' – White miners strike.
1923	1923 S. Rhodesia gets self-government.	Urban Areas Act controls flow of Non-whites into towns.
1924		Nationalist–Labour Pact defeats SAP. Hertzog becomes Premier.
1925		Afrikaans becomes an official language.
1926		Colour bar entrenched in Mines and Works Act.
1929	1929 Wall Street Crash.	'Black Peril' election.
1931		Statute of Westminster confirms self-governing status.
1932		United Transkeian Territories General Council formed. Gold Standard abandoned.
1933	1933 Rise of Hitler.	
1934		Fusion of Nationalist and SA Parties to form United Party. Malan forms 'purified' Nationalist Party.
1936–7	1935 Italians invade Ethiopia. 1936 German–Japanese anti-Comintern pact. Spanish Civil War. 1937 Rome–Berlin Axis. 1939 Second World War.	Hertzog's Segregation Laws.

Some Principal Officials

Dutch East India Company 1652–1795	J. A. van Riebeeck	1652–62
	Simon van der Stel	1678–99
	W. A. van der Stel	1699–1707
	M. P. de Chavonnes	1714–24
First British Occupation 1795–1803	Major-General J. H. Craig	1795–7
	Earl Macartney	1797–8
	Major-General F. Dundas	1798–9
	Sir George Yonge	1799–1801
	Major-General F. Dundas	1801–3
Batavian Republic 1803–6	J. A. de Mist (Commissioner-General)	1803–4
	Lt-General J. W. Janssens (Governor)	1803–6
Second British Occupation 1806–71	Major-General D. Baird	1806–7
	Lt-General H. G. Grey	1807
	Earl of Caledon	1807–11
	Lt-General H. G. Grey	1811
	Lt-General Sir J. F. Cradock	1811–14
	Lt-General Lord Charles Somerset	1814–26
	Major-General Sir R. S. Donkin (acting)	1820–1
	Major-General Sir Benjamin D'Urban	1834–8
	Andries Stockenström (Lt-Governor)	1836–9
	Major-General Sir G. T. Napier	1838–44
	Lt-General Sir Peregrine Maitland	1844–7
	Major-General Sir Harry Smith	1847–52
	Lt-General Sir George Cathcart	1852–4
	Sir George Grey	1854–61
	Sir P. E. Wodehouse	1862–70

Some Principal Officials

Second British Occupation 1806–71	Sir Bartle Frere	1877–80
	Major-General Sir Garnet Wolseley	1879–80
	Sir Hercules Robinson	1881–9
	Sir Hercules Robinson (Lord Rosmead)	1895–7
	Sir Alfred Milner	1897–1901
	Sir Alfred Milner (Lord Milner, Governor of Transvaal)	1902–5
Premiers of Union and Republic of South Africa	General Louis Botha	1910–19
	General J. C. Smuts	1919–24
	General J. B. M. Hertzog	1924–39
	General J. C. Smuts	1939–48
	Dr D. F. Malan	1948–54
	J. G. Strydom	1954–8
	Dr H. F. Verwoerd	1958–66
	B. J. Vorster	1966–

Further Reading

ARMSTRONG, H. C., *Grey Steel (J. C. Smuts)*, Penguin Books, 1939.

BARBER, JAMES, *South African Foreign Policy: 1945–1970*, Oxford University Press, 1973.

BENSON, MARY, *Chief Albert Lutuli of South Africa*. Oxford University Press, 1963.

  The Struggle for a Birthright, Penguin Books, 1966.

BRITISH COUNCIL OF CHURCHES, *The Future of South Africa*. 1965.

BUNTING, BRIAN, *The Rise of the South African Reich*, Penguin Books, 1964.

CALPIN, G. H., *Indians in South Africa*, Shuter & Shooter, Pietermaritzburg, 1949.

Cambridge History of the British Empire – South Africa. Vol. VIII, Cambridge University Press, 1936.

CARLSON, JOEL, *No Neutral Ground*, Davis-Poynter, 1973.

CARTER, GWENDOLIN M., *The Politics of Inequality: South Africa since 1948*, Thames & Hudson, 1958.

CLARK, J. DESMOND, *The Prehistory of Southern Africa*, Penguin Books, 1959.

DAVENPORT, T. R., *The Afrikaner Bond 1880–1911*, Oxford University Press, 1966.

DAVIDSON, BASIL, *Old Africa Rediscovered*, Gollancz, 1959.

DE KIEWIET, C. W., *A History of South Africa: Social and Economic*, Oxford University Press, 1941.

  The Imperial Factor in South Africa, Cambridge University Press, 1937.

DESMOND, COSMOS, *The Discarded People*, Penguin Books, 1973.

DUGARD, JOHN (ed.), *The SWA–Namibia Dispute*, University of California Press, 1973.

DUNDAS, SIR CHARLES, *South West Africa: The Factual Background*, S.A. Institute of International Affairs, 1946.

FAGAN, B., *South Africa during the Iron Age*, Thames & Hudson, 1965.

Further Reading

FIRST, RUTH, *South West Africa*, Penguin Books, 1963.

FIRST, RUTH, STEELE, J., and GURNEY, C., *The South African Connection*, Penguin Books, 1973.

FORDHAM, PAUL, *The Geography of African Affairs*, Penguin Books, 1965.

FREISLICH, RICHARD, *The Last Tribal War*, C. Struik, Cape Town, 1962.

GALBRAITH, JOHN S., *Reluctant Empire 1834–54*, University of California Press, 1963.

GOODFELLOW, C. F., *Great Britain and the South African Confederation 1870–81*, Oxford, 1966.

HAILEY, LORD, *An African Survey*, Oxford University Press, 1938.

HALPERN, J., *South Africa's Hostages: Basutoland, Bechuanaland and Swaziland*, Penguin Books, 1965.

HANCOCK, W. K., *Smuts: I The Sanguine Years 1870–1919*, 1962: *II The Fields of Force 1919–1956*, Cambridge University Press, 1968.

HELLMANN, ELLEN (ed.). *Handbook on Race Relations in South Africa*. Oxford University Press, 1949.

HEPPLE, ALEX, *South Africa: A Political and Economic History*, Pall Mall Press, 1966.
Verwoerd, Penguin Books, 1967.

HOAGLAND, JIM, *South Africa*, Allen & Unwin, 1973.

HORRELL, MURIEL, *Action, Reaction and Counteraction*, South African Institute of Race Relations, 1963.
Legislation and Race Relations, South African Institute of Race Relations, 1966.

HORWITZ, RALPH, *The Political Economy of South Africa*, Weidenfeld & Nicolson, 1967.

HUNTER, M., *Reaction to Conquest*, Oxford University Press, 1936.

JOSEPH, HELEN, *If this be Treason*, Deutsch, 1963.

JOSHI, P. S., *The Tyranny of Colour: A Study of the Indian Question in South Africa*, Durban, 1942.

KUPER, LEO, *Passive Resistance in South Africa*, Cape, 1956.

LAZAR LEONARD, *Namibia, Africa Bureau*, 1972.

LEGUM, COLIN and MARGARET, *South Africa: Crisis for the West*, Pall Mall Press, 1964.

LEWIN, JULIUS, *Politics and Law in South Africa*, Merlin Press, 1963.

LOCKHART, J. G., and WOODHOUSE, THE HON C. M., *Rhodes*, Hodder & Stoughton, 1963.

LUTHULI, A. J., *Let my People Go: An Autobiography*, Collins, 1962.

MACCRONE, I. D., *Race Attitudes in South Africa*, Oxford University Press, 1937.

MACMILLAN, W. M., *Africa Emergent*, Penguin Books, 1949.
Bantu, Boer and Briton, Faber, 1929
The Cape Colour Question, Faber, 1927.

MARAIS, J. S., *The Cape Coloured People 1652–1937*, Longmans, 1939.
Maynier and the First Boer Republic, Cape Town, 1944.
The Fall of Kruger's Republic, Oxford University Press, 1961.

MARKS, SHULA, *The Reluctant Rebellion 1906–1908*, Oxford University Press, 1970.

MARQUARD, LEO, *The Story of South Africa*, Faber, 1966.

MATHEWS, A. S., *Law, Order and Liberty in South Africa*, University of California Press, 1971.

MBEKI, GOVAN, *The Peasants' Revolt*, Penguin Books, 1964.

MILLIN, S. G., *Rhodes*, Chatto & Windus, 1933.
The People of South Africa, Constable, 1951.

MORRIS, D. R., *The Washing of the Spears*, Sphere Books, 1966.

MUTWA, C., *My People*, Anthony Blond, 1969.

NEAME, L. E., *The History of Apartheid*, Pall Mall Press, 1962.

OLIVER, ROLAND and FAGE, J. D., *A Short History of Africa*, Penguin Books, 1962.

OLIVER, ROLAND (ed.), *The Dawn of African History*, Oxford University Press, 1961.
The Middle Age of African History, Oxford University Press, 1967.

OMER-COOPER, J. D., *Zulu Aftermath*, Longmans, 1966.

PATON, ALAN, *J. H. Hofmeyr*, Oxford University Press, 1965.

PATTERSON, S., *Colour and Culture in South Africa*, Routledge & Kegan Paul, 1953.

PEART-BINNS, J., *Ambrose Reeves*, Gollancz, 1973.

PERHAM, M., and CURTIS, L., *The Protectorate of South Africa*, Oxford, 1935.

PIENAAR, S., and SAMPSON, A., *South Africa: Two Views of Separate Development*, Oxford University Press, 1960.

PIROW, OSWALD, *James Barry Munnik Hertzog*, Allen & Unwin, 1958.

PLAATJE, S. I. T., *Native Life in South Africa*, P. S. King & Son, 1916.

RANGER, T. O., *Revolt in Southern Rhodesia*, Heinemann, 1967.

RITTER, E. A., *Shaka Zulu*, 1955.

Further Reading

ROBERTSON, JANET, *Liberalism in South Africa*, Oxford University Press, 1971.

ROBINSON, R., and GALLAGHER, J., *Africa and the Victorians*, Macmillan, 1961.

ROSKAM, K. L., *Apartheid and Discrimination*, A. W. Sythoff. Leyden, 1960.

ROUX, EDWARD, *Time Longer than Rope*, University of Wisconsin Press, 1964.

SACHS, ALBIE, *Justice in South Africa*, Heinemann, 1973.

SAMPSON, ANTHONY, *The Treason Cage*, Heinemann, 1955.

SIMONS, H. J., and R. E., *Class and Colour in South Africa 1850–1950*, Penguin Books, 1969.

SMUTS, J. C., *Africa and Some World Problems*, Clarendon Press, Oxford, 1939.

SMUTS, JUN., J. C., *Jan Christiaan Smuts*, Cassell, 1952.

STONE, JOHN, *Colonist or Uitlander? The British Immigrant in South Africa*, Oxford University Press, 1973.

SPILHAUS, M., *South Africa in the Making*, Juta, Cape Town. 1966.

TATZ, C. M., *Shadow and Substance in South Africa*, Pietermaritzburg, 1962.

THEAL, G. M., *History of South Africa 1795–1827*, 5 Volumes, Allen & Unwin, 1908–10.

THOMAS, E. MARSHALL, *The Harmless People*, Penguin Books, 1959.

THOMPSON, L. M., *The Unification of South Africa 1902–1910*, Heinemann, 1960.

THOMPSON, L. M., *Politics in the Republic of South Africa*, Little, Brown & Co., Boston, 1968.

THOMPSON, L. M. (ed.), *African Societies in Southern Africa before 1880*, Heinemann, 1969.

UNESCO. *Apartheid: Its Effects on Education, Science, Culture and Information*.

VAN DER HEEVER, C. M., *General J. B. M. Hertzog*, ABP Bookstore, Johannesburg, 1946.

WALKER, E., *A History of Southern Africa*, Longmans, 1959.
The Great Trek, A. & C. Black, 1934.

WALSHE, PETER, *The Rise of African Nationalism in South Africa: The ANC, 1912–1952*, University of California Press, 1971.

WELLINGTON, J. H., *Southern Africa: A Geographical Study*, 2 Volumes, Cambridge University Press, 1955.

WELLINGTON, J. H., *South West Africa and the Human Issues*, Cape, 1970.

WELSH, DAVID, *Roots of Segregation*, Oxford University Press, 1972.

WILLCOX, A. R., *The Rock Art of South Africa*, Nelson & Sons, 1963.

WILSON, FRANCIS, *Labour in South African Gold Mines*, Cambridge University Press, 1972.

Migrant Labour in South Africa, Johannesburg, 1972.

WILSON, M. and THOMPSON, L. (ed.), *The Oxford History of South Africa*, Vol. I to 1870, 1969: Vol. II 1870–1966, Oxford University Press, 1971.

The above is a small selection from the great number of books on South Africa. Abundant material is also to be found in many periodicals and pamphlets, including:

The *Journal of African History* (London); *African Affairs*; the publications of the South African Institute of Race Relations including their annual *Survey of Race Relations* (ed. Muriel Horrell), their quarterly *Journal of Race Relations* and many pamphlets and Fact papers; the SABRA *Journal of Race Affairs* and pamphlets; the *Africa Digest* of the Africa Bureau (London) and their pamphlets; the quarterly *Africa South* 1956–1960 (ed. Ronald Segal); the quarterly *Optima* (the Anglo-American Corporation of South Africa); the weekly *Press Digest* (Jewish Board of Deputies, Johannesburg); the *Digest of South African Affairs*, pamphlets and Fact papers issued by the South African Information Services; the publications issued by various sections of the United Nations Organization.

Index

433

Index

Index

Index

Index

Index

More about Penguins and Pelicans

Penguinews, which appears every month, contains details of all the new books issued by Penguins as they are published. From time to time it is supplemented by *Penguins in Print*, which is a complete list of all titles available. (There are some five thousand of these.)

A specimen copy of *Penguinews* will be sent to you free on request. For a year's issues (including the complete lists) please send 50p if you live in the British Isles, or 75p if you live elsewhere. Just write to Dept EP, Penguin Books Ltd, Harmondsworth, Middlesex, enclosing a cheque or postal order, and your name will be added to the mailing list.

In the U.S.A.: For a complete list of books available from Penguin in the United States write to Dept CS, Penguin Books Inc., 7110 Ambassador Road, Baltimore, Maryland 21207.

In Canada: For a complete list of books available from Penguin in Canada write to Penguin Books Canada Ltd, 41 Steelcase Road West, Markham, Ontario

The Beginners

Joel, David, and Rachel Glickman are determined not to repeat their parent's mistakes, and are resolved to find a code of behaviour in the confusion of post-war South Africa – scene of racial conflict, social upheaval, and dazzling opportunity.

Dan Jacobson charts their voyages of self-discovery – with their setbacks, triumphs, ideals achieved or renounced – on a huge canvas with a host of characters and settings in South Africa, Israel, England, and Eastern Europe. His sustained narrative brilliance makes *The Beginners* a masterpiece.

The Price of Diamonds

For all his partner's big talk Gottlieb is sure that it is he, not Fink, who is really the man of action and dangerous secret deals. And to prove it he kept the illicit uncut diamonds that he had acquired by chance – a gesture with unexpected and dangerous consequences . . .

'A gem of a comedy as effortless and delightful as *The Diary of a Nobody*' – *The Times Literary Supplement*

The Trap *and* A Dance in the Sun

'And don't you forget that you're a kaffir and I'm a white man and the police will believe what I say . . . not what you tell them.'

The Trap and *A Dance in the Sun* are stories of suspense set under the high skies of the sun-seized South African veld; stories which vividly demonstrate the inadequacy of liberal values in the face of evil.

A Penguin Book

The Grass is Singing

Doris Lessing

The Grass is Singing was Doris Lessing's first novel and
brought her immediate recognition. A story of white people
in Rhodesia, it is both an accurate picture of Africa as it
appears to the average settler and a subtle study of a
doomed marriage.

'Original and striking ... full of those terrifying touches of
truth, seldom mentioned but instantly recognized. By any
standards, this book shows remarkable power and
imagination' – *New Statesman*

A Penguin Modern Classic

Cry, The Beloved Country

Alan Paton

'*Cry, The Beloved Country* approaches the racial problems of South Africa with an intelligence, a simplicity and a compassionate sincerity which make its reading an absorbing and deeply moving experience. Alan Paton has thought deeply and impartially and has put his heart into his subject, but he has made it bigger than argument or emotion; I don't think you will soon forget the resigned sorrow of its closing pages' – *Observer*

'Mr Paton's record of a simple Zulu parson's search for his delinquent son in the maelstrom of Johannesburg is as moving in the biblical simplicity of its style and drama as it is imaginatively disinterested as an account of the problems of race relations. This is as remarkable a novel for its facts as for its truth' – *Guardian*

Penguin African Library

Rhodesia

WHITE RACISM AND IMPERIAL RESPONSE

Martin Loney

The late 1950s and early 1960s saw the rapid and, in most cases, peaceful decolonization of Africa. But today Rhodesia remains colonized, no longer controlled by the imperial power, but still governed by white settlers. Martin Loney describes the history of the colony and of the continuous African opposition to the invaders.

Central to his theme is the development of the power of the intransigent white rulers; in his words, 'this book is about the historical development of that power, the systematic use which has been made of it to build a prosperous white society in Africa, and the consequent impoverishment of the African population. It is also about the complicity of the British governments, Labour and Conservative, in this process.'

In its assessment of the British sell-out and of the growing sense of national identity on the part of the African population, this is a book which will upset many of the comfortable ideas held about Rhodesia in this country.

Penguin African Library

The South African Connection

WESTERN INVESTMENT IN APARTHEID

Ruth First, Jonathan Steele, Christabel Gurney

Does investment in South Africa help to bring about modernization and to raise the standard of living for Africans or not ? The question is asked often enough: this book provides the answer.

The authors base their findings on a careful investigation into the activities of a number of major companies and on their thorough knowledge of conditions in South Africa. Looking at the reality concealed behind the polite generalities uttered by those seeking to defend investment there, they show what actually happens to Africans and to the political scene in South Africa as a result of it.

'The fundamental case made by this book is that there is a powerful political-industrial complex, predominantly British, which fuels the engines of apartheid' – *Observer*

'The most comprehensive account yet published of South Africa's dependence on Western and especially British capitalism' – *Sunday Times*

'A mine of information and a minefield of controversy' – *The Times*

'Those who rely on an economic resolution of the South African problem should certainly read this book' – *Economist*

NOT FOR SALE IN THE U.S.A.

The Penguin African Library